T0331064

NAVIGATING THE FACTOR ZOO

Bridging the gap between theoretical asset pricing and industry practices in factors and factor investing, Zhang et al. provides a comprehensive treatment of factors, along with industry insights on practical factor development.

Chapters cover a wide array of topics, including the foundations of quantamentals, the intricacies of market beta, the significance of statistical moments, the principles of technical analysis, and the impact of market microstructure and liquidity on trading. Furthermore, it delves into the complexities of tail risk and behavioral finance, revealing how psychological factors affect market dynamics. The discussion extends to the sophisticated use of option trading data for predictive insights and the critical differentiation between outcome uncertainty and distribution uncertainty in financial decision-making. A standout feature of the book is its examination of machine learning's role in factor investing, detailing how it transforms data preprocessing, factor discovery, and model construction. Overall, this book provides a holistic view of contemporary financial markets, highlighting the challenges and opportunities in harnessing alternative data and machine learning to develop robust investment strategies.

This book would appeal to investment management professionals and trainees. It will also be of use to graduate and upper undergraduate students in quantitative finance, factor investing, asset management and/or trading.

Michael Zhang is the founder of Super Quantum Fund. He has over 20 years of experience in quantitative investing. He publishes in the most prestigious academic journals and has been extensively cited. He holds a PhD from MIT, an MSc, and two bachelor's degrees from Tsinghua University.

Tao Lu is the CEO of Super Quantum Fund. He has extensive practical experience in portfolio management through quantitative methods and leading quantitative research teams. He holds a PhD from the Chinese University of Hong Kong and two bachelor's degrees from Tsinghua University.

Chuan Shi is a co-founder of Beijing Liangxin Investment Management, specializing in factor investing, portfolio allocation, and risk management. He holds a PhD from MIT and bachelor's and master's degrees from Tsinghua University. He is the lead author of *Factor Investing: Methodology and Practice*.

NAVIGATING THE FACTOR ZOO

The Science of Quantitative Investing

Michael Zhang, Tao Lu and Chuan Shi

Routledge
Taylor & Francis Group

LONDON AND NEW YORK

First published 2025
by Routledge
4 Park Square, Milton Park, Abingdon, Oxon OX14 4RN

and by Routledge
605 Third Avenue, New York, NY 10158

Routledge is an imprint of the Taylor & Francis Group, an informa business

British Library Cataloguing-in-Publication Data
A catalogue record for this book is available from the British Library

ISBN: 978-1-032-76843-4 (hbk)
ISBN: 978-1-032-76841-0 (pbk)
ISBN: 978-1-003-48020-4 (ebk)

DOI: 10.4324/9781003480204

Typeset in Bembo
by Taylor & Francis Books

CONTENTS

FIGURES

TABLES

PREFACE

"It is difficult to make predictions, especially about the future."

(Danish physicist and Nobel laureate Niels Bohr)

Generations of financial researchers and practitioners tried to predict the financial market. Few of them succeeded.

Eugene Fama, an American economist known for his work on the Efficient Market Hypothesis (EMH), wrote several papers that discuss the unpredictable nature of the market. Two of his most influential papers are:

- Fama, Eugene F. (1965). "The Behavior of Stock-Market Prices". *Journal of Business*, 38(1): 34–105. In this paper, Fama suggests that stock prices follow a random walk, making them unpredictable based on past price information. This laid the foundation for the development of the EMH.
- Fama, Eugene F. (1970). "Efficient Capital Markets: A Review of Theory and Empirical Work". *Journal of Finance*, 25(2): 383–417. In this seminal paper, Fama provides a comprehensive review of the existing theory and empirical work on market efficiency up to that time. He argues that the market is efficient in reflecting all available information, making it difficult for investors to consistently outperform the market on a risk-adjusted basis.

These papers, among others, form the basis of Fama's influential work on the EMH, which suggests that the market is generally unpredictable because of its efficiency in incorporating available information into asset prices.

At the same time, Warren Buffett, the renowned investor and CEO of Berkshire Hathaway, has been quoted as saying, "I'd be a bum on the street with a tin cup if the markets were always efficient." The statement reflects Buffett's skepticism about the EMH.

Indeed, the market cannot be efficient if some investors, such as Warren Buffett and Jim Simons, can consistently beat the market over the course of some 30 years. The question is: how?

This book delves into the hidden ingredients that enable quantitative trading to outperform the market. Ironically, these hidden ingredients, or "factors", were developed by Eugene Fama and his fellow financial economists, who themselves do not believe that the market can be consistently outperformed.

The term "factors" is ubiquitous in finance and asset management. It has been a major focus in asset pricing literature and an active research area within the industry for the past 50 years. However, confusion usually comes when we read academic journals where the term "factors" seems to have a very different meaning from what industry practitioners refer to. From academia's point of view, factors are *market-wide*, which explains the cross-sectional variation of assets' returns, and assets have different returns because of their different *exposure* to the factors. The classical yet famous single-factor model is the Capital Asset Pricing Model (CAPM), which states that the market excess return is the single factor and assets' returns are determined by their systematic exposure (beta) to the market. In the multi-factor space, the Fama-French three-factor model (FF3) starts the race, complementing the market factor with HML (high-minus-low) and SMB (small-minus-big), which are respectively the spread between stock returns of high book-to-market value and low book-to-market value, and the spread between the returns of small market capitalization stocks versus big market capitalization stocks. Following the literature, Carhart (1997) four-factor model complements the FF3 with an additional momentum factor (MOM). Since then, market excess return, HML, SMB, and MOM have become consensus factors within the academic world. Later developments are the liquidity factor (Pástor and Stambaugh 2003) and the tail risk factor (Almeida et al. 2017) etc. In parallel, Fama-French came up with another five-factor model by complementing the FF3 with two additional factors called RMW (robust-minus-weak), which is the spread of returns of firms with robust vs weak operational profitability, and CMA (conservative-minus-aggressive), which is the spread of returns of firms that invest conservatively vs those that invest aggressively.

In contrast, the terminology in the industry is much less rigorous and loosely defined. In this context, they seem to be referring to *variables* or *attributes* of assets that are associated with their future returns. Unlike the academic factors, factors in the industry are not considered market-wide measures. For example, the volatility of stocks correlates with stocks' next-period returns, so volatility could be treated as a factor. While both academia and industry try to use factors to capture *cross-sectional variation*, which essentially tries to answer the question why different assets have different returns during a certain period, the definitions, motivations, treatments, and uses of factors are vastly different, leading to confusions about what exactly factors are, their uses and limitations, etc.

Structure of this Book

We aim to offer a map of factor investing in this book. Each chapter covers an important direction of factor development. Chapter 1 starts with the current landscape in factor investing. It contrasts the definitions, treatments, and identifications of factors between academia and industry, with a phenomenon on the numerous factors being used known as the "factor zoo". Chapter 2 introduces fundamental analysis and a new trend of combining fundamentals with quantitative analysis, known as the "Quantamentals". Chapter 3 studies how various statistical moments relate to risk and are treated as factors. Chapter 4 deals with a crucial risk concept, systematic risk, or beta, as a factor. Chapter 5 introduces factors from price history and technical indicators, with a special focus on trend and jump analysis. Chapter 6 examines microstructure and a broad range of liquidity metrics, from early studies on volume impacts to contemporary advancements in trade time metrics and liquidity resilience. Chapter 7 discusses tail risk, a topic gaining increasing traction. Chapter 8 focuses on factors from behavioral finance, which is a very broad and hot topic on its own. In Chapter 9, we examine how other asset classes like commodities and options may affect equities' returns. Chapter 10 focuses on recent advances in our understanding of distribution uncertainty. Chapter 11 discusses factor development based on alternative data. Finally, in Chapter 12, we discuss various ways of how machine learning may contribute to factor investing. The Epilogue concludes our journey through the factor zoo and offers our reflection on the multifaceted world of factor investing.

The Philosophy of Scientific Investing

Two authors of this book, Zhang and Lu, come with both academic backgrounds—as business school professors—and industry experience, having co-founded a quantitative hedge fund named Super Quantum Fund. Shi manages a hedge fund called Beijing Liangxin Investment Management. This book is written with practitioners in mind, including those from private or public equity funds, asset managers, brokers, financial advisors, and regulators. We hope it serves as a practical guide to factor investing from a scientific perspective, linking flourishing academic research with the industry's practical implementations. The book aims to provide practitioners with a synthesis and formal treatment of factors used in the industry. It also explains how these factors relate to academic foundations with sound economic rationale.

While many market participants in the quantitative trading space emphasize the value of (1) identifying more factors, and (2) developing more complex models, we hold the view that the science behind these factors and models is even more important. Based on our research in academia and practice in the financial market through the Super Quantum Fund, we developed a framework for students and asset managers to gain a deeper understanding of factor investing. In this book, we show how such an understanding can bring consistent returns that transcend both bull and bear markets.

The pyramid's apex comprises *Finance*, encompassing risk management, trading execution, compliance, and operations. Every financial institution should possess this layer to ensure the proper execution of investment strategies to serve investors.

The second layer, *Technology*, relies on inductive reasoning and should be present in all quantitative funds. It incorporates financial engineering aspects such as factor creation, machine learning, and portfolio optimization.

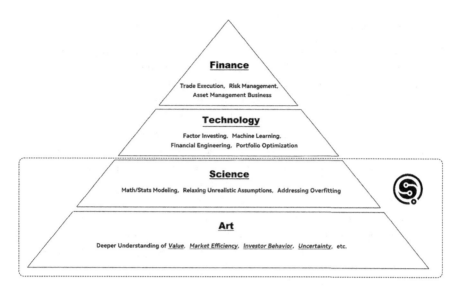

FIGURE 0.1 The Super Quantum Pyramid of Quantitative Investment
Figure shows the Super Quantum pyramid of quantitative investment. It has four layers: Finance, Technology, Science, and Art.

Following this is the *Science* layer, emphasizing the significance of deductive reasoning. It involves creating theoretical and methodological tools to tackle issues unaddressed in the *Technology* layer. For instance, data-driven decision-making is sometimes criticized for its inability to foresee future outcomes: "Predicting future events based on historical occurrences is akin to driving while only looking in the rear-view mirror". To circumvent this limitation, the *Science* layer must develop a solid theory before validating it with data.

The base of the pyramid is *Art*, requiring hypotheses formulated on powerful intuition and an in-depth understanding of financial markets. This layer necessitates a thorough grasp of the inherent uncertainties in the market. As either humans or their devised models constitute market participants, a resilient quantitative strategy must account for trading outcomes that may diverge from logical predictions.

Each layer in the pyramid is crucial, building upon the foundation beneath it to create a holistic framework that fuses intuition, theory development, technological infrastructure, and financial judiciousness to generate superior investment outcomes.

It is clear, from this figure, that financial engineering, machine-learning models, factors, etc. are just a small part of the whole framework. Developing better models should go beyond the Technology layer and push the frontiers of the Science and the Art layers.

GitHub Repository

While writing this book, we developed an open-source code project: the Factor Investing Research Engine (FIRE). We invite our readers to contribute to this project. You can find the project on GitHub at this link: https://github.com/fire-institute/fire. Our goal is for FIRE to progressively encompass all the factor topics discussed within and beyond this book, translating factor research ideas into executable code and ensuring their scientific validity through validations.

While a book remains static once printed, ideas should be dynamic. With FIRE, we can continuously update and expand on new research topics, delve deeper into issues mentioned in the book, and explore fresh insights. The book will remain a living document.

We hope that FIRE serves as a bridge between us, the authors, and you, the readers. We look forward to discussing topics related to factor investing and gaining new inspiration through our interactions. Perhaps these interactions will lead to a series of follow-up works.

ACKNOWLEDGMENTS

This book is not just a product of our efforts, but a testament to the collective spirit and dedication of all those who have been involved, directly or indirectly.

We are deeply indebted to our spouses and children, who have shown endless patience and understanding during the countless hours we dedicated to this project. Their sacrifices and encouragement have been the bedrock of our perseverance. We also thank our colleagues for their invaluable contributions throughout the journey of writing this book. Their unwavering support and insightful feedback have been pillars of strength and inspiration, without which this work would not have been possible.

Our gratitude extends to our academic peers and mentors, whose rigorous critiques and thought-provoking discussions have greatly enriched the content of this book. We are particularly thankful for the collaborative environment provided by our respective institutions (Super Quantum Fund, Beijing Liangxin Investment Management, Chinese University of Hong Kong, Tsinghua University, Southern University of Science and Technology), which has been fundamental in the development of our ideas. Our colleagues, Baochen Qiao and Renjie Liao, from Super Quantum Fund, created an open-source platform on GitHub, called FIRE (Factor Investing Research Engine), that accompanies this book.

We would like to thank Erik Brynjolfsson, Shane Greenstein, Campbell Harvey, Terrence Hendershott, Yuriy Nevmyvaka, Michael Saunders, and Feng Zhu for their endorsement and valuable suggestions for this book.

We acknowledge the broader community of researchers and professionals in our field. The body of work they have created has been a source of knowledge and motivation, prompting us to contribute to the ongoing dialogue with this book.

To everyone who has played a part in this journey, we offer our heartfelt thanks.

Michael Zhang, Tao Lu, and Chuan Shi

References

Almeida, C., K. Ardison, R. Garcia, and J. Vicente (2017). Nonparametric tail risk, stock returns, and the macroeconomy. *Journal of Financial Econometrics* 15(3), 333–376.

Carhart, M. M. (1997). On persistence in mutual fund performance. *Journal of Finance* 52(1), 57–82.

Fama, E. F. (1965). The behavior of stock-market prices. *Journal of Business* 38(1), 34–105.

Fama, E. F. (1970). Efficient capital markets: A review of theory and empirical work. *Journal of Finance* 25(2), 383–417.

Pástor, L. and R. F. Stambaugh (2003). Liquidity risk and expected stock returns. *Journal of Political Economy* 111(3), 642–685.

1

FACTOR INVESTING

In the complex world of financial markets, factors offer a systematic approach to investment by focusing on measurable characteristics that have historically been linked to higher returns. Factors such as value, size, momentum, quality, and volatility allow investors to construct portfolios with a structured methodology, providing a sense of clarity amidst the market's inherent unpredictability.

Quantitative models play a crucial role in factor investing, enabling investors to screen and select securities that exhibit desired factor characteristics. By using historical data and statistical methods, investors can identify which factors are likely to contribute to performance in different market conditions. The increasing use of machine learning and artificial intelligence has further refined these models, allowing for a more nuanced understanding and application of factors.

One of the key benefits of factor investing is the potential for risk management through diversification. By investing in multiple factors, one can mitigate the impact of any single factor underperforming. This approach does not guarantee protection against losses but is intended to achieve a more stable performance over time.

While no investment strategy can offer complete certainty, factor investing provides a disciplined framework that helps mitigate some of the randomness and emotion in investment decisions. By relying on evidence-based factors, investors can make more informed choices with a clearer understanding of the risks and potential returns.

1.1. Background

Factor investing is a strategy in the financial market that involves identifying specific drivers of returns. Factors are quantifiable characteristics of securities that can explain the risk and return profile of an asset or portfolio. The concept is that certain underlying factors or characteristics drive the expected return of an

DOI: 10.4324/9781003480204-1

investment. They can be understood as *features* in machine learning or *independent variables* or *predictors* in regression analysis.

Factors in investing are fundamental traits or features that are common across a broad set of securities that can help explain their performance and risk profile. These factors are often grounded in academic research and can be economic (e.g., growth, inflation), statistical (e.g., volatility, momentum), or behavioral (e.g., investor sentiment).

Factors are important because they provide a framework for portfolio construction and risk management that is more nuanced than traditional asset-class-based investing. They allow investors to:

- **Target Returns:** By understanding the factors that drive returns, investors can construct portfolios that are more likely to meet their return objectives.
- **Manage Risks:** Factors can expose hidden risks in a portfolio that might not be apparent when looking only at asset classes.
- **Improve Diversification:** Factors can help identify and invest in uncorrelated sources of potential returns, reducing risk through better diversification.
- **Enhance Transparency:** Factor investing offers a clear and transparent method to track the performance and risk profile of an investment strategy.

A "factor" in math means a part that helps make up a whole. For example, the factors of 15 are 3 and 5 because $3 \times 5 = 15$. Similarly, when we "factor" investments, we break down the returns into different parts that contribute to the total performance.

To picture factor investing, think of returns in a multi-dimensional space. Each dimension represents a different factor affecting the returns. By looking at each dimension, we can see how various aspects of the financial world impact an investment's performance.

Dimensions are analogous to the different sources of risk and return that can affect an asset's performance. When analyzing an investment, we are essentially trying to understand its behavior in a space defined by multiple dimensions, each aligned with a specific factor.

Each factor can be thought of as an axis in this multidimensional space. Common factors like size, value, momentum, quality, and volatility act as vectors or directions in this space. Just as in a three-dimensional physical space, where you have axes for length, width, and height, in factor investing, the axes might be these various characteristics of stocks.

When constructing a portfolio, we are projecting our investment onto these various factor dimensions. The projection onto each axis (factor) gives us a sense of the portfolio's sensitivity to that factor. For instance, a high projection on the "value" axis suggests a portfolio heavily weighted towards value stocks.

By analyzing the factor exposures of a portfolio, investors can understand the drivers of performance. If a portfolio outperforms, factor analysis can help determine which factors contributed to this outperformance. For example, if the value factor had strong returns over a period, and the portfolio was heavily projected onto the value dimension, this factor likely played a significant role in the portfolio's performance.

In practice, multi-factor models quantify the contribution of each factor to expected returns using statistical methods. Regression analysis, for instance, can be used to estimate the sensitivity of an asset's returns to each factor, often expressed as beta coefficients. These coefficients measure the extent to which the asset moves in relation to a unit change in the factor.

Traditional multi-factor models in finance are often constructed using linear regression, which assumes that the return of an asset is a linear combination of various factors. However, the assumption that factors are orthogonal to each other (meaning that they are uncorrelated and therefore provide independent information) is an ideal that often does not hold true in practice.

In theory, having orthogonal factors in a multi-factor model is desirable because it simplifies the analysis and interpretation of the model. Orthogonal factors would mean that each factor explains a distinct portion of asset returns, and there is no overlap in the information that each factor provides. This would allow for clear attribution of performance to each factor.

However, in the real world, financial factors often exhibit some degree of correlation. Many factors are empirically correlated to some extent. For example, the value and size factors may be related since smaller companies might also be value companies. Correlation among factors can lead to multicollinearity in regression models, which can inflate the variance of the estimated coefficients and make the model less stable and more sensitive to changes in the model's inputs. To address the issue of non-orthogonality, statistical techniques such as principal component analysis (PCA) can be used to transform correlated factors into a set of uncorrelated factors. These uncorrelated factors are linear combinations of the original factors and are orthogonal by construction. Another technique is factor rotation, which also aims to create factors that are more interpretable and less correlated with each other. This can help in better understanding the unique contribution of each factor.

The advent of machine-learning tools has significantly advanced the field of factor investing by allowing for the discovery and exploitation of complex, non-linear relationships between factors and asset returns. Traditional linear models, such as multiple regression, are limited to linear relationships and assume that the impact of a one-unit change in a factor on asset returns is constant, regardless of the level of the factor. Machine-learning models, on the other hand, can capture more nuanced interactions and non-linear effects.

Machine learning includes a variety of algorithms capable of modeling non-linear relationships. Decision trees, for example, can capture non-linear patterns by splitting the data into branches based on factor thresholds. Ensemble methods like random forests or gradient-boosting machines combine multiple decision trees to improve predictive performance and capture complex factor interactions. At the same time, machine learning can automatically perform feature engineering, which involves creating new features from existing ones to better capture the underlying patterns in the data. For instance, it could involve transforming factors through polynomial expansion to capture non-linear effects or interaction terms to capture the combined effect of multiple factors. Techniques like principal component analysis (PCA) and t-distributed stochastic neighbor embedding (t-SNE) can reduce the dimensionality of the data, helping uncover the underlying structure and relationship between factors that may not be apparent in higher-dimensional space. Machine-learning models, such as Lasso and Ridge regression, include regularization techniques that penalize the complexity of the model. This not only helps in preventing overfitting but also in dealing with multicollinearity among factors by shrinking less important factor coefficients toward zero.

Although machine-learning models, especially the more complex ones, are often considered "black boxes", there is a growing field of model interpretability aimed at understanding the decisions made by these models. Techniques such as SHAP (SHapley Additive exPlanations) and LIME (Local Interpretable Model-agnostic Explanations) can help quantify the contribution of each factor to the predictions made by a machine-learning model.

In summary, factor investing models help dissect the complex financial returns into more understandable components. By examining each dimension separately, investors can make more informed decisions about where to allocate their capital to optimize their risk-adjusted returns.

The rest of this chapter is organized as follows. Section 1.2 discusses the role of quants, or quantitative analysts, who are central to developing factor models in finance. Section 1.3 introduces the motivation for understanding factors. Section 1.4 discusses the current landscape of factor investing. In Section 1.5, we compare the definitions and treatments of factors between academia and industry practitioners. Section 1.6 explains the process of identifying factors. Section 1.7 discusses the consensus factors in the asset pricing literature. Section 1.8 provides a broad classification of factors being used in the industry. Section 1.9 discusses factors from the perspective of them as explainers or predictors. Finally, Section 1.10 concludes with a summary table that compares key differences.

1.2. Quant

Factors and factor models are often developed by quantitative analysts, who are commonly referred to as quants. The word "quant" is probably one of the most frequently used prefixes in numerous finance programs offered by universities or job titles from various financial institutions in the past 20 years. Adding the word quant in front of an academic program or a job role seems to give some kind of prestige, at least to the applicants seeking a career in the finance field. From an educational perspective, we observe innovative combinations of terms such as *quantitative, mathematical, computational,* and *engineering* integrated into novel program names like Quantitative Finance, Financial Engineering, Computational Finance, and Mathematical Finance. From a job role perspective, we see quantitative analysts, quant researchers, quantitative portfolio managers, financial engineers, quantitative developers, etc. Furthermore, this quant prefix seems to appear everywhere in banks, and financial institutes like insurance companies, asset management firms, and hedge funds, covering different parts of the firms like front office quants, risk quants, quant developers, etc. What is quant? What are the so-called quant skills? What are the quant skills that are taught by most programs from universities? What are the quant skills required by different roles like banks or hedge funds? The answer lies in the P Quant vs Q Quant distinctions.

Whenever they hear the word quant, most people will assume it refers to investment banks' (like Goldman Sachs or Morgan Stanley) quantitative research that deals with derivatives and structured products pricing if the role sits in the front office. This is unsurprising since this was the focus of the traditional finance programs offered by most universities with the prefix quant or other similar words we mentioned. The origin traces back to the emergence of derivatives and structured products popular since the late 1990s and early 2000s which gave rise to demand for heavy mathematical tools that were previously only used in science and engineering. The quant in this respect is usually referred to as the Q Quant which generally covers quantitative researchers working on derivatives valuation, a function mostly found in the sell side. The term risk-neutral measure is usually represented by the letter Q in the literature. Derivative pricing is based on hedge arguments, which means the perfectly hedged instrument/portfolio is essentially risk-free. With hedges, risk-averse individuals would behave like risk-neutral ones in the Q world. The transformation from the actual world (the P world) to the Q world lies in the *risk premium*, $(r - r_f)$ where r is the expected rate of return of a security in the real world, whereas r_f is the risk-free rate (the rate of return in a hedged, or risk-free world). The concept of risk premium is a core idea in quantitative finance, and it has key implications in both the P and Q worlds. Q Quants aim to price a security (mainly derivatives) fairly. The pricing requires the calibration of stochastic processes based on the underlying stocks' prices and other information such as dividends etc. The main idea is to *extrapolate the present* from available information.

Alternatively, P Quants refer to quantitative investors from the buy side such as quantitative hedge funds (e.g., Citadel, Two Sigma, AQR Capital, etc.) that focus on constructing quantitative portfolios by some kind of combination of statistics and machine-learning techniques for trading purposes. The use of P comes from an *objective* probability measure to model possible states in the future. In this spectrum, multivariate statistics and advanced econometrics are used for estimation to determine what securities to purchase and to sell to get the highest chance of a positive profit-and-loss profile. This results in rigorous portfolio construction, trading strategy, and risk management. In short, it is to model the future based on current information for profit-making purpose.

Quantitative factor investing belongs to the P Quant world since we want to find factors that could predict positive returns and trade on them. Nevertheless, the Q world might complement in some way. This is because some factors might need techniques from Q world for fair pricing, especially those related to derivatives. We will see an example of the jump factor which applies variance swap pricing technique from the Q world in Chapter 9.

Although the P world and Q world seem to be very different, there are occasions when the two worlds intersect. One example is derivatives hedging where fund managers in the P world need to use the "Greeks" calculated from the Q world to manage their trading book's risk. Another example can be given in the context of statistical arbitrage, where arbitragers use the fair prices of derivatives from the Q world as equilibrium and bet on real-price deviations from the equilibrium in the hope of price reversion.

1.3. Factor Investing and Value Investing

Factor investing and value investing are two distinct approaches within the investment world. Factor investing is a broad strategy that aims to utilize multiple factors—quantifiable characteristics of securities that can explain differences in returns—to construct and manage a portfolio. It is typically systematic and relies on a rules-based approach to identify and capitalize on these factors, such as size, value, momentum, quality, and low volatility, among others.

Value investing was made well-known and significant by Benjamin Graham and David Dodd, often referred to as the "fathers of value investing". Their seminal work, *Security Analysis*, first published in 1934, laid the intellectual foundation for this investment philosophy. Benjamin Graham later elaborated on these concepts in his book *The Intelligent Investor*, which was first published in 1949 and has since been widely regarded as one of the most important books on investing. Warren Buffett, perhaps the most famous proponent of value investing, was a student of Benjamin Graham at Columbia Business School and worked for Graham before starting his own investment partnership. Buffett's success at Berkshire Hathaway has made him an iconic figure in the investment world and has further popularized the value-investing approach. His annual letters to shareholders of Berkshire Hathaway are read extensively for insights into the practical application of value-investing principles.

Value investing focuses on finding securities that appear undervalued compared to their intrinsic value, often assessed through fundamental analysis. Value investing is epitomized by the search for stocks trading at a discount to their book value or with low price-to-earnings ratios, and it frequently involves a long-term horizon, with investors willing to wait for the market to realize the true value of these assets.

Despite their distinct characteristics, factor investing and value investing can exhibit similarities in certain aspects: Both strategies are grounded in the idea of rational investment, meaning they both rely on the analysis of financial data to make investment decisions. They reject speculative approaches that are based on hype without underlying financial justification. Both styles often use financial metrics to select investments. While factor investing may use a broader set of factors, value investing specifically focuses on value indicators such as the Price-To-Earnings (P/E) ratio, Price-To-Book (P/B) ratio, and dividend yield. The value factor is indeed one of the key factors in factor investing, illustrating a direct overlap. Both approaches typically take a long-term view of investing. Factor investors believe that certain factors will deliver superior returns over the long term, while value investors wait for the market to recognize and correct the undervaluation of the assets they have purchased. Both strategies aim to manage risk, though they may do so differently. Factor investing manages risk through diversification across different factors, while value investing often considers a margin of safety when purchasing undervalued assets, which can provide a buffer against errors in valuation or unforeseen market downturns. At times, both factor and value investors may take contrarian positions. For example, buying an undervalued stock in a downtrend is a contrarian move typical of value investing. Similarly, a factor investor might invest in stocks with high exposure to the value factor when growth stocks are in favor, which is also a contrarian stance. While factor investing is known for its quantitative approach, modern value investing has also incorporated more quantitative methods, blurring the lines between the two. As a result, many value investors now use quantitative tools to screen for undervalued stocks or to assess risk. Most importantly, both factor and value investors operate under the premise that markets can be inefficient in the short term, which can create opportunities for superior returns. Both styles seek to exploit inefficiencies such as mispricing and irrational behavior to generate long-term returns.

In essence, factor and value investing are not mutually exclusive and can sometimes be integrated into a comprehensive investment strategy. While factor investing often employs quantitative models, possibly incorporating machine learning to discern complex relationships, value investing may combine quantitative metrics with qualitative assessments of a company's financial health. Both strategies aim to outperform the market, but they do so through different lenses— one through diversified exposure to proven risk factors and the other through the identification of undervalued assets poised for appreciation.

Table 1.1 outlines some key differences between factor investing and value investing.

We can examine how factor investing works by examining and explaining Warren Buffett's Berkshire Hathaway performance by six factors (see Table 1.2) (Frazzini, Kabiller, and Pedersen 2018). The six factors are respectively excess market return, size factor, value factor, momentum factor, betting against beta factor, and quality factor.

From April 1980 to March 2017, as can be seen in the center panel, if a simple one-factor model (MKT, the market factor only) is applied to explain Berkshire's portfolio excess return, the alpha (intercept) of the model is 5.8% with a t-statistic of 3.09 (an absolute value of t-statistics above 2.0 can be considered statistically significant). If a four-factor model is used, with the market factor (MKT), the size factor (SMB), the value factor (HML) and the momentum factor (UMD) combined, the resulting alpha is still statistically significant at a t-statistic of 2.46. Suppose a five-factor model is used, that is, adding the Betting-Against-Beta (BAB), the alpha is further reduced, and the t-statistic falls to 1.62. If all the six factors are included in the model, the alpha becomes 0.3% with a t-statistic of 0.16, which is no longer significant. It is found that the two main factors that make the alpha insignificant are the BAB and the quality factor (QMJ). These six factors explain away Warren Buffet's alpha and at the same time can explain 61% of the variations of the model, suggesting significant explanatory power.

TABLE 1.1 Factor Investing vs Value Investing

	Factor Investing	Value Investing
Definition	Investing strategy that targets specific drivers of returns across asset classes.	Investing strategy that involves picking stocks that appear to be trading for less than their intrinsic value.
Investment Focus	Multiple factors (e.g., value, size, momentum, quality, volatility).	Typically focuses on identifying undervalued stocks.
Approach	Systematic, rules-based approach to portfolio construction.	Often involves qualitative analysis and fundamental research to identify undervalued stocks.
Diversification	Seeks to diversify across various factors to reduce risk and enhance returns.	May concentrate on a smaller number of holdings believed to be undervalued.
Quantitative Emphasis	High; typically involves complex statistical models and may use machine-learning techniques.	Moderate to high; relies on quantitative measures of value, but may also include qualitative assessment.
Time Horizon	Can vary; some factors may work better over different time horizons.	Long term; value investors may hold stocks for several years until they reach their perceived intrinsic value.
Market Conditions	Designed to perform across various market conditions depending on the factor exposure.	May perform better in bear markets when undervalued stocks can become more pronounced, or when the market corrects and value stocks may be favored.
Investor Psychology	Less driven by emotions.	Often contrarian, going against prevailing market sentiments to buy undervalued stocks.
Performance Attribution	Returns are attributed to factor premiums and their respective weights within the portfolio.	Returns are attributed to the realization of the asset's intrinsic value over time.

According to the factor model decomposition, Buffett's success can be attributed to the six factors. Moreover, the consistency in exposure to high-value, high-quality and low-beta stocks highlights his emphasis on value investing.

1.4. Current Landscape in Factor Investing

1.4.1. Smart Beta vs Factor Investing

One popular term we encounter in the industry is smart beta strategy. It is worth understanding what this term means and how it comes about.

The term "smart beta" originally referred to alternative index construction rules as opposed to market-capitalization weighted indexes. Beta refers to market exposure that originates from the Capital Asset Pricing Model (CAPM) which states that the expected excess return of any security is determined by its systematic (beta) exposure to the market-risk premium (i.e., the expected market return over the

TABLE 1.2. Berkshire Hathaway Performance Analysis

	Berkshire Stock, 10/1976–3/2017				13F Portfolio, 4/1980–3/2017				Private Holdings, 4/1980–3/2017			
Alpha	13.4%	11.0%	8.5%	5.4%	5.8%	4.5%	3.0%	0.3%	7.0%	4.9%	3.9%	3.5%
	(4.01)	(3.30)	(2.55)	(1.55)	(3.09)	(2.46)	(1.62)	(0.16)	(1.98)	(1.40)	(1.10)	(0.91)
MKT	0.69	0.83	0.83	0.95	0.77	0.85	0.86	0.95	0.30	0.39	0.40	0.42
	(11.00)	(12.74)	(12.99)	(12.77)	(22.06)	(23.81)	(24.36)	(23.52)	(4.46)	(5.63)	(5.72)	(5.03)
SMB		-0.29	-0.30	-0.13		-0.19	-0.19	-0.05		-0.26	-0.25	-0.23
		(-3.11)	(-3.19)	(-1.17)		(-3.73)	(-3.79)	(-0.95)		(-2.65)	(-2.56)	(-1.95)
HML		0.47	0.31	0.40		0.28	0.19	0.25		0.28	0.21	0.22
		(4.68)	(2.82)	(3.55)		(5.20)	(3.25)	(4.32)		(2.63)	(1.80)	(1.85)
UMD		0.06	-0.02	-0.05		-0.01	-0.06	-0.09		0.08	0.04	0.04
		(1.00)	(-0.25)	(-0.80)		(-0.36)	(-1.66)	(-2.58)		(1.24)	(0.62)	(0.51)
BAB			0.33	0.27			0.19	0.15			0.15	0.14
			(3.79)	(3.04)			(4.08)	(3.18)			(1.61)	(1.53)
QMJ				0.47				0.37				0.07
				(3.06)				(4.55)				(0.43)
$\bar{R}^2$	0.20	0.25	0.27	0.29	0.52	0.58	0.59	0.61	0.05	0.08	0.08	0.08
Obs	486	486	486	486	444	444	444	444	399	399	399	399

Source Values excerpted from Frazzini, Kabiller, and Pedersen (2018).

risk-free rate). One key result of CAPM is that the optimal portfolio offering the highest reward-to-risk ratio (the so-called Sharpe ratio) is the market-capitalization (market-cap) weighted portfolio. Because of the cost-effectiveness of *passive tracking*, ETFs tracking various market indexes have flourished in the market since then. However, with unrealistically rigorous assumptions of CAPM such as frictionless markets and unlimited long-short restrictions, etc., and abundant empirical evidence pointing to the rejection of the model, deviations from passive tracking strategies start to gain traction. These give rise to the idea of smart beta, which could be interpreted as *smart* or *alternative* exposure to the market in contrast to the pure market-cap weighting strategy.

With smart beta schemes, portfolio weights are optimized according to specified objectives by using alternative weighting methods. Popular examples include risk parity, maximum diversification, minimum variance, and equal-weighting schemes. We introduce them briefly here.

Risk parity is an investment strategy that focuses on allocating capital based on risk, rather than on market capitalization or other traditional methods. The goal is to balance the portfolio so that each asset class contributes equally to the overall risk of the portfolio. This contrasts with a more traditional approach where asset allocation might be based on market value, potentially leading to concentration in certain asset classes and, consequently, a higher risk exposure to those areas.

In the context of smart beta, which refers to investment strategies that deviate from the traditional market capitalization-weighted indexes to seek improved returns or lower risk, risk parity can be a guiding principle. Smart beta strategies use alternative methods to construct their portfolios, often based on factors such as value, size, momentum, dividend yield, and volatility.

Risk parity can be integrated into smart beta strategies by ensuring that the portfolio isn't overly reliant on any single factor (or small set of factors) that could lead to disproportionate risk. For instance, a smart beta fund might be constructed to have exposure to both low-volatility stocks and high-dividend stocks, but through risk parity, the fund would allocate its assets so that each of these factors contributes equally to the portfolio's risk profile. This is done by adjusting the investment weights according to the risk each asset or factor brings to the portfolio.

The rationale behind risk parity in the smart beta context is to create a more robust portfolio that can withstand different market conditions. By not overexposing the portfolio to any single source of risk, it may perform more consistently across various market environments. This is particularly appealing to investors who wish to minimize the impact of market volatility and are looking for a more stable return profile over the long term.

Marginal contribution to risk of an asset within a portfolio is defined as

$$w_i \frac{\partial \sigma_p}{\partial w_i}, \tag{1.1}$$

with w_i being the weight of asset i within a portfolio and σ_p the portfolio volatility (the standard deviation of returns)

$$\sigma_p = \sqrt{\Sigma_i w_i^2 \sigma_i^2 + \Sigma_i \Sigma_{j \neq i} w_i w_j \sigma_{ij}}. \qquad (1.2)$$

Since $\Sigma_i w_i \frac{\partial \sigma_p}{\partial w_i} = \frac{1}{\sigma_p} \Sigma_i w_i \left(w_i \sigma_i^2 + \Sigma_{j \neq i} w_j \sigma_{ij} \right) = \sigma_p$, the term $w_i \frac{\partial \sigma_p}{\partial w_i}$ is called the marginal contribution to risk as the sum (over all i's) equals the portfolio risk (volatility). The purpose of the risk parity scheme is to choose the weight w_i (for $i = 1, \ldots, n$) such that the marginal contribution to risk is equalized across assets.

Risk parity in Bridgewater's "All-Weather" investment strategy

Risk parity differs from modern portfolio theory which suggests minimizing variance based on a fixed level of expected return. The risk parity method allows capital allocation on a risk-weighted basis to diversify investment (across asset classes), viewing the risk and return of the entire portfolio as one.

The concept of risk parity originated from Bridgewater Associates, a global investment management firm. The firm created a very famous "All-Weather" investment strategy, which formed the foundation of risk parity. The strategy tries to answer the question "What kind of investment portfolio would perform well across all environments?", and it turns out this can be achieved by *balancing* the risk of assets.

Under this framework, assets (stocks and bonds) are balanced according to environmental conditions, such as inflation and growth periods, etc. By equalizing each asset's contribution to risk in a portfolio, the underperformance of some assets could be mitigated by others to a large extent. The term "risk parity" became popular after the successful implementation of the All-Weather investment strategy. It remains one of the most widely used smart beta schemes in the industry.

Maximum diversification scheme aims to maximize the diversification index (DI) by choosing w_i. DI is defined as

$$DI = \left(\frac{\Sigma_i w_i \sigma_i}{\sqrt{\Sigma_{i,j} w_i w_j \sigma_{ij}}} \right). \qquad (1.3)$$

The numerator of DI is the weighted average of volatility while the denominator is the portfolio's volatility. To understand its intuition, we take the example of a two-asset case. Suppose there is a perfect correlation (Pearson's correlation of one) between two assets, i.e., no diversification effect. It can easily be shown that the portfolio standard deviation is the weighted sum of the two assets' standard deviations: $\sigma_p = \sqrt{w_1^2 \sigma_1^2 + w_2^2 \sigma_2^2 + 2 w_1 w_2 \sigma_1 \sigma_2 (1)} = w_1 \sigma_1 + w_2 \sigma_2$. In this case, Equation (1.3) will equal one, which is also the lower bound. When we extend the problem to multiple assets, we can see that the numerator of Equation (1.3) is always greater than the denominator. If there is a strong internal diversification within a portfolio, the value of DI will be higher. Therefore, maximizing DI means maximizing the diversification effect within a portfolio.

TOBAM and Amundi: A Story on Maximum Diversification Ratio (MDR)

TOBAM is a French asset management company that is credited with developing the concept of the Maximum Diversification Ratio (MDR). The idea behind MDR is to construct a portfolio that maximizes the diversification across its holdings. TOBAM's philosophy posits that diversification, more than any other component, is key to achieving better risk-adjusted returns. This is backed by the idea that markets are not always efficient and that risk can be reduced more effectively through diversification than through traditional asset allocation strategies.

The Maximum Diversification Ratio is calculated as follows:

$$MDR = \frac{Portfolio\ Volatility}{Weighted\ Average\ Volatility\ of\ Individual\ Securities}$$

where *Portfolio Volatility* is the standard deviation of the portfolio's returns and *Weighted Average Volatility of Individual Securities* is the sum of the products of each security's weight in the portfolio and its volatility.

The numerator represents the risk (volatility) of the entire portfolio, while the denominator represents the sum of risks if each asset was held in isolation, weighted by their respective portfolio weights. The work was published in 2006 in the United States Patent and Trademark Office and later in 2008 in the *Journal of Portfolio Management*.

TOBAM's MDR approach uses quantitative methods to assess the diversification of each asset in the portfolio. It then constructs a portfolio that maximizes this diversification measure.

In 2012, Amundi, the largest asset manager in Europe, entered a strategic partnership with French asset management company TOBAM. Amundi provides the platform and distribution channels that help bring TOBAM's approach to a wider base of investors. Together, they have created and offered investment solutions that aim to maximize the diversification benefits for investors.

The MDR-based products have been met with interest from investors looking for alternative ways to construct their portfolios, especially in times of increased market volatility and correlation between asset classes.

Minimum variance, as its name suggests, tries to minimize a portfolio's variance by choosing an optimal weight vector. One can imagine that under this scheme, most weights will be allocated to lower volatility stocks like utilities. Stocks with lower covariances with others will also have higher weights as well.

The equal-weighting scheme is the easiest. It assigns the same weights to all constituents within a portfolio. Despite its straightforward interpretation, this scheme suffers from a liquidity issue since all stocks (liquid or illiquid) are financed equally. When a portfolio has a high capital base and insufficient stocks, the market impact on some illiquid stocks can be prohibitively expensive.

Note that all schemes mentioned above are based on weighting within a portfolio instead of picking the stocks, which involves much more activeness. Smart beta as an alternative weighting scheme can be regarded as somewhere between passive and active management.

The term smart beta later evolved to refer to enhanced-return strategies that involve using factors to outperform a benchmark index. In factor investing, we choose the factors we would like to be exposed to in each environment. ETFs and custom indices that mimic different factors emerge for this purpose. The famous factor ETFs are, for instance, the iShares issued by Blackrock and custom indices produced by MSCI Barra.

1.4.2. The Factor Zoo

Factor ETFs and custom indices are based on broad concepts like value, size, momentum, volatility, quality, etc. They are sometimes termed "styles" instead of "factors" since each of them is composed of many variables (or attributes) or a combination/formula of variables. For example, value consists of various fundamental variables from financial statements or balance sheets like book-to-price ratio, earnings-to-price ratio, book values, sales, earnings, cashflow, etc., and some extended calculations like free cashflow which involves sales revenue, operating costs, taxes, and operating capital in the calculation. These variables are equivocally included as factors in the industry. With multiple styles and many variables within styles, together with ongoing unrelenting efforts to discover new factors, the rate of factor production becomes so fast and out-of-control that many of them become redundant or replicates of others. Professor John Cochrane, a famous financial economist, describes this phenomenon as the "factor zoo".

"Factor Zoo" by John Cochrane

John Cochrane was formerly a professor of economics and finance at the University of Chicago. He serves full-time as the Rose-Marie and Jack Anderson Senior Fellow at the Hoover Institution at Stanford University. His book, *Asset Pricing*, is the standard textbook for graduate courses on asset pricing in finance. It earned him the TIAA-CREF Institute Paul A. Samuelson Award.

Cochrane was active in the media and contributed to the debate on the financial crisis during 2008. His blog *The Grumpy Economist* humorously commented on the issues which drew criticism from Paul Krugman, who won the

Nobel Memorial Prize in Economic Sciences in 2008, leading Cochrane to write a response on his website. The response was later published in *The Wall Street Journal*.

In his 2011 presidential address to the American Finance Association, Cochrane coined the term *zoo of factors*. This was to describe the uncontrolled explosive growth of factors in the industry in a humorous way, which is how the term *factor zoo* came.

Cochrane is the son-in-law of the famous financial economist Eugene Fama, who won the Nobel Memorial Prize in Economic Sciences in 2013 and is one of the most prominent figures in asset pricing literature.

1.4.3 Multiple Hypothesis Testing and False Discoveries

One cause of the "factor zoo" in finance is the phenomenon of multiple hypothesis testing (MHT) and the resultant false discoveries. MHT refers to the practice of testing multiple null hypotheses using the same dataset. In empirical asset pricing and factor investing, the mining of hundreds or even thousands of factors from the same historical data exemplifies a multiple hypothesis testing problem. When testing several hypotheses simultaneously, it's possible to encounter some false discoveries merely by chance.

Consider the scenario where 100 independent factors (i.e., 100 null hypotheses) are tested simultaneously, and one factor shows a t-statistic of 2.0. In this case, we cannot assert that the factor is significant at the 5% significance level. This is because, even if all 100 null hypotheses are true (meaning their expected excess returns are zero), there's still a 99% chance of encountering a t-statistic greater than 2.0 purely by chance. Hence, using the conventional threshold of 2.0 for the t-statistic to determine significance will inevitably lead to many false discoveries or false rejections. This type of error, where a true null hypothesis is incorrectly rejected, is statistically known as a Type I error.

In recent years, to secure publications in top-tier journals, scholars have indulged in data snooping, excessively chasing low p-values (a practice known as p-hacking). Unfortunately, due to deliberate or unintentional data manipulation, the use of lax statistical methods, misinterpretations of p-values, and neglect of the inherent economic logic of factors, many factors concocted under utilitarian motives fail to hold up after publication, as discussed by McLean and Pontiff (2016). Correspondingly, Smart Beta ETF funds also suffer from the problem of p-hacking (Huang et al. forthcoming).

At the 2017 American Finance Association (AFA) meeting, Professor Campbell Harvey, then AFA president, dissected this phenomenon in his speech "The Scientific Outlook of Financial Economics". Advocating for a scientific approach and integrity, Harvey urged scholars to acknowledge and reevaluate the research culture in empirical asset pricing (Harvey 2017).

Professor Campbell R. Harvey

Professor Campbell R. Harvey is a distinguished academic figure in the realm of finance, particularly celebrated for his expertise in investment finance and international finance at Duke University's Fuqua School of Business. With a PhD from the University of Chicago, Professor Harvey has devoted his career to dissecting the intricacies of financial markets and instruments. His scholarly pursuits have firmly established him as a leader in the field, fostering a deeper understanding of market dynamics through his teaching and prolific research.

In the sphere of factor investing, Professor Harvey's contributions are particularly noteworthy. Harvey has delved into the temporal aspects of factor premiums, shedding light on their performance across various economic conditions. This exploration has armed investors with valuable insights about the timing and reasons behind the outperformance of certain factors. Moreover, he has been at the forefront of critiquing the rapid expansion of factors within academic circles. Harvey has argued for more rigorous statistical methods to curb data mining practices and to prevent the recognition of spurious factors that falter outside of sample data.

His innovative methodologies for assessing financial factors have underscored the necessity of solid statistical techniques to circumvent false discoveries in finance. This has been especially significant in a world where investment strategies are increasingly data-driven. Harvey's influence extends beyond academia into the realm of practical finance, where he has educated numerous investment professionals on the nuances of factor investing. His ability to distill complex research into practical investment advice has altered the landscape of factor investing.

Moreover, Campbell Harvey and his long-time collaborator Yan Liu have made significant contributions to this research agenda, which encompasses frequentist and Bayesian methods. In their seminal paper "… and the Cross-Section of Expected Returns" (Harvey, Liu, and Zhu 2016), they mainly flagged the issue, arguing that multiple testing may contribute to the proliferation of factors or asset pricing anomalies. In their subsequent work "Lucky Factors" (Harvey and Liu 2021a), they proposed a general testing framework that nests most asset pricing environments and systematically addresses the issue of multiple testing. In an attempt to generalize the Type I and Type II error trade off to multiple testing, they took their insights to the prominent yet perplexing performance evaluation literature and provided a different answer to the question: "how many fund managers outperform?" (see Harvey and Liu 2020, 2022). Finally, borrowing the idea of prior anchoring from the Bayesian literature on multiple testing adjustments, they proposed a new frequentist approach to forming robust estimates in a panel data setup, as exemplified in Harvey and Liu (2018, 2019).

Addressing MHT and false discoveries has long been a focus in other disciplines, as noted by Ioannidis (2005), while finance has been relatively late to the game.

However, the good news is that both the academic and professional worlds are now recognizing this issue. Regarding the severity of this issue, it is crucial for the academic community to discuss it with an open mind. For instance, Chen (2021) and Jensen, Kelly, and Pedersen (2023) have pointed out that the problem may not be as severe as previously thought. Nevertheless, as Harvey and Liu (2021b) attest, the issue remains under-identified since we only observe published factors, unaware of the total number attempted. As a result, acknowledging this methodological issue and deriving convincing conclusions through sound priors is the right approach to research.

1.5. Factors? What Are They?

We have so far seen the loose definition of factors from an industry point of view, i.e., any variables that seem to drive (or correlate to) future returns on assets. Nevertheless, when we read asset-pricing literature from academic journals, the term "factors" seems to have a completely different meaning. A related and omnipresent term "alpha" also refers to different things between industry and academia. To reconcile the differences, it is worth a brief review of factor models in the asset-pricing literature.

The linear factor model representation of assets' expected returns roots deeply in the theory of asset pricing, which shows the equivalence between the stochastic discount factor (SDF) representation, the mean-variance efficient portfolio, and the linear factor model in terms of pricing assets' returns in the cross-section. While a full treatment of all the necessary mathematical derivation is beyond the scope of this book, a brief introduction about its background is essential to explain why identifying factors and specifying the linear factor model are of paramount importance for both academia and the asset management industry to analyze assets' returns. For a comprehensive discussion of the asset pricing theory, interested readers are referred to the authoritative book of Cochrane (2005).

In the spirit of Ross's (1976) arbitrage pricing theory (APT), the data-generating process of assets' excess returns is governed by

$$r = \mathrm{E}[r] + \beta\nu + e \tag{1.4}$$

where the $N \times 1$ vector r represents assets' excess returns, the $N \times K$ matrix β represents factor exposures (also referred to as factor loadings), assuming there are a total number K of factors, the $K \times 1$ vector ν is the zero-mean factor innovations, and the $N \times 1$ vector e is the zero-mean idiosyncratic errors, such that $\mathrm{E}[e|\nu] = 0$. According to the APT, the expected excess return $\mathrm{E}[r]$ can be decomposed as

$$\mathrm{E}[r] = \alpha + \beta\lambda, \tag{1.5}$$

where the $K \times 1$ vector λ is the factors' risk premia, and the $N \times 1$ vector α represents pricing errors. It is worth mentioning that Equation (1.5) indicates that the expected excess return of a given asset is determined by its exposure to a set of factors and the risk premia of those factors (plus an error term), and it explains why assets have different excess expected returns in the *cross-section*. This cross-sectional equation is both the heart and soul of empirical asset pricing and factor investing.

While theory provides a framework for studying assets' returns under (1.5), it does not offer much guidance on which factors should be included on the right-hand side of the equation. Regarding the identification of factors, there are two main approaches and both have gained a lot of attention. The first approach assumes either factors or factor exposures are known and observable. Academia and the industry take different stances in this regard. Specifically, academia considers that factors are tradable portfolios that are constructed by using some firm characteristics, such as the HML (the value factor) and SMB (the size factor) factors of Fama and French (1993) (which are built by using the book-to-market ratio and the market cap). In this case, factor realizations are the excess returns of those tradable portfolios, and factor exposures are determined by regressing assets' excess returns on factors. A related but different stance commonly adopted in the industry (e.g. the MSCI Barra model) assumes that factor exposures are observable. In this case, industry practice uses firm characteristics (usually after necessary normalization) directly as factor exposures β, and factors' risk premia can be obtained by regressing assets' return on the factor exposures.

These two distinct perspectives also clarify the different interpretations of the term "factors" as used by academia and industry, a distinction we emphasize throughout this chapter. In academia, "factors" refer to tradable portfolios. For example, the value factor, often represented as HML (High-Minus-Low), is constructed by forming two portfolios from the universe of stocks: one portfolio contains stocks with high book-to-market ratios (value stocks), and the other contains stocks with low book-to-market ratios (growth stocks). The performance of the high book-to-market portfolio minus the performance of the low book-to-market portfolio is considered the HML factor return, capturing the excess returns of value stocks over growth stocks. In contrast, within the industry, the term pertains to firm characteristics which, though not explicitly stated, serve as the factor exposures within the framework of a linear factor model. The second approach, as pioneered by Chamberlain and Rothschild (1983) and Connor and Korajczyk (1986), assumes both factors and factor exposures are latent. In this case, a statistical technique such as principal component analysis is employed to identify the factor model, and the factors are called statistical factors.

This book adopts the first approach for the following two reasons. First, the finance literature has proposed a plethora of tradable portfolios (constructed by using corresponding firm characteristics) as factors, and they have either risk-based or behavioral finance explanations. Categorizing them into different classes and providing a detailed description for each category will give the readers a comprehensive understanding of the most important and prevailing factors discovered by academia in the past several decades. Second, although the statistical factor model is conceptually appealing as it does not require factors to be known and observable, it is very hard to estimate accurately given the small sample size and low signal-to-noise ratio nature of asset return data. Besides, the statistical factor model assumes that all relevant and priced risk factors are reflected in asset returns and can be captured by the specified factors. However, in practice, this assumption may not hold true, especially if certain risk factors are weak or if markets are less integrated, giving rise to the omitted variable problem (Giglio and Xiu 2021). These limitations undermine the effectiveness and reliability of traditional statistical factor models in capturing the true risk structure of asset pricing.

When factors are tradable portfolios, factor realizations f can be written as the sum between the population mean $E[f]$ and factor innovations ν_t, i.e., $f = E[f] + \nu$, and it can be shown that factors' risk premia $\lambda = E[f]$. To see this, the no-arbitrage condition implies that α in Equation (1.5) is zero (i.e., no pricing errors), a condition equivalent to the existence of a stochastic discount factor m of the form $m = a - b'(f - E[f])$, satisfying the fundamental equation $E[mr] = 0$. Without loss of generality, we can normalize m such that $E[m] = 1$, which means that a takes the value of 1, and therefore m becomes $m = 1 - b'(f - E[f])$.

To derive the linear factor model, start with $E[mr] = 0$ and write,

$$0 = E[mr] = E[m]E[r] - \text{cov}(r, f')b$$

$$= E[r] - \text{cov}(r, f')b. \tag{1.6}$$

Therefore, we can write

$$E[r] = \text{cov}(r, f')b. \tag{1.7}$$

Next, plugging the definition of $\beta' \equiv \text{cov}(r, f')\text{var}(f)^{-1}$ into (1.7) gives

$$E[r] = \text{cov}(r, f')\text{var}(f)^{-1}\text{var}(f)b$$

$$= \beta'\text{var}(f)b. \tag{1.8}$$

where $\lambda \equiv \text{var}(f)b$ are the risk premia of the factors. To see the meaning of λ, multiplying f' on both sides of $m = 1 - b'(f - E[f])$ and then taking expectation and then transposing would yield,

$$E[mf] = E[f] - \text{var}(f)b. \tag{1.9}$$

Since factors are tradable portfolios and therefore f represents their excess returns, it follows that $E[mf] = 0$. Plugging this into (1.9) gives $E[f] = \text{var}(f)b \equiv \lambda$, or $\lambda = E[f]$, i.e., the risk premium of a tradable factor is the expected value of its excess return, and $f = \lambda + \nu$.

Finally, plugging (1.5) into (1.4) and using the fact that $f = \lambda + \nu$, we can re-write the data generating process of assets' excess returns as

$$r = \alpha + \beta f + e. \tag{1.10}$$

It can also be written for individual asset i's excess return at time t as,

$$r_{it} = \alpha_i + \sum_{k=1}^{K} \beta_{ik} f_{kt} + e_{it}, \tag{1.11}$$

where β_{ik} is the factor loading of asset i on factor k and f_{kt} is the factor k's excess return realization at time t. In general, the number of factors K is much smaller than the number of assets N. The term alpha (α) refers to the *intercept* of a factor model (Equation (1.11). It is the part of the excess return that is not explained or captured by the factors (also commonly referred to as "mispricing" in academia). This definition contrasts with the industry definition of alpha which basically means the *outperformance* of a strategy over a market benchmark index.

With the help of Equation (1.11), we next explain how academia and industry estimate a factor model differently. For academia, since factors are tradable portfolios, factor realizations f are assumed to be known. Therefore, one only needs to run *time-series* regression of each individual asset's excess return on factor realizations over time periods $t = 1, \ldots, T$. The estimated regression coefficients are estimates of factor exposures for this particular asset, and the intercept term is the estimate of the pricing error α_i.

For industry practice, on the other hand, firm characteristics are treated as factor exposures. As a result, Equation (1.11) changes to

$$r_{it} = \gamma_t + \sum_{k=1}^{K} \beta_{ik} f_{kt} + e_{it}. \tag{1.12}$$

Note that the intercept term in Equation (1.12) is no longer α_i but changed to γ_t (we use something other than α deliberately to emphasize that it is not a pricing error). Equation (1.12) is a *cross-sectional* regression across different assets but for a given time period t; that is, we regress cross-sectionally assets' excess returns on the factor exposures to estimate factor returns for time t. The regression coefficients derived are estimates of factor returns. However, as we have mentioned, the intercept term from the cross-sectional regression shall not be interpreted as a pricing error because it is the same for all assets in the cross-section. Instead, the residual term e_{it} from the regression is the estimate of the pricing error.

Although academia and industry have different definitions for the term factor and use different methods to estimate factor models, the actual differences between the two perspectives are not as significant as they seem. Both aim to find firm characteristics that can help explain the cross-sectional differences in assets' expected returns and eliminate pricing errors. In essence, the goal of factor investing is to find useful factors under the core formula $E[r] = \alpha + \beta\lambda$, and presenting factors of different categories to readers is precisely the objective of this book.

1.6. Factor Identification Process

So far, we have been dealing with factors $f_{1t}, \ldots, f_{Kt}$ as if they are known. One question we may ask is: how are they determined to be valid? On the technical side, academics have a standard procedure that the industry also follows closely. However, before we move on to addressing the mathematical procedure of factor identification, let us first briefly explain the standards that common factors should satisfy.

The generality of linear factor models introduces certain perils to empirical research, suggesting that one can seemingly add any factor to a model at whim. Financial titan Eugene Fama jestingly referred to factor models as a "fishing license", mocking the act of factor mining within the multifactor paradigm. To ensure there's substantive economic rationale behind factors and to prevent factor research from degenerating into a mere data mining exercise, a true and valid factor should satisfy the following six criteria (Shi, Liu, and Lian 2020). First and foremost, it should possess a strong intuitiveness, having a logical foundation viewed either from a risk lens or through behavioral finance. Persistence is equally crucial, ensuring that the factor remains effective over time, even after it has been publicly disclosed. Another vital attribute is its ability to provide incremental predictive power to assets' returns, offering a unique perspective not captured by other factors. Moreover, the factor's robustness is paramount, demanding insensitivity to varying construction methods and parameters, and proving resistant in diverse robustness tests. In a practical sense, the factor should be highly investable, translating on-paper returns into actionable strategies with manageable transaction costs. Lastly, its pervasive nature across different asset classes or consistency within a single asset class across various countries speaks to its universal applicability and relevance in the investment landscape. All the different categories of factors introduced in this book meet the aforementioned criteria.

Now, let us turn to the technical part. We first introduce the rigorous procedure in the asset pricing literature and then discuss industry variations. Recall that for academia, factors are considered as tradable portfolios that are constructed by some corresponding firm characteristics (or attributes). When a researcher identifies a potential factor that explains the cross-sectional variation of returns, the first step is to construct a market-wide measure to represent it. This is best explained by an example and let us use the Small–Minus–Big (SMB) factor (also known as the size factor) by Fama and French (1992, 1993) for demonstration. In their work, Fama and French first sort all firms by market capitalizations (for a specified universe) in ascending order. Put differently, market capitalization is the firm characteristic used to construct the size factor. The sorted firms are divided into three quantiles and each quantile is formed into an equal-weighted (or value-weighted) portfolio. The first portfolio is composed of all smallest-sized stocks while the third portfolio is composed of all largest-sized stocks. An SMB premium is the difference between the returns of the small and the big portfolios measured in the next period (usually one month). Then, firms are sorted again with the small and big portfolios rebalanced. The returns spread is observed again in another period and the procedure continues. Following this procedure, we will have a time series of SMB premiums over time.

Nowadays, the asset pricing literature usually applies 10 quantiles to sort stocks (instead of three quantiles) according to a specified attribute, then uses quantile ten portfolio's return minus the quantile one portfolio's return (equal-weighted or value-weighted) as the spread. We denote the time series of spreads as SP_t for brevity. One can add this factor to the right-hand side of Equation (1.11), and run time series regression to estimate assets' exposures on this particular factor. Given that this approach constructs factors by first sorting stocks in the cross-section based on a particular attribute, and then allocating them into different portfolios, it is also referred to as the *portfolio sort* method in the academic community.

Eugene Fama and Kenneth French

Eugene Fama and Kenneth French are probably the most recognizable figures in the asset pricing space. They are American economists and professors at the University of Chicago Booth School of Business and Dartmouth College, respectively.

Fama is well known for his work on efficient markets, especially the Efficient Market Hypothesis (EMH) which states the three forms of market efficiency: the strong form, semi-strong form, and the weak form. The work of efficient markets has been influential in the development of index funds like Exchange Traded Funds (ETF) and passive investing strategies.

Fama is also a key figure in empirical finance. His co-work with James MacBeth on the Fama-MacBeth regression (Fama and MacBeth 1973) is a standard in the literature in estimating the relationship between asset returns and various factors. In corporate finance, Fama also introduced the concept of the agency cost of debt.

Fama received numerous awards for his contributions to financial economics, including the Nobel Memorial Prize in Economic Sciences in 2013.

To test the validity of factors, the Fama and MacBeth (1973) procedure is the standard in all empirical works. The procedure has the following steps:

i. For each stock i, run a time series regression of excess return r_{it} on SP_t using $t = 1, \ldots, T$ observations to estimate β_i, and there will be N estimated betas $(\hat{\beta}_i)$ from the N time-series regressions

$$r_{it} = \alpha_i + \beta_i SP_t + e_{it}, \tag{1.13}$$

ii. For each time point $t = 1, \ldots, T$, run a cross-sectional regression of all stocks' excess returns on the $\hat{\beta}_i$ using $i = 1, \ldots, N$ observations. We get estimated $\hat{\lambda}_t$ from each regression and there are T of them $(\hat{\lambda}_1, \ldots \hat{\lambda}_T)$ from the T cross-sectional regressions

$$r_{it} = \gamma_t + \lambda_t \hat{\beta}_i + e_{it}, \tag{1.14}$$

where γ_t is the intercept (the constant from regression) and e_{it} are the errors (there are n of them for each t)

iii.   Assuming the estimated $\hat{\lambda}_t$ are independent and identically distributed (i.i.d.), we can compute the t-statistics since we have T observations which allow us to compute the standard errors

$$t_\lambda = \frac{\bar{\lambda}}{\hat{\sigma}_\lambda / \sqrt{T}}, \tag{1.15}$$

where $\bar{\lambda} = \frac{\sum_{t-1}^{T} \hat{\lambda}_t}{T}$ is factor average return, serving as the estimate of factors' risk premium and $\hat{\sigma}_\lambda = \frac{\sum_{t-1}^{T} (\hat{\lambda}_t - \bar{\lambda})^2}{T-1}$ is the standard error. t_λ tells us the statistical significance of the factor average return. For large samples, we look for its absolute value to be greater than 2.0.

One might wonder why we do not use SP_t directly as the estimate of the factor premium but go through the cross-sectional regressions. The reason behind it is to extract the *unit* factor premium, i.e., the expected return of a portfolio that has exactly one unit exposure to this factor (so its beta to this factor is 1). By running the cross-sectional regression as Equation (1.14), λ_t corresponds to the factor premium of such a portfolio (see Figure 1.1 for an illustration of $\beta = 1$ to this specific factor) at each time period $t = 1, \ldots, T$.

Suppose we have many potential factors, and we wish to pick the most important one out of them, we can apply the ranking procedure to each of them to get the "spreads" correspondingly. Then we apply the Fama-MacBeth procedure for each of them to see which t_λ has the highest absolute value. This

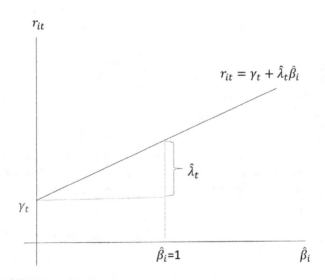

FIGURE 1.1. Factor Premium from Cross-sectional Regression

searching process is sometimes informally called the "Fama-MacBeth race" in the literature for factor identification.

Having discussed the portfolio sort and the Fama-MacBeth procedure to identify significant factors within the academic world, we now turn our focus to industry treatment. As a reminder, for industry, the term factor refers to the firm characteristics or attributes that implicitly serve as the factor exposures in a factor model. For example, industry will view the earnings-to-price ratio (EP), rather than the tradable portfolio constructed by sorting stocks using EP, as the factor. In assessing the factor's validity, the standard evaluation tool is known as the Information Coefficient (IC). To illustrate the idea of IC, suppose we are interested in testing whether a particular factor (say EP) of stocks drives their future returns. The IC of the EP factor is defined as

$$\mathrm{corr}\left(EP_{i,t}, R_{i,t+1}\right), \tag{1.16}$$

where $EP_{i,t}$ and $R_{i,t+1}$ are respectively the earning-to-price ratio of stocks $i = 1, \ldots, n$ at time t and returns of the stocks $i = 1, \ldots, n$ for the next period $t + 1$. $\mathrm{corr}(X, Y)$ is simply the Pearson correlation defined as

$$\mathrm{E}[r] = \mathrm{cov}(r, f')b.$$

In addition to the cumulative IC plot, we can also compute the mean and standard deviation of the IC_t

$$IC_{mean} = \frac{IC_1 + \ldots IC_{T-1}}{T - 1}.$$

$$IC_{std} = \sqrt{\frac{1}{T - 2} \sum_{t=1}^{T-1} (IC_t - IC_{mean})^2}. \tag{1.18}$$

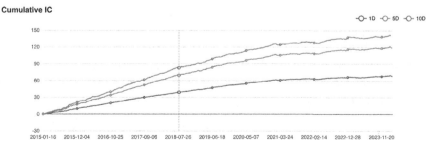

Cumulative IC

FIGURE 1.2. Example of a Cumulative IC Chart
Source: Super Quantum Fund

The information coefficient's information ratio, denoted IC_{IR}, is defined as

$$IC_{IR} = \frac{IC_{mean}}{IC_{std}}. \tag{1.19}$$

A high IC_{IR} indicates that the average IC is high and/or its standard deviation is low.

1.7. Consensus Factors

Having described the factor identification procedure in the last section, we now briefly review the key consensus factors in the academic world. This contrasts with the factor zoo phenomenon in the industry.

The first yet most impactful factor model is the Capital Asset Pricing Model (CAPM). It states that market expected excess return is the single factor that explains the cross-sectional variation of assets' expected excess returns fully,

$$E[r_i] = \alpha_i + \beta_i \, E[r_m]. \tag{1.20}$$

If CAPM holds, then the α_i estimated from the sample should be insignificantly different from zero in a statistical sense since all assets' returns should be explained solely by their regression coefficients β_i. The beta here is called the systematic exposure of asset i to the market factor. Securities with higher betas are expected to have higher returns to compensate for the higher level of risk, and conversely, securities with lower betas are expected to have lower returns due to their lower level of risk.

Capital Asset Pricing Model (CAPM) and Betting-Against-Beta (BAB)

CAPM was developed by William Sharpe, John Lintner, and Jack Treynor in the 1960s. The origin traces back to Harry Markowitz who invented the efficient frontier (or Modern Portfolio Theory).

The main contribution of CAPM is the systematic risk concept, measured by the beta coefficient. The concept of beta is still widely used in the industry, which states the co-movement of a security's return with the market. While traditional finance tells us *high risk high return*, CAPM is the first to point out that NOT all risks are priced. Instead, only the undiversifiable or systematic risk is compensated, highlighting the role of diversification in finance.

The "Betting-Against-Beta" (BAB) factor is an investment strategy that comes from the observation that lower-beta securities may offer better risk-adjusted returns than higher-beta securities, which contradicts the prediction of the CAPM (Frazzini and Pedersen 2014).

> The BAB factor strategy involves going long (buying) on low-beta assets and shorting (selling) high-beta assets, with the aim of profiting from this anomaly. The idea is that by doing so, one can create a portfolio that has an overall beta of zero, which theoretically should not have any market risk (as measured by beta) and thus should earn the risk-free rate. However, in practice, these portfolios have been shown to earn higher returns than the risk-free rate, suggesting that lower-beta securities are providing higher risk-adjusted returns.
>
> This phenomenon can be partially explained by leverage constraints. Some investors cannot use leverage or prefer not to. These investors, seeking higher returns, may disproportionately invest in high-beta assets, pushing their prices up and their future returns down. Conversely, since lower-beta assets are less attractive to these investors, they may be underpriced, leading to higher future returns. Moreover, behavioral biases might cause investors to overpay for high-beta assets that have the potential for large gains during market upswings. As a result, high-beta assets might be overvalued and low-beta assets undervalued.
>
> Therefore, the BAB factor suggests that, in contradiction to CAPM, securities with lower betas might not only be less risky but also might be associated with higher returns when adjusted for that risk.

The main contribution of CAPM is its introduction of systematic exposure, aka beta, stating that not all risks are priced but only systematic risk, which is the covariance of a security's return with the market return (scaled by the variance of market returns), is priced. The market factor is *market-wide* in the sense that it is the same for all assets. The CAPM model gives us clear definitions of factor, alpha and beta: A factor is a market-wide risk that is the same for every asset, the exposure to the factor risk needs to be compensated by the factor risk premium. Assets have different returns because of their different exposures (betas) to the factor.

Although CAPM's key concept of diversification is very popular, the fact that a single factor drives all cross-sectional variation of returns seems too rigid. Fama and French (1992) introduced size and book-to-market values which drive excess returns that cannot be explained by market beta alone. Fama and French (1993) formalized the small-minus-big (SMB) and high-minus-low (HML) factors which respectively represent the spread of returns between the small-market capitalization stocks and the big-market capitalization stocks, and the spread of returns between the high book-to-market value stocks and the low book-to-market value stocks. The Fama-French 3-factor (FF3) model then becomes the standard which complements the CAPM by adding the size and the value factors,

$$E[r_i] = \alpha_i + \beta_{i1} E[r_m] + \beta_{i2} \text{SMB} + \beta_{i3} \text{HML}. \qquad (1.21)$$

Carhart (1997) introduces the fourth factor based on Jegadeesh and Titman (1993)'s work on momentum. It is the difference between the previous 12-month returns of winners and losers, skipping the most recent month's returns in order to avoid the serial correlation problem. The four-factor model is usually abbreviated as FF3+MOM in the literature, which represents another standard model,

$$E[r_i] = \alpha_i + \beta_{i1}E[r_m] + \beta_{i2}\text{SMB} + \beta_{i3}\text{HML} + \beta_{i4}\text{MOM}. \qquad (1.22)$$

Though not as widely adopted as the FF3 and the MOM factor, Pástor and Stambaugh (2003) identify an additional liquidity factor which relates stocks' excess return reversal from previous order flows. A high reversal indicates lower liquidity and thus requires a higher-risk premium. This five-factor model is sometimes abbreviated to FF3 + MOM + LIQ in literature,

$$E[r_i] = \alpha_i + \beta_{i1}E[r_m] + \beta_{i2}\text{SMB} + \beta_{i3}\text{HML} + \beta_{i4}\text{MOM} + \beta_{i5}\text{LIQ}. \quad (1.23)$$

Fama and French (2015) develop another five-factor model (FF5) on top of their FF3 model by adding the profitability factor (RMW) and the investment factor (CMA). RMW stands for robust-minus-weak, the difference between the returns of firms with robust (high) and weak (low) operating profitability. CMA stands for conservative-minus-aggressive, the difference between the returns of firms investing conservatively and those investing aggressively,

$$E[r_i] = \alpha_i + \beta_{i1}E[r_m] + \beta_{i2}\text{SMB} + \beta_{i3}\text{HML} + \beta_{i4}\text{RMW} + \beta_{i5}\text{CMA}.$$
$$(1.24)$$

The set of standard models is critical because it helps us identify whether an identified factor is original, or just a replication of existing factors. When a new factor is identified, the typical step is to run the portfolio sort test, i.e., to perform a ranking (for a specified universe) of stocks into 10 deciles, calculate the difference between the returns of the top decile (equal-weighted or value-weighted) versus the bottom decile for the subsequent period. This is performed period-wise to get a time series of spreads. Then run a time series regression of the spreads on a chosen standard model, say FF3 + MOM + LIQ with an intercept. If the intercept is significantly different from zero, it means that the spreads are not fully explained by an existing model. This gives some validity to the newly identified factor.

1.8. Industry Factors

Now, we turn our attention to industry practice. Since the definitions and the identification of factors are less rigorous than the asset pricing literature the number of factors becomes so numerous, a phenomenon known as the factor zoo as mentioned before. There is no consensus on what those factors are, and we do not even have a standard classification for them. An informal and non-exhaustive classification based on our observation and experience is presented here.

The first category could be securities' sensitivity to macroeconomic variables like interest rates, currency, credit spreads, commodity prices, etc. Macroeconomic variables could be understood as risk barometers of the general market environment. For instance, a looming black-swan event is likely associated with a strengthening US dollar and heightened credit spreads, etc. As a result, the sensitivity of stocks to macroeconomic variables is usually treated as a factor in the industry.

The second category relates to firms' fundamentals like leverage ratios from the balance sheet or financial ratios from the income statement, etc. Scores constructed from single or multiple financial ratios can also serve as factors. A well-known example is the Piotroski F-score, which combines nine measures to assess the strength of a company's financial position. Using fundamentals as factors in a quantitative model is different from the approach of fundamental analysts who use only fundamental information to make investment decisions. Combining fundamentals into quantitative models gives rise to an innovative term called "Quantamentals". This will be further discussed in Chapter 2.

The third category is statistical properties. Based on investors' risk preferences, asset pricing theories address questions like risk aversion and how they can be reflected in statistical moments. Furthermore, advanced techniques like regression and time series analysis can also draw relevant information from data. Chapter 3 will discuss how statistical moments can be interpreted as factors and review the new trends.

A fourth category relates to the microstructure of the market. Important factors can be volume price moves, turnovers, high-low-open-close behavior, liquidity, order flow, etc. Deeper research into high frequency data like tick levels and bid-ask spreads could reflect buyers' versus sellers' motives that drive securities' returns in the short-run.

The fifth category is technical indicators. They range from simple moving averages and relative strength index (RSI) to more involved measures like Bollinger bands and stochastic oscillators, etc. Since technical indicators aim to identify trends, they may contain information driving returns and serve as factors. Other pattern-based indicators like channel breakthroughs or head-and-shoulders, and so on, can also be factors as believers' concerted action on those patterns could become self-reinforcing.

Behavioral finance, the last category, is a broad topic that can only be loosely defined. Many such models have their roots in the prospect theory, reference-dependent preference, and bounded rationality. We will discuss various topics in Chapter 8.

When evaluating new factors, industry practitioners often check their correlation with existing factors in their factor database. Ideally, the new factor should not have a correlation higher than a specified threshold (say 80%) with any existing factors in the database.

1.9. Factors as Predictors: Two Considerations

We discuss the notion of factors from the perspectives of both academia and industry. From an academic point of view, factors help to explain the cross-sectional variation in excess returns. From an industry perspective, factors are attributes that serve as factor exposures and the objective is to use factors as predictors of future returns.

Regarding prediction, the following aspects should be considered. First, the time span of factor effectiveness. There is a life cycle for the factors, roughly the discovery stage, the usage stage, the crowded stage, and finally the phase out stage. When a factor is newly discovered, it should be very effective as no one else has traded it. With more people discovering it, the factor will become *crowded* and the gains will dissipate over time. Eventually, its effectiveness will wear out, and it will be phased out. In this book, we will show examples of factors that have worked in the past and are working even now. However, when they are used by readers, they will become crowded, and their effectiveness will likely be diminished. To beat the market, readers will need to improve and update these factors and discover new ones.

Second, factors are not universal, i.e., some factors may work in some markets but not in others. Factors working in the US market in the past may not be simply transferred to work in other markets. Market efficiency, market structure, trading friction, government regulations, stock market participant composition, and many other factors may have an impact.

1.10. Conclusion

In this chapter we have introduced the nature of quant and factor investing. Factor investing is critical in helping us understand where outperformance (excess return) comes and its decomposition. We have also contrasted all pertinent terms between the understanding of academia versus common practice in the industry. Academically, factors are tradable portfolios that capture common (market-wide) risks and require premia for exposure. From an industry point of view, factors (loosely) refer to stocks' individual attributes that correlate with future returns.

A closely related term "alpha" also means different things between the two communities. From academia, it means the intercept that cannot be explained by a factor model. In this sense, alpha is highly dependent on the choice of the factor model. For industry practitioners, alpha simply refers to outperformance above a specific benchmark. Academia aims to find a factor model that fully explains the cross-sectional variation of securities' returns, i.e., alpha close to zero in a statistical sense, while industry practitioners aim to find factors such that the investment strategy has the highest outperformance, i.e., highest alpha.

We also briefly review the key consensus models in the asset pricing literature including CAPM, FF3, FF3 + MOM, FF3 + MOM + LIQ, FF5, as well as the procedure for identifying factors via the quintile approach and the Fama-MacBeth procedure. For industry practitioners, while the quintile approach is also widely adopted, there are additional evaluation metrics like the information coefficient (IC) and the

TABLE 1.3. Summary of Factors' Concepts within Academia vs Industry

	Academia	Industry
Factors	Tradable portfolios that carry market-wide risks and need to be compensated by factor risk premium	Individual asset-based attributes /variables that correlate with future returns, and serve as factor exposures
Alpha	Intercept from a factor model, the excess return not explained by the factors	Outperformance of a strategy over the market benchmark
Goal	To find a perfect factor model that captures cross-sectional variation of returns fully, i.e. intercept not statistically different from zero	To explore as many valid factors as possible to gain outperformance over the market benchmark
Factor Identification	Portfolio sort, Fama-MacBeth regression, etc.	Portfolio sort, information coefficient (IC), ICIR, correlation analysis, etc.
Consensus Factors/ Models	CAPM, FF3, FF3+MOM, FF3 +MOM+LIQ, FF5 etc.	Factor zoos covering many broad categories: 1 macroeconomics 2 fundamentals 3 statistical moments 4 microstructure 5 technical analysis 6 behavioral finance

information ratio of information coefficient (ICIR). Because of the relatively loose definition of factors within the industry, the growth of factors has become so rapid that the phenomenon of an enormous factor pool is referred to as the factor zoo. Using a non-exhaustive approach, we have presented a rough classification of industry factors based on our observation. A summary contrasting all terms, identifications, treatments, and classifications of factors is given as Table 1.3.

References

Carhart, M. M. (1997). On persistence in mutual fund performance. *Journal of Finance* 52(1), 57–82.

Chamberlain, G. and M. Rothschild (1983) Arbitrage, factor structure, and mean-variance analysis on large asset markets. *Econometrica* 51(5), 1281–1304.

Chen, A. Y. (2021). The limits of p-hacking: Some thought experiments. *Journal of Finance* 76(5), 2447–2480.

Cochrane, J. H. (2005). *Asset pricing.* (Revised ed.). Princeton University Press.

Connor, G.and R. A.Korajczyk (1986). Performance measurement with the arbitrage pricing theory: A new framework for analysis. *Journal of Financial Economics* 15(3), 373–394.

Fama, E. F. and K. R. French (1992). The cross-section of expected stock returns. *Journal of Finance* 47(2), 427–465.

Fama, E. F. and K. R. French (1993). Common risk factors in the returns on stocks and bonds. *Journal of Financial Economics* 33(1), 3–56.

Fama, E. F. and K. R. French (2015). A five-factor asset pricing model. *Journal of Financial Economics* 116(1), 1–22.

Fama, E. F. and J. D. MacBeth (1973). Risk, return, and equilibrium: Empirical tests. *Journal of Political Economy* 81(3), 607–636.

Frazzini, A. and L. H. Pedersen (2014). Betting against beta. *Journal of Financial Economics* 111 (1), 1–25.

Frazzini, A., D. Kabiller, and L. H. Pedersen (2018). Buffett's alpha. *Financial Analysts Journal* 74(4), 35–55.

Giglio, S. and D. Xiu (2021). Asset pricing with omitted factors. *Journal of Political Economy* 129(7), 1947–1990.

Harvey, C. R. (2017). Presidential address: The scientific outlook in financial economics. *Journal of Finance* 72(4), 1399–1440.

Harvey, C. R. and Y. Liu (2018). Detecting repeatable performance. *Review of Financial Studies* 31(7), 2499–2552.

Harvey, C. R. and Y. Liu (2019). Cross-sectional alpha dispersion and performance evaluation. *Journal of Financial Economics* 134(2), 273–296.

Harvey, C. R. and Y. Liu (2020). False (and missed) discoveries in financial economics. *Journal of Finance* 75(5), 2503–2553.

Harvey, C. R. and Y. Liu (2021a). Lucky factors. *Journal of Financial Economics* 141(2), 413–435.

Harvey, C. R. and Y. Liu (2021b). Uncovering the iceberg from its tip: A model of publication bias and p-hacking. Working paper.

Harvey, C. R. and Y. Liu (2022). Luck versus skill in the cross section of mutual fund returns: Reexamining the evidence. *Journal of Finance* 77(3), 1921–1966.

Harvey, C. R., Y. Liu, and H. Zhu (2016). … and the cross-section of expected returns. *Review of Financial Studies* 29(1), 5–68.

Huang, S., Y. Song, and H. Xiang (forthcoming). The smart beta mirage. *Journal of Financial and Quantitative Analysis*.

Ioannidis, J. P. A. (2005). Why most published research findings are false. *PLoS Medicine* 2 (8), 696–701.

Jegadeesh, N. and S. Titman (1993). Returns to buying winners and selling losers: Implications for stock market efficiency. *Journal of Finance* 48(1), 65–91.

Jensen, T. I., B. T. Kelly, and L. H. Pedersen (2023). Is there a replication crisis in finance? *Journal of Finance* 78(5), 2465–2518.

McLean, R. D. and J. Pontiff (2016). Does academic research destroy stock return predictability? *Journal of Finance* 71(1), 5–32.

Pástor, Ľ. and R. F. Stambaugh (2003). Liquidity risk and expected stock returns. *Journal of Political Economy* 111(3), 642–685.

Ross, S. A. (1976). The arbitrage theory of capital asset pricing. *Journal of Economic Theory* 13 (3), 341–360.

Shi, C., Y. Liu, and X. Lian (2020). *Factor Investing: Methodology and Practice* (in Chinese). Beijing, P. R. China: Publishing House of Electronics Industry.

2

QUANTAMENTALS

The quantamental approach to investing represents a confluence of two distinct philosophies: fundamental and quantitative analysis. This merger is a relatively recent development in the history of financial markets, emerging as a response to evolving market dynamics, technological advancements, and the continuous quest for competitive advantage.

For much of the twentieth century, fundamental analysis was the cornerstone of investment decision-making. Pioneered by Benjamin Graham and David Dodd in the 1930s, this approach focuses on evaluating a company's intrinsic value by examining its financial statements, management quality, competitors, and broader economic factors. Investors who adhered to this school of thought believed in the principle that the stock market may misprice securities in the short run, but that these prices would eventually reflect their *true* value over time.

As computational power increased in the latter part of the twentieth century, quantitative analysis began to gain prominence. Quantitative, or quant, investors use mathematical models to identify trading opportunities, relying on the analysis of historical data, statistical patterns, and often the assumption of market inefficiencies. The approach took off with the advent of computers in the 1970s and 1980s, as they allowed for the processing of large data sets and the execution of complex mathematical models that were previously unfeasible.

The explosion of big data and advancements in machine learning algorithms further pushed the boundaries of quantitative investing. Quants were no longer restricted to structured financial data; they could now incorporate a plethora of unstructured data—from satellite images to social media sentiment—into their models. Machine learning allowed for the identification of non-linear patterns and subtle correlations that might be invisible to human analysts.

Despite the strengths of both fundamental and quantitative approaches, each has its limitations. Fundamental analysis can be subjective and often fails to capitalize

DOI: 10.4324/9781003480204-2

on short-term market inefficiencies, while quantitative models can miss the bigger picture, becoming too reliant on historical data and sometimes overlooking significant structural changes in businesses or economies.

The global financial crisis of 2008 served as a catalyst for change, highlighting the weaknesses of both strategies—particularly the risk of relying too heavily on historical data and models. In response, a more sophisticated strategy began to emerge that combined the best of both worlds.

Quantamental investing takes the depth and qualitative insights of fundamental analysis and enhances it with the precision, speed, and data-processing capabilities of quantitative methods. This hybrid approach allows investors to leverage large datasets and powerful computing to inform and enhance traditional valuation models, aiming for more accurate, timely, and actionable insights.

Investors now use quantitative tools to process fundamental data more efficiently, while also employing fundamental insights to guide and inform their quantitative models. This synergy aims to capture market inefficiencies more effectively, manage risk better, and ultimately, achieve superior returns.

As we move forward, the quantamental approach continues to evolve, driven by continuous innovation in technology and data analytics. It represents an adaptive strategy in an ever-changing investment landscape, where the integration of diverse skill sets and knowledge domains appears to be a defining factor for success.

The rest of this chapter is organized as follows. Section 2.1 discusses the nature of quantamental strategies. We provide some examples and case studies in Section 2.2. Section 2.3 begins with a brief introduction to fundamental analysis, with a focus on the general framework of firm valuation. Section 2.4 gives an overview of popular fundamental variables or ratios that industry practitioners usually use as factors. Section 2.5 discusses recent advances in the asset pricing literature on using fundamental information, namely mispricing, earnings announcements, speculative sentiment, short sales, fund flows, joint venture/alliance, and cashflow. Section 2.6 concludes.

2.1. The Nature of Quantamentals

We discussed the "factor zoo" phenomenon in Chapter 1. Within that huge pool of factors in the industry, many are related to fundamental information taken from firms' balance sheets or financial statements. Unlike fundamental analysts who rely on these data to make buy/sell recommendations, factor investment would treat those fundamental ratios or extended calculations as factors. These factors would be complemented by quantitative models including machine learning to form portfolios or investment decisions.

The concept of quantamentals represents a sophisticated fusion of quantitative analysis and fundamental principles, marking a significant evolution in investment strategies. In the realm of quantamentals, the traditional approach of fundamental analysis, which meticulously examines a company's financial health, market position, and growth potential, is seamlessly integrated with the precision and computational power of quantitative methods. This integration allows for a more nuanced and dynamic analysis, leveraging the vast amount of data and the computational capabilities available today.

Quantitative models, particularly those powered by machine-learning algorithms, excel in identifying patterns and correlations within large datasets that might elude human analysts. By incorporating fundamental data—such as earnings, revenue growth, debt levels, and other financial metrics—into these models, investors can achieve a more comprehensive understanding of a company's intrinsic value.

Quantamental analysis is applied in portfolio construction and management by integrating the deep, qualitative insights of fundamental analysis with the systematic, data-driven processes of quantitative models. This approach begins with the selection of securities based on traditional valuation metrics such as P/E ratios, cash-flow analysis, and balance-sheet strength. However, instead of relying solely on these factors, quantamental managers leverage advanced analytics, machine-learning algorithms, and big data to further refine and test the robustness of their investment theses. They may use quantitative techniques to identify patterns in market data that signal when a fundamentally strong company is undervalued or to detect early warning signs of deteriorating fundamentals not yet reflected in financial statements. In managing the portfolio, quantamental strategies dynamically adjust holdings to optimize risk–return profiles based on real-time quantitative signals while adhering to a foundation of solid fundamental valuation. This results in a more disciplined, data-informed portfolio that can adapt to market changes more swiftly, potentially providing a hedge against volatility and enhancing overall performance.

As we delve deeper into this chapter, we will explore the foundational elements of fundamental analysis, highlighting how traditional valuation frameworks can be enhanced through quantitative methodologies. We will then examine the specific fundamental variables and ratios that have gained prominence in factor investing, shedding light on how these elements are transformed into actionable insights through advanced modeling techniques. The subsequent sections provide a comprehensive overview of the latest developments in asset pricing theory as they pertain to fundamental information, offering a glimpse into the future of investment strategies shaped by the principles of quantamentals.

2.2. Examples and Case Studies

Quantamental strategies are being employed by a variety of investment firms, from hedge funds to mutual funds, and are often considered proprietary, making specific details about their implementation and outcomes less publicly available. However, we can look at some examples that illustrate how quantamental strategies might be applied in the real world and their potential outcomes compared to traditional methods.

2.2.1. Enhancing Value Investing with Quantamental Analysis

A traditional value investment firm might focus on stocks with low price-to-earnings ratios, seeking undervalued companies. A quantamental manager could enhance this strategy by integrating quantitative signals, such as sentiment analysis from social media or news trends, to time their purchases or sales better. In a real-world scenario, this could mean identifying when negative sentiment is a temporary market overreaction, providing a buying opportunity for a fundamentally sound company. The quantamental approach could lead to outperformance during market recoveries as the firm can better capitalize on these mispriced opportunities.

2.2.2. Risk Management in Market Downturns

During the 2008 financial crisis, traditional investment strategies experienced significant drawdowns. A quantamental investor might have incorporated real-time quantitative data, like credit default swap spreads or market liquidity measures, along with fundamental analysis to reduce exposure to financial stocks before the worst of the crisis hit. The outcome of a quantamental strategy, in this case, could have been a more resilient portfolio that navigated the downturn with fewer losses, demonstrating the advantage of combining quantitative indicators with fundamental foresight.

2.2.3. Quantamental Approach in ESG Investing

Environmental, social, and governance (ESG) investing is another area where quantamental strategies are being applied. A traditional ESG approach might exclude companies based on certain criteria. A quantamental investor might use quantitative data, such as natural language processing on company reports and news articles, to score and rank companies on ESG performance more accurately. This could lead to the selection of ESG leaders who are not only compliant with sustainability criteria but also positioned for better financial performance, potentially leading to superior returns relative to traditional ESG portfolios.

2.2.4. Sector Rotation Based on Economic Indicators

Sector rotation strategies typically involve moving investments from one industry to another based on economic cycles. A quantamental investor might improve this strategy by using machine learning to analyze a wide array of economic indicators and market data to predict sector performance more accurately. For instance, by analyzing consumer sentiment, inventory levels, and logistic data, a quantamental approach might have anticipated the tech sector's resilience during the COVID-19 pandemic, shifting allocation towards tech stocks ahead of the broader market recognition of the tech-enabled shift in consumer and business behavior.

These examples illustrate how quantamental strategies could provide an edge over traditional methods by incorporating a broader range of data inputs and using advanced analytics to interpret those inputs. The outcomes of these approaches are often enhanced risk-adjusted returns, better-timed entry and exit points in investments, and more robust risk management practices. However, as with any investment strategy, quantamental approaches are not without their risks and challenges, including the potential for overfitting models to historical data and the need for constant adaptation to changing market conditions.

2.2.5. Case Study 1: Bridgewater Associates

Bridgewater Associates, founded by Ray Dalio in 1975, has long been recognized for its distinctive culture of radical transparency and its systematic approach to understanding the economic machine. While Bridgewater is primarily known for its macroeconomic investing style, the firm has also been associated with quantamental strategies in the way it applies its deep understanding of economic fundamentals through a rigorous, systematic framework.

The firm's investment philosophy is rooted in what Dalio calls "principled decision-making". Bridgewater seeks to understand the fundamental economic drivers and relationships that dictate how markets should behave over the long term. This involves extensive research into economic indicators, monetary policies, and various macroeconomic factors that can influence global financial markets.

On the quantitative side, Bridgewater employs sophisticated statistical tools and algorithms to process vast amounts of data related to these economic fundamentals. The firm uses this data to validate its understanding of economic relationships and to test its theories against historical market behavior. The algorithms are also used to help identify and manage risk, forecast market movements, and inform portfolio allocation decisions.

Bridgewater's flagship fund, the Pure Alpha fund, is a good illustration of the firm's approach. The fund aims to achieve positive returns through all market environments by betting on macroeconomic trends. This involves going both long and short across 150 different economic markets, including debt, stock indices, currencies, and commodities, all based on insights gleaned from Bridgewater's fundamental and systematic research.

The firm also operates the "All Weather" fund, which is based on Dalio's concept of risk parity. The "All Weather" fund is designed to perform well across various economic environments by balancing the portfolio based on the volatility of its assets, rather than the traditional method of allocation based on dollar amounts. This requires a deep understanding of the fundamentals driving asset volatilities and correlations, combined with quantitative models to balance the portfolio accordingly.

While Bridgewater might not label itself as a quantamental investor in the traditional sense, the firm's blend of deep economic theory, empirical research, and systematic application of these insights through advanced quantitative methods puts it in line with the ethos of quantamental investing.

2.2.6. Case Study 2: D.E. Shaw

D.E. Shaw is a pioneering investment firm that has evolved to embody a quantamental approach to investing, which leverages the strengths of both quantitative and fundamental analysis. The firm's reputation was originally built on its quantitative trading expertise, employing sophisticated mathematical models and computational algorithms to predict market movements. These techniques, grounded in statistical analyses and machine learning, are designed to identify patterns that might elude traditional analysis.

In addition to its quantitative prowess, D.E. Shaw incorporates fundamental analysis into its investment process. This involves a meticulous examination of company financials, evaluating management quality, and understanding the conditions within industries and the broader economic environment. By doing so, D.E. Shaw aims to assess the intrinsic value of securities, which complements the insights provided by its quantitative models.

D.E. Shaw allocates a significant portion of its focus to discretionary investment activities, which are characterized by the pursuit of profitable opportunities identified by its seasoned professionals. These strategies are underpinned by human analysis, which is adept at uncovering and exploiting pricing inefficiencies across a diverse range of asset classes, encompassing both public and private markets. The firm's discretionary investment teams are distinguished by a meticulous and systematic investment process, aimed at discovering unique profit opportunities that exhibit a low correlation with broader market trends and macroeconomic factors.

The firm's investment philosophy is predicated on a collaborative approach, leveraging the specialized knowledge and expertise of its investment teams, which is crucial for adapting to the dynamic nature of financial markets. This collaborative spirit extends to several strategies employed by the firm, which integrate elements of both systematic and discretionary methods. For instance, a quantitative forecast might initially overlook an anomalous market event that the firm's analysts are aware of, or conversely, a fundamental perspective may require validation through quantitative tools for a more robust analysis.

The integration of quantitative and fundamental approaches allows D.E. Shaw to capitalize on the strengths of both methods. The quantitative side provides a powerful tool for processing large datasets and identifying hidden patterns, while the fundamental side offers context and a deeper understanding of the economic and business realities that drive market dynamics.

Risk management is another critical facet of the firm's quantamental strategy. D.E. Shaw employs quantitative models to understand and optimize portfolios across various risk factors. At the same time, the firm remains cognizant of the fundamental risks that cannot be easily quantified, such as geopolitical events or shifts in regulatory landscapes, ensuring a comprehensive approach to managing potential downsides.

D.E. Shaw operates a range of investment strategies, reflecting the versatility of its quantamental approach. From algorithmic trading and market-making to global macro and long/short equity, the firm navigates different market segments by applying its combined quantitative and fundamental insights.

The firm's quantamental strategy is indicative of its intent to achieve a more holistic understanding of the financial markets, aiming to exploit market inefficiencies and generate returns for investors.

2.3. Introduction to Fundamental Valuation of Firms

Before delving into the nuances of quantamental analysis, it is instructive to outline a foundational valuation framework commonly employed by industry practitioners to ascertain a firm's value.

Predominantly, the discounted cash flow (DCF) model and the residual income model stand as the pillars of firm valuation. These methodologies focus on forecasting a company's earnings for a period of up to 15 years. For the first five years, the projection is based on the most recent five-year growth rate, reflecting confidence in the company's short-term growth potential. For the following five to ten years, the growth assumption is adjusted to a more conservative rate, taking into account the likely impact of increased competition and changing industry conditions that could weaken the company's market position. This phase is critical in evaluating a firm's resilience to new market entrants and its ability to maintain its profit margins. Profit margins are often measured by the gross profit margin, calculated as

$$1 - \frac{Cost\ of\ Goods\ Sold}{Sales}. \tag{2.1}$$

However, to understand the full impact of investment in research and development (R&D) on sales performance, one would need to look beyond the gross profit margin and consider operating profit or net profit margins, where R&D expenses are factored into the equation.

Sales growth emerges as a pivotal driver in sustaining a firm's competitive edge. Herein, the turnover ratio, an indicator of asset efficiency in generating sales, assumes a vital role. This metric, akin to profit margins, undergoes a phased projection: an adherence to recent actuals in the first five years, followed by a gradual decline reflective of increasing market competition over the next decade.

Another cornerstone of fundamental analysis is the leverage ratio. As a firm expands, capital is required. Debt will usually increase as a firm expands and thus leverage will be higher. Analysts closely examine the current ratio as an indicator of a company's potential leverage position, recognizing that optimal leverage levels differ markedly among industries. Sectors such as banking and real estate typically exhibit higher leverage ratios, an outcome necessitated by their unique operational demands.

Sales growth and profit margins are viewed as dynamic ratios, which can be projected using data from income statements. Conversely, turnover and leverage ratios are seen as more static measures, reflecting the financial state captured in balance sheets.

After the 15-year mark, it is common practice for analysts to use a terminal growth rate that aligns with a country's GDP growth when valuing a company. This approach is based on the principle that a company's growth will eventually stabilize and move in tandem with the broader economy. Consequently, the valuation hinges critically on the expected duration of the company's competitive edge, as reflected by the diminishing rate of profit margins from the sixth to the fifteenth year. A gradual decline in these margins suggests strong barriers to entry or proprietary assets, such as patents, which signal a durable competitive moat and, in turn, contribute to an enhanced valuation within the framework of quantamental analysis.

2.4. Performance of Fundamental Factors

Transitioning from the foundational principles of firm valuation and the strategic interplay of quantamental analysis, we now turn our focus to the practical application of these concepts within the realm of factor investing.

MSCI classifies factors into six categories: Value, Size, Low Volatility, High Yield, Quality, and Momentum and Growth. This classification scheme not only simplifies the complex market landscape but also highlights the multifaceted nature of securities analysis. In this nuanced framework, the Value, Size, Dividend Yield, and Quality factors are intimately linked with fundamental variables, offering a bridge between traditional financial analysis and quantitative methods. By examining these factors through the lens of fundamental analysis, investors can gain deeper insights into the intrinsic characteristics that drive asset returns.

The Value factor measures the relative cheapness of securities' prices to their fundamental values, identifying securities that appear undervalued when juxtaposed against their intrinsic worth. This factor is quantified through an array of metrics such as the book-to-price ratio, earnings-to-price ratio, and comprehensive financial measures such as book values, sales figures, earnings, cash earnings, net profit, cash flow, and more. These indicators collectively paint a vivid picture of a security's financial standing relative to its market valuation.

The Size factor encapsulates the empirical observation that smaller firms, as defined by their market capitalization, often outperform larger counterparts in terms of cross-sectional returns. This phenomenon is typically quantified using metrics such as full market capitalization or free-floating market capitalization, providing a straightforward yet powerful lens through which to assess investment opportunities.

Meanwhile, the High Yield factor champions the notion that securities with higher dividend yields typically have higher returns than their counterparts with lower dividend yields. This factor underscores the tangible rewards of income-generating assets, making it a critical consideration for yield-focused investors.

Quality, as a factor, delves into the overall healthiness of a firm, evaluating aspects such as debt levels, consistency in earnings growth (evidenced by metrics like return on equity, ROE), dividend growth stability, the solidity of the balance sheet, financial leverage, the reliability of accounting practices, the caliber of management, and the predictability of cash flows. High-quality firms, characterized by these attributes, are posited to offer more reliable investment prospects, reflecting prudent management and operational excellence.

Table 2.1 organizes and summarizes the performance of some selected fundamental variables used to construct factors in US stocks as identified in the empirical research literature. Specifically, these factors belong to the abovementioned four categories, i.e., Value, Size, High Yield, and Quality, and for each variable, the table lists its name,

TABLE 2.1. Fundamental Variables Identified in the US Market

Category	Variable	Source	Period	t-statistic
Value	Book-to-Market Ratio	Fama and French (1992)	1963–1990	5.71
	Earnings-to-Price Ratio	Basu (1977)	1957–1971	N/A
	Enterprise Multiple	Loughran and Wellman (2011)	1963–2009	6.54
Size	Market Cap	Banz (1981)	1926–1975	3.07
High Yield	Divide Yield	Litzenberger and Ramaswamy (1979)	1936–1977	6.33
Quality	Return on Equity	Haugen and Baker (1996)	1979–1993	4.50
	Return on Asset	Balakrishnan, Bartov and Faurel (2010)	1976–2005	6.45
	Book Leverage	Fama and French (1992)	1963–1990	5.34
	Earnings Consistency	Alwathainani (2009)	1971–2002	2.67

source, empirical period, and the *t*-statistic of the mean excess return of the associated factor. The *t*-statistic of a given factor either comes from portfolio sort analysis or Fama-MacBeth regression. For a full treatment of a much larger scope of factors, interested readers are referred to the open-source asset pricing project (www.openassetpricing.com) initiated by Chen and Zimmermann (2022).

2.5. Recent Advances in Fundamental Data as Factors

Having discussed the general effectiveness of commonly used fundamental variables as factors, this section discusses some advances in using fundamental information. These advances were shown to be significant in driving asset returns.

2.5.1. Mispricing

One key use of fundamental data is to compare whether the market price is trading relatively expensive or cheap to the firm's fair value. This is determined by some models using fundamental factors. A large deviation is termed "mispricing", which is a key topic in quantamental investing.

Stambaugh, Yu and Yuan (2015) determine mispricing by combining 11 return anomalies: Financial distress (Campbell et al. 2008), O-score bankruptcy probability (Ohlson 1980), net stock issues (Ritter 1991, Loughran and Ritter 1995, Fama and French 2008), composite equity issues (Daniel and Titman 2006), total accruals

(Sloan 1996), net operating assets (Hirshleifer et al. 2004), momentum (Jegadeesh and Titman 1993), gross profitability (Novy-Marx 2013), asset growth (Cooper, Gulen, and Schill 2008), returns on assets (Fama and French 2006), and investment-to-assets ratio (Titman, Wei, and Xie 2004, Xing 2008). The mispricing measure is a composite rank based on these 11 anomalies. For each anomaly, the highest rank is assigned to the value of the anomaly variable associated with the lowest average abnormal return. The higher the rank, the greater the relative degree of overpricing according to the given anomaly variable. A stock's composite rank is just the arithmetic average of its ranking percentile for each of the 11 anomalies.

Robert F. Stambaugh

Robert F. Stambaugh is a prominent academic known for his contributions to the field of finance, particularly in asset pricing, mutual fund performance, and investment strategies. He is especially noted for his work on the challenges of estimating future stock returns and the issues related to predicting mutual fund performance.

Stambaugh is currently a professor at the Wharton School of the University of Pennsylvania, where he has made significant contributions to the understanding of financial markets through his research. Some of his well-known work includes:

Predictive Regressions: Stambaugh has addressed the statistical biases that can occur when using historical returns to predict future returns, particularly the issue known as the "Stambaugh bias". This bias arises when simultaneously estimated predictive regressions involve lagged dependent variables that are also predictors. His work helps in understanding the limitations of using historical data to forecast returns.

Liquidity and Asset Pricing: He has conducted research that examines the role of liquidity in asset pricing, suggesting that assets' illiquidity should be factored into their expected returns.

Mutual Fund Performance: Stambaugh has analyzed mutual fund performance and the challenges involved in evaluating the skills of fund managers, including the impact of expenses and the difficulty of distinguishing skill from luck in fund returns.

Bayesian Analysis of Financial Markets: He has also made contributions to the Bayesian analysis of financial markets, which involves using Bayesian statistical methods to interpret and predict market behavior.

Stambaugh's research has been published in leading academic journals, and he is widely cited in both academic and practitioner circles. His work not only advances the theoretical framework of financial economics but also has practical implications for investment strategy and policy.

Various attempts have been made to use different fundamental variables to construct some measures that reflect the financial healthiness of stocks. An early and popular one is Alman (1968) which develops a formula to predict the probability of bankruptcy for a firm within two years. The formula is known as the Alman Z-score:

$$Z = 1.2X_1 + 1.4X_2 + 3.3X_3 + 0.6X_4 + X_5, \tag{2.2}$$

where X_1 is working capital / total assets; X_2 is retained earnings / total assets; X_3 is earnings before interest and taxes / total assets; X_4 is market value of equity / total liabilities; X_5 is sales / total assets. If Z exceeds 2.99, the stock is deemed to be in a relatively safe zone; a Z-score ranging from 1.81 to 2.99 falls into a gray area, which is indeterminate and does not offer a clear signal; a score below 1.81 indicates the distress zone, suggesting higher financial risk.

A more comprehensive and equally popular metric is the F-score of Piotroski (2000). F-score is a number between 0 and 9 assigned to a firm to assess its financial strength, with 9 being the highest. The score is based on nine criteria (each 1 point) in three groups:

Group 1: Profitability

1. Return on Assets (ROA) (1 if positive in the current year);
2. Operating Cash Flow (1 if positive in the current year);
3. Change in ROA (1 if current ROA is higher than that of the previous year);
4. Accruals (1 if operating cashflow/total assets is higher than ROA in the current year);

Group 2: Leverage, Liquidity and Source of Funds

1. Change in Leverage ratio (1 if the ratio is lower in the current year than that of the previous year);
2. Change in current ratio (1 if the ratio in the current year is higher than that of the previous year);
3. Change in the number of shares (1 if no new shares were issued during the last year);

Group 3: Operating Efficiency

1. Change in gross margin (1 if it is higher in the current year than that of the previous year);
2. Change in asset turnover ratio (1 if it is higher in the current year than that of the previous year)

An F-score of 8 to 9 is considered financially strong and a score of 0 to 2 is considered financially weak. Empirically, using data from 1976 to 1996, Piotroski (2000) finds that stocks with high F-scores outperform stocks with low F-scores. The average annual return of the high-minus-low portfolio is over 23%, with a t-statistic of 5.59.

The mispricing measures, Altman Z-score and Piotroski F-score are either based on rankings or pre-determined rules for aggregation (a weighted sum or simple scoring sum). The *strong* and *weak* zones are somewhat arbitrary. Using a pure statistician's perspective, Bartram and Grinblatt (2018) look for mispricing in the market. The authors determine fair values of stocks from *peers*, which are the predictions of monthly cross-sectional regressions of market capitalizations on all firm-level accounting items. Regression residuals tell which firm is under/overpriced and the market portfolio will be fairly priced since residuals sum to zero for a regression that is run with a constant. A broad range of accounting items are chosen including asset levels, dividends, stockholders' equity, net income, invested capital, debt, income taxes, liabilities, cash, payables, accruals, etc. Details can be found in the appendix of their paper. In the empirical study for a period between 1987 and 2012, Bartram and Grinblatt (2018) find that the average monthly return spread between the least and most underpriced stock quintiles is 0.42%, which is equivalent to an annualized return spread of 5.0%. With a t-statistic of 2.38, the result is both economically and statistically significant.

2.5.2. Earnings Announcements

The examination of the impact of earnings announcements on cross-sectional stock returns constitutes another significant research avenue.

Savor and Wilson (2016) state that firms on average experience stock price increases during periods when they are scheduled to report earnings. Non-announcing firms, and the market in general, will respond more to announcements offering more informative signals about consolidated earnings, such as those by firms making announcements early in a given period. The response should be stronger when more firms are reporting since this provides a more precise signal of aggregate cash-flow news. The sensitivity of non-announcing firms to announcements will also increase with the time that has elapsed since the firm's last earnings announcement. In this context, exposure to announcement risk is a proxy for aggregate cash-flow risk which should command a risk premium. The announcement risk premium is quite persistent across stocks: those with high (low) historical announcement returns continue to earn high (low) returns on future announcement dates. Non-announcing firms, particularly those that have not reported their earnings for an extended period, exhibit a heightened reaction to new announcements compared to those that have disclosed their earnings more recently.

Complementing this line of inquiry, Akbas (2016) delves into the interplay between earnings announcements and trading volume. The study highlights that stocks marked by unusually low trading activity in the week leading up to the earnings announcements tend to reveal more adverse earnings surprises. This effect is more pronounced among stocks with higher short-selling constraints. The unusual volume is to compare a stock's average daily turnover over the week (five days [−6, −2] prior to an earnings announcement date) versus the stock's previous 10 weeks of turnover (totaling 50 days, [−61, −12]), where daily turnover is defined as daily total shares traded divided by the number of shares outstanding. Stock is classified as a low (high) volume stock if its event period volume is in the bottom (top) 20% of its 10-week reference period volume.

Both strands of research pertaining to earnings announcements offer potential factors for consideration by closely tracking the scheduled announcement dates of stocks. The implementation of Savor and Wilson's (2016) findings necessitates additional data, such as the identification of relevant *peer* companies, to facilitate proper application.

2.5.3. Speculative Sentiment

An important factor in asset pricing is speculative sentiment. Attempts are being made to capture it by extracting information from trade-related fundamental data. Devault, Sias, and Starks (2019) study institutional and individual investors' demand shocks. They find that sentiment metrics capture institutional rather than individual investors' demand shocks. Their further investigation reveals the underlying economic mechanisms and concludes that common institutional investment styles, such as risk management and momentum trading, can explain a significant portion of the relationship between sentiment and institutional investors.

In their study, Devault, Sias, and Starks (2019) leverage the foundational work of Baker and Wurgler (2006) to gauge investor sentiment, a methodology that merits its own discussion. Baker and Wurgler (2006) utilize six investor sentiment proxies to synthesize a comprehensive measure of investor sentiment. These proxies encompass closed-end fund discounts, NYSE share turnover, the number of IPOs, average first-day IPO returns, the proportion of equity issues in total debt and equity issues, and the dividend premium (the disparity between the average market-to-book ratios of dividend payers versus nonpayers).

To distill the common information embedded within these six variables, the authors employ principal component analysis (PCA). Specifically, changes in investor sentiment are captured by the first principal component of the alterations in these six proxies. Empirical findings indicate that this principal component accounts for 49% of the sample variance, demonstrating significant representativeness. However, a potential issue with this indicator is the difficulty in distinguishing the effects of investor sentiment from those of economic cycles. To address this, Baker and Wurgler (2006) further utilize various variables reflective of economic cycles as explanatory variables, with the baseline investor sentiment indicator as the dependent variable. By regressing and then taking the residuals for a neutralization process, they extract the principal component factors from the covariance matrix of the residuals to construct an *orthogonalized* sentiment index. For this orthogonalized investor sentiment measure, empirical results show that the first principal component explains 53% of the sample variance.

Subsequent empirical research has shown that investor sentiment is closely related to many market anomalies. For instance, Stambaugh, Yu and Yuan (2012) utilize the investor sentiment index to examine the long/short portfolios of the 11 anomalies mentioned earlier, as well as the performance of the long and short legs under different investor sentiment states, thus offering a more detailed discussion on the link between investor sentiment and mispricing. By comparing the long and short legs, rather than just the performance of the long/short portfolios, they make some intriguing discoveries. Among the 11 anomalies, ten show significantly lower future expected returns on the short leg during periods of high investor sentiment compared to periods of low sentiment. In contrast, the performance of the long leg differs markedly from that of the short leg, with no significant differences observed across different investor sentiment states for all anomalies. Hence, the differential performance of anomalies under various sentiment states is primarily driven by the short leg. These findings suggest that while investor sentiment as an aggregated indicator may not serve directly as a factor, given its close association with anomalies, it can be utilized to enhance factor performance.

2.5.4. Short Sales

Another trade-related fundamental data is short sales interest. Engelberg, Reed, and Ringgenberg (2018) delve into the intricate dynamics of short-selling risk and its pronounced impact on the cross-section of stock returns. They unveil that a long/short portfolio formed based on short-selling risk earns significant alpha (9.6% per annum) against the Fama and French (2015) five-factor model. The study elucidates how elevated short-selling risk can stymie arbitrageurs' efforts to rectify mispricing, leading to diminished future returns for the affected stocks. This insight provides a compelling explanation for the enigmatic observation that short interest data, despite being public, can predict future stock returns. The researchers' findings shed light on the nuanced interplay between short-selling dynamics and market efficiency, offering valuable perspectives for both practitioners and academics in the field of finance.

A similar attempt using short interest to predict aggregate stock returns is Rapach, Ringgenberg, and Zhou (2016). The work indicates that short sellers are informed traders who can anticipate future aggregate cash flows and associated market returns. Further international evidence in this regard from other countries is available in Gorbenko (2023). With solid evidence that short-sales data correlate to cross-sectional returns, they could serve well as factors in quantamental analysis.

2.5.5. Fund Flows

A mutual fund's stock holdings might also be a quantamental factor. A mutual fund's fund flow (MFFLow) measure, proposed by Edmans, Goldstein and Jiang

(2012), captures the total dollar amount of each stock sold by the funds, scaled by its dollar volume, if all of the funds in question were to sell their stocks in proportion to their initial holdings. Conditioning on the outflow of fund j being greater than 5%, i.e., $\frac{F_{j,t}}{TA_{j,t-1}} < -5\%$, the definition of this measure is

$$
MFFlow_{i,t} = \sum_{j}^{m} \frac{F_{j,t} \times SHARES_{i,j,t-1} \times PRC_{i,t-1}}{TA_{j,t-1} \times VOL_{i,t}}, \tag{2.3}
$$

where

$F_{j,t}$: Net dollar flow to each mutual fund in the quarter t,
$SHARES_{i,j,t-1}$: Shares held by each fund at the end of the last quarter,
$PRC_{i,t-1}$: Price of stock i at the end of the last quarter,
$TA_{j,t-1}$: Total asset value of each fund at the end of the last quarter, and
$VOL_{i,t}$: The dollar volume of each stock over the quarter.

However, Wardlaw (2020) points out the flaw of the above approach which is inadvertently a direct function of a stock's actual realized return during the outflow quarter, and thus not orthogonal to other fundamentals. Wardlaw's findings cast doubt on the industry's common practice of using fund flows as a factor to predict stock returns.

2.5.6. Economically-linked Firms

In the interconnected web of economic activities and business operations, companies often find themselves linked, directly or indirectly, through various forms of corporate relationships. These connections, whether stemming from supply chain interactions, industry affiliations, collaborative partnerships, or shared resources, constitute the intricate network of inter-firm linkages. Such economic ties can lead to mutual influences on performance or mirror broader market trends, with stock returns often exhibiting a lead–lag effect. This effect arises when one set of assets reacts to information or events sooner or more swiftly than another, resulting in a temporal lag in price adjustments for the latter. This phenomenon reflects the uneven dissemination of information across the market and offers another avenue for quantamental analysis.

Harnessing the lead–lag effect in returns involves identifying these inter-firm connections and using the returns of leading firms as predictive variables for forecasting the future returns of lagging firms. This dynamic can be seen as a form of *momentum*, where the focal company (the lagging firm) and its associated leading firms (the connected entities) play pivotal roles. The relationships between these entities represent spillover effects, shedding light on the underlying economic mechanisms and market behaviors driving asset price dynamics.

The empirical investigation of the lead–lag effect typically begins with quantifying the links between companies from an economic perspective. This has been a long-standing area of academic research and Table 2.2 offers a list of studies that are the most relevant. Once these links are established, predictive variables can be constructed as weighted averages of the returns of connected companies, with weights determined by the strength of the linkage,

$$x_{i,t} = \frac{\sum_{j \in S} LINK_{i,j,t} \times RET_{j,t}}{\sum_{j \in S} LINK_{i,j,t}}, \tag{2.4}$$

where S represents the set of firms that are linked to the focal company i, $LINK_{i,j,t}$ measures the strength of the linkage between the focal company and the linked firm j, while $RET_{j,t}$ is the return of firm j. By adopting a strategy that involves taking long positions in stocks with high $x_{i,t}$ and short positions in those with low $x_{i,t}$ empirical results have demonstrated the potential to achieve significant excess returns (see Table 2.2). This suggests that the web of corporate linkages contains valuable information about asset returns, offering a rich vein of insights for quantamental analysis.

2.5.7. Cashflow

From fundamental analysis, we have heard the phrase "cash is king", underscoring *cashflow* as a crucial fundamental variable. Ball et al. (2016) points out that cash-based operating profitability outperforms measures of profitability that include accruals. Investors can increase a strategy's Sharpe ratio by adding a cash-based operational profitability factor to the investment opportunity set more than by adding both an accruals factor and a profitability factor that includes accruals. A cash-driven operating profitability measure (purging accruals from operating profitability) provides a significantly stronger predictor of future returns. The computation of a cash-based operating profit could serve well as a quantamental factor with the formulae,

$$Operating\ profitability = Revenue - Cost\ of\ goods\ sold$$

$$(COGS) - Selling,\ general\ and\ administrative$$

$$expenses\ (SG\&A), \tag{2.5}$$

TABLE 2.2. Economic Links between Firms

Economic Link	Source	Period	t-statistic
supplier–customer link	Cohen and Frazzini (2008)	1981–2004	4.93
conglomerate link	Cohen and Lou (2012)	1977–2009	5.51
firm–partner link	Cao, Chordia, and Lin (2016)	1991–2012	4.51
technology link	Lee et al. (2019)	1963–2012	5.47
geographic link	Parsons, Sabbatucci, and Titman (2020)	1970–2013	5.11
shared analyst coverage link	Ali and Hirshleifer (2020)	1984–2015	6.23

and

$$Cash - based\ operating\ profitability = Operating\ profitability-$$

$$\Delta(\text{Accounts receivable}) - \Delta(\text{Inventory}) - \Delta(\text{Prepaid expenses})$$

$$+\Delta(\text{Deferred revenue}) + \Delta(\text{Trade accounts payable}) + \Delta(\text{Accrued expenses}),$$

$$(2.6)$$

where Δ represents the change of a variable on a year-to-year basis, and the variables are explained next:

Δ(Accounts receivable): The change in accounts receivable from one accounting period to the next. If accounts receivable increase, it means the company has sold more on credit and hasn't yet received that cash, thus cash profit is lower.

Δ(Inventory): The change in inventory levels. An increase in inventory represents more cash tied up in stock that has not been sold, decreasing cash profit.

Δ(Prepaid expenses): The change in prepaid expenses. An increase indicates that the company has paid in advance for goods/services, which reduces the current period cash flow.

Δ(Deferred revenue): The change in deferred revenue (unearned revenue). An increase in deferred revenue means that the company has received cash for services or goods to be provided in the future, which increases cash profit.

Δ(Trade accounts payable): The change in trade accounts payable. An increase in accounts payable means that the company owes more to suppliers, which is essentially an interest-free loan and increases current cash profit.

Δ(Accrued expenses): The change in accrued expenses. An increase in accrued expenses indicates expenses that have been recognized but not yet paid, conserving cash in the current period and thus increasing cash profit.

In their empirical study that ranges from 1963 to 2014, Ball et al. (2016) report that the long/short portfolio constructed by using cash-based operating profitability earns an average annualized return of 4.88%, with a t-statistic of 6.29.

2.6. Conclusion

In this chapter, we delved into the innovative realm of quantamental investing, a strategy that elegantly marries the depth of fundamental analysis with the precision of quantitative methods. We embark on this exploration by providing an outline of the foundational principles underlying the fundamental valuation of corporations, accompanied by a catalog of essential fundamental variables routinely employed in factor investing.

Our discussion extends beyond the traditional scope to encompass a selection of contemporary research that employs fundamental data in crafting quantamental factors. This includes areas such as the identification of mispriced assets, the implications of earnings announcements, the impact of speculative sentiment, the dynamics of short sales, the insights gleaned from the flow of funds, the economic links among firms, and the analysis of cash flows. Each of these components offers a unique lens through which the financial health and potential of a firm can be assessed.

Given the widespread utilization of fundamental data derived from income statements and balance sheets, there is a natural anticipation of a diminishing return on the corresponding factors over time. This anticipated erosion of effectiveness underscores the need for innovative research directions that explore the integration of novel forms of fundamental data with trade-related data. For instance, the examination of short-sale interest and fund flows, along with their potential transformations, could unveil new dimensions in quantamental analysis. These emerging data sources, when synergized with traditional financial metrics, promise to enrich the analytical toolkit available to investors. This forward-looking perspective on the fusion of diverse data forms represents a promising frontier in the evolution of factor investing.

Quantamental investing is a field that inherently requires a melding of diverse expertise, drawing from finance, economics, statistics, computer science, and more. Professionals engaged in this approach need a robust understanding of financial markets and investment principles to evaluate securities and market trends through a fundamental lens. At the same time, a solid foundation in economics allows them to place these individual opportunities within the broader context of market cycles and economic indicators. Importantly, the rigor of statistical analysis underpins their ability to detect patterns and test investment hypotheses, while computer science expertise is indispensable for managing and analyzing the vast datasets that inform quantamental strategies. This skill set is complemented by an ability in data analysis, including the handling of both structured and unstructured data, which is crucial for gleaning actionable insights from the sea of information available today. Moreover, as machine learning and artificial intelligence play an increasingly vital role in predictive modeling, familiarity with these fields is becoming a core component of the modern investor's toolkit. Finally, all this technical acumen must be balanced with a keen sense of risk management and an appreciation for the psychological factors at play in financial markets, which can often mean the difference between success and failure in investment outcomes. In practice, quantamental teams are typically composed of individuals who specialize in these areas—financial analysts, quantitative analysts, data scientists, programmers, risk managers, and occasionally behavioral scientists—each bringing their unique perspective to inform a cohesive investment strategy that is greater than the sum of its parts.

References

Akbas, F. (2016). The calm before the storm. *Journal of Finance* 71(1), 225–266.

Ali, U. and D. Hirshleifer (2020). Shared analyst coverage: Unifying momentum spillover effects. *Journal of Financial Economics* 136(3), 649–675.

Alman, E. (1968). Financial ratios, discriminant analysis and the prediction of corporate bankruptcy. *Journal of Finance* 23(4), 189–209.

Alwathainani, A. M. (2009). Consistency of firms' past financial performance measures and future returns. *The British Accounting Review* 41(3), 184–196.

Baker, M. and J. Wurgler (2006). Investor sentiment and the cross-section of stock returns. *Journal of Finance* 61(4), 1645–1680.

Balakrishnan K., E. Bartov, and L. Faurel (2010). Post loss/profit announcement drift. *Journal of Accounting and Economics* 50 (1), 20–41.

Ball, R., J. Gerakos, J. T. Linnainmaa, and V. Nikolaev (2016). Accruals, cash flows, and operating profitability in the cross section of stock returns. *Journal of Financial Economics* 121(1), 28–45.

Banz, R. W. (1981). The relationship between return and market value of common stocks. *Journal of Financial Economics* 9(1), 3–18.

Bartram, S. M. and M. Grinblatt (2018). Agnostic fundamental analysis works. *Journal of Financial Economics* 128 (1), 125–147.

Basu, S. (1977). Investment performance of common stocks in relation to their price-earnings ratios: A test of the efficient market hypothesis. *Journal of Finance* 32(3), 663–682.

Campbell, J. Y., J. Hilscher, and J. Szilagyi (2008). In search of distress risk. *Journal of Finance* 63(6), 2899–2939.

Cao, J., T. Chordia, and C. Lin (2016). Alliances and return predictability. *Journal of Financial and Quantitative Analysis* 51(5), 1689–1717.

Chen, A. Y. and T. Zimmermann (2022). Open source cross-sectional asset pricing. *Critical Financial Review* 27(2), 207–264.

Cohen, L. and A. Frazzini (2008). Economic links and predictable returns. *Journal of Finance* 63(4), 1977–2011.

Cohen, L. and D. Lou (2012). Complicated firms. *Journal of Financial Economics* 104(2), 383–400.

Cooper, M. J., H. Gulen, and M. J. Schill (2008). Asset growth and the cross-section of stock returns. *Journal of Finance* 63(4), 1609–1651.

Daniel, K. D. and S. Titman (2006). Market reactions to tangible and intangible information. *Journal of Finance* 61(4), 1605–1643.

Devault, L., R. Sias, and L. Starks (2019). Sentiment metrics and investor demand. *Journal of Finance* 74(2), 985–1024.

Edmans, A., I. Goldstein, and W. Jiang (2012). The real effects of financial markets: The impact of prices on takeovers. *Journal of Finance* 67(3), 933–971.

Engelberg, J. E., A. V. Reed, and M. C. Ringgenberg (2018). Short-selling risk. *Journal of Finance* 73(2), 755–786.

Fama, E. F. and K. R. French (1992). The cross-section of expected stock returns. *Journal of Finance* 47(2), 427–465.

Fama, E. F. and K. R. French (2006). Profitability, investment and average returns. *Journal of Financial Economics* 82(3), 491–518.

Fama, E. F. and K. R. French (2008). Dissecting anomalies. *Journal of Finance* 63(4), 1653–1678.

Fama, E. F. and K. R. French (2015). A five-factor asset pricing model. *Journal of Financial Economics* 116(1), 1–22.

Gorbenko, A. (2023). Short interest and aggregate stock returns: International evidence. *Review of Asset Pricing Studies* 13(4), 691–733.

Haugen, R. A. and Nardin L. Baker (1996). Commonality in the determinants of expected stock returns. *Journal of Financial Economics* 41(3), 401–439.

Hirshleifer, D., K. Hou, S. H. Teoh, and Y. Zhang (2004). Do investors overvalue firms with bloated balance sheets? *Journal of Accounting and Economics* 38, 297–331.

Jegadeesh, N. and S. Titman (1993). Returns to buying winners and selling losers: Implications for stock market efficiency. *Journal of Finance* 48(1), 65–91.

Lee, C. M. C., S. T. Sun, R. Wang, and R. Zhang (2019). Technological links and predictable returns. *Journal of Financial Economics* 132(3), 76–96.

Litzenberger R. H. and K. Ramaswamy (1979). The effect of personal taxes and dividends on capital asset prices: Theory and empirical evidence. *Journal of Financial Economics* 7(2), 163–195.

Loughran, T. and J. R. Ritter (1995). The new issues puzzle. *Journal of Finance* 50 (1), 23–51.

Loughran, T. and J. W. Wellman (2011). New evidence on the relation between the enterprise multiple and average stock returns. *Journal of Financial and Quantitative Analysis* 46(6), 1629–1650.

Novy-Marx, R. (2013). The other side of value: The gross profitability premium. *Journal of Financial Economics* 108(1), 1–28.

Ohlson, J. A. (1980). Financial ratios and the probabilistic prediction of bankruptcy. *Journal of Accounting Research* 18(1), 109–131.

Parsons, C. A., R. Sabbatucci, and S. Titman (2020). Geographic lead–lag effects. *Review of Financial Studies* 33(10), 4721–4770.

Piotroski, J. D. (2000). Value investing: The use of historical financial statement information to separate winners from losers. *Journal of Accounting Research* 38, 1–41.

Rapach, D. E., M. C. Ringgenberg, and G. Zhou (2016). Short interest and aggregate stock returns. *Journal of Financial Economics* 121(1), 46–65.

Ritter, J. R. (1991). The long-run performance of initial public offerings. *Journal of Finance* 46(1), 3–27.

Savor, P. and M. Wilson (2016). Earnings announcements and systematic risk. *Journal of Finance* 71(1), 83–138.

Sloan, R. G. (1996). Do stock prices fully reflect information in accruals and cash flows about future earnings? *The Accounting Review* 71(3), 289–315.

Stambaugh, R. F., J. Yu, and Y. Yuan (2012). The short of it: Investor sentiment and anomalies. *Journal of Financial Economics* 104(2), 288–302.

Stambaugh, R. F., J. Yu, and Y. Yuan (2015). Arbitrage asymmetry and the idiosyncratic volatility puzzle. *Journal of Finance* 70(5), 1903–1948.

Titman, S., K. C. J. Wei, and F. Xie (2004). Capital investments and stock returns. *Journal of Financial and Quantitative Analysis* 39(4), 677–700.

Wardlaw, M. (2020). Measuring mutual fund flow pressure as shock to stock returns. *Journal of Finance* 75(6), 3221–3243.

Xing, Y. (2008). Interpreting the value effect through the q-theory: An empirical investigation. *Review of Financial Studies* 21(4), 1767–1795.

3
STATISTICAL MOMENTS AS FACTORS

In the realm of factor investing, factors are fundamentally about using variables to characterize specific attributes of an asset's returns. If we can identify an attribute that predicts the future returns of an asset, then we have found an effective factor.

Starting from a simple perspective, we might begin by analyzing the historical returns of a single stock. Viewing these returns as samples from a specific distribution offers an intuitive approach. This distribution could be influenced by a variety of elements, including market styles, asset fundamentals, and investor preferences. Although we might not be able to deduce this distribution directly from theory, we can describe it through an empirical and parametric approach.

One of the most basic parametric methods is the method of moments. For example, for a normal distribution, the method of moments requires only the mean and variance to fully characterize the distribution. While the asset returns in the real market are not perfectly normal, they often exhibit characteristics similar to a normal distribution: most returns fluctuate around zero, with less frequent large fluctuations and exceedingly rare extreme returns.

3.1. Why do Moments Matter?

The historical development of using statistical moments as factors in finance is deeply intertwined with the evolution of modern portfolio theory (MPT) and asset pricing models. Below is a brief discussion of the key milestones. The use of statistical moments in finance can be traced back to Harry Markowitz's seminal paper on portfolio selection (Markowitz 1952). In this work, Markowitz proposed that investors are concerned with two moments of the distribution of returns: the mean (as a measure of expected returns) and the variance (as a measure of risk). This laid the foundation for the mean–variance optimization framework that is central to MPT. With variance being used as a proxy for risk, the problem becomes a mean–variance optimization

DOI: 10.4324/9781003480204-3

problem. This means investors prefer expected return (the first moment) but are averse to variance (the second central moment).

Harry Markowitz

Harry Markowitz was an influential figure in the field of economics and finance, renowned for his development of modern portfolio theory (MPT), a framework that fundamentally changed the way investors and financial professionals approach portfolio construction, risk management, and asset allocation. Born on August 24, 1927, Markowitz's academic journey led him to the University of Chicago, where he earned a PhD in economics. It was his doctoral dissertation, later published as "Portfolio Selection" in the *Journal of Finance* in 1952, that introduced the concepts that would earn him a Nobel Prize in Economic Sciences in 1990.

The essence of Markowitz's modern portfolio theory is the idea that an investor can achieve optimal portfolio construction by maximizing expected return for a given level of risk. This approach was a significant departure from the then-prevailing wisdom that focused on assessing each investment's risk and return in isolation. Markowitz's key insight was that by diversifying a portfolio—combining assets whose prices do not move in perfect synchrony—an investor could reduce the portfolio's overall volatility and improve its return potential.

His theory introduced the concept of the *efficient frontier*, representing the set of portfolios that provide the best possible expected return for a given level of risk. This concept has become a cornerstone of investment management and financial analysis, illustrating the trade-off between risk and return and guiding investors in their quest for the most efficient asset mix.

After his groundbreaking work on MPT, Markowitz continued to apply mathematical techniques to the field of finance, including the use of linear programming, thanks to his collaboration with George Dantzig at the RAND Corporation. Throughout his career, Markowitz held various academic and industry positions and has continued to contribute to economics and operations research.

Harry Markowitz's contributions have had a lasting impact on the finance industry, shaping investment strategies and asset management practices worldwide. His ideas have been widely adopted and remain integral to the practice of finance, influencing everything from individual portfolio management to the construction of complex financial instruments and the strategic allocation of institutional investments. Markowitz passed away on June 22, 2023, leaving behind a rich legacy in both academic and practical aspects of finance.

Building upon MPT, the CAPM further cemented the importance of the first two moments in asset pricing (Sharpe 1964, Lintner 1965, Mossin 1966). The CAPM suggests that the expected return of an asset is determined by its systematic risk (beta), which is essentially the covariance of the asset return with the market return standardized by the market variance. Beta became a key factor in explaining returns.

William F. Sharpe

William F. Sharpe is an American economist who is most famous for his work on the capital asset pricing model (CAPM), which earned him a share of the Nobel Memorial Prize in Economic Sciences in 1990, along with Harry Markowitz and Merton Miller. Born on June 16, 1934, Sharpe's contributions have significantly shaped modern financial theory, particularly in the areas of investment, pricing models, and the understanding of financial market behavior.

Sharpe's CAPM, introduced in a 1964 paper titled "Capital Asset Prices: A Theory of Market Equilibrium under Conditions of Risk", provides a formula that calculates the expected return on an investment while considering its risk relative to the market. The model essentially links the expected return of an investment to its beta, a measure of the asset's volatility in relation to the market. According to CAPM, the expected return on a security is equal to the risk-free interest rate plus a risk premium, which is based on the premium of the market times the beta of the security.

The CAPM was a breakthrough because it offered a way to assess the trade-off between risk and return, which is central to the decision-making process for investors. It has become a fundamental tool in the field of finance for pricing risky securities and generating estimates of the expected return considering both the risk of the security and the time value of money.

Sharpe also developed what is known as the Sharpe Ratio, a measure to calculate the risk-adjusted return of an investment. This ratio has become a standard gauge for comparing the performance of investment funds or portfolios with different risk characteristics. It is calculated by subtracting the risk-free rate from the return of the portfolio and dividing the result by the portfolio's standard deviation, which is a measure of its volatility. A higher Sharpe Ratio indicates a more desirable risk-adjusted return.

Beyond these seminal contributions, Sharpe has written extensively on investment funds, asset management, and retirement planning. He has held academic positions at the University of Washington, the University of California at Irvine, and, most notably, at Stanford University's Graduate School of Business.

Throughout his career, Sharpe has been recognized not only for his theoretical work but also for his efforts to make finance more accessible and practical for individuals and institutions. His work has influenced the way financial advisors and institutions manage assets, construct portfolios, and understand market behavior. William Sharpe's enduring impact on finance continues to inform both the theory and practice of investment management around the world.

Suppose we assume each investor has a utility function $u(x)$ for the non-negative payoff x, and we perform a Taylor-expansion for the utility function around the mean $\bar{x}$ up to the fourth moment,

$$u(x) = u(\bar{x}) + u'(\bar{x})(x - \bar{x}) + \frac{u''(\bar{x})(x - \bar{x})^2}{2!} +$$

$$\frac{u'''(\bar{x})(x - \bar{x})^3}{3!} + \frac{u''''(\bar{x})(x - \bar{x})^4}{4!} + \dots , \tag{3.1}$$

taking expectation of both sides gives

$$E[u(x)] = u(\bar{x}) + \frac{u''(\bar{x})E[(x - \bar{x})^2]}{2!} + \frac{u'''(\bar{x})E[(x - \bar{x})^3]}{3!} +$$

$$\frac{u''''(\bar{x})E\left[(x - \bar{x})^4\right]}{4!} \dots \tag{3.2}$$

Here the first term on the right-hand-side is the utility value of the mean $\bar{x}$, the second term $E[(x - \bar{x})^2]$ is the variance with a coefficient of $\frac{u''(\bar{x})}{2!}$. Modern portfolio theory posits that investors wish to minimize the variance for a given level of expected return, thus we can assume that the coefficient $u''(\bar{x})$ should be negative for risk aversion individuals, i.e., the utility function should be concave in shape. For the third moment, it relates to skewness, i.e., the asymmetry of outcome. In the finance literature, it is found that investors prefer lottery outcomes, that is, games that could provide extremely positive outcomes albeit with very small probabilities, are generally preferred. This could be translated into the coefficient for the third moment, $u'''(\bar{x})$, being positive. The fourth moment measures the denseness of the tail of a distribution, i.e., how likely the so-called blackswan events happen in the finance world, which is generally referred to as the "tail risk". Empirical evidence has shown that investors have an aversion towards tail risk, and thus the associated coefficient in the utility function, $u'''(\bar{x})$, should be negative in sign. Tail risk has been gaining traction in recent years; we dedicate Chapter 7 for a full discussion.

The above discussion suggests that statistical moments are good candidates as factors. Generally speaking, investors prefer odd moments, i.e., all derivatives of $u(x)$ of odd orders should be positive, but dislike even moments, i.e., all derivatives of $u(x)$ of even orders should be negative.

Chapter 3 is organized as follows. Section 3.2 gives a brief review of random variables and moments. Section 3.3 discusses variance as risk, and shows that it can be decomposed into systematic vs unsystematic components. Section 3.4 introduces the low-risk anomaly and offers some explanation to this phenomenon. Section 3.5 describes recent advancement on this topic, which covers semi-variance, semi-beta and coskewness. Section 3.6 concludes.

3.2. Basic Concepts about Moments

3.2.1. Random Variables

From elementary statistics, a random variable X is a variable whose value depends on the outcomes of a random experiment. Formally speaking, it is a real-valued function mapping from the sample space Ω into the real line R, $X\colon \Omega \to R$. In finance, asset returns are regarded as random variables, their possible outcomes are random and are real numbers (real-valued).

A random variable is *discrete* if it is countable (either finite or infinite), its probability distribution can be described by a probability mass function (PMF) which assigns a probability to each possible value of $P(X = x_i)$. When the value of a random variable X is uncountably infinite, we call it a *continuous* random variable, and its distribution is described by a probability density function (PDF) which assigns probabilities to it being in an interval or intervals and the probability of X being equal to a single point is zero. We usually use $f_X(x)$ to denote the PDF. Note that if X is continuous, $P(X = x) = 0$ for any single value of x.

Any random variable X (discrete or continuous) can also be described by the cumulative distribution function (CDF), which is defined as the probability of X being less than or equal to a particular value x. We usually use $F_X(x)$ to denote the CDF, i.e., $F_X(x) = P(X \leq x)$.

The range of values for which the probability density of a random variable X is greater than zero is called the "support". In finance, we usually model asset returns as continuous random variables since their possible outcomes cannot be *counted* and are infinite. If we assume returns are normally distributed, then the support will be the real line $\mathbb{R}$ since normally distributed random variables can range from $-\infty$ to $+\infty$.

Given the distribution of a random variable X, we can define the first moment of it as the expectation (or mean μ_x) as

$$E[X] \equiv \mu_x = \sum_i P(X = x_i)x_i, \tag{3.3}$$

if X is discrete; and

$$E[X] \equiv \mu_x = \int_{-\infty}^{+\infty} x f(x)\,dx, \tag{3.4}$$

if X is continuous.

3.2.2. Mean and Variance

The expected value (or mean) measures the weighted average of possible outcomes with the weights being the probabilities. Given that the true distribution of a random variable is often unknown, samples are utilized to estimate moments. Utilizing historical samples of size n to estimate the mean results in the sample mean $\bar{x}$, which assumes each historical outcome has an equal probability of $1/n$,

$$\bar{x} = \frac{\sum_i^n x_i}{n}. \tag{3.5}$$

The mean gives us the *average* of possible outcomes (see Figure 3.1). If we want to know how dispersed the outcomes are around the mean, we need the second *central* moment with the word "central" emphasizing the dispersion is around the mean. The second central moment is defined as $E\left[(X - \mu_x)^2\right]$ and is also called variance, often denoted by σ_x^2 or var(x). If we use historical samples to estimate it, the sample variance estimator is,

$$\hat{\sigma}_x^2 = \frac{\sum_i^n (x_i - \bar{x})^2}{n - 1}. \tag{3.6}$$

Note that the denominator of Equation (3.6) is $n - 1$ instead of n because the equation involves the sample mean $\bar{x}$ which is also estimated instead of the true μ_x. Intuitively, we lose one degree of freedom because of $\bar{x}$. It can be shown that using $n - 1$ as the denominator leads to an unbiased estimator of the variance, assuming that all x_i are independent and identically distributed (i.i.d).

From the variance formula, we see that it measures the *average* dispersion of outcomes around the mean. Outcomes higher than or lower than the mean are treated equally since we take squares of them. The next question is, how do we measure the *asymmetry* of a distribution? It is the third moment.

3.2.3. Skewness and Kurtosis

The third central moment, defined as $E[(X - \mu_x)^3]$, is the measure of the lopsidedness of the distribution. Any symmetric distribution has a third central moment (if defined) of zero. Besides, the *standardized* third central moment is called skewness,

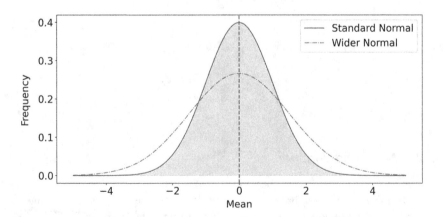

FIGURE 3.1 Mean and Variance

$$\text{skewness}(X) = \text{E}\left[\left(\frac{X - \mu_x}{\sigma_x}\right)^3\right].\tag{3.7}$$

As one can imagine, raising outcomes to the third power is sign-preserving, i.e., the outcome higher than the mean is still positive, while the outcome lower than the mean is negative. Moreover, by raising outcomes to the third power, extreme outcomes will become dominant in values. We can therefore picture that positive skewness refers to a sharp tail on the right side (some probabilities for extremely positive outcomes) while negative skewness refers to a sharp tail on the left side (some probabilities for extremely negative outcomes), see Figure 3.2. The unbiased sample estimator for the third central moment is

$$\frac{n\sum_{i=1}^{n}(x_i - \bar{x})^3}{(n-2)(n-1)}.\tag{3.8}$$

Similarly, the fourth central moment $\text{E}\left[(X - \mu_x)^4\right]$ indicates the degree of central *peakedness* or, equivalently, the *fatness* of the outer tails. The *standardized* fourth central moment is called the kurtosis,

$$\text{kurtosis}(X) = \text{E}\left[\left(\frac{X - \mu_x}{\sigma_x}\right)^4\right].\tag{3.9}$$

Raising the difference between the outcome and the mean to the fourth power will treat both positive and negative outcomes equally. Therefore, kurtosis measures the *denseness* or *thicknesses* of the extreme outcomes on both sides. Distributions with high kurtosis are called fat tails. We usually use the normal distribution as a reference for comparison. Distributions that have the same kurtosis as the normal distribution are called mesokurtic. Those with higher kurtosis than normal are termed leptokurtic,

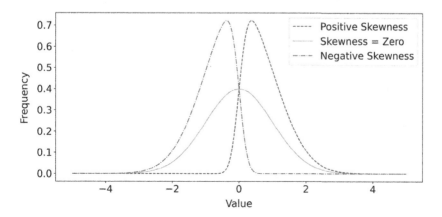

FIGURE 3.2. Skew Asymmetry

while those with lower kurtosis than the normal distribution are termed platykurtic (see Figure 3.3). The unbiased sample estimator for kurtosis is more complicated, and it is defined as,

$$\frac{n(n+1)\sum_{i=1}^{n}(x_i - \bar{x})^4}{(n-3)(n-1)(n-1)}.$$

(3.10)

3.2.4. Moments and Asset Returns

The subsequent discussion turns to the impact of moments of different orders on the expected returns of stocks. While the academic evidence for kurtosis is not particularly abundant or compelling, substantial research has been conducted on how volatility—more precisely, variance (standard deviation)—and skewness affect stock returns. This section briefly introduces some of the representative findings.

For volatility, van Viet and de Koning (2016) analyze 86 years of US stock data, from 1929 to 2015. In the empirical study, they utilize the volatility of monthly returns over the past three years as a factor. Additionally, to exclude the impact of extremely low market capitalization and illiquidity, they consider only the top 1,000 stocks by market cap for each period and divide them into deciles based on the factor's value (hence, each decile comprises 100 stocks). The portfolios are rebalanced quarterly.

Their results indicate that over the extensive backtesting period, the decile with the lowest volatility yields an average annualized return of 10.2%. In contrast, the highest volatility decile has an average annualized return of only 6.4%. Taking into account the effect of compound interest, the annualized difference of 3.8% in returns of the two groups leads to the lower volatility group's cumulative return being 18 times greater than that of the higher volatility group. These findings demonstrate a negative correlation between volatility and stock returns. However, it is noteworthy that, although the low-volatility portfolios significantly outperformed the high-volatility ones, the relationship between volatility and average returns is not monotonic when viewed across deciles.

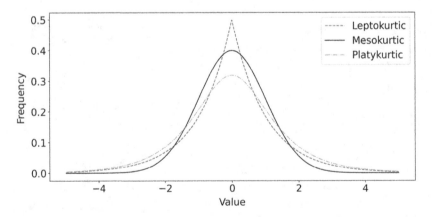

FIGURE 3.3. Kurtosis

Furthermore, Blitz and van Vliet (2007) examine this phenomenon on a global scale. Their findings from 1986 to 2006 show that a portfolio strategy of going long on low-volatility stocks and short on high-volatility stocks in large market cap stocks achieves an average annualized return of 12%, with a *t*-statistic of 3.0.

We turn to examine skewness next. Most investors favor stocks that exhibit positive skewness in returns due to their potential for occasional large payouts. Conversely, stocks characterized by negative skewness are generally less desirable, as they are prone to significant drops in value. Nonetheless, it is important to distinguish between types of skewness. Stocks that demonstrate a high level of *systematic skewness* are valued for their resilience during downturns, offering protection against losses. In contrast, stocks with high *idiosyncratic skewness* are attractive for their capacity to deliver substantial returns independent of overall market trends, akin to a lottery-like windfall.

Previous studies exploring the theoretical connection between skewness and asset pricing have led to the development of different models. Some of these models suggest that only systematic skewness should be associated with a risk premium, as discussed in works by Rubinstein (1973), Kraus and Litzenberger (1976), and Harvey and Siddique (2000). Other models argue that the total skewness, encompassing both systematic and idiosyncratic components, plays a role in security pricing, a view supported by research from Brunnermeier, Gollier, and Parker (2007), Barberis and Huang (2008), and Mitton and Vorkink (2007). The primary distinction between these models lies in their underlying assumptions about investor preferences.

Bali, Engle, and Murray (2016) investigate its relationship with stock returns. Behavioral finance theory suggests that investors' pursuit of stocks with positive skewness can lead to their overpricing, resulting in lower expected returns. If this hypothesis is correct, then strategies that short stocks with high skewness and go long on those with low skewness could realize significant abnormal returns.

Utilizing US stock data from 1963 to 2012, Bali, Engle, and Murray (2016) conduct an extended analysis of skewness. Specifically, they consider using different frequency data (daily vs. monthly) and skewness calculated over various lookback windows. In constructing the factors, they also consider both equal weighting and market value weighting schemes. The relationship between skewness and returns depends significantly on how the factor is constructed. For instance, using daily frequency data and a one-month window to calculate the skewness factor, the average returns of the equally weighted decile portfolios show a significant negative correlation with skewness. However, this correlation reverses when market value weighting is applied, indicating that the empirical results of the skewness factor constructed this way are not robust, potentially due to high estimation errors of skewness.

After further considering the persistence of the skewness factor and controlling for other variables in a Fama-MacBeth regression analysis, Bali, Engle, and Murray (2016) recommend using monthly returns and a longer historical window to estimate skewness and construct the related factor. In this case, skewness is negatively correlated with the expected stock returns. For example, when calculating skewness using the past year's monthly returns and constructing portfolios with market value weighting, the portfolio that goes long on the lowest skewness and short on the highest yields an average monthly return of 0.34% (with a *t*-statistic of 2.49). This result remains economically and statistically significant after controlling for the Fama and French (1993) three factors and the momentum factor of Carhart (1997).

Langlois (2018) explores the roles of systematic and idiosyncratic skewness in explaining expected stock returns. The author develops a new methodology to forecast the cross-sectional ranks of systematic and idiosyncratic skewness, which are easier to predict than their actual values. The study finds that a predicted systematic skewness risk factor carries a significant risk premium ranging from 7% to 12% per year. This premium is robust to the inclusion of other factors such as downside beta, size, value, momentum, profitability, and investment factors. However, the role of idiosyncratic skewness in pricing stocks is less robust. The paper also examines the determinants of systematic and idiosyncratic skewness and finds that they differ.

3.2.5. Partial Moments

Lower Partial Moments (LPM) are a set of measures in finance that capture the downside risk of an investment or portfolio. Unlike standard deviation, which considers both upside and downside volatility, LPMs focus only on the downside, or negative returns, relative to a target or threshold level, such as the risk-free rate or an investor's minimum acceptable return.

Lower Partial Moments can be categorized into different orders:

1. Zeroth-order LPM (LPM0) measures the probability of returns falling below the threshold.
2. First-order LPM (LPM1) sums the absolute differences below the threshold, representing the expected shortfall.
3. Second-order LPM (LPM2) squares the differences below the threshold, which emphasizes larger deviations and is related to downside variance or semivariance.

LPM is generally calculated for the nth order,

$$LPM_n = \int_{-\infty}^{t} (t - r)^n f(r) dr \qquad (3.11)$$

where t is the target return threshold, r is the actual return, $f(r)$ is the probability density function of the returns, and n is the order of the LPM.

Bawa (1975) and Bawa and Lindenberg (1977) develop a CAPM that integrates LPM, yielding equilibrium values for asset pricing adaptable to any probability distribution. This LPM-based CAPM encompasses the traditional model, promising at least comparable explanatory power for market data. The framework also extends to offer a decision criterion for capital investment projects. Fishburn's

(1977) work is foundational in the area of mean-risk analysis, which includes discussions on Lower Partial Moments as a risk measure. Harlow and Rao (1989) generalize the mean–variance framework to include Lower Partial Moments and test its empirical performance.

Similarly defined, Upper Partial Moments (UPMs) are statistical tools used in finance to measure the potential upside or positive deviation of an investment's returns above a specified target or benchmark. Unlike traditional risk metrics, which often focus on downside risk, UPMs isolate the part of an investment's volatility that represents opportunities rather than risks.

UPMs can help investors understand the extent to which an investment has outperformed a benchmark. By focusing solely on the upper tail of the return distribution, investors can assess the potential for outperformance and the frequency and magnitude of positive excess returns. Investors seeking to maximize returns can use also UPMs in the optimization process to tilt portfolios towards assets or strategies that have historically offered more frequent or more significant upside deviations from a benchmark. Related to risk control, UPMs can be integrated into risk-adjusted performance metrics, such as the Sortino Ratio or Omega Ratio, which consider only downside risk in the denominator. These metrics provide a more nuanced view of performance by focusing on the "good" variability that investors welcome. UPMs cater to investors with asymmetric risk preferences, who may be more interested in maximizing gains than in minimizing losses. This is particularly relevant for investors with mandates or objectives that prioritize capital appreciation over capital preservation. UPMs can also be used to study behavioral aspects of finance, such as investor optimism and the preference for investments with lottery-like payoffs (i.e., low probability of high returns). Finally, financial products, such as structured notes or option-based strategies, can be designed using UPMs to target returns above a certain level, providing investors with tailored solutions that align with their investment goals and risk tolerance.

Partial moments have received considerable attention in the context of portfolio selection (Jarrow and Zhao 2006, Brogan and Stidham 2008, Ling et al. 2014) and asset pricing (Ang, Chen, and Xing 2006, Anthonisz 2012, Kelly and Jiang 2014, Guastaroba et al. 2016).

Recently, Huang, Li, and Yao (2022) introduce a novel approach to index-linked investment strategies by applying LPMs and UPMs to measure portfolio deviations from a benchmark, incorporating a balance parameter to link the two measures in creating enhanced index and index-tracking models. The study demonstrates through simulation and empirical analysis using six global indices that the proposed models can outperform traditional models in terms of returns, with the index tracking model achieving stable performance akin to the mean absolute deviation model.

3.2.6. Comments

Simple moment estimates have identified factors that appear to possess predictive information about asset returns. In practical applications, there are many adjustable parameters for users to choose from, such as lookback periods and frequencies (e.g., annually, monthly, or daily). These are not mere variations in parameters; they reflect different attributes of assets and influence investors' perceptions of these assets, resulting in different selections of stocks by these factors.

Capturing the volatility characteristics of shorter periods can leverage higher-frequency data, such as using day-level returns to measure annual volatility, or using minute-level returns to measure daily volatility. Additionally, whether to exclude outliers can affect the factor values. For instance, an anomalous fluctuation in an asset on a given day, if consistently included in rolling calculations, could significantly impact the volatility values derived. The decision to exclude should be based on the properties that one aims to capture and the reasons behind the anomalous returns.

Here, we have outlined some calculation details, but there are many more actionable aspects. With clear objectives and the right empirical procedures, further enhancements in the predictive power of factors can likely be achieved. Moment estimates of asset returns can serve as a starting point for us, prompting further contemplation on whether moments can delineate additional distinct dynamics of assets' returns.

3.3. Variance as Risk: Systematic vs Unsystematic

In the previous discussions, we relied solely on assets' raw returns for statistical analysis, i.e., calculating the corresponding moments. This raises a pertinent question: are raw returns the optimal measure for capturing the properties of an asset? This inquiry is further motivated by the fact that, when charting the distribution of returns for a typical asset, it is often observed that there are protrusions at the tails of the distribution, indicating significant deviations from the mean. This phenomenon warrants an investigation into its origins. For example, are these deviations systematic or unsystematic? Do systematic and unsystematic shifts convey different types of information? After pondering these questions, we are inclined to revisit the factor pricing models mentioned earlier in the book. It is worth investigating, once factors are controlled, whether the distribution of unsystematic return could also (or perhaps more effectively) reveal the inherent characteristics of an asset.

3.3.1. Idiosyncratic Risk

The notion of systematic risk vs. unsystematic risk stems from the Capital Asset Pricing Model (CAPM) discussed before. To repeat ourselves, under CAPM, we can express the excess return of an asset as,

$$r_{i,t} = \alpha_i + \beta_i r_{m,t} + \varepsilon_{i,t}, \tag{3.12}$$

where $r_{i,t}$ is the excess return of stock i over the risk-free rate and $r_{m,t}$ is the market excess return (i.e., market factor). If CAPM holds, α_i should be zero for all assets and the excess return of any asset i should be determined solely by its exposure, i.e., β_i, to the market factor.

If we take variance of both sides of Equation (3.12), the risk (variance) of asset i can be decomposed into systematic and unsystematic parts,

$$\sigma_{i,t}^2 = \beta_i^2 \sigma_{m,t}^2 + \sigma_{\varepsilon,t}^2. \tag{3.13}$$

It is clear from Equation (3.13) that the systematic risk is $\beta_i^2 \sigma_{m,t}^2$, which is the part of risk driven by the market, scaled by asset i's (squared) systematic exposure. The remaining risk, $\sigma_{(s,t)}^2$, is known as the unsystematic risk, or *idiosyncratic* risk, of that specific asset, as it is driven by the unique characteristic of asset i.

We should make it clear that the decomposition of systematic vs unsystematic risks is not independent of the choice of the factor model. If we use the Fama and French (1993) three-factor model instead of CAPM as the pricing model, then we have the following regression model about the excess return of a given asset,

$$r_{i,t} = \alpha_i + \beta_{i,1} r_{m,t} + \beta_{i,2} SMB_t + \beta_{i,3} HML_t + \varepsilon_{i,t}. \tag{3.14}$$

In this case, the variance of residuals, $\varepsilon_{i,t}$, will be different from those calculated based on CAPM. From a factor-investing perspective, instead of using the variance of the total return (i.e., asset's excess return over risk-free rate) to construct the factor, we can use the standard deviation of the idiosyncratic return, i.e., the idiosyncratic volatility, to construct the factor.

3.3.2. Idiosyncratic Volatility and Asset Return

Traditional financial theory posits that idiosyncratic volatility can be offset through diversification and, therefore, should not be correlated with asset returns. However, Ang et al. (2006) challenge this view by demonstrating that stocks with higher idiosyncratic volatility tend to have lower future returns, indicating a negative correlation between the two. Specifically, the paper uses the Fama and French (1993) three-factor model as a benchmark and calculates the return residuals and idiosyncratic volatility using daily return data from the previous month. Based on US stock data from 1963 to 2000, the study finds that going long on the low idiosyncratic volatility group while simultaneously going short on the high idiosyncratic volatility group yields a significant average monthly excess return of 1.06%, with a t-statistic of 3.10. This result indicates a significant negative correlation between idiosyncratic volatility and asset return.

Since its publication, Ang et al. (2006) has become one of the most cited articles in the *Journal of Finance*, highlighting the academic community's significant interest. Three years later, in another investigation, Ang et al. (2009) confirm the robustness of their previous findings with additional empirical evidence from the US and globally.

The work of Ang et al. (2006) sparks extensive debate in the academic world. Contrary studies are not in short supply; for instance, Fu (2009) argues for a positive correlation between idiosyncratic volatility and returns, suggesting that the negative correlation found by Ang et al. (2006) is due to a reversal in returns among a small subset of stocks with high idiosyncratic volatility. Additionally, Anderson, Bianchi, and Goldberg (2015) voice skepticism about the negative correlation between idiosyncratic volatility and expected returns.

Empirical research often risks falling into the trap of data snooping, so conflicting results are not surprising. The academic consensus on the relationship between idiosyncratic volatility and expected returns is still unsettled. Studies support all positions, whether positive, negative, or no significant correlation. However, more findings point to a negative correlation between idiosyncratic volatility and returns, a phenomenon termed the idiosyncratic volatility puzzle.

To unravel this puzzle, Stambaugh, Yu, and Yuan (2015) conduct a study from the perspective of arbitrage asymmetry, with elegant empirical results. They divide stocks into quintiles based on valuation and discover that within the most overvalued group, there is a negative correlation between idiosyncratic volatility and asset return. Conversely, in the most undervalued group, a positive correlation between the two is found. The most fascinating part follows: arbitrage asymmetry leads to insufficient market arbitrage for the most overvalued stocks, making the negative correlation between idiosyncratic volatility and asset return in this group stronger than the positive correlation in the most undervalued group. This results in an overall negative correlation between idiosyncratic volatility and asset return in the cross-section, consistent with the idiosyncratic volatility anomaly discovered by Ang et al. (2006).

3.3.3. Comments

Compared to moment estimates using raw returns, moment estimates that account for idiosyncratic volatility or return distributions provide additional insights, often yielding superior results in terms of return predictability. While several pricing models have been enumerated, a broader spectrum of pricing models could be harnessed for interpretative purposes. Researchers should thoughtfully choose factor models that are most fitting for dissecting returns, customized for the particular stock markets or collections of stocks they are examining. This approach enables more accurate decomposition and more effectively serves the research objectives, enhancing both the granularity and applicability of the analysis.

3.4. Explanation of Low-Risk Anomaly

Conventional financial theories suggest that higher-risk assets should be compensated by higher expected returns. Yet, from the discussions presented, whether through the use of second and third moments of raw returns or the calculation of idiosyncratic volatility, high-risk assets appear to be associated with lower expected returns. This pervasive phenomenon is known as the low-risk anomaly.

Numerous attempts have been made to explain the reason behind this anomaly, one of which relates to investors' preference for lottery-like payoffs. Behavioral finance theory has uncovered that individuals frequently misestimate the likelihood of probabilistic events. For example, there's a tendency for investors to over-estimate the probability of rare occurrences, which underpins gambling behavior and motivates them to seek lottery-like stocks.

The fact that investors are looking for a lottery-like payoff has been well docu-mented in the literature. This gives rise to skewness being a valid factor. Since investors like assets with a positive skewness, those assets are prone to being over-priced, leading to lower future returns. The preference for lottery payoff also extends to using maximum returns over a historical period as a factor. The logic is that assets with high maximum returns in a past period could be overpriced. This is because investors usually perceive them to have a higher probability of extremely positive outcomes. In this regard, Bali, Cakici, and Whitelaw (2011) provide an empirical study. Using US stock data from 1962 to 2005, they construct a MAX variable by using the maximum daily return of a given stock in the previous month and find that the difference between returns on the portfolios with the highest and lowest maximum daily returns is -1.03% (with a *t*-statistic of -2.83).

In addition to the variables previously discussed, low CAPM beta serves as another proxy for low risk. The negative correlation between low beta and returns is docu-mented in the seminal paper by Frazzini and Pedersen (2014) titled "Betting Against Beta". This study uncovers that low beta stocks in 20 stock markets, including the United States, exhibit higher future expected returns. They argue that the underlying reason for this phenomenon is attributed to the leverage constraints faced by inves-tors. However, Bali et al. (2017) posit that the pursuit of lottery-like stocks by indi-vidual investors is a significant contributor to the low beta anomaly. They highlight that individual investors display a pronounced preference for stocks experiencing substantial short-term surges, typically associated with higher betas, leading these stocks to be overvalued and subsequently underperform in future returns. An examination of the investor composition indicates that the low beta anomaly is more pronounced in stocks with a lower proportion of institutional investors and less effective in those with a substantial institutional presence. The dominance of indivi-dual investors, characterized by their strong preference for lottery-like stocks, con-trasts with the more rational approach of institutional investors. This dichotomy further underscores the notion that the demand for lottery-type stocks among indi-vidual investors is a key driver of the low beta anomaly.

3.5. Recent Advances in Moments

3.5.1. Good vs Bad Volatility

Having examined the volatility of returns, it prompts consideration of whether the predictive information carried by asset volatility differs across various scenarios.

Specifically, is the interpretation of volatility distinct between periods of upside movements and those of downside movements?

Upside and downside movements both play a role in the volatility observed in assets. However, it is noteworthy that investors tend to disregard the volatility stemming from upside movements, focusing instead on the volatility associated with downside movements. This implies that the volatility of upside movements is not typically viewed as a risk warranting additional attention. Against this backdrop, efforts have been initiated to delineate the differing implications of volatility's upside versus its downside effects.

One example in this regard is Bollerslev, Li, and Zhao (2020), which decompose the realized variation for stocks into realized up and down semi-variance, or the "good" and "bad" volatilities. Denoting p_T as the natural logarithmic price of an arbitrary asset on day T, a generic jump diffusion process proposes a logarithmic price to follow:

$$p_T = \int_0^T \mu_\tau d\tau + \int_0^T \sigma_\tau dW_\tau + J_T. \tag{3.15}$$

Let $p_t, p_{t+1/n}, \ldots, p_{t+1}$ be the observed $n+1$ equally spaced log-prices over times of trading day $[t, t+1]$ and define intraday returns $r_{i+i/n} = p_{t+i/n} - p_{t+(i-1)/n}$. Then the daily realized variance (RV) for day t is

$$RV_t = \sum_{i=1}^n r_{t-1+i/n}^2. \tag{3.16}$$

In the limit of $n \to \infty$, $RV_t \to \int_{t-1}^t \sigma_s^2 ds + \sum_{t-1 \leq \tau \leq t} J_\tau^2$. Decomposing (RV)s into positive and negative intraday returns yields

$$RV_t^+ = \sum_{i=1}^n r_{t-1+i/n}^2 \mathbb{1}_{[r_{t-1+i/n>0}]}, \quad RV_t^- = \sum_{i=1}^n r_{t-1+i/n}^2 \mathbb{1}_{[r_{t-1+i/n0}]}, \tag{3.17}$$

where $\mathbb{1}_{[x]}$ is the indicator function which equals 1 if condition x is satisfied and 0 otherwise. A signed jump (SJ) for day t is therefore defined as,

$$SJ_t = RV_t^+ - RV_t^-. \tag{3.18}$$

In the limit of $n \to \infty$, $RV_t^+ \to \int_{t-1}^t \sigma_s^2 ds + \sum_{t-1 \leq \tau \leq t} J_\tau^2 \mathbb{1}_{J_\tau > 0}$, $RV_t^- \to \int_{t-1}^t \sigma_s^2 ds + \sum_{t-1 \leq \tau \leq t} J_\tau^2 \mathbb{1}_{J_\tau 0}$ and,

$$SJ_t = \sum_{t-1 \leq \tau \leq t} J_\tau^2 \mathbb{1}_{J_\tau > 0} - \sum_{t-1 \leq \tau \leq t} J_\tau^2 \mathbb{1}_{J_\tau 0}. \tag{3.19}$$

Since different stocks could have different magnitudes of jumps, (SJ) is usually normalized by RV and eventually the relative signed jump (RSJ) is defined as,

$$RSJ_t = \frac{SJ_t}{RV_t}. \tag{3.20}$$

Utilizing the aforementioned mathematical models, Bollerslev, Li, and Zhao (2020) employ intraday high-frequency return data spanning from 1993 to 2013 to investigate the relationship between RSJ and asset return. The empirical findings indicate that by going long on portfolios with the lowest RSJ and short on those with the highest RSJ, one could achieve a weekly excess return of 0.29% (equating to an annualized excess return of approximately 15%), with a corresponding t-statistic of 5.83. Considering the construction of RSJ, a lower value implies higher downside volatility of the asset. Thus, these results suggest that investors pay more attention to downside risks and demand higher risk compensation for them.

3.5.2. Semi-beta

The previous section's risk decomposition, which focuses on the asset's volatility itself, results in semi-variance representing upside and downside risks, and empirical findings also indicated investors' heightened concern for downside risks. Inspired by this, a similar approach can be applied to decompose an asset's systematic risk, shifting the focus from asset volatility to asset beta. With this in mind, Bollerslev, Patton, and Quaedvlieg (2022) conduct a more detailed decomposition of the covariance between assets and the market factors, introducing the concept of semi-beta. Before delving into this paper, however, we first briefly discuss the pioneers of beta decomposition, Ang, Chen, and Xing (2006).

Ang, Chen, and Xing (2006) posit that assets with high downside risks yield the lowest returns during periods when investors' returns are low, necessitating risk compensation and, hence, higher expected returns for assets with high downside risks. To test this hypothesis, they employ the following method to compute the downside beta,

$$\beta_i = \frac{\text{cov}(r_i, r_m | r_m < \mu_m)}{\text{var}(r_m | r_m < \mu_m)}, \tag{3.21}$$

where r_i and r_m represent the excess returns of the asset and the market, respectively, while μ_m is the mean market excess return. In other words, downside beta is defined as the conditional beta when market excess returns are below the mean. Similarly, upside beta can also be calculated. Empirical results show that stocks with higher realized downside beta have significantly higher future returns, indicating a positive correlation and thus validating the importance of downside risk in stock returns. In other words, identifying stocks with greater future downside risks could potentially yield significant excess returns.

Following on from its predecessor, Bollerslev, Patton, and Quaedvlieg (2022) considered the signs of both asset and market returns, instead of merely conditioning on the sign of market returns, thus allowing for a more granular segmentation of the original beta. Starting from the definition of covariance and considering the signs of both asset and market returns, the original covariance can be decomposed into four parts (for derivation simplicity, it is assumed that both returns are demeaned),

$$\text{cov}(r_i, r_m) = \text{E}[r_i r_m | r_i < 0, r_m < 0] + \text{E}[r_i r_m | r_i > 0, r_m > 0] +$$

$$\text{E}[r_i r_m | r_i \langle 0, r_m \rangle 0] + \text{E}[r_i r_m | r_i > 0, r_m < 0]. \quad (3.22)$$

Let N, P, M^+ and M^- represent the four components on the right-hand-side of Equation (3.22), respectively. The N, P, M^+, and M^- semicovariance components refer to the portions of total covariation defined by both returns being positive ("P"), both returns being negative ("N"), mixed sign with positive market return ("M^+"), and mixed sign with negative market return ("M^-").

Then, beta can be decomposed accordingly,

$$\beta_i = \frac{\text{cov}(r_i, r_m)}{\text{var}(r_m)} = \frac{N + P + M^+ + M^-}{\text{var}(r_m)} = \beta_i^N + \beta_i^P - \beta_i^{M^+} - \beta_i^{M^-}. \quad (3.23)$$

Note that in the expression above, $\beta_i^{M^+}$ is defined as $-M^+/\text{var}(r_m)$ and $\beta_i^{M^-}$ is defined as $-M^-/var(r_m)$,, hence the minus sign before the last two terms in the equation. Given investors' aversion to downside risk, the two betas representing downside risk (i.e., β_i^N and $\beta_i^{M^-}$ should be priced accordingly. Besides, since β_i^N represents risk, it therefore should carry a positive risk premium. On the other hand, since $\beta_i^{M^-}$ represents hedging assets which perform well during market downturns, it therefore should have a negative risk premium.

Empirically, the aforementioned semi-betas are latent variables, not directly observable, and can only be estimated. According to Bollerslev, Patton, and Quaedvlieg (2020), the realized semi-betas serve as consistent estimators of the true semi-betas. The empirical results confirm the authors' hypothesis, indicating that the two downside betas are significantly priced, albeit in opposite directions (consistent with the expected direction), while the two upside betas are not priced.

3.5.3. Coskewness

Another related measure is the coskewness. From CAPM, investors holding asset i are compensated for the covariance of asset i's returns with the market. In a skew-awareness world, however, investors should also be compensated for residual coskewness, which is defined as the covariance of the CAPM residuals and the square of market excess returns:

$$coskew_{i,t} = cov\left(\varepsilon_{i,t}, r_{m,t}^2\right), \tag{3.24}$$

where $\varepsilon_{i,t} = \alpha_i + \varepsilon_{i,t}$ of Equation (3.12).

The work related to coskewness dates back to the 1970s. Kraus and Litzenberger (1976) posit that the diminishing absolute risk aversion of investors implies a positive third derivative of the utility function, suggesting a preference for positive skewness. Harvey and Siddique (2000) formalize this notion into a model, indicating a negative skewness premium. Theoretical derivations reveal that the residual coskewness of an asset is negatively correlated with its CAPM-alpha (i.e., the pricing error from the CAPM model). This theoretical model implies that when investors care about skewness, CAPM-alpha is closely related to residual coskewness. Therefore, residual coskewness could be a key factor in explaining the cross-section.

The empirical challenge, however, lies in the ex-ante estimate of residual coskewness. A natural attempt in this regard is to use implied skewness that is derived from option prices, similar to implied volatility. Schneider, Wagner, and Zechner (2020) first test how closely the implied skewness is related to true residual coskewness through simulation analysis. They generate data for 2,000 companies, then sort stocks into 10 groups based on implied skewness, and calculate the average residual coskewness for different groups. The results indicate a strong and negative relationship between the two. Empirically, with real US stock data from 1996 to 2014, Schneider, Wagner, and Zechner (2020) further confirm the same pattern. As a result, implied skewness derived from option prices is a good proxy for residual coskewness. In addition, they turn their attention to examining the relationship between residual coskewness and other low-risk anomalies using principal component analysis and regression analysis. Specifically, they extract the first principal component of four low-risk anomalies and investigate whether residual coskewness could explain this principal component. The results show that the former could almost entirely account for this principal component. Extensive empirical evidence suggests that residual coskewness can explain low-risk anomalies, not merely by coincidence but because it is related to the core driving force of low-risk anomalies, corroborating the implications of the theoretical model discussed earlier. For low-risk anomalies, Schneider, Wagner, and Zechner (2020) may offer a potential resolution to the debate: low-risk anomalies cease to exist when residual coskewness is added to the pricing model.

3.6. Conclusion

In this chapter, we examined simple statistical moments as factors. Contrary to conventional wisdom and the traditional understanding of finance, the relationship between variance (a common measure of volatility) and asset return is negatively related, leading to the well-known low volatility anomaly. This anomaly can be partially explained by investors' preference for lottery-like payouts, a concept within the realm of behavioral finance, which will be thoroughly discussed in Chapter 8.

Variance can be decomposed into systematic and idiosyncratic components through a factor model. The systematic component is associated with market exposure, i.e., beta, a subject that merits its own discussion in Chapter 4. Idiosyncratic risk is contingent upon the factor model chosen. A vast body of empirical research on the US stock market and other global markets has demonstrated that idiosyncratic volatility, as a factor, is even more potent than the volatility of returns itself. However, given that the construction of this factor is not independent of the factor model chosen, readers are encouraged to explore alternative benchmark models in their analyses. We have also delved into recent advancements in employing moments as factors, such as differentiating between upside and downside volatility, semi-beta, and coskewness.

It is undeniable that statistical moments and their extensions will remain a fundamental aspect of the factor universe. Future research directions could unfold in two main areas. First, instead of relying on historical sample statistics, one avenue involves applying Bayesian techniques to the moment estimation process to derive potentially better estimators. Additionally, by broadening our perspective, we can also apply moment estimation techniques to stock attributes beyond returns. For instance, stock trading volume could be used to compute similar metrics or conduct analogous analyses, offering fresh insights into factor research.

Upon completing this chapter, it becomes evident that various moments of asset returns hold significant potential for generating factors. However, caution is warranted as more technical manipulations, such as employing more complex estimation methods or experimenting with different variables, may gradually obscure the logical understanding of factors. Hence, when investigating similar factors, it is crucial to continually seek the underlying meaning of the chosen variables and the source of returns behind the factors. Admittedly, pinpointing the source of returns often lacks a singular correct answer. Yet, each time we arrive at a more reasoned and profound explanation, it likely indicates a deeper understanding of a particular factor.

References

Anderson, R. M., S. W. Bianchi, and L. R. Goldberg (2015). In search of statistically valid risk factors. *Quantitative Finance* 15(3), 385–393.

Ang, A., J. Chen, and Y. Xing (2006). Downside risk. *Review of Financial Studies* 19(4), 1191–1239.

Ang, A., R. J. Hodrick, Y. Xing, and X. Zhang (2006). The cross-section of volatility and expected returns. *Journal of Finance* 61(1), 259–299.

Ang, A., R. J. Hodrick, Y. Xing, and X. Zhang (2009). High idiosyncratic volatility and low returns: International and further US evidence. *Journal of Financial Economics* 91(1), 1–23.

Anthonisz, S. A. (2012). Asset pricing with partial-moments. *Journal of Banking and Finance* 36(7), 2122–2135.

Bali, T. G., S. J. Brown, S. Murray, and Y. Tang (2017). A lottery-demand-based explanation of the beta anomaly. *Journal of Financial and Quantitative Analysis* 52(6), 2369–2397.

Bali, T. G., N. Cakici, and R. F. Whitelaw (2011). Maxing out: Stocks as lotteries and the cross-section of expected returns. *Journal of Financial Economics* 99(2), 427–446.

Bali, T. G., R. F. Engle, and S. Murray (2016). *Empirical Asset Pricing: The Cross Section of Stock Returns*. Wiley.

Barberis, N., and M. Huang. (2008). Stocks as lotteries: The implications of probability weighting for security prices. *American Economic Review* 98, 2066–2100.

Bawa, V. S. (1975). Optimal rules for ordering uncertain prospects. *Journal of Financial Economics* 2(1), 95–121.

Bawa, V. S. and E. B. Lindenberg (1977). Capital market equilibrium in a mean-lower partial moment framework. *Journal of Financial Economics* 5(2), 189–200.

Blitz, D. and P. van Vliet (2007). The volatility effect. *Journal of Portfolio Management* 34(1), 102–113.

Bollerslev, T., S. Z. Li, and B. Zhao (2020). Good volatility, bad volatility, and the cross section of stock returns. *Journal of Financial and Quantitative Analysis* 55(3), 751–781.

Bollerslev, T., A. J. Patton, and R. Quaedvlieg (2020). Realized semicovariances. *Econometrica* 88(4), 1515–1551.

Bollerslev, T., A. J. Patton, and R. Quaedvlieg (2022). Realized semibetas: Disentangling "good" and "bad" downside risks. *Journal of Financial Economics* 144(1), 227–246.

Brogan, A. J. and S. Stidham Jr. (2008). Non-separation in the mean–lower-partial-moment portfolio optimization problem. *European Journal of Operations Research* 184(2), 701–710.

Brunnermeier, M. K., C. Gollier, and J. A. Parker. (2007). Optimal beliefs, asset prices and the preferences for skewed returns. *American Economic Review* 97, 159–165.

Carhart, M. M. (1997). On persistence in mutual fund performance. *Journal of Finance* 52(1), 57–82.

Fama, E. F. and K. R. French (1993). Common risk factors in the returns on stocks and bonds. *Journal of Financial Economics* 33(1), 3–56.

Fishburn, P. C. (1977). Mean-risk analysis with risk associated with below-target returns. *The American Economic Review* 67(2), 116–126.

Frazzini, A. and L. H. Pedersen (2014). Betting against beta. *Journal of Financial Economics* 111(1), 1–25.

Fu, F. (2009). Idiosyncratic risk and the cross-section of expected stock returns. *Journal of Financial Economics* 91(1), 24–37.

Guastaroba, G., R. Mansini, W. Ogryczak, and M. G. Speranza (2016) Linear programming models based on omega ratio for the enhanced index tracking problem. *European Journal of Operations Research* 251(3), 938–956.

Harlow, W. V. and R. K. S. Rao (1989). Asset pricing in a generalized mean-lower partial moment framework: Theory and evidence. *Journal of Financial and Quantitative Analysis* 24 (3), 285–311.

Harvey, C. R. and A. Siddique (2000). Conditional skewness in asset pricing tests. *Journal of Finance* 55(3), 1263–1295.

Huang, J., Y. Li, and H. Yao (2022). Partial moments and indexation investment strategies. *Journal of Empirical Finance* 67(C), 39–59.

Jarrow, R. and F. Zhao (2006) Downside loss aversion and portfolio management. *Management Science* 52 (4), 558–566.

Kelly, B. and H. Jiang (2014) Tail risk and asset prices. *Review of Financial Studies* 27 (10), 2841–2871.

Kraus, A. and R. H. Litzenberger (1976). Skewness preference and the valuation of risk assets. *Journal of Finance* 31(4), 1085–1100.

Langlois, H. (2018) Measuring skewness premia. HEC Paris Research Paper No. FIN-2018-1256. Available at SSRN: http://dx.doi.org/10.2139/ssrn.3141416.

Ling, A., J. Sun, and X. Yang (2014). Robust tracking error portfolio selection with worst-case downside risk measures. *Journal of Economic Dynamics and Control* 39, 178–207.

Lintner, J. (1965). The valuation of risk assets and the selection of risky investments in stock portfolios and capital budgets. *The Review of Economics and Statistics*, 47(1), 13–37.

Markowitz, H. (1952). Portfolio selection. *Journal of Finance* 7(1), 77–91.

Mitton, T., and K. Vorkink. (2007). Equilibrium underdiversification and the preference for skewness. *Review of Financial Studies* 20, 1255–1288.

Mossin, J. (1966). Equilibrium in a capital asset market. *Econometrica* 34(4), 768–783.

Rubinstein, M. (1973). The fundamental theorem of parameter-preference security valuation. *Journal of Financial and Quantitative Analysis* 8, 61–69.

Sharpe, W. F. (1964). Capital asset prices: A theory of market equilibrium under conditions of risk. *Journal of Finance* 19(3), 425–442.

Schneider, P., C. Wagner, and J. Zechner (2020) Low-risk anomalies? *Journal of Finance* 75 (5), 2673–2718.

Stambaugh, R. F., J. Yu, and Y. Yuan (2015). Arbitrage asymmetry and the idiosyncratic volatility puzzle. *Journal of Finance* 70(5), 1903–1948.

van Viet, P. and J. de Koning (2016). *High Returns from Low Risk: A Remarkable Stock Market Paradox*. Wiley.

4

MARKET BETA

4.1. Background

In the context of investing, alpha and beta are fundamental concepts commonly used in portfolio management and performance measurement. Beta is a measure of the volatility—or systematic risk—of a security or a portfolio in comparison to the market as a whole. On the other hand, alpha represents the excess return on an investment relative to the return of a benchmark index or the expected performance given the asset's beta. Alpha is often interpreted as the value that a portfolio manager adds or subtracts from a fund's return. In other words, an alpha of zero suggests that the investment has earned a return commensurate with the risk (beta) it has taken. Positive alpha indicates outperformance on a risk-adjusted basis, while negative alpha indicates underperformance.

In Chapter 1, we discussed the Capital Asset Pricing Model (CAPM), which posits that the cross-sectional variation of assets' returns is solely dependent on their systematic exposure to the market factor, measured by beta. A straightforward method to estimate beta is by conducting a regression of the assets' excess returns on the market's excess return using historical data.

However, estimating beta is inherently challenging. First, beta naturally changes over time, and it is difficult for people to accurately predict these changes *ex-ante* due to the underlying uncertainties of financial markets (this point will be further elaborated in Chapter 10 on uncertainty). Therefore, it may be impossible to ever truly obtain real-time precise estimates of beta. Instead, one can only attempt to find a feasible estimation method for the problem at hand. Table 4.1 provides a summary of the challenges.

This chapter provides an in-depth exploration of various beta estimation methods and their respective applications. Specifically, Section 4.2 presents the concept of instrumental variables. Sections 4.3 and 4.4 delve into conditional beta and dynamic conditional beta, respectively. Section 4.5 dissects and interprets beta from the

DOI: 10.4324/9781003480204-4

TABLE 4.1. Challenges of Estimating Beta

Challenge	Description
Historical Data Dependency (Non-Stationarity)	Beta calculations rely on historical price data, which may not be indicative of future trends due to the ever-changing nature of financial markets.
Time Frame Selection	The time frame for calculating beta can significantly influence its value, with shorter time frames possibly missing the full extent of market responsiveness and longer periods potentially including obsolete data.
Market Benchmark Relevance	An accurate beta depends on using a relevant market index as a benchmark. An inappropriate index can lead to misleading beta estimates.
Structural Changes	Changes within a company, such as mergers, acquisitions, or strategy shifts, can alter its risk profile and, consequently, its beta.
Statistical Noise	Estimating beta using statistical methods like OLS regression can be distorted by outliers and noise in the data.
Leverage Effects	A company's level of debt can influence its beta, as changes in financial leverage affect the company's risk profile.
Liquidity	The trading frequency and bid–ask spreads associated with a security's liquidity can complicate beta estimation.
Regime Shifts	Changes in economic conditions, such as moving from a bull to a bear market or vice versa, can affect the relevance of historical beta estimates.
Globalization and Integration	International events can impact local markets, making it more complex to choose an appropriate benchmark and interpret beta correctly.

perspectives of continuity and discontinuity. Section 4.6 introduces the two most important factors related to beta, namely the BAB (Betting-Against-Beta) and BAC (Betting-Against-Correlation) factors. Finally, Section 4.7 summarizes the key take-aways of this chapter.

4.2. Instrumental Variables

The concept of beta fundamentally represents the estimated values of parameters in a regression model. When measuring beta, one standard approach is to regress the dependent variable y on independent variables (or regressors) x. The goal of regression is to estimate the conditional expectation function of the form (assuming no intercept),

$$\mathrm{E}[y|x] = \beta' x. \tag{4.1}$$

In the simplest one regressor case, both x and β are scalars and we have

$$y = \beta x + u, \tag{4.2}$$

where u is the error term. Ordinary least square (OLS) method seeks to find β such that the sum of squared error (u_t^2) is minimized for sample y_t and x_t, $t = 1, \ldots, T$. The OLS estimator of β is

$$\beta = \frac{\text{cov}(y, x)}{\text{var}(x)}. \tag{4.3}$$

In the regression model (4.2), one key assumption is that the error term u has no association with x, such that the estimate of β (denoted by $\hat{\beta}$) reflects purely the effect of a change in x to y. In mathematics,

$$\frac{dy}{dx} = \beta + \frac{du}{dx}. \tag{4.4}$$

The second term du/dx is assumed to be zero because u is not a function of x. However, if u is associated with x, the second term will no longer be zero and thus $\hat{\beta}$ will incorporate the effect of du/dx, which is no longer a consistent estimator of β. A consistent estimator means that as the sample size is increased indefinitely, the resulting sequence of estimates (in our case $\hat{\beta}$) will converge to the true parameter (β) with probability one. An inconsistent estimator cannot be used since there is no hope of getting the true parameter even if we were to spend the effort to collect an infinite number of samples.

To address the inconsistency, the instrumental variable (IV) method seeks to identify an instrumental variable z that ideally exhibits a strong correlation with x while remaining uncorrelated with the error term u. Under this approach, the beta of y with respect to the instrument variable z is

$$\beta_{IV} = \frac{dy/dz}{dx/dz}. \tag{4.5}$$

Regressing y on z yields a slope estimate of $(z'z)^{-1}z'y$ (the numerator). Similarly, regressing x on z yields a slope estimate of $(z'z)^{-1}z'x$ (the denominator). Dividing the former by the latter, we have the IV estimator $\hat{\beta}_{IV}$,

$$\hat{\beta}_{IV} = \frac{(z'z)^{-1}z'y}{(z'z)^{-1}z'x} = (z'x)^{-1}z'y, \tag{4.6}$$

which is a consistent estimator for β.

4.3. Conditional Beta

Grant (1977), Jagannathan and Wang (1996), Lewellen and Nagel (2006) and Boguth et al. (2011) showed that unconditional alphas are biased estimates of the true alphas if betas vary systematically with the market risk premium or market volatility. Cederburg and O'Doherty (2016) found that betas of portfolios sorted on past firms' beta vary substantially over time, mainly due to the shifting cross-sectional variation in firm betas. Lewellen and Nagel (2006) and Boguth et al. (2011) show that if the conditional CAPM holds, the unconditional alpha for a particular asset can be approximated by

$$\alpha_i^U \approx cov\left(\beta_{i,t}, \mathrm{E}_{t-1}\left[R_{m,t}\right]\right) - \frac{\mathrm{E}\left[R_{m,t}\right]}{\sigma_m^2} cov\left(\beta_{i,t}, \sigma_{m,t}^2\right), \qquad (4.7)$$

where $\beta_{i,t}$ is the asset's conditional beta, $\mathrm{E}\left[R_{m,t}\right]$ and $\mathrm{E}_{t-1}\left[R_{m,t}\right]$ are unconditional and conditional market expected excess returns, and σ_m^2 and $\sigma_{m,t}^2$ are unconditional and conditional market volatilities. From Equation (4.7), a negative bias in unconditional alpha arises when the conditional beta is negatively correlated to the expected market excess return and/or positively correlated to market volatility. According to Boguth et al. (2011), the latter effect could be particularly large, leading to substantial bias in unconditional alphas.

The conditional CAPM implies that

$$\alpha_{i,t} \equiv \mathrm{E}\left[R_{i,t}|I_{t-1}\right] - \beta_{i,t}\mathrm{E}\left[R_{m,t}|I_{t-1}\right] = 0, \qquad (4.8)$$

where $R_{i,t}$ is asset i's excess return during period t, $R_{m,t}$ is the excess market return, I_{t-1} is the investor information set at the end of period $t-1$. Shanken (1990), Ferson and Schadt (1996), and Ferson and Harvey (1999) model beta as a linear function of instrumental variables such as the aggregate dividend yield and default spreads. Boguth et al. (2011) further built on the literature by incorporating lags of realized betas as additional instrumental variables,

$$R_{i,\tau} = \alpha_i^{IV} + \left(\gamma_{i,0} + \gamma_{i,1}' Z_{i,\tau-1}\right)R_{m,\tau} + u_{i,t}, \qquad (4.9)$$

where τ indexes quarters, $R_{i,\tau}$ is the quarterly excess returns, $R_{m,\tau}$ is the quarterly market excess returns, and $Z_{i,\tau-1} \subseteq I_{t-1}$ is a vector of instruments, which means $\beta_{i,\tau}^{IV} \equiv \gamma_{i,0} + \gamma_{i,1}' Z_{i,\tau-1}$.

What should the instrumental variables ($Z_{i,\tau-1}$) be? Boguth et al. (2011) show that lagged betas from prior estimation windows are typically good predictors of beta. Equation (4.9) can be estimated by regression,

$$R_{i,\tau} = \alpha_i^{IV1} + \gamma_{i,0}R_{m,\tau} + \gamma_{i,1}' Z_{i,\tau-1}R_{m,\tau} + u_{i,t}. \qquad (4.10)$$

Boguth et al. (2011) also suggest a two-step IV method that can generate more direct evidence of the relation between the conditioning variables and betas. Indexing each quarter as τ, the following regression (using daily returns of quarter τ) can be estimated for each τ,

$$r_{i,j} = \alpha_i + \beta_{i,0}r_{m,j} + \beta_{i,1}r_{m,j-1} + \beta_{i,2}\left[\frac{r_{m,j-2} + r_{m,j-3} + r_{m,j-4}}{3}\right] + \varepsilon_{i,j},$$

(4.11)

where $r_{i,j}$ is the excess return for a given asset i on day j and $r_{m,j}$ is the excess market return on day j of quarter τ. The beta estimate for quarter τ is given by

$$\hat{\beta}_{i,\tau} \equiv \hat{\beta}_{i,0} + \hat{\beta}_{i,1} + \hat{\beta}_{i,2}.$$

(4.12)

In the first stage of the two-stage IV estimation, the estimated quarterly betas are regressed on a set of lagged instruments,

$$\hat{\beta}_{i,\tau} = \delta_{i,0} + \delta'_{i,1}Z_{i,\tau-1} + e_{i,\tau}.$$

(4.13)

The fitted betas $\tilde{\beta}_{i,\tau} = \delta_{i,0} + \delta'_{i,1}Z_{i,\tau-1}$ are then used in the second stage,

$$R_{i,\tau} = \alpha_i^{IV2} + \left(\phi_{i,0} + \phi_{i,1}\tilde{\beta}_{i,\tau}\right)R_{m,\tau} + v_{i,t}.$$

(4.14)

The two-stage method is a restricted version in which $\beta_{i,\tau}^{IV2} \equiv \phi_{i,0} + \phi_{i,1}\tilde{\beta}_{i,\tau}$ is constrained to be linear in the fitted first-stage beta. Equation (4.14) can be estimated by regression,

$$R_{i,\tau} = \alpha_i^{IV2} + \phi_{i,0}R_{m,\tau} + \phi_{i,1}\tilde{\beta}_{i,\tau}R_{m,\tau} + v_{i,t}.$$

(4.15)

The conditional betas, either using one-stage $\beta_{i,\tau}^{IV} \equiv \gamma_{i,0} + \gamma'_{i,1}Z_{i,\tau-1}$ or two-stage, $\beta_{i,\tau}^{IV2} \equiv \phi_{i,0} + \phi_{i,1}\tilde{\beta}_{i,\tau}$ require the specification of instrumental variables $Z_{i,\tau-1}$, which is a matter of insights and experience. The $k+1$ from the regression in Equation (4.10) (one-stage) or Equation (4.15) (two-stage) reflects the ability of a given set of instruments to describe beta dynamics. Moreover, regressing beta estimates on instrumental variables in the first stage of the two-stage approach (Equation (4.13)) should produce more accurate estimates of the conditional beta coefficients $(\delta'_{i,1})$ when compared to the one-stage approach of which the coefficients are from return-based regression (Equation (4.10)).

4.4. Dynamic Conditional Beta

The conditional beta discussed in the last section depends heavily on instrumental variables which may be difficult to find or non-existent. To avoid the specification of economic variables while also not making unrealistic assumptions like rolling samples or state-space formulation, Engle (2016) proposes the dynamic conditional beta which is built on his earlier work on dynamic conditional correlation (Engle 2002).

Suppose we have a vector z_t of $k+1$ dimension: $z_t = \left(y_t, x_t'\right)', t = 1, \ldots, T$, where $x_t' = \left(x_{1,t}, \ldots, x_{k,t}\right)$ are the explanatory variables of dimension k. The problem is to find the conditional distribution of y given x. Denote $H_{zz,t}$ as the covariance matrix of z_t, which can be expressed as the following partitioned matrix,

$$H_{zz,t} = \begin{pmatrix} H_{yy,t} & H_{yx,t} \\ H_{xy,t} & H_{xx,t} \end{pmatrix} \tag{4.16}$$

OLS tells us that

$$\beta_t = H_{xx,t}^{-1} H_{xy,t}. \tag{4.17}$$

The betas from Equation (4.17) are called the dynamic conditional betas (DCB).

If we can estimate $H_{zz,t}$ from samples $t = 1, \ldots, T$, $H_{xy,t}$ and $H_{xx,t}$ will naturally come out. Engle (2002) proposes one way to estimate dynamic conditional covariance. Before we get into the details, it is worth reviewing univariate volatility modeling first. The earliest and most used models are the autoregressive model for conditional heteroskedasticity (ARCH) proposed by Engle (1982), and the generalized autoregressive model for conditional heteroskedasticity (GARCH) proposed by Bollerslev (1986).

DCBs are an extension of the traditional concept of beta, which measures the sensitivity of an asset's returns to the returns of a benchmark, typically the overall market. While traditional beta is considered to be static over time, DCBs allow for the possibility that the risk exposure of an asset to the market can change over time due to evolving market conditions, the firm's financial policies, macroeconomic factors, or other variables.

The idea behind DCBs stems from the recognition that financial markets are complex, and the relationships between assets and their benchmarks are not necessarily stable. These betas are estimated using models that account for this time variation in risk exposures.

In a DCB model, several features are considered. The model takes into account periods of fluctuating market volatility, which can influence how sensitive an asset's returns are to the movements of the market. It also includes the impact of a firm's leverage on its beta, recognizing that financial risk affects overall risk exposure.

Moreover, dynamic models can identify regime shifts where beta might change significantly, such as during market crises versus more stable times. They can also integrate macroeconomic variables that might influence the market risk profile of an asset.

To estimate DCBs, econometric techniques like the Kalman filter are often employed, allowing the beta to be updated as new information comes to light. This approach is sophisticated and requires a substantial amount of data to accurately reflect the beta's dynamics.

For investors and risk managers who must adapt to changing market conditions, DCBs offer a more refined and adaptable tool for risk assessment and investment decision-making. This approach moves beyond the limitations of static risk measures and provides a dynamic framework for understanding and managing market risk.

Robert Engle

Robert Engle is a Nobel laureate, an American economist and professor at New York University's Stern School of Business. He is best known for his work on time-varying volatility, the development of the autoregressive model on conditional heteroskedasticity (ARCH) model and its extensions known as GARCH (Generalized ARCH). The impact of ARCH is far-reaching. Its extension, GARCH, is still the standard in both academia and industry for modeling the time-varying volatility of asset returns.

In addition to ARCH and GARCH, Engle also made significant contributions to the study of systemic risk and financial crises. He developed the concept of conditional value-at-risk (CVaR), which rectifies VaR's insufficiency to satisfy the subadditivity property as a risk measure (more on this in Chapter 7).

Engle received numerous awards in economics and finance, including the Nobel Memorial Prize in Economic Sciences in 2003, which he shared with Clive Granger for time-series econometrics. He is a fellow of the Econometric Society and the American Academy of Arts and Sciences.

4.4.1. Review of ARCH and GARCH

Consider a univariate random variable a_t, an $\mathrm{ARCH}(m)$ is of the form,

$$a_t = \sigma_t \varepsilon_t, \sigma_t^2 = \alpha_0 + \alpha_1 a_{t-1}^2 + .. + \alpha_m a_{t-m}^2,$$

$$\alpha_0 > 0, \alpha_1 \geq 0, \ldots, \alpha_m \geq 0. \tag{4.18}$$

The goal is to estimate parameters $\alpha_0, \alpha_1, \ldots, \alpha_m$. The term ε_t is called the innovation and its conditional distribution based on information set F_{t-1} needs to be specified. Popular assumptions for $\varepsilon_t | F_{t-1}$ the standard normal distribution with density function

$$f(\varepsilon_t) = \frac{1}{\sqrt{2\pi}} \exp\left(-\frac{\varepsilon_t^2}{2}\right), \tag{4.19}$$

or the Student's t-distribution with density

$$f(\varepsilon_t) = \frac{\Gamma\left[\frac{\nu+1}{2}\right]}{[\pi\nu]^{\frac{1}{2}}\Gamma\left(\frac{\nu}{2}\right)} \left[1 + \frac{\varepsilon_t^2}{\nu}\right]^{-\frac{\nu+1}{2}}, \tag{4.20}$$

where ν is the degree of freedom and $\Gamma(z) = \int_0^\infty t^{z-1} e^{-t} dt$ is the gamma function.

Parameters of Equation (4.20) can be estimated by maximum likelihood estimation (MLE). Under MLE, we aim to find the set of parameters such that the probability (likelihood) of observing a particular sample set $\{a_1, \ldots, a_T\}$ is maximized.

Depending on the distribution assumption of $\varepsilon_t|F_{t-1}$, the likelihood function (and thus the resulting parameters) will be different. For example, if we assume $\varepsilon_t|F_{t-1}\tilde{N}(0,1)$, then $a_t|F_{t-1}\tilde{N}(0,\sigma_t^2)$ with density

$$f(a_t) = \frac{1}{\sigma_t\sqrt{2\pi}}\exp\left(-\frac{a_t^2}{2\sigma_t^2}\right), \tag{4.21}$$

The joint likelihood L of observing $\alpha_0, \alpha_1, \ldots, \alpha_m$ will be the product of densities $f(a_t)$

$$L = \prod_{t=1}^{T}\frac{1}{\sigma_t\sqrt{2\pi}}\exp\left(-\frac{a_t^2}{2\sigma_t^2}\right). \tag{4.22}$$

In MLE, we usually apply a logarithmic transformation to the likelihood function since optimization will become easier to deal with. The optimized result will not be affected since the logarithm is a monotonic increasing transformation that will reserve the same optimized solution. The log-likelihood function L is

$$L = -\sum_{t=1}^{t}\left[\ln(\sigma_t) + \frac{a_t^2}{2\sigma_t^2}\right]. \tag{4.23}$$

Note that we exclude $\sqrt{2\pi}$ because it is a constant and will not affect the optimization. Maximizing Equation (4.23) is equivalent to minimizing $\sum_{t=1}\left[\ln(\sigma_t) + \frac{a_t^2}{2\sigma_t^2}\right]$ by choosing $\alpha_0, \alpha_1, \ldots, \alpha_m$ with $\sigma_t^2 = \alpha_0 + \alpha_1 a_{t-1}^2 + .. + \alpha_m a_{t-m}^2$. We will not go through the MLE formulation under the Student's t-distribution assumption of $\varepsilon_t|F_{t-1}$ since the derivation is similar.

The main problem of ARCH is that volatility persistence behavior can only live up to the lag period (see Equation (4.18)), i.e., any shocks longer than m will have no impact on σ_t^2. In the real world where volatility seems to persist for a long time, a large m is needed for ARCH to properly reflect empirical returns' behavior. This gives rise to the GARCH model which includes an extra persistence term, the lag of volatility, as a modification of ARCH. A GARCH(m, s) is of the general form

$$a_t = \sigma_t\varepsilon_t$$
$$\sigma_t^2 = \alpha_0 + \Sigma_{i=1}^{m}\alpha_i a_{t-i}^2 + \Sigma_{j=1}^{s}\beta_j\sigma_{t-j}^2, \tag{4.24}$$

with $\alpha_0 > 0, \alpha_i \geq 0, \beta_j \geq 0$, and $\Sigma_{i=1}^{\max(m,s)}(\alpha_i + \beta_i) < 1$.

As we can see from Equation (4.24), a shock older than m lags is already reflected in the recursive nature of σ_t^2, resulting in shorter lags m and s to adequately fit the empirical returns' behavior. In finance practice, a GARCH(1,1) model is usually sufficient. Like ARCH, $\varepsilon_t|F_{t-1}$ can be assumed normal or Student's t

distributed under GARCH. The MLE procedure is also similar by just adjusting the σ_t^2 specification in the objective function.

4.4.2. Dynamic Conditional Covariance (DCC)

After reviewing ARCH and GARCH in the univariate case, we are now in a good position to extend the framework to multivariate settings. Consider a k-dimensional random variables α_1 with covariance matrix Σ_t. Its correlation matrix is given by

$$\rho_t = D_t^{-1}\Sigma_t D_t^{-1}, \tag{4.25}$$

with

$$D_t = diag\left\{\sigma_{11,t}^{1/2}, \ldots, \sigma_{kk,t}^{1/2}\right\}, \tag{4.26}$$

where $\sigma_{jj,t}$ is the marginal (univariate) variance of asset $j = 1, \ldots, k$, k that can be individually fit with a univariate model like $\mathrm{GARCH}(1,1)$.

The DCC model takes advantage of the fact that correlation matrices are easier to handle than covariance matrices since correlations are bounded between -1.0 and 1.0. It divides covariance modeling into two steps: The first step is to obtain the volatility series, and the second step is to model the dynamic dependence of the correlation matrices ρ_t.

Denote $\eta_t = (\eta_{1t}, \ldots, \eta_{kt})'$ to be the marginally standardized innovation vector, i.e. $\eta_{it} = a_{it}/\sqrt{\sigma_{ii,t}}$. The correlation matrix of a_t, ρ_t is also the covariance matrix of η_t. Engle (2002) defines a Q_t process which looks like a general GARCH form,

$$Q_t = (1 - \theta_1 - \theta_2)\bar{Q} + \theta_1 Q_{t-1} + \theta_2 \eta_{t-1}\eta_{t-1}', \tag{4.27}$$

where $\bar{Q}$ is the unconditional covariance matrix of η_t, and we can use samples η_t, $t = 1, \ldots, T$ to estimate it; θ_is are non-negative real numbers satisfying $0 < \theta_1 + \theta_2 < 1$. The purpose is to find $\Theta = [\theta_1, \theta_2]$. Since η_t is not bounded between -1.0 and 1.0, Q_t cannot be a correlation matrix because it is not bounded as well. Therefore, to get a dynamic correlation matrix, Q_t needs to be normalized by its diagonal,

$$\rho_t = J_t Q_t J_t, \tag{4.28}$$

$$J_t = diag\left\{q_{11,t}^{-1/2}, \ldots, q_{kk,t}^{-1/2}\right\}, \tag{4.29}$$

where $q_{ii,t}^{-1/2}$ denotes the (i,i)th element of Q_t. Once we get ρ_t, the dynamic covariance matrix can be calculated by left-multiplying and right-multiplying ρ_t with D_t, expressed as

$$\Sigma_t = D_t \rho_t D_t. \tag{4.30}$$

To make the whole idea concrete, let us demonstrate the maximum likelihood method for estimating the DCC assuming $\varepsilon_t | F_{t-1}$ follows the multivariate Student's t-distribution. The Student's t density function for $\varepsilon_t | F_{t-1}$ with degree of freedom ν is

$$f(\varepsilon_t | \nu, F_{t-1}) = \frac{\Gamma\left[\frac{\nu+k}{2}\right]}{[\pi(\nu-2)]^{\frac{k}{2}}\Gamma\left(\frac{\nu}{2}\right)} \left[1 + (\nu-2)^{-1}\varepsilon_t'\varepsilon_t\right]^{-\frac{\nu+k}{2}}. \tag{4.31}$$

Since $a_t = (\Sigma_t)^{1/2}\varepsilon_t$ (the multivariate analogue of univariate case: $a_t = \sigma_t\varepsilon_t$), we have the density of a_t as

$$f(a_t | \nu, \Sigma_t) = \frac{\Gamma\left[\frac{\nu+k}{2}\right]}{[\pi(\nu-2)]^{\frac{k}{2}}\Gamma\left(\frac{\nu}{2}\right)|\Sigma_t|^{\frac{1}{2}}} \left[1 + (\nu-2)^{-1}a_t'\Sigma_t^{-1}a_t\right]^{-\frac{\nu+k}{2}}. \tag{4.32}$$

The joint likelihood function is and the log-likelihood is

$$\sum_{t=1}^{T}\{\log\left(\Gamma\left[\frac{\nu+k}{2}\right]\right) - \frac{k}{2}\log(\pi(\nu-2)) - \log\left(\Gamma\left(\frac{\nu}{2}\right)\right) - \frac{1}{2}\log(|\Sigma_t|) -$$
$$\frac{\nu+k}{2}\log\left(1 + (\nu-2)^{-1}a_t'\Sigma_t^{-1}a_t\right)\}. \tag{4.33}$$

We also choose to estimate the degrees of freedom ν as its optimal value is unknown, thereby expanding our parameter vector for optimization to $\{\theta_1, \theta_2, \nu\}$ which influences Σ_t. The following outlines the algorithmic steps:

1. For a given sample $a_1, \ldots, a_T$ where each a_t represents the return of k-dimensional assets, apply a GARCH(1,1) model to each a_{it} for $i = 1, \ldots, k$ to obtain a_{it} for $t = 1, \ldots, T$, and $i = 1, \ldots, k$.
2. Compute $\eta_t = (\eta_{1t}, \ldots, \eta_{kt})'$ where $\eta_{it} = a_{it}/\sqrt{\sigma_{ii,t}}$.
3. Initialize with $\{\theta_1, \theta_2, \nu_0\}$ to estimate an initial version of Q_1 using Equation (4.27).
4. Derive Q_1 using Equation (4.27), ρ_t using Equation (4.28) and Σ_t using Equation (4.30) for $t = 1, \ldots, T$.
5. Optimize the parameter vector $\{\theta_1, \theta_2, \nu\}$ by maximizing the log-likelihood function Equation (4.33) with the obtained Σ_t from step 4.

To estimate the dynamic conditional beta (DCB), apply the above DCC methodology to $z_t = (y_t, x_t')'$ for $t = 1, \ldots, T$, which yields $H_{zz,t}$. From there, $H_{xy,t}$

and $H_{xx,t}$ can be easily derived using the partition Equation (4.16). Subsequently, DCB is computed in accordance with Equation (4.17).

4.5. Continuous and Discontinuous Beta

So far, we have focused on the conditional estimation of beta using the instrument variable approach or the dynamic conditional approach under a general ARCH/GARCH formulation. There are other beta analyses.

A prominent one is Bollerslev, Li, and Todorov (2016). The article investigates how individual equity prices respond to market price movements, distinguishing between continuous (smooth intraday co-movements) and discontinuous risks (jumps during the day and overnight returns). Accordingly, it defines three intraday beta measures for stocks, and they are the continuous beta, the discontinuous beta, and the overnight beta. Betas like those could be a great fit for our factor purpose if they carry significant risk premia and exhibit low correlations among each other.

With high-frequency data for almost 1,000 stocks over two decades, the authors' findings reveal significant risk premiums for discontinuous and overnight betas, but not for continuous intraday beta. This suggests that markets price the risks associated with large, abrupt price changes differently from more gradual, continuous price movements. The implications are significant for understanding market risk premiums and for the construction of investment strategies that account for different types of market risks.

4.5.1. Continuous Beta

Continuous beta reflects the smooth intraday co-movements of individual equity prices with the market. Unlike its counterparts that deal with jumps and abrupt changes, continuous beta captures the more regular, ongoing price movements that occur during the trading day. Bollerslev, Li, and Todorov (2016) suggest that these types of movements are viewed differently by investors compared to more sudden changes, implying a distinction in risk perception and pricing. Notably, the risk premiums associated with continuous beta do not appear to be priced in the cross-section, indicating that the market does not reward investors for the risks associated with continuous intraday price movements to the same extent as it does for jumps and overnight movements.

4.5.2. Discontinuous Beta

Discontinuous beta is concerned with intraday price discontinuities or jumps during the active part of the trading day. These jumps represent abrupt changes in stock prices that can significantly impact an investor's portfolio. The estimation of discontinuous beta assumes a positive relationship between these jumps in individual stocks and the market, aiming to capture the risk associated with these sudden movements. The framework for discontinuous beta involves comparing the jumps in individual stocks with those in the market to understand the systematic risk posed by these abrupt changes.

4.5.3. Overnight Beta

Overnight beta deals with the price changes that occur from the close of one trading day to the opening of the next. These movements are considered discontinuous and can be significant, as they capture all the information and events that occur while the market is closed. The estimation of overnight beta is similar to that of discontinuous beta but focuses on the overnight jump returns, considering them as a separate category of risk. This distinction is crucial because the dynamics of overnight returns can be different from those during the trading day, influenced by after-hours news, global market developments, and other factors that can lead to significant price adjustments at the opening of the next trading day.

4.6. Beta-related Factors

In the preceding sections, we have explored various methods for estimating beta. This section shifts our focus to factors constructed based on beta. Among these, the most renowned factors are Betting-Against-Beta (BAB) and Betting-Against-Correlation (BAC), with BAB garnering the most attention and controversy. Understanding these factors and approaching the debates surrounding them with an open mind is crucial for enriching and refining our factor construction methodologies.

4.6.1. Betting-Against-Beta (BAB)

According to CAPM, a security that has a higher beta should be compensated with a higher return. Nevertheless, we usually see lower beta securities turn out to have higher risk-adjusted returns and the empirical evidence dates back to the 1970s.

Black, Jensen, and Scholes (1972) observe from real market data that the Security Market Line (SML) is much flatter than predicted by the CAPM, indicating that the relationship between risk and return cannot be adequately explained by CAPM alone. Through empirical analysis using time series and cross-sectional regressions, they substantiate this hypothesis. Particularly, their study groups stocks into deciles based on market beta estimates and conducts time series regression analysis. Their empirical findings reveal that, across different historical periods, alpha is significantly nonzero and negatively correlated with beta. This means that stocks with higher betas tend to have negative alphas. Based on these findings, they augment CAPM with an additional zero-beta factor, and this two-factor model is also referred to as the Black CAPM.

Forty years after the introduction of the Black CAPM, Frazzini and Pedersen (2014) propose the Betting-Against-Beta (BAB) factor, offering a different perspective on the negative correlation between alpha and beta. Besides, the authors identify leverage constraints as a key reason behind the BAB phenomenon. By utilizing the Treasury-Eurodollar (TED) spread as a proxy for the ease of financing, they find that wider TED spreads, indicating easier financing, are associated with lower future BAB returns; conversely, narrower TED spreads, suggesting tighter financing conditions, predict higher BAB returns.

The "TED spread" is a financial indicator that represents the difference between the interest rates on short-term United States government debt (usually measured using three-month Treasury bills) and interbank loans (measured using the three-month LIBOR, or London Interbank Offered Rate). The acronym "TED" is derived from "Treasury-Eurodollar", with the latter referring to the dollar-denominated deposits held at banks outside of the United States, which is what LIBOR is based on. Treasury Bills (T-Bills) are short-term government securities with a maturity of typically three months. They are considered virtually risk-free because they are backed by the full faith and credit of the U.S. government. Eurodollar Deposits (represented by LIBOR) are U.S. dollars deposited in commercial banks outside the United States. The LIBOR is a benchmark rate that some of the world's leading banks charge each other for short-term loans. It represents the interest rate banks are willing to pay for these deposits. LIBOR has been replaced by the Secured Overnight Financing Rate, or SOFR. Unlike LIBOR, SOFR represents the cost of borrowing for a broader variety of market participants and is based on actual transactions in overnight lending markets.

The TED spread measures the difference between the interest rate on short-term U.S. government debt (perceived as risk-free) and the interest rate on funds in the banking system (which includes credit risk). A wider TED spread indicates that lenders believe the risk of interbank loans (credit risk) is increasing relative to risk-free government debt. This can be a sign of tightening credit conditions because banks are charging more for loans to each other due to perceived higher risk, and hence, it may be more difficult for companies to obtain financing. Conversely, a narrower TED spread suggests that credit risk is perceived to be lower, and financing conditions are more relaxed. This is because the difference between what banks charge each other for loans and what is charged for risk-free loans is smaller.

In the context of market beta, when the TED spread is wider (indicating higher perceived risk and tighter credit conditions), it is associated with higher future returns on the BAB strategy. The BAB strategy involves buying low-beta assets and selling high-beta assets, betting that the low-beta assets will outperform on a risk-adjusted basis. If financing conditions are tight, high-beta assets might perform worse due to their higher risk and cost of capital, leading to better performance of the BAB strategy. Conversely, when the TED spread is narrower (indicating lower perceived risk and easier financing conditions), the BAB strategy might yield lower returns as high-beta assets are not penalized as heavily by financing costs.

Frazzini and Pedersen (2014) also examine how different levels of leverage constraints influence investors' preferences, revealing that investors with higher constraints (such as mutual funds and individual investors) tend to favor high-beta stocks, while those with fewer constraints (like hedge funds, LBOs, and Berkshire Hathaway) prefer low-beta stocks. Defining Ψ as the degree of funding constraint,

Frazzini and Pedersen (2014) demonstrate that the relationship between alpha and beta follows $\alpha = \Psi(1 - \beta)$.

Additionally, Blitz, Falkenstein, and van Vliet (2014) discuss leverage constraints from the fundamental assumptions of CAPM. CAPM imposes no leverage restrictions for investors, who all aim to maximize returns per unit of risk (i.e., the tangency portfolio), and can adjust their desired return levels through borrowing and lending. In reality, however, leverage is constrained; the cost of borrowed funds can be high, or terms may not permit leveraging, preventing investors from freely adjusting their leverage levels. As a result, investors seeking higher returns are forced to take on more market risk by pursuing high-beta stocks, leading to their overvaluation. Blitz and van Vliet (2007) argue that the same constraints on using leverage, or the aversion to it, prevent smart (or sophisticated) investors from eliminating the low-beta anomaly.

Next, we navigate back to the BAB factor. Let $\hat{\beta}_{it}$ be the estimated beta of stock i at time t. To construct the factor, stocks are ranked in ascending order on $\hat{\beta}_{it}$. Let z be the $n \times 1$ vector of beta ranks, then $z_i = \text{rank}(\hat{\beta}_{it})$. Besides, let $\bar{z}$ be the average rank in the cross-section. The ranked stocks are assigned to one of two portfolios: low-beta and high-beta. The low- (high-) beta portfolio is composed of all stocks with a beta below (above) its median. In each portfolio, stocks are weighted by the ranked betas, and therefore stock weights in the high- and low-beta portfolios are

$$w_H = k(z - \bar{z})^+,$$

$$w_L = k(z - \bar{z})^-, \tag{4.34}$$

where k is a normalizing constant, while x^+ and x^- indicate the positive and negative elements of a vector x. According to Equation (4.34), it is easy to see that stocks with lower betas have larger weights in the low-beta portfolio, and stocks with higher betas have larger weights in the high-beta portfolio. By construction, $1_n' w_H = 1$ and $1_n' w_L = 1$ with n being the number of stocks in the cross-section.

Finally, both portfolios are rescaled to have a beta of one at portfolio formation. The BAB factor is then constructed as a self-financing, beta-neutral portfolio. It involves taking a long position in the low-beta portfolio and short selling the high-beta portfolio. The excess return of the BAB factor is therefore,

$$r_{t+1}^{\text{BAB}} = \frac{1}{\beta_t^L}\left(r_{t+1}^L - r_f\right) - \frac{1}{\beta_t^H}\left(r_{t+1}^H - r_f\right), \tag{4.35}$$

where $r_{t+1}^L = r_{t+1}' w_L$ and $r_{t+1}^H = r_{t+1}' w_H$ are the returns of the low- and high-beta portfolios, and $\beta_t^L = \beta_t' w_L$ and $\beta_t^H = \beta_t' w_H$.

Empirical evidence from various markets has supported the hypothesis proposed by Frazzini and Pedersen (2014). In the industry, BAB has become a hallmark of defensive investment strategies, garnering widespread acclaim from institutional investors.

Objectively speaking, despite the clear theoretical framework and empirical evidence supporting the BAB factor, its construction methodology—both the ex-ante estimation of beta values and the beta-neutral constraint applied during the portfolio formulation process—differ markedly from the more conventional approach of constructing factors based on direct sorting of firm characteristics, such as the Fama-French factors. As we will see later, these differences have become focal points for criticism of the BAB factor.

It is also helpful to mention that, by construction, the BAB factor is a market-wide measure that captures the risk premium of low-beta stocks in excess of high-beta stocks, rather than firm-level characteristics that can be used directly to sort and pick stocks. In order to utilize the BAB factor for stock selection, we need to transform it into individual asset measures. One way to accomplish this is by calculating the assets' exposure to this factor through a regression analysis. This involves running a regression of each asset's excess return on the BAB factor. Then, this exposure can be used to select stocks.

4.6.2. Criticism on BAB

Previously, we have touched upon the unique construction method of the BAB factor, which has sparked considerable debate. A notable critique comes from Novy-Marx and Velikov (2022) in their provocatively titled paper, "Betting Against Betting Against Beta" (BABAB), which challenges BAB on three fronts: (1) the use of rank weighting in portfolio construction; (2) achieving beta neutrality through leverage; and (3) employing different time windows to calculate the standard deviation of the correlation coefficient when estimating beta.

Novy-Marx and Velikov (2022) point out that using ranks as weights in BAB is nearly equivalent to equal weighting, which significantly elevates the role of small and micro-cap stocks in the portfolio, contrary to Frazzini and Pedersen's (2014) intention to give higher weights to stocks with extreme beta values. Furthermore, Frazzini and Pedersen's (2014) approach of leveraging low-beta long positions and de-leveraging high-beta short positions to construct a zero-beta (beta neutral) hedge portfolio also approximates equal weighting. Combining these factors, Novy-Marx and Velikov (2022) argue that the BAB factor's construction method results in an excessive weight on ultra-small-cap companies and high exposure to profitability and investment factors. Since the size, profitability, and investment factors have been proven effective in the US stock market, this significantly enhances the performance of the BAB factor.

Regarding the third critique, Novy-Marx and Velikov (2022) highlight that Frazzini and Pedersen (2014) use different time windows to calculate volatility and correlation coefficients when estimating beta, leading to a biased estimation method that inadvertently supports their proposed theory. Correcting this bias nullifies the theory.

To see this, recall that for a dependent variable y and an independent variable x, the OLS estimator of beta is:

$$\beta = \frac{\text{cov}(y, x)}{\text{var}(x)} \tag{4.36}$$

Besides, the correlation coefficient of the two variables is:

$$\rho_{xy} = \frac{\text{cov}(x, y)}{\sigma_x \sigma_y} \tag{4.37}$$

Plugging Equation (4.37) into Equation (4.36) reveals the close relationship between beta and correlation as well as the standard deviations of the variables of interest,

$$\beta = \frac{\text{cov}(y, x)}{\text{var}(x)} = \frac{\rho_{xy} \sigma_x \sigma_y}{\sigma_x^2} = \rho_{xy} \frac{\sigma_y}{\sigma_x}. \tag{4.38}$$

Now, we are ready to address the third concern regarding Frazzini and Pedersen (2014). The authors use one-year and five-year windows to calculate volatility and correlation coefficients, respectively. With the help of Equation (4.38), simple algebraic manipulation reveals the relationship between their beta (denoted by β_i^{FP}) and the beta computed by using the traditional approach,

$$\beta_i^{FP} \equiv \rho_i^{(5)} \frac{\sigma_i^{(1)}}{\sigma_m^{(1)}} = \left(\rho_i^{(5)} \frac{\sigma_i^{(5)}}{\sigma_m^{(5)}} \right) \left(\frac{\sigma_m^{(5)} \sigma_i^{(1)}}{\sigma_m^{(1)} \sigma_i^{(5)}} \right) = \left(\frac{\sigma_i^{(1)} / \sigma_i^{(5)}}{\sigma_m^{(1)} / \sigma_m^{(5)}} \right) \beta_i^{(5)}, \tag{4.39}$$

where the superscripts 1 and 5 denote one-year and five-year rolling windows, respectively, and therefore $\beta_i^{(5)}$ represents the beta computed by the traditional approach with a five-year window of historical data. Equation (4.39) shows that the beta estimate of Frazzini and Pedersen (2014) is equivalent to the traditionally derived beta multiplied by a coefficient: the ratio of the asset's $\sigma_i^{(1)} / \sigma_i^{(5)}$ to the market's $\sigma_m^{(1)} / \sigma_m^{(5)}$. Novy-Marx and Velikov (2022) empirically find that when the market itself is highly volatile, the elasticity between the asset's $\sigma_i^{(1)} / \sigma_i^{(5)}$ and the market's $\sigma_m^{(1)} / \sigma_m^{(5)}$ is less than 1; conversely, when the market is less volatile, the elasticity is greater than 1. This implies that β_i^{FP} is lower than the traditionally calculated beta during high market volatility periods and higher during low volatility periods. As a result, using β_i^{FP} for individual assets leads to a market-wide beta unequal to 1 (its value fluctuates over time with a mean slightly above 1), indicating that β_i^{FP} is not a reasonable estimator.

4.6.3. Betting-Against-Correlation (BAC)

Another factor closely associated with BAB is the Betting–Against-Correlation (BAC) factor. A review of Equation (4.38) reveals that beta is intricately linked with both correlation and volatility. Asness, Frazzini, and Gormsen (2020) provide a framework to isolate different components in the beta expression and construct a Betting-Against-Correlation (BAC) factor by focusing on the correlation component.

Cliff Asness and AQR

Cliff Asness is a co-founder of AQR Capital Management, a global investment management firm that is known for its emphasis on systematic and quantitative investing strategies. Asness completed his PhD in finance at the University of Chicago, where he studied under Eugene Fama. Asness's dissertation contributed to the development of what is now known as "factor investing". Asness has been a leading figure in researching and advocating for this investment style, which seeks to capture these risk premia in a systematic way.

Asness's contributions to factor investing include both academic and practical applications.

Academic Contributions: Asness's research has helped to empirically validate the existence and persistence of various factors in different markets. His academic work has been published in numerous peer-reviewed journals, contributing to the body of knowledge on topics such as momentum and value investing.

Practical Applications: At AQR, Asness has been instrumental in applying quantitative research to real-world investing. AQR uses factor-based strategies to manage assets for institutional investors, including pension funds, insurance companies, and endowments.

Innovation in Strategies: Under Asness's leadership, AQR has been at the forefront of developing innovative investment products that utilize factor-investing strategies. These include mutual funds, hedge funds, and other vehicles designed to provide investors with exposure to targeted factors.

Risk and Return Models: Asness has contributed to the understanding of how factors can be combined to manage risk and improve returns. His work has helped investors understand the behavior of factor returns over time and through different market conditions.

Cliff Asness's influence in the field is significant due to his dual role as both a scholar and a practitioner. His firm, AQR Capital Management, is considered one of the pioneers in applying factor-investing principles systematically and at scale, which has had a considerable impact on the asset management industry.

The construction of the BAC factor is very similar to that of the BAB factor, except that volatility should be controlled for BAC. As a result, the procedure runs a dependent double portfolio sort, first based on volatility and then on correlation. Specifically, for each time t, the BAC factor is constructed according to the following steps:

1. Sort assets in ascending order based on the estimate of volatility and assign them to one of the five quintiles. Within each quintile, assets are then ranked based on the estimate of correlation with the market and assigned to one of two portfolios, i.e., low- and high-correlation portfolios.

Assets with low correlation with market have a higher weight in the low correlation portfolio. Let z^q be the $n_q \times 1$ vector of correlation ranks within each volatility quintile $q = 1, 2, 3, 4, 5$ and $\overline{z^q} = 1'_{n_q} z^q / n_q$ be the average rank, where n_q is the number of assets in volatility quintile q and 1_{n_q} is a vector of ones with size n_q. The portfolio weights of the low-correlation portfolios in each volatility quintile are given by:

$$w_L^q = k^q (z^q - \overline{z^q})^-, \tag{4.40}$$

where k^q is a normalizing constant equal to $2/1'_{n_q} |z^q - \overline{z^q}|$ and x^- indicates the negative elements of a vector x. By construction, $1'_{n_q} w_L^q = 1$.

2. Similarly, assets with high correlation with the market have a larger weight in the high correlation portfolio. The portfolio weights of the high correlation portfolios in each volatility quintile are given by:

$$w_H^q = k^q (z^q - \overline{z^q})^+, \tag{4.41}$$

where x^+ indicates the positive elements of a vector x. By construction, $1'_{n_q} w_H^q = 1$.

The excess return to BAC in each volatility quintile is given by

$$r_{t+1}^{BAC(q)} = \frac{1}{\beta_t^{L,q}} \left(r_{t+1}^{L,q} - r_f \right) - \frac{1}{\beta_t^{H,q}} \left(r_{t+1}^{H,q} - r_f \right), \tag{4.42}$$

where $r_{t+1}^{L,q} = r_{t+1}^{q'} w_L^q$ and $r_{t+1}^{H,q} = r_{t+1}^{q'} w_H^q$ are the returns of the low- and high-correlation portfolios, and $\beta_t^{L,q} = \beta_t^{q'} w_L^q$ and $\beta_t^{H,q} = \beta_t^{q'} w_H^q$ are the corresponding betas of each asset in quintile q.

3. Finally, the return of the BAC factor is,

$$r_{t+1}^{BAC} = \frac{1}{5} \sum_{q=1}^{5} r_{t+1}^{BAC(q)}. \tag{4.43}$$

Note that by construction, the BAC portfolio is still beta-neutral. However, it is not correlation-neutral. Similar to the BAB factor, the BAC measure is again a market-wide measure. It captures the risk premium associated with the BAC effect. To use it for stock selection, we also need to transform it into individual asset measures, such as running a time-series regression of an asset's excess return on the BAC factor and using the estimated beta as the factor for stock selection.

Recall that in Section 3.4, we mentioned that Bali et al. (2017) posit that the pursuit of lottery-like stocks by individual investors, rather than the theory related to leverage constraint, is a significant contributor to the low beta anomaly, especially the BAB factor. The BAC paper of Asness, Frazzini, and Gormsen (2020) is in response to this critique. Intuitively, as BAC is relatively unrelated to volatility and lottery demand, if BAC realizes significant excess returns, it would support the leverage constraint theory. On the contrary, if BAC performs poorly, it would be evidence for the lottery demand hypothesis.

The empirical findings of Asness, Frazzini, and Gormsen (2020) indicate that the BAC factor yields significant and robust excess returns. To test the leverage constraint hypothesis, the authors examine the impact of margin loan balances on both BAB and BAC factors, and find that both factors performed significantly better when prior margin loans were lower, indicating higher leverage constraints, providing strong evidence in support of the leverage constraint hypothesis. To assess the influence of lottery preferences, the study introduces quarterly changes in casino dividends (normalized by GDP) as a proxy for gambling preferences. The results show a significant effect on the MAX effect but no significant impact on the BAB factor. These findings suggest that the leverage constraint hypothesis is a plausible explanation for BAB, while the lottery preference hypothesis remains inconclusive.

4.7. Conclusion

In this chapter, we delved into the pivotal concept of systematic risk, captured by beta, which is fundamental to understanding market dynamics. The temporal instability of beta complicates its estimation beyond mere regression analysis on historical data, challenging conventional wisdom. In addition, the phenomenon known as the beta anomaly, which contradicts the CAPM's assertion that higher beta correlates with higher returns, is well-documented in academic circles. We explored several methodologies for calculating conditional beta, ranging from the basic technique of employing a rolling window with a predetermined lag to more sophisticated approaches such as the instrumental variable method and dynamic conditional beta within the GARCH framework. Furthermore, we examined techniques to delineate the sensitivity of stock returns to market movements, segregating them into intraday continuous, discontinuous, and overnight components.

Beyond various estimation methodologies, we also delved into the application of beta as a factor, with the BAB and BAC factors emerging as the most significant. However, given the debates surrounding their construction methods and underlying rationales, we advocate for a rational and dialectical approach towards these factors. While they have yielded significant excess returns in the US stock market and numerous global equity markets, it's crucial not to take them for granted. Embracing diverse perspectives with an open mind and conducting independent analyses can deepen our understanding of these factors, ultimately broadening our horizons in factor investing research.

Beta remains a compelling, central topic with significant practical implications, and it is poised to continue as such for the foreseeable future, with numerous avenues for further exploration. One potential path involves expanding the logic of instrumental variables to identify additional instruments with robust economic rationales as exogenous variables for beta estimation. Another promising direction is to employ Bayesian techniques, such as Bayesian regression, for modeling conditional beta. Additionally, considering beta as following a stochastic process that requires calibration with market data represents another innovative approach. These methodologies collectively strive to accurately capture securities' instantaneous reactions to market fluctuations, emphasizing the need for precise and dynamic beta estimation in financial modeling and risk management.

References

Asness, C., A. Frazzini, and N. J. Gormsen (2020). Betting against correlation: Testing theories of the low-risk effect. *Journal of Financial Economics* 135(3), 629–652.

Bali, T. G., S. J. Brown, S. Murray and Y. Tang (2017). A lottery-demand-based explanation of the beta anomaly. *Journal of Financial and Quantitative Analysis* 52(6), 2369–2397.

Black, F., M. C. Jensen, and M. Scholes (1972). The Capital Asset Pricing Model: Some Empirical Tests. In *Studies in the Theory of Capital Markets*. M. C. Jensen (editor), New York: Praeger, 79–121.

Blitz, D., E. Falkenstein, and P. van Vliet (2014). Explanations for the volatility effect: An overview based on the CAPM assumptions. *Journal of Portfolio Management* 40(3), 61–76.

Blitz, D. and P. van Vliet (2007). The volatility effect. *Journal of Portfolio Management* 34(1), 102–113.

Boguth, O., M. Carlson, A. Fisher, and M. Simutin (2011). Conditional risk and performance evaluation: Volatility timing, overconditioning, and new estimates of momentum alphas. *Journal of Financial Economics* 102(2), 363–389.

Bollerslev, T. (1986). Generalized autoregressive conditional heteroskedasticity. *Journal of Econometrics* 31(3), 307–327.

Bollerslev, T., S. Z. Li, and V. Todorov (2016). Roughing up beta: Continuous versus discontinuous betas and the cross section of expected stock returns. *Journal of Financial Economics* 120(3), 464–490.

Cederburg, S. and M. S. O'Doherty (2016). Does it pay to bet against beta? On the conditional performance of the beta anomaly. *Journal of Finance* 71(2), 737–774.

Engle, R. F. (1982). Autoregressive conditional heteroskedasticity with estimates of the variance of United Kingdom inflation. *Econometrica* 50(4), 987–1007.

Engle, R. F. (2002). Dynamic conditional correlation: A simple class of multivariate generalized autoregressive conditional heteroskedasticity models. *Journal of Business & Economic Statistics* 20(3), 339–350.

Engle, R. F. (2016). Dynamic conditional beta. *Journal of Financial Econometrics* 14(4), 643–667.

Ferson, W. E. and C. R. Harvey (1999). Conditioning variables and the cross section of stock returns. *Journal of Finance* 54(4), 1325–1360.

Ferson, W. E. and R. W. Schadt (1996). Measuring fund strategy and performance in changing economic conditions. *Journal of Finance* 51(2), 425–461.

Frazzini, A. and L. H. Pedersen (2014). Betting against beta. *Journal of Financial Economics* 111 (1), 1–25.

Grant, D. (1977). Portfolio performance and the "cost" of timing decisions. *Journal of Finance* 32(3), 837–846.

Jagannathan, R. and Z. Wang (1996). The conditional CAPM and the cross-sectional of expected returns. *Journal of Finance* 51(1), 3–53.

Lewellen, J. and S. Nagel (2006). The conditional CAPM does not explain asset-pricing anomalies. *Journal of Financial Economics* 82(2), 289–314.

Novy-Marx, R. and M. Velikov (2022). Betting against betting against beta. *Journal of Financial Economics* 143(1), 80–106.

Shanken, J. A. (1990). Intertemporal asset pricing: An empirical investigation. *Journal of Econometrics* 45(1–2), 99–120.

5

TECHNICAL ANALYSIS FACTORS

In the realm of financial markets, investors and traders seek to gain an edge through various methods of analysis to make informed decisions. Among these methods, technical analysis stands out as a powerful tool used to predict future market movements based on past market data, primarily price and volume. This chapter delves into the intricate world of technical analysis, exploring its fundamental concepts, the rationale behind its effectiveness, and the various factors that play a critical role in its application.

Technical analysis, at its core, is built on the premise that market prices reflect all known information and that patterns in price movements tend to repeat themselves over time. This form of analysis is often contrasted with fundamental analysis, which focuses on evaluating a security's intrinsic value based on economic and financial factors. Technical analysts, sometimes referred to as chartists, rely on charts and other tools to identify patterns and trends that can suggest future activity.

5.1. Nature of Technical Analysis

Technical analysis has been an integral part of financial practice for decades and is still widely used by speculative investors.

5.1.1. Publications

Publications related to technical analysis are marked by both extensive guides for practitioners and critical examinations of the methodology's efficacy. Murphy's (1999) *Technical Analysis of the Financial Markets* stands out as a comprehensive guide to the field, offering a thorough overview of trading methods and applications. Its breadth covers the foundational concepts of chart types,

DOI: 10.4324/9781003480204-5

trend identification, and the use of technical indicators, making it a fundamental resource for both novice and seasoned traders.

Complementing Murphy's practical approach, Aronson (2006) provides a critical, empirically-driven perspective in *Evidence-based Technical Analysis*. Aronson rigorously scrutinizes various technical analysis strategies through the lens of the scientific method, focusing on statistical inference to validate trading signals. His work serves as a counterbalance to the often uncritical acceptance of technical analysis techniques, demanding a more evidence-based approach to their application in trading.

While the aforementioned works focus on the mechanisms and legitimacy of technical analysis, Malkiel's (1973) seminal book, *A Random Walk Down Wall Street*, offers a more skeptical view of the practice. Malkiel argues against the predictability of stock movements based on past data, suggesting that stock prices evolve according to a random walk and thus cannot be reliably predicted through technical analysis or any other method. Despite its critical stance, the book has contributed to the debate on market efficiency and the feasibility of various trading strategies, including technical analysis.

Schwager's (1989) "Market Wizards" series of books provides anecdotal evidence through a collection of interviews with successful traders. These narratives reveal how technical analysis, among other tools, plays a role in the trading strategies of market experts. Schwager's work does not merely chronicle trading successes; it also explores the psychological and methodological aspects of trading, offering readers insights into the practical application of technical analysis and risk management.

In *The Evolution of Technical Analysis: Financial Prediction from Babylonian Tablets to Bloomberg Terminals*, Lo and Hasanhodzic (2010) provide a comprehensive historical account of the development of technical analysis. Their investigation starts from the ancient techniques of the Babylonians and traces the evolution of chart-based analysis through the centuries, highlighting how each era's intellectual advancements have shaped the methods used by traders and analysts. The authors examine the adaptation of technical analysis to reflect the prevailing market conditions and technologies, an aspect crucial to its continued relevance. They discuss the early contributions of Dutch and Japanese traders to technical analysis, including the development of candlestick charting, and detail the impact of Charles Dow's work, which laid the foundation for what is known today as the Dow Theory. Lo and Hasanhodzic's book emphasizes that technical analysis is more than a set of heuristic trading rules; it represents a complex interplay of market psychology and behavioral economics. This point of view aligns with Lo's (2017) "Adaptive Market Hypothesis", suggesting that the resilience and adaptability of technical analysis are attributable to its capacity to integrate psychological insights and respond to changing market dynamics. As part of the literature on technical analysis, Lo and Hasanhodzic's work provides a historical context that is often missing from academic and practitioner debates.

Andrew W. Lo and Adaptive Market Hypothesis

Andrew Wen-Chuan Lo is an influential economist and finance academic known for his work on the Efficient Market Hypothesis and the Adaptive Market Hypothesis, among other topics. He is a professor at the MIT Sloan School of Management and the director of the MIT Laboratory for Financial Engineering. His research has spanned various areas, including financial engineering, computational finance, behavioral economics, and risk management.

Professor Lo has made several significant contributions to financial theory and practice, including:

Adaptive Market Hypothesis (AMH): Lo proposed the AMH as an alternative to the traditional efficient market hypothesis (EMH), which posits that financial markets are always perfectly efficient, and prices fully reflect all available information. The AMH suggests that market efficiency is not a static condition but can vary over time as a result of the interactions of various market participants, each adapting to changes in the investment environment using heuristics or simple rules of thumb. The AMH integrates principles from evolutionary biology into the study of financial markets and acknowledges the impacts of human behavior on market dynamics.

Financial Engineering and Quantitative Analysis: Lo has been a pioneer in the field of financial engineering, developing new statistical tools and models for the analysis of financial markets. He has contributed to the development of algorithms and quantitative strategies for trading and investment.

Hedge Fund Replication: Lo has conducted extensive research on hedge funds, including work on creating replicable strategies that can mimic the returns of hedge funds without investing in them directly.

Non-standard Risk Measures: He has worked on alternative risk measures to better capture the risks in hedge funds and other alternative investments, moving beyond traditional measures like volatility and beta.

Cancer Research Funding: In recent years, Lo has applied his financial expertise to the challenge of funding drug development, particularly for cancer. He has proposed the use of "cancer megafunds" as a way to raise large amounts of capital for early-stage drug research by issuing bonds and shares backed by a diverse portfolio of drug development efforts.

Professor Lo's work is highly interdisciplinary, drawing on psychology, economics, artificial intelligence, and biology to understand the mechanisms driving market behavior and to develop practical tools for financial risk management. He has published extensively, with articles appearing in top academic journals, and he is also a successful author, with books that address both academic and general audiences.

His academic honors and awards are numerous, and he serves on the editorial boards of several academic journals. Lo's teaching and research have had a significant impact on how economists and financial professionals understand and approach financial markets.

Collectively, these publications paint a picture of technical analysis as a field with a rich tapestry of methodologies, from systematic and evidence-based approaches to heuristic and experience-based practices. The literature underscores the ongoing discourse on technical analysis and the need for a nuanced understanding of its principles, applications, and limitations within the broader context of financial market trading.

5.1.2. Caveat

Many traders, particularly novices, initially approach the market from a technical analytical perspective, aspiring to discern patterns in the price and volume trajectories of ascending and descending stocks. They aim to identify common characteristics that might suggest a probabilistic outcome of future asset price movements, either upwards or downwards. This approach is somewhat reminiscent of the astrological belief where a solar eclipse is perceived as a precursor to unfortunate events. The perceived efficacy of these technical patterns is often amplified by a cognitive phenomenon known as "selective recall" or "confirmation bias", a concept explored within behavioral finance. This bias leads individuals to remember successful predictions while neglecting the unsuccessful ones, a topic that is elaborated upon in Chapter 8. Moreover, the methodologies employed in summarizing these patterns can lead to overfitting, akin to certain deep learning models, primarily because many technical indicators are utilized without a thorough understanding of the underlying reasons driving these trends or how investors react post-trend.

Despite the tendency of chartists to attribute specific meanings to these patterns, categorizing them as bullish or bearish signals, many purported patterns lack a logical foundation or rigorous empirical backing. Consequently, due to its inherently subjective nature, technical analysis has not attained the level of academic rigor and acceptance that more conventional methodologies like fundamental analysis have achieved.

The challenge in scientifically validating technical analysis primarily stems from two aspects. First, the patterns themselves may be flawed in the sense that they do not guarantee long-term profitability. For instance, while stocks on an upward trajectory may exhibit similar characteristics, a larger proportion of stocks fitting these technical indicators might not experience growth or may even plummet. Should an investor construct a portfolio comprising stocks that meet these indicators, the overall performance might be negative, despite some stocks appreciating in value. Additionally, while a strategy may be effective under normal conditions, extreme market volatility could result in significant losses, potentially eradicating long-term gains.

When discussing technical indicators, it is crucial to acknowledge that while numerous indicators can be effectively applied, and some have indeed been widely used and proven reliable over time, greater emphasis should be placed on the applicability and usefulness of these indicators. It is essential to scientifically evaluate and analyze the source of returns and to understand the market logic reflected by these indicators.

5.1.3. Key Components of Technical Analysis

Technical analysis relies on several key components to forecast future market movements. Among the most recognized chart patterns is the head and shoulders formation, which is considered a reliable indicator of a potential reversal in the prevailing trend. This pattern is typified by a peak (the head), flanked by two slightly lower peaks (the shoulders), which ideally occur on similar volume levels. The subsequent break below the neckline—the support level that connects the lows after the two shoulders—can be seen as confirmation of a shift from a bullish to a bearish market. This pattern, alongside other forms of chart analysis, is complemented by various technical indicators like the RSI and moving averages, which help traders gauge momentum and trend strength. Support and resistance levels play a crucial role, marking the thresholds where price movements are likely to stall or reverse due to concentrated demand or supply. Volume is another cornerstone of technical analysis, providing additional clues to the conviction behind price movements. Collectively, these elements provide traders with a toolkit for navigating financial markets, deciphering market psychology, and making strategic trading decisions.

The initial phase of technical analysis is marked by the adoption of charting methodologies, including point, line, and bar charts. These tools serve the primary purpose of visually extracting trends and patterns from the plethora of market data. Among the myriad of patterns recognized, a select few have gained prominence for their reliability and frequency of occurrence:

1. The Head-and-Shoulders (HS) pattern emerges when a stock's price ascends to a peak before retreating to the base of the preceding upward movement. This forms the first "shoulder", and the base is also known as the "neckline". The price then climbs above the initial peak to form the "head", subsequently falling back to the original base level. A final ascent to the level of the first peak, followed by a decline, completes the formation (i.e., the second "shoulder"). Figure 5.1 illustrates the HS configuration. It is renowned for its ability to forecast a shift from bullish to bearish trends.

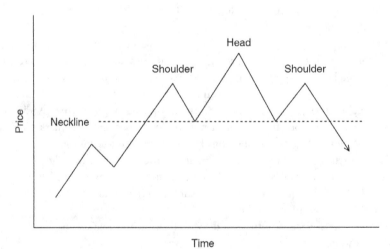

FIGURE 5.1. Illustration of the Head-and-Shoulders Configuration

Conversely, the Inverse Head-and-Shoulders (IHS) signifies the reverse process, where the price initially dips to a trough, rebounds, and then falls below the initial trough to establish a deeper one before rising once more. A third trough, shallower than the second, precedes a significant upward movement, making the IHS a reliable indicator for predicting a bearish-to-bullish trend reversal. Figure 5.2 illustrates the IHS configuration.

2. Broadening Top (BT) is a broadening top pattern, which means that the stock price undergoes several minor reversals followed by a substantial decline. This is a bearish pattern. In contrast, Broadening Bottom (BB) is the reverse of BT in which the stock price undergoes several minor reversals followed by a substantial surge, and hence a bullish signal. Figure 5.3 illustrates these two patterns.

3. Triangle patterns, known for their continuation trait, take the form of ascending, descending, or symmetrical shapes. They are formed when upper

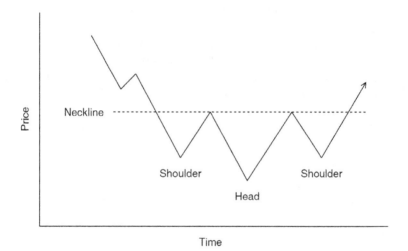

FIGURE 5.2. Illustration of the Inverse Head-and-Shoulders Configuration

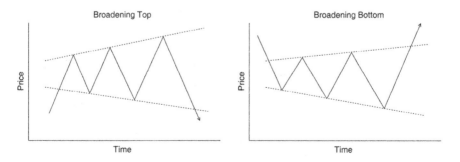

FIGURE 5.3. Illustration of Broadening Top and Bottom

trendlines meet lower trendlines at the apex on the right side. An upper trendline is formed by connecting the highs, while a lower trendline is formed by connecting the lows. Bullish (bearish) signals can be seen when the triangle breaks on the upside (downside) with heavy volume. Figure 5.4 shows three types of triangle patterns, i.e., ascending, descending, and symmetrical shapes.

4.   Rectangles represent periods of consolidation within an uptrend or downtrend, hinting at the continuation of the prevailing trend. A bullish (bearish) rectangle is confirmed by a breakout above (below) the consolidation range, indicating the likely resumption of the uptrend (downtrend). Figure 5.5 illustrates both uptrend and downtrend rectangle patterns.

5.   The Double Top or Bottom pattern is a potent indicator of market sentiment reversal. A double top (bottom) is an extremely bearish (bullish) pattern after the stock price reaches a high (low) price two consecutive times with a moderate decline (rise) between the two highs (lows). It is confirmed once the price falls below (or rises above) a support (resistance) level equal to the lowest (highest) between the two prior highs (lows). Figure 5.6 demonstrates double top and bottom patterns.

6.   Moving Averages (MAs) play a crucial role in smoothing out short-term price fluctuations to reveal underlying trends. The concept of MAs has given rise to various trend-following strategies, including the widely utilized moving average crossover technique.

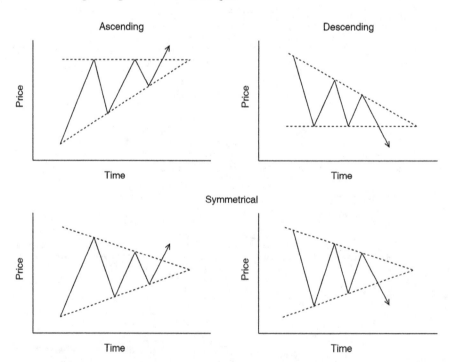

FIGURE 5.4. Illustration of Triangle Patterns

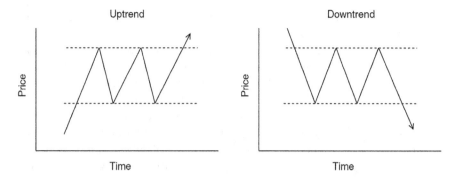

FIGURE 5.5. Illustration of Rectangle Patterns

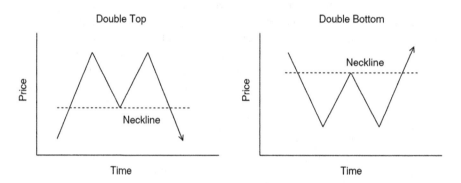

FIGURE 5.6. Illustration of Double Top and Bottom Patterns

The stock technical patterns mentioned above have been widely adopted by traders, stemming from rules of thumb established through experience, many of which were formulated even before the advent of computers. Thus, they are primarily based on the visual shapes and structures found in charts. With the advent of more powerful computing resources and sophisticated technologies, complemented by enhanced data quality, we are now in a position to empirically test these traditional rules to evaluate whether these rudimentary experiences retain any predictive power over asset returns.

However, computing these patterns is not straightforward, as they do not have a fixed-time window like many of the factors we have discussed previously. For example, a Head-and-Shoulders pattern could form over 20 trading days or perhaps take as long as 200 trading days to develop. This necessitates a time-scaling approach to asset price trends. Common methods involve using various time windows for scaling and employing mathematical techniques for pattern recognition. Furthermore, with the maturation of deep learning-based image recognition algorithms, the application of such algorithms in identifying technical indicators holds good potential for the future.

The third stage marks the significance of technical analysis to be *quantifiable*, the development of technical indicators. In the 1950s and 1960s, technical analysts began to develop technical indicators using historical prices (including intraday) and volumes. The relative strength index (RSI), moving average convergence divergence (MACD), and Stochastic Oscillator are examples of classic yet famous indicators. These indicators help to identify overbought and oversold conditions and potential trend reversals. We will have a comprehensive discussion in Section 5.2.

By quantifying technical indicators, computer-based technology is also a natural extension of technical analysis. As seen before, technical patterns can be quite subjective as to the location of critical points like the shoulders in the HS or IHS patterns. These points are also the trendlines that form the triangle and rectangle etc. Computer algorithms make it harder to identify those points as stock prices can be noisy with many spikes. One work trying to bridge the gap between technical analysis and quantitative finance is Lo, Mamaysky, and Wang (2000). In their work, the authors try to smooth out the price noise through nonparametric kernel regressions. After this, the technical patterns can then be easily automated with the smoothed series. For a long empirical study covering years 1962 to 1996 for each of the technical patterns described above, the authors found that the conditional returns (after a pattern is identified) were significantly different from the unconditional returns for 7 out of the 10 patterns. Empirical results showed substantial support for technical indicators using Nasdaq as samples.

The key evolution of technical analysis is its integration with factor investing. With a growing recognition of the importance of integrating technical analysis with fundamental analysis, there has been development of the quantitative methods that combine both approaches. The goal of this chapter is to analyze technical indicators' effectiveness as factors.

Chapter 5 is organized as follows. Section 5.2 walks through four categories of technical indicators, namely the momentum indicators, the volume indicators, the trend indicators, and the volatility indicators. Section 5.3 discusses recent advances in the trend factor. Section 5.4 concludes.

5.2. Technical Indicators

The term "momentum" is very popular both in academia and in industry. In Chapter 1, we discussed some consensus asset pricing models with the momentum factor being the key factor introduced by Carhart's (1997) four-factor model (FF3 + MOM). In that context, the momentum factor refers to the spread of returns between winners and losers for the past twelve-month period (usually excluding the recent month).

From an industry's standpoint, momentum refers to strong price performances which can be measured by relative returns on 3-month, 6-month, and 12-month horizons, etc. In technical analysis, momentum is a category of indicators that reflect a continuing trend. This can be captured by some kind of moving average of prices, and/or complemented with volume analysis. In this chapter, we discuss momentum in the context of technical analysis, i.e. momentum indicators.

In addition to momentum indicators which utilize the historical price data, volume indicators complement price data with volume data for a clearer market direction. Trend indicators apply different horizons of price movement to identify short-, medium-, and long-term trends. Volatility indicators measure dispersion or range of price moves over some specified windows.

5.2.1. Momentum Indicators

A key component of technical analysis is the momentum indicators. There are many momentum indicators. We introduce a few as factors in a non-exhaustive way.

Awesome Oscillator (AO)

Introduced by a famous trader, Bill Williams, AO is calculated by the difference between two Simple Moving Averages (SMA), usually the 34-day SMA and the 5-day SMA of median prices, where median is simply the average of day-high and day-low. Assuming security prices of up to day n lags are $P_t, \ldots, P_{t-n+1}$, $SMA_t(n)$ is given by

$$SMA_t(n) = \frac{P_t + \ldots + P_{t-n+1}}{n}. \tag{5.1}$$

Note that once we observe P_{t+1}, we can update the $SMA_{t+1}(n+1)$,

$$
\begin{aligned}
SMA_{t+1}(n+1) &= \frac{P_{t+1} + P_t + \cdots + P_{t-n+1}}{n+1} \\
&= \frac{P_{t+1} - SMA_t(n) + SMA_t(n) + P_t + \cdots + P_{t-n+1}}{n+1} \\
&= SMA_t(n) + \frac{P_{t+1} - SMA_t(n)}{n+1}
\end{aligned} \tag{5.2}
$$

Equation (5.2) shows us a recursive formula to update $SMA_{t+1}(n+1)$ when we get a new data point P_{t+1}. It is simply the previous $SMA_t(n)$ adjusted by the *shock* which is the difference between the new data and the previous SMA, weighted by $1(n+1)$. In the SMA framework, the shock carries equal weight with other data points.

Bill Williams and Trading Fractal

Bill Williams was a renowned trader, educator, and author who contributed significantly to the field of technical analysis and trading psychology. Born in 1932, he was known for his work on applying chaos theory to the financial markets and creating several technical indicators that are still widely used by traders today.

Williams developed his unique approach by combining his understanding of psychology, his study of chaos theory, and his practical experience in trading. He believed that traditional technical analysis methods did not adequately account for the seemingly random and chaotic nature of the financial markets. Instead, he proposed that the market's movements were a result of natural structures that could be understood through the analysis of fractals and chaos theory.

One of the key concepts introduced by Bill Williams is the idea of the "Trading Fractal", which is a pattern that repeats itself at different scales within the market. A fractal in trading is a natural phenomenon that can be observed in the form of recurring patterns and can be used to predict potential market reversals.

Bill Williams created several popular technical analysis indicators, including:

Alligator Indicator: Designed to help traders identify the presence of a trend and its direction.

Awesome Oscillator (AO): Intended to measure market momentum and confirm trends or signal the possibility of a trend reversal.

Accelerator Oscillator (AC): Used to confirm the acceleration or deceleration of market momentum.

Market Facilitation Index (MFI): Aims to measure the efficiency of price movement by comparing the price changes to volume.

Williams' indicators are often used together to provide a comprehensive picture of market conditions and to help traders make more informed decisions. He authored several books, including *Trading Chaos* and *New Trading Dimensions*, which outline his trading philosophy and methods.

Bill Williams' contributions to technical analysis have left a lasting legacy, with his indicators and theories still being taught in trading courses and used by traders around the world to analyze and interpret market behavior.

Percent Price Oscillator (PPO)

PPO is the difference between two Exponential Moving Averages (EMA), usually 12-day EMA and 26-day EMA, divided by the 26-day EMA. The EMA formula is,

$$EMA_{t+1}(n+1) = EMA_t(n) + \left[\left(\frac{2}{n+1} \right) \times (P_{t+1} - EMA_t(n)) \right]. \quad (5.3)$$

Compared to SMA, EMA updates the latest estimate by two times the shock. Since EMA can only be computed recursively, EMA_0 can be either set at P_0 or the average of $P_0, \ldots, P_t$, to start the recursion.

Relative Strength Index (RSI)

Developed by Welles Wilder in 1978, RSI measures the magnitude of recent gains to losses over a specified lookback period, usually 9-day or 14-day. The formula is:

$$RSI = 100 - \frac{100}{1 + \frac{average\ gain}{average\ loss}} \qquad (5.4)$$

where average gain/loss is the average positive/negative returns over the specified lookback period.

J. Welles Wilder Jr.

J. Welles Wilder Jr. is an influential figure in the field of technical analysis, best known for his development of several popular technical indicators that many traders incorporate into their market analysis and trading strategies. Wilder is a mechanical engineer by training, which influenced his systematic approach to trading and the development of his indicators.

Wilder started his career in real estate before moving into the commodities market. His interest in the financial markets led him to create precise trading systems and methodologies. The indicators he developed are renowned for their mathematical rigor and effectiveness in various market conditions.

Some of the key technical indicators developed by Welles Wilder include:

Relative Strength Index (RSI): A momentum oscillator that measures the speed and change of price movements, typically used to identify overbought or oversold conditions in the trading of an asset.

Average True Range (ATR): A volatility indicator that measures market volatility by decomposing the entire range of an asset price for that period.

Parabolic SAR (Stop and Reverse): A trend-following indicator that provides potential stop-loss levels and can indicate the direction of the trend.

Directional Movement Index (DMI): An indicator that consists of the Average Directional Index (ADX), Plus Directional Indicator (+DI), and Minus Directional Indicator (-DI). It is used to determine trend strength and direction.

Wilder detailed these indicators and his trading system in his groundbreaking book *New Concepts in Technical Trading Systems*, published in 1978. The book is not only a compendium of his indicators but also an exposition on Wilder's trading philosophy and the importance of discipline and risk management in trading.

Welles Wilder's work has had a profound and lasting impact on technical analysis. His systematic and quantitative approach to trading was revolutionary at the time and remains highly relevant today. His indicators are embedded in most technical analysis software and are commonly used by traders around the globe, a testament to his legacy in the world of trading.

Stochastic Oscillator (SO)

Developed by George Lane, SO measures the relative location of the current close price to the high—low range of a lookback period, usually 14 days. The formula is:

$$SO = (current\ close - lowest\ low)/(highest\ high - lowest\ low). \quad (5.5)$$

where highest high is the highest intraday price of the lookback period and lowest low is the lowest intraday price of the lookback period.

George C. Lane

George C. Lane was a securities trader, author, educator, and the creator of the Stochastic Oscillator, which is a momentum indicator that has become one of the core tools in the field of technical analysis.

Lane developed the Stochastic Oscillator in the late 1950s. The indicator measures the momentum of price movements by comparing the closing price of a security to the range of its prices over a certain period of time. The idea behind this indicator is based on Lane's observation that, as prices increase, closing prices tend to be closer to the upper end of the price range; conversely, as prices decrease, closing prices tend to be near the lower end of the price range.

The Stochastic Oscillator is plotted on a scale of 0 to 100 and consists of two lines: the %K line, which measures the current price level relative to the high–low range over a set number of periods; and the %D line, which is a moving average of the %K line. Traditionally, readings above 80 are considered overbought, while readings below 20 are considered oversold.

George Lane's Stochastic Oscillator is used not only to predict the turning points in the price of an asset but also to confirm trends and signal potential entry and exit points. It has become a staple in chart analysis, often used in conjunction with other forms of technical analysis to enhance the accuracy of predictions regarding market behavior.

Aside from his famous Stochastic Oscillator, Lane also contributed to the field of technical analysis through his teachings and seminars, helping traders understand the importance of market psychology and the use of technical indicators to make informed trading decisions. His work has left a lasting imprint on the technical analysis community, providing traders with tools to navigate the complexities of market trends and momentum.

True Strength Index (TSI)

Developed by William Blau, TSI is a double smoothing of price changes, based on two EMAs, usually 13-day and 25-day:

$$TSI = \frac{double\ smoothed\ PC}{double\ smoothe\ dabsolute\ PC} \qquad (5.6)$$

where PC is the price change, i.e., current price minus prior price, the first smoothed PC is the 25-period EMA of PC, and the double smoothed PC is the 13-period EMA of the first smoothed PC.

Absolute PC is the absolute value of PC. The first absolute smoothed PC is the 25-day EMA of absolute PC. The double smoothed absolute PC is the 13-period EMA of the first absolute smoothed PC.

William Blau

William Blau was a well-regarded technical analyst and trader who made significant contributions to the field of technical analysis through the creation of various innovative indicators and the authoring of insightful literature. While Blau may not be as widely recognized as some of his contemporaries like J. Welles Wilder or George Lane, his work is highly regarded among technical analysts for its depth and practical applicability.

One of Blau's key contributions is the development of the Stochastic Momentum Index (SMI), which is an advancement of the classic Stochastic Oscillator created by George Lane. Blau's SMI was designed to provide a more refined and accurate representation of market momentum. It differs from the traditional Stochastic Oscillator by incorporating a range that is centered on zero, which helps to reduce volatility and the likelihood of false signals.

In addition to the SMI, Blau devised several other technical indicators, including the Double Smoothed Stochastic (DSS) and the True Strength Index (TSI). The DSS is an oscillator that aims to eliminate the choppiness inherent in traditional stochastic indicators, providing a smoother and more reliable signal. The TSI is a momentum oscillator that combines price movement and volatility; it's designed to identify trends by determining the direction and magnitude of price movements.

William Blau's book *Momentum, Direction, and Divergence* is a comprehensive resource that delves into his technical indicators and trading theories. Published in 1995 as part of the "Wiley Trader's Exchange" series, the book is highly regarded for its clear explanations of complex concepts and practical strategies for traders.

Blau's work, especially his focus on momentum and smoothing techniques to improve the responsiveness and accuracy of technical indicators, has been influential in the development of trading strategies and is still referenced by traders and analysts today. His indicators are commonly included in technical analysis software and continue to be used as part of trading systems to analyze and interpret market behavior.

Ultimate Oscillator (UO)

Developed by Larry Williams, UO captures momentum across three different time-frames, usually 7-day, 14-day, and 28-day. Buying power is defined as $BP_t = close_t - \min(low_t, close_{t-1})$, true range is defined as $TR_t = \max(high_t, close_{t-1}) - \min(low_t, close_{t-1})$..

Define $A_l = \dfrac{\sum_{t-l}^{t} BP_s}{\sum_{t-l}^{t} TR_s}$ then UO is defined as

$$UO = (4A_7 + 2A_{14} + A_{28})/7. \tag{5.7}$$

Larry Williams

Larry Williams is a prominent figure in the field of financial market trading, known for his work as a commodities and stock trader, as well as an author and educator. Born on October 6, 1942, he has had a long and distinguished career, gaining recognition for his trading performance and the development of various trading indicators and concepts.

Williams first made headlines in the trading community when he won the 1987 World Cup Championship of Futures Trading from the Robbins Trading Company. He turned $10,000 into over $1.1 million (11,376% return) in a 12-month competition, which is an achievement that has contributed greatly to his fame as a trader.

He has developed several widely used indicators and trading tools, including:

Williams %R: This is a momentum indicator, similar to the Stochastic Oscillator, that measures overbought and oversold levels. It compares the close of a commodity to the high-low range over a set period of time, typically 14 days.

Ultimate Oscillator: This indicator combines short, intermediate, and long-term market trends in one oscillator, aiming to reduce volatility and false signals associated with other oscillators that only reflect a single time frame.

Williams Accumulation/Distribution (A/D): This tool aims to provide insight into market supply and demand by looking at the relationship between the price, its movement, and volume.

Larry Williams has also authored numerous books on trading and has provided education for traders through courses and seminars. Some of his well-known books include "How I Made One Million Dollars Last Year Trading Commodities", "Long-Term Secrets to Short-Term Trading", and "The Secret of Selecting Stocks for Immediate and Substantial Gains".

In addition to his indicators and books, Williams is also known for his theories related to economic cycles and the impact of seasonal trends on market prices. He has conducted research on historical market patterns and developed the "Williams % Range" and "Cycle Forecast" indicators to capitalize on these patterns.

His daughter, Michelle Williams, gained public attention when she competed in the same futures trading competition as her father and won in 1997, using the same methods he teaches.

Throughout his career, Larry Williams has been a highly influential trader and his contribution to the field of technical analysis and trading education has left a lasting legacy. His trading methods and indicators remain popular among traders seeking to understand and capitalize on market trends and cycles.

5.2.2. Volume Indicators

Volume indicators complement price movement with volume data. Again, we introduce a few in a non-exhaustive way as factors.

Chaikin Money Flow (CMF)

Developed by Marc Chaikin, CMF is an average of money flow volume over a pre-specified period, usually 20-day. Money flow multiplier is defined as:

$$MFM = \frac{[(close - low) - (high - close)]}{high - low}. \tag{5.8}$$

It is then multiplied by volume to get the money flow volume (MFV). A 20-day CMF is then calculated by the sum of MFV over 20 days, divided by the sum of volume for the same period.

Marc Chaikin

Marc Chaikin is a seasoned stock market professional and the creator of several widely used technical analysis tools. With over 50 years of experience in the industry, Chaikin's work has made a significant impact on the field of technical analysis, particularly in the area of volume indicators.

One of Chaikin's key contributions is the Chaikin Money Flow (CMF) indicator, which combines price and volume to measure the buying and selling pressure for a given period. The CMF adds value to the analysis by incorporating the concept that the closing price should reflect whether buyers or sellers are in control of the market. The indicator oscillates around a zero line, with positive values indicating buying pressure (accumulation) and negative values indicating selling pressure (distribution).

Another prominent tool developed by Chaikin is the Chaikin Oscillator, which refines the Accumulation/Distribution Line by pairing it with the Moving Average Convergence Divergence (MACD) methodology. The Chaikin Oscillator takes the difference between the 3-day and 10-day exponential moving averages of the Accumulation/Distribution Line, thereby providing insights into the momentum behind buying and selling pressure.

Marc Chaikin also established Chaikin Analytics, a stock research and analysis firm that offers tools and market insights based on his proprietary indicators. The firm's analytics platform is designed to help investors make more informed trading decisions by providing a suite of indicators and models, such as the Chaikin Power Gauge, which is a quantitative model that combines various factors including financial metrics, earnings performance, price volume activity, and expert opinions to provide an overall rating for stocks.

Chaikin's work is particularly notable for the way it has helped bridge the gap between fundamental and technical analysis. By including volume and accumulation/distribution analysis with price movement, his indicators offer a more comprehensive view of market dynamics, which is valuable for both short-term traders and long-term investors.

His contributions to the field have made Chaikin a respected name in technical analysis, and his tools continue to be used by traders and investors looking to understand market sentiment and identify potential trends.

Money Flow Index (MFI)

Developed by Gene Quong and Avrum Soudack, MFI is similar to the RSI in calculation, but it measures the strength of positive money flow to negative money flow instead of the price over a specified period, usually 14-day.
Typical price is found daily by

$$TP = (high + low + close)/3. \tag{5.9}$$

Raw money flow (RMF) is defined by multiplying TP by volume.

Money flow ratio (MFR) is defined as the 14-day positive RMF divided by 14-day negative RMF, where a positive (negative) money flow means that the change in typical price over the preceding day is positive (negative). The money flow index is defined as

$$MFI = 100 - \frac{100}{1 + MFR}. \tag{5.10}$$

Force Index (FI)

Developed by Alexander Elder, force index 1-day is the change of price (over preceding day) multiplied by current volume. Force index over a period, usually 13-day, is simply the 13-day EMA of force index 1-day.

Alexander Elder

Dr. Alexander Elder is an influential figure in the world of trading, recognized for his expertise in trading psychology and technical analysis. He was born in Russia and spent his early years in Estonia before defecting to the United States while working as a doctor on a Soviet ship. His journey ultimately led him to New York City, where he became a professional trader.

One of his most notable contributions to the field is his book *Trading for a Living*, which was first published in 1993. This work has become one of the quintessential reads for traders, covering a multitude of critical trading aspects such as psychology, discipline, trading tactics, and money management. Notably, *Trading for a Living* also introduces traders to various technical analysis methods and trading indicators.

Among the technical tools Elder has developed is the Force Index, an indicator that combines price movements with volume to measure the buying and selling pressure behind market trends. The Force Index is particularly useful for identifying potential reversals and can be used to confirm trend strength, as it helps to identify the force of every market move.

Elder's work emphasizes the importance of understanding oneself to become successful in trading, acknowledging that personal psychology can have a significant impact on financial decision-making. He has written other books as well, including *Come Into My Trading Room* and *The New Trading for a Living*, which is an updated and expanded edition of his original classic, providing new insights and reflecting changes in the markets and technology.

In addition to his writing, Dr. Elder is also known for his role as an educator in trading. He conducts classes and workshops, has been a speaker at conferences around the globe, and operates a firm that offers educational materials for traders. His comprehensive approach and emphasis on the psychological aspects of trading have made his teachings invaluable to traders of all experience levels.

5.2.3. Trend Indicators

Trend indicators are very similar to momentum indicators but combine averages of different horizons. We introduce a few commonly used indicators.

Know Sure Thing (KST)

Developed by Martin Pring, KST is simply a weighted average of four SMAs of returns:

$R1$: $SMA(10)$ of 10-day returns
$R2$: $SMA(10)$ of 15-day returns
$R3$: $SMA(10)$ of 20-day returns
$R4$: $SMA(15)$ of 30-day returns

$$KST = R1 + R2 \times 2 + R3 \times 3 + R4 \times 4. \tag{5.11}$$

Martin J. Pring

Martin J. Pring is a prominent figure in the field of technical analysis, best known for his extensive research and published works on the subject. With a career spanning several decades, Pring has contributed significantly to the understanding and application of technical analysis in financial markets.

Pring's most influential work is perhaps his book *Technical Analysis Explained*, which is widely regarded as a definitive guide to the discipline. First published in the 1980s, this book has been updated multiple times to incorporate new developments in the field and remains a staple text for both novice and experienced traders looking to deepen their knowledge of market analysis techniques.

In *Technical Analysis Explained*, Pring covers a wide range of topics, including the basic principles of technical analysis, chart patterns, indicators, and the psychology behind market movements. His comprehensive approach aims to provide readers with the tools they need to interpret market trends and make informed trading decisions.

Beyond authoring books, Pring has also produced educational courses, video materials, and articles on various aspects of technical analysis and market psychology. He is known for his ability to explain complex concepts in a way that is accessible to traders at all levels.

One of Pring's notable contributions to technical analysis is his work on market momentum and the development of various indicators, such as the Price Momentum Oscillator (PMO) and the Know Sure Thing (KST) oscillator. These tools are designed to help traders identify momentum shifts in the market, which can be a precursor to trend changes.

Throughout his career, Martin Pring has been a respected educator and thought leader in the field of technical analysis. His teachings and tools have equipped countless traders with the analytical skills necessary to navigate the complexities of financial markets.

Moving Average Convergence Divergence (MACD)

Developed by Gerald Appel, MACD line is defined as 12-day EMA of price minus 26-day EMA of price. A signal line is defined as the 9-day EMA of the MACD line. The difference of MACD versus the signal line (MACD-sig) is a bullish (bearish) signal if the value is positive (negative).

Gerald Appel

Gerald Appel is a highly influential figure in the field of technical analysis, particularly known for creating one of the most popular technical indicators in use today: the Moving Average Convergence Divergence (MACD). Appel's introduction of the MACD in the late 1970s revolutionized the way traders and analysts assess market momentum and trends.

The MACD is a trend-following momentum indicator that shows the relationship between two moving averages of a security's price. Typically, it is calculated by subtracting the 26-period EMA from the 12-period EMA. The result of this subtraction is the MACD line. A nine-day EMA of the MACD, called the "signal line", is then plotted on top of the MACD line, which can function as a trigger for buy and sell signals. Traders may also look at the divergence or convergence between the MACD and price, as well as crossovers between the MACD line and the signal line, to inform their trading decisions.

Beyond the MACD, Appel has authored or co-authored numerous books on investing and market analysis, where he shares his insights and methods for interpreting markets. His books cover a wide range of topics, from technical analysis basics to more advanced trading strategies and systems.

Aside from his writing, Gerald Appel has also been involved in money management. He founded Signalert Corporation, an investment advisory firm that manages client funds and provides financial guidance, emphasizing technical analysis and conservative investment strategies.

Appel's work extends into market research and investment systems, and he has developed various tools and indicators that are used by technical analysts worldwide. His contributions have made him a respected name in the investment community, and his methods are widely adopted for trading and market analysis.

Commodity Channel Index (CCI)

Developed by Donald Lambert, CCI measures the current close relative to an average price level over a specified period, usually 20-day. CCI is defined as

$$CCI_t = \frac{TP_t - SMA_t(20)}{0.015 \times MD_t},$$
(5.12)

where MD is the mean-deviation of TP:

$$MD_t = \frac{\sum_{t-20}^{t} abs(TP_t - SMA_t(20))}{20}.$$
(5.13)

Donald Lambert

Donald Lambert is the creator of the Commodity Channel Index (CCI), which is a versatile technical analysis indicator used to identify new trends or warn of extreme conditions. Lambert introduced the CCI in the October 1980 issue of *Commodities Magazine* (now known as *Futures Magazine*).

The CCI was originally developed to spot cyclical turns in commodities, but it has since been applied to a variety of other investment vehicles such as stocks, indices, and forex. The indicator is designed to measure the variation of a security's price from its statistical mean. High values show that prices are unusually high compared to average prices whereas low values indicate that prices are unusually low.

The calculation of the CCI involves several steps. It starts with the determination of the Typical Price for each period, which is the average of the high, low, and close prices. The Typical Price is then compared to a moving average of the Typical Price, and the difference is compared to the average deviation from the moving average. This final value is the CCI, which is typically displayed as an oscillator that moves above and below a zero line.

Lambert set the constant at 0.015 to ensure that approximately 70 to 80 % of CCI values would fall between −100 and +100. This scaling gives the CCI its characteristic oscillating appearance. Traders use these levels to identify overbought and oversold conditions. For example, a CCI reading over +100 can indicate that an asset is entering overbought territory, while a reading below −100 can indicate that an asset has become oversold.

While Lambert's CCI remains a popular tool among technical traders, there is not as much publicly available biographical information on Lambert himself compared to other well-known figures in the field of technical analysis. His main legacy lives on in the continued use of the CCI by traders around the world to inform their trading decisions.

5.2.4. Volatility Indicators

In contrast to previous indicators which try to predict bullish or bearish signals, volume indicators deal with the risk aspect. We introduce a few commonly used ones in what follows.

Mass Index (MI)

Developed by Donald Dorsey, MI uses the high-low range to identify trend reversals based on range expansions. A single EMA is calculated based on the 9-day EMA of the high-low differential. Then a double EMA is calculated from the 9-day EMA of the single EMA. The EMA ratio is defined as the ratio of the single EMA divided by the double EMA. Mass Index is then computed as the 25-day sum of the EMA ratio.

Donald Dorsey
Donald Dorsey is a technical analyst known for developing the Mass Index, an indicator used in the field of technical analysis to predict trend reversals based on range expansion over time. The Mass Index is premised on the concept that reversals in the price trend are likely to occur when the range between high and low prices widens.

The indicator does not predict the direction of the price trend but rather the likelihood of a trend reversal occurring. Dorsey proposed that a reversal can be anticipated when the Mass Index goes above a certain level (typically set at 27) and then falls back below a lower threshold (commonly set at 26.5). This phenomenon is referred to as a "reversal bulge".

The Mass Index is calculated by first determining the nine-period EMA of the range between the high and low prices, then calculating a nine-period EMA of that EMA, and finally dividing the first EMA by the second EMA. The sum of these values for a certain number of periods (usually 25) forms the Mass Index.

Dorsey's work on the Mass Index was an attempt to refine the use of volatility in technical analysis by focusing on the range expansion as a signal of a potential change in price trend direction. His research and development of the Mass Index contributed to the broader field of technical analysis by providing traders and analysts with another tool for market assessment.

Beyond the Mass Index, there is limited public information available on Donald Dorsey's broader career and other contributions he may have made to technical analysis or the field of finance. His specific background details are not as well-documented as some of the other figures in the field of technical analysis. Nonetheless, the Mass Index remains a part of the technical analyst's toolkit, particularly for those who specialize in identifying potential trend reversals.

Average True Range (ATR)

Developed by Welles Wilder, ATR aims to identify volatility from gaps and limit moves which could not otherwise be captured by a pure high-low range. The True Range (TR) is calculated by the maximum of

- current high minus the current low,
- absolute value of current high minus previous close, and
- absolute value of current low minus previous close.

ATR is then the rolling average of 14-day daily TRs.

Ulcer index (UI)

Developed by Peter Martin and Byron McCann, UI measures volatility based on the drawdown over a specified look-back period. Percent drawdown is defined as the current close divided by the 14-day maximum close, then minus one. The percent drawdown is squared and averaged over a 14-day period, of which the square root is defined as the Ulcer index.

Peter Martin and Byron McCann

Peter Martin and Byron McCann are recognized for their contribution to the field of finance through the development of the Ulcer Index. The Ulcer Index is a stock market risk measure or investment metric designed to give a sense of the downside risk, or "stress" of holding a stock or market index.

The Ulcer Index was introduced by Peter Martin and Byron McCann in their 1989 book, "The Investor's Guide to Fidelity Funds". The primary goal of the Ulcer Index is to measure the depth and duration of drawdowns in price from earlier highs. Unlike other measures of risk that focus on volatility or standard deviation, the Ulcer Index specifically accounts for the fact that investors tend to be more concerned about the actual losses incurred rather than price fluctuations that occur above the highest value reached (which would be considered unrealized gains).

The term "ulcer" was used metaphorically to describe the emotional distress or the "gut-wrenching" feeling investors experience when the value of their investments falls and remains below the peak for a period of time. The Ulcer Index is calculated by taking the percentage drawdowns (or retracements from the peak) and squaring the result to give more weight to larger drawdowns. Then, it averages those squared figures over a certain period, typically 14 days, and takes the square root of that average to produce the index.

The Ulcer Index has been adopted by many investors as a tool to assess the risk of mutual funds, stocks, and other investment vehicles. It helps investors understand not just how much an investment's price may fall, but also how long it will likely take to recover to previous highs—both critical factors in investment decision-making.

Peter Martin and Byron McCann's development of the Ulcer Index added a significant tool to the suite of indicators that investors can use to gauge market risk and make more informed decisions about their investment portfolios.

5.3. Advanced Trend Factor

So far, we have discussed simple trend factors like KST, MACD and CCI that involve multiple moving averages. Given the observation that phenomena such as short-term reversals, intermediate-term momentum, and long-term reversals coexist in the US stock market, in a more rigorous setting, Han, Zhou, and Zhu (2016) formalize these short-, intermediate-, and long-term trends or reversals simultaneously into an advanced trend factor by exploiting information from moving average prices over various time windows.

Like SMA, the moving average ($A_{jt,L}$) on the last trading day of month t of lag L is defined as

$$A_{jt,L} = \frac{P^t_{j,d-L+1} + P^t_{j,d-L+2} + \ldots + P^t_{j,d-1} + P^t_{j,d}}{L} \tag{5.14}$$

where $P^t_{j,d}$ is the closing price for stock j on the last trading day d of month t, and L is the lag length. To ensure stationarity of the MA signals, $A_{jt,L}$ is normalized by the closing price on the last trading day of the month,

$$\tilde{A}_{jt,L} = \frac{A_{jt,L}}{P^t_{j,d}}. \tag{5.15}$$

The $A_{jt,L}$ signal is used to predict the monthly expected stock returns cross-sectionally. The process involves two steps:

i. For each month t, run a cross-sectional regression of stock j returns on observed $\tilde{A}_{jt,L}$ signals to obtain the time-series of the coefficients $\tilde{A}_{jt,L}$:

$$r_{j,t} = \beta_0 + \sum_i \beta_{L_i,t} \tilde{A}_{jt-1,L_i} + \varepsilon_{j,t}, j = 1, \ldots, n, \tag{5.16}$$

where n is the number of stocks, L_i used are 3-, 5-, 10-, 20-, 50-, 100-, 200-, 400-, 600-, 800-, 1000-days.

ii. The expected return for month $t + 1$ is estimated to be:

$$\mathrm{E}_t\left[r_{j,t+1}\right] = \sum_i \mathrm{E}_t\left[\beta_{L_i,t+1}\right] \tilde{A}_{jt,L_i}, \tag{5.17}$$

where $\mathrm{E}_t\left[\beta_{L_i,t+1}\right] = \frac{1}{12} \sum_{m=1}^{12} \beta_{L_i,t+1-m}$, which is the average of the estimated

loadings on the trend signals over the past 12 months.

The expected return for each stock for month $t + 1$, i.e., $\mathrm{E}_t\left[r_{j,t+1}\right]$, is then used as factors directly. A succinct overview of the above procedure can be given as follows. The process of computing the advanced trend factor initially identifies the moving averages of each stock across various temporal scales; these moving averages are treated as indicators that are related to stock returns, and cross-sectional regressions yield their coefficients for each period. Utilizing a rolling window approach, the mean coefficient for each moving average indicator is calculated over this time frame, dynamically capturing which level of moving average is most effective for predicting the next period's stock returns. In this regard, the direction of beta indicates momentum or reversal, while the magnitude of beta indicates the strength of the prediction. Ultimately, the stock return for the next period is forecasted using the mean coefficients and the most recent values of the indicators.

Empirically, the study constructs long portfolios of the top quintile of stocks sorted by expected returns and short portfolios of the bottom quintile at the end of each month. The performance difference between the long and short portfolios reflects the profitability of the trend factor. Based on empirical data from 1930 to 2014, the trend factor exhibits an average monthly return of 1.30% (with a *t*-statistic over 15.0), which significantly surpasses traditional momentum and reversal factors.

Furthermore, this factor also demonstrates exceptional performance during periods of momentum crashes (Daniel and Moskowitz 2016). This can be attributed to the low correlation between the factor and traditional momentum and reversal factors. As the method dynamically exposes the portfolio to different levels of moving average indicators through rolling regression, it is conceivable that during the backtesting period, it is more exposed to long and short-term reversal factors, rather than medium-term momentum factors.

To quantitatively compare the new trend factor with traditional momentum and reversal factors, Han, Zhou, and Zhu (2016) employ the mean-variance spanning tests of Huberman and Kandel (1987). The results indicate that the new trend factor captures the cross-section of stock returns that traditional momentum and reversal factors cannot explain. This means that the excess returns generated by the trend factor cannot be achieved by merely exposing a portfolio to those traditional momentum and reversal factors.

To alleviate concerns about potential overfitting in their methodology, the authors note that the moving average windows used to construct the trend factor are not the result of optimization and are backed by sound business logic. Secondly, by dividing the backtesting period into decades and observing the performance of the trend factor within these intervals, it is evident that the factor's returns are remarkably robust. This robustness suggests that the factor is unlikely to be a product of data mining. Additionally, as an out-of-sample test, Han, Zhou, and Zhu (2016) examine the effectiveness of the trend factor in the stock markets of other G7 countries (France, the UK, Germany, Italy, Canada, and Japan). Significant excess returns from the trend factor are observed in all these countries, with monthly CAPM-α exceeding 1% in all but Germany. Although the performance of the trend factor is not as pronounced as in the US market, such results support the notion that the trend factor is not a result of data mining.

Finally, in a related subsequent study, Liu, Zhou and Zhu (forthcoming) applied this trend factor to the Chinese stock market. Moreover, considering the differences in the investor structures between China and the US, in constructing the factor, they took into account not only the moving average (MA) of prices but also the MA of trading volumes. This factor achieved an average monthly excess return of 1.43% in the Chinese stock market (with a *t*-statistic exceeding 6.0). Furthermore, using this factor, they enhanced the three-factor model of Liu, Stambaugh, and Yuan (2019) for China, resulting in a four-factor model that could explain 60 common anomalies in the Chinese stock market.

5.4. Conclusion

In this chapter, we introduce technical indicators as factors. We discussed four classes of technical indicators: momentum, volume, trend, and volatility indicators in a non-exhaustive manner. In respect of the trend factor, we highlighted recent work in the literature on how to extract information from various moving averages.

Technical pattern indicators are relatively straightforward topics to begin with in quantitative factor investing. The process of coding and calculating these factors is comparably simple, and because the primary source of returns is the imbalance of supply and demand, the yields are not exceptionally high.

From a statistical testing standpoint, it is easier to consider the predictive power of these factors as significant. Nonetheless, it is hoped that readers will ponder more deeply about how various technical factors influence the supply and demand relationship of assets, how they affect investors' perceptions of assets, and how they reflect some intrinsic characteristics of the assets themselves. A better understanding of the principles behind these factors, along with a more comprehensive grasp of market dynamics, allows for sensible adjustments and modifications to these factors. This can lead to a more accurate expression of the essential attributes of assets that one wishes to capture.

Furthermore, combining technical indicators with other variables that have a more logical financial market rationale is a promising and potentially fruitful avenue of research. Technical indicators primarily capture micro-level logic driven by investors. Fluctuations in the broader market environment, or the impact of unconventional information on different assets, can influence the performance of technical factors developed based on normal market logic. Therefore, considering how market logic might affect the performance of technical factors will undoubtedly play a significant role in the development and improved application of such factors.

References

Aronson, D. (2006). *Evidence-based Technical Analysis: Applying the Scientific Method and Statistical Inference to Trading Signals*. John Wiley & Sons.

Carhart, M. M. (1997). On persistence in mutual fund performance. *Journal of Finance* 52(1), 57–82.

Daniel, K. and T. J. Moskowitz (2016). Momentum Crashes. *Journal of Financial Economics* 122(2), 221–247.

Han, Y., G. Zhou, and Y. Zhu (2016). A trend factor: Any economic gains from using information over investment horizons? *Journal of Financial Economics* 122(2), 352–375.

Huberman G. and S. Kandel (1987). Mean-variance spanning. *Journal of Finance* 42(4), 873–888.

Liu, J., R. F. Stambaugh, and Y. Yuan (2019). Size and value in China. *Journal of Financial Economics* 134(1), 48–69.

Liu, Y., G. Zhou, and Y. Zhu (forthcoming). Trend Factor in China: The Role of Large Individual Trading. *Review of Asset Pricing Studies*.

Lo, A. W. (2017). *Adaptive Markets: Financial Evolution at the Speed of Thought*. Princeton University Press.

Lo, A. W. and J. Hasanhodzic (2010). *The Evolution of Technical Analysis: Financial Prediction from Babylonian Tablets to Bloomberg Terminals*. Bloomberg Press.

Lo, A. W., H. Mamaysky, and J. Wang (2000). Foundations of technical analysis: Computational algorithms, statistical inference, and empirical implementation. *Journal of Finance* 55(4), 1705–1765.

Malkiel, B. G. (1973). *A Random Walk Down Wall Street: The Time-Tested Strategy for Successful Investing*. W. W. Norton & Company.

Murphy, J. J. (1999). *Technical Analysis of the Financial Markets: A Comprehensive Guide to Trading Methods and Applications*. New York Institute of Finance.

Schwager, J. D. (1989). *Market Wizards: Interviews with Top Traders*. New York: Harper & Row.

6

MICROSTRUCTURE AND LIQUIDITY

6.1. Microstructure

6.1.1. Background

Market microstructure and liquidity have long been crucial components in understanding the complexities of financial markets. These elements shed light on the trading mechanisms, price formation, and information flow that all contribute to the liquidity of assets. In the context of factor investing, where the goal is to explain and predict asset returns using various risk factors, incorporating microstructure and liquidity can provide a more nuanced approach. This chapter explores how microstructure and liquidity are used to develop financial factors, with examples from seminal and recent academic literature.

The theoretical underpinnings of market microstructure relate to the study of how trades are executed, and their consequent impact on market prices. Seminal works in this field include Garman (1976), who develop a model of market microstructure with implications for the variance of prices, and Glosten and Milgrom (1985), who explore how asymmetric information affects prices and spreads. These foundational studies set the stage for understanding how liquidity and trading processes influence asset pricing.

Kyle (1985) considers a market with three distinct types of participants: informed traders, uninformed traders, and market makers. Informed traders possess private information about the true value of an asset, which they leverage to their advantage. Uninformed traders, often called noise traders, execute trades based on liquidity needs or other non-informational factors. Market makers provide liquidity by setting prices and standing ready to buy or sell.

A key insight from Kyle's model is the dynamic nature of price discovery. Informed traders strategically buy or sell the asset based on their private information, influencing

DOI: 10.4324/9781003480204-6

the asset's price. Their trades send signals that market makers and other participants decipher, leading to price adjustments that reflect the new information. This interaction underpins informationally efficient markets where prices at any moment represent all available information.

Kyle's work also underscores the concept of liquidity in a market marked by asymmetric information. Liquidity emerges as a function of how market makers price the risk of potentially trading with someone holding superior information. The more risk-averse the market makers, the less liquid the market, as evidenced by wider bid–ask spreads and reduced market depth.

Market depth refers to the capacity of a market to absorb relatively large market orders without impacting the price of the security. It is an indicator of the "thickness" or liquidity of the market for a particular security. Depth is typically associated with the ability of the market to sustain a certain level of trading activity while maintaining price stability.

In practical terms, market depth can be observed through an order book on a trading platform, where buy and sell orders are listed by price level. A market with good depth will have a balanced and substantial volume of orders both above and below the current market price, indicating that there are plenty of buyers and sellers waiting to transact. This creates a buffer for new orders, meaning that large transactions can be executed without causing a significant change in price.

A deeper market means that larger orders are required to change the price by a given amount, while a shallow market can see prices fluctuate more significantly with smaller orders. Market depth is an important aspect of the market microstructure that reflects the liquidity and efficiency of the market. It is particularly relevant for institutional investors and traders who deal in large volumes and require substantial liquidity to execute their trades with minimal slippage (the difference between expected transaction prices and the prices at which trades are actually executed).

The Kyle model introduces the concept of "Kyle's lambda", which quantifies the price impact of trades. This measure becomes a fundamental tool in understanding the influence of information flow on prices and has implications for trading costs and market volatility.

Albert S. "Pete" Kyle

Albert S. "Pete" Kyle is a notable figure in the field of financial economics, particularly known for his contributions to the understanding of market microstructure and the role of information in financial markets. Kyle is a distinguished academic whose work has had a profound impact on both the theoretical and empirical aspects of finance.

Kyle's most celebrated contribution is his 1985 paper, "Continuous Auctions and Insider Trading", which introduces what is now known as the Kyle Model. This model has become a central framework for analyzing the effects of informational asymmetry on financial markets. The model describes a setup with three types of market participants: informed traders, who have access to private information about the future value of a security; uninformed traders, who trade for reasons unrelated to information; and market makers, who provide liquidity by facilitating trades and setting prices.

The Kyle Model demonstrates how informed traders use their private information to trade profitably, and in doing so, how they impact prices, leading to the dissemination of information through the market. This has implications for the liquidity of assets and the efficiency of pricing, as market makers adjust the prices they set to manage the risk of trading with better-informed traders. The model's introduction of "Kyle's lambda" provided a measure of the price impact per unit of trading, becoming a vital tool for assessing market liquidity and the cost of trading.

Kyle's work extends beyond his 1985 paper. His research interests cover a wide range of topics in financial economics, including market microstructure, the dynamics of speculative markets, the role of information in finance, and the design of financial markets. His insights help to understand not just how markets work under normal conditions, but also how they can become dysfunctional, as in the case of market crashes and bubbles. Kyle's model significantly shapes the field of market microstructure by providing a clear and tractable model that illustrates how information asymmetry influences trading behavior, price formation, and liquidity. It lays the groundwork for further research into the implications of trading with asymmetric information and influences both theoretical and empirical studies in finance.

Kyle has also contributed to the literature on market manipulation, examining how traders can influence prices through their trades and the legal and economic implications of such activities. His work in this area informs regulatory policies aimed at ensuring fair and efficient markets.

In recognition of his substantial contributions to the field, Kyle has received numerous accolades and is highly regarded by both academics and practitioners. His research continues to inform the design and regulation of financial markets, as well as the strategies employed by participants in these markets. The principles derived from his work are considered foundational in finance, making him one of the leading scholars in the study of financial markets and their mechanisms.

6.1.2. Feedback Trading and Mispricing

Exploring the market microstructure of assets is akin to using a microscope to scrutinize the conditions under which assets are traded. This detailed analysis aids in understanding how each investor makes trading decisions based on market information and how these trading actions subsequently affect the price movements of assets. It also sheds light on how, within the same market context, different assets can exhibit distinct microstructural characteristics.

Zhang and Zhang (2015) explore the consequences of the increasing popularity of online stock trading and the influx of relatively inexperienced investors into the financial markets. This study builds upon Kyle's (1985) model by incorporating the impact of internet-facilitated feedback trading strategies. The authors use a dynamic equilibrium framework to study the impact of feedback trading strategies adopted by uninformed online traders.

The results of the study indicate that uninformed online traders who adopt feedback strategies (feedback traders) are not able to outperform those who do not follow such strategies (noise traders). Furthermore, feedback trading does not affect market equilibrium, the speed at which information is incorporated into prices, or the equilibrium strategy and expected profit of informed traders. However, if uninformed traders collectively adopt aggressive feedback trading strategies, they bear a higher risk. Therefore, it is important to manage and contain the risks associated with these uninformed traders. The paper also discusses the implications for regulating and designing internet trading systems. It highlights the importance of considering the risks posed by uninformed traders and suggests that online trading systems do not increase market volatility or impose costs on informed traders. The speed of information incorporation into prices is not affected by the adoption of online trading systems, indicating that the stability and liquidity of the market remain intact.

The above model was developed with the assumption that the market is semi-strong efficient. However, mispricing often exists in real financial markets. Zhang and Zhang (forthcoming) explore the impact of feedback trading strategies on market instability and profitability when mispricing exists. They argue that incorporating initial market mispricing into their analysis is crucial to understanding the outcomes of feedback trading.

The paper develops a stylized continuous-time model of feedback trading and provides closed-form solutions to assess the degree of price divergence from the efficient level. Comparing this paper with Kyle's (1985) model, both studies investigate the impact of trading strategies on market equilibrium. However, the approach differs in terms of incorporating market mispricing. While Kyle's model focused on information asymmetry between informed and uninformed traders in a semi-strong efficient market, the Zhang and Zhang (forthcoming) study relaxes the market efficiency assumption and incorporates mispricing explicitly.

The findings suggest that feedback trading, when combined with initial market mispricing, can lead to significant market volatility, resulting in financial bubbles and crashes. The impact, profitability, and policy implications of different algorithm trading strategies depend on the initial mispricing: (1) Regardless of the extent to which the price strays from its efficient level, it is destined to converge back to the liquidation value when the position is closed. (2) The impact of algorithmic traders on the market is not universally detrimental. Feedback trading acts as a double-edged sword; it can either correct pricing inaccuracies and enhance market efficiency or it can exacerbate pricing errors and result in greater price discrepancies. Profitability arises from feedback trading that diminishes pricing inaccuracies, whereas feedback trading that amplifies them will incur financial losses. (3) When an asset is overvalued, even a modest amount of feedback trading that exacerbates mispricing may render the price excessively sensitive to changes in trading volume. This can give rise to extreme price fluctuations, creating bubbles and precipitating crashes.

The development of such a model enables the identification of new factors that affect market outcomes. For example, these insights generated from the model can be crucial for market participants in determining when and how to deploy their algorithmic trading strategies. Understanding the dynamics of when mispricing and volatility interact with each other can help participants better prepare for potential bubbles and crashes. The study finds that different algorithmic trading strategies might have varying impacts based on whether the market is initially underpriced or overpriced. Market participants could use insights from the model to tailor their strategies in accordance with the initial market conditions. The model may also provide predictive insights into how certain algorithmic strategies will behave under different market conditions, which can be valuable for liquidity providers, market makers, and traders.

6.1.3. Key Concepts

Next, we outline some key concepts in market microstructure:

1. **Liquidity**: In the realm of market microstructure, liquidity refers to the ease with which an asset can be transacted—purchased or sold—with minimal impact on its prevailing market price. The microstructural elements such as the depth of the order book, the bid–ask spread, and the volume of trading play pivotal roles in shaping liquidity. This concept stands as a cornerstone within market microstructure studies, warranting further exploration and discussion due to its critical influence on market dynamics.
2. **Bid-ask spread**: The bid price represents the highest price a buyer is willing to pay for the security while the ask price represents the lowest price a seller is willing to accept. Bid–ask spread is the amount by which the ask price exceeds the bid price for an asset. This spread represents a transaction cost inherently tied to liquidity; a narrower spread signifies higher liquidity, rendering the asset more liquid.
3. **Market depth**: It refers to a market's ability to absorb relatively large market orders without significantly impacting the price of the security. It is gauged by the volume and distribution of pending buy (bid) and sell (ask) orders across various price levels. Market depth, by considering the size and volume of orders at each price level, serves as a liquidity metric, with greater depth implying a reduced likelihood of substantial trades markedly affecting the security's price.
4. **Order types**: The taxonomy of order types includes market orders, which are executed forthwith at the best prevailing price, and limit orders, which are executed at a specified price or better. Stop orders, conversely, are contingent on the security reaching a predetermined price threshold. Analyzing the nature and volume of each order type can provide insights into traders' intentions and market sentiment.
5. **Price discovery**: The process of price discovery, through which market prices are established based on the interplay of supply and demand, is significantly influenced by market microstructure. Noteworthy price discovery events often stem from the influx of pivotal information such as economic

data, news events, corporate earnings reports, and shifts in investor sentiment. An in-depth analysis of the price discovery process can reveal insights into the performance of various market participants, the velocity and efficacy of price discovery, and the potential for overreaction and price reversals.

6. **High-frequency trading (HFT) and its impact on liquidity**: HFT, characterized by the execution of a multitude of orders in mere fractions of a second through sophisticated algorithms, often enhances market liquidity by narrowing the bid–ask spread. The inclusion of HFT behaviors in market microstructure analysis is imperative for a more accurate quantification of microstructural features. HFT and its impact on market liquidity have been the subject of extensive academic research, with seminal works such as those by Hendershott, Jones, and Menkveld (2011) establishing a positive relationship between HFT and liquidity, as these traders provide lower bid–ask spreads and enhance price efficiency. Brogaard (2010) supports these findings, indicating that HFT contributes to market quality by providing immediacy and reducing transaction costs for other participants. However, the flash crash of May 2010 cast HFT in a different light, with research by Kirilenko et al. (2017) showing that while HFT did not cause the crash, the high-speed trading strategies employed exacerbated price volatility by withdrawing liquidity in times of market stress. This dual nature of HFT—both as a liquidity provider and a potential source of liquidity evaporation—has been a focal point in the literature, leading to debates on the stability and resilience of liquidity provided by HFT. In the appendix to this chapter, we include a list of the top HFT hedge funds.

From a quantitative finance perspective, the aforementioned concepts can be empirically quantified using high-frequency tick trading data. A thorough comprehension of each concept's definition, coupled with a meticulous analysis tailored to varying market conditions and asset classes, is essential for accurately capturing the trading characteristics of assets. Furthermore, a deeper understanding and synthesis of various trading features may facilitate the identification of profitable quantitative factors by inferring underlying asset attributes.

The goal of this chapter is to promote factors from the perspective of market microstructure. In particular, we touch on the concept of liquidity in more detail in Section 6.2, followed by the introduction of the probability of information-based trading factors in Section 6.3. Section 6.4 reviews recent advances in liquidity measures and liquidity factors. A summary of this section is provided in Section 6.5.

6.2. Liquidity

Liquidity is a key area of research on market microstructure. It refers to the ease and speed with which an asset can be bought or sold without affecting its market price. Trading volume and turnover ratio, defined as the total number of shares traded during a period divided by the average number of shares outstanding for the same period, are direct measures of a stock's liquidity, along with bid–ask spread and market depth as mentioned before. High trading volume, turnover ratio, market depth, and low bid–ask spread indicate a stock has high liquidity.

Initial research on market liquidity focused on the bid–ask spread as a primary measure of liquidity. Demsetz (1968) is a seminal work in exploring the determinants of the bid–ask spread, attributing it to the costs of dealing, including inventory holding costs and the risk of adverse selection. Copeland and Galai (1983) further develop this concept, detailing how the bid–ask spread compensates market makers for the risk of trading with better-informed participants.

Further studies introduced additional liquidity measures. Roll (1984) proposes an implicit measure of the effective bid-ask spread, highlighting the impact of trade sizes on price movements. Subsequently, Amihud (2002) introduces an illiquidity ratio that considers the price impact per dollar of trading volume, offering a different perspective by focusing on the transaction cost aspect of liquidity.

Market microstructure theory, as discussed by O'Hara (1995), examines how the trading process affects price formation, liquidity, and market efficiency. This field has expanded the understanding of liquidity by considering the roles of different market participants, trading mechanisms, and information asymmetries.

The relationship between liquidity and asset pricing has been a critical area of study. Amihud and Mendelson (1986) posit that less liquid assets offer higher expected returns as compensation for their higher trading costs. This is further supported by empirical studies such as those by Pástor and Stambaugh (2003), who develop a liquidity-based asset pricing model, demonstrating that liquidity risk is priced in asset returns. Liquidity's role in financial stability has been highlighted by Brunnermeier and Pedersen (2009), who introduce the concept of liquidity spirals, where funding liquidity and market liquidity are interrelated, potentially leading to market crises. This line of research has shown the importance of liquidity management and regulation. The Global Financial Crisis (2007–2008) brought liquidity to the forefront of financial research. Studies by Acharya and Viswanathan (2011) and others explore the systemic risk implications of liquidity, with particular focus on the interconnectedness of institutions and markets. Goyenko et al. (2009) argue that high-quality liquidity proxies derived from daily data could enable the examination of liquidity trends over extended periods and across various nations. They present novel liquidity metrics and evaluate them against established standards like effective spread, realized spread, and price impact. The findings indicate that these new measures of liquidity hold up favorably when compared to the traditional benchmarks, reinforcing the prevailing belief in academic literature that liquidity proxies are indeed reflective of actual liquidity conditions.

Some popular liquidity measures include:

1. **Tightness:** It is broadly defined as transaction costs represented by the difference in bid and ask prices. Spread can be described using various definitions. The *quoted spread* is the straightforward gap between the bid and ask prices at a given moment in the marketplace. Conversely, the *effective spread* represents the gap between the executed transaction price and the mid-point

between the bid and ask prices, also known as the midpoint price. Considering factors like large-volume trades that progress through the order book, concealed orders, or the private matching of orders by market makers, the effective spread is often viewed as a more accurate measure of market liquidity compared to the quoted spread. Two widely used indicators of market liquidity are the Percent Effective Spread (PES) and the Relative Quoted Spread (RQS),

$$PES = 2 \times \frac{|P_t - Midpoint\ Price_t|}{Midpoint\ Price_t}, \qquad (6.1)$$

and

$$RQS = \frac{Ask_t - Bid_t}{Midpoint\ Price_t}. \qquad (6.2)$$

Goyenko et al. (2009) propose two related measures. The first one is effective spread (ES) defined as,

$$ES = 2 \times (|\ln(P_k) - \ln(Midpoint_k)|) \qquad (6.3)$$

where P_k is the price of the kth trade and $Midpoint_k$ is the midpoint of the consolidated highest bid price and lowest ask price prevailing at the time of the kth trade and the second one is realized spread (RS),

$$RS = \begin{cases} 2 \times [\ln(P_k) - \ln(P_{k+5})] & \text{when the } k\text{th trade is a buy} \\ 2 \times [\ln(P_{k+5}) - \ln(P_k)] & \text{when the } k\text{th trade is a sell} \end{cases}, \qquad (6.4)$$

where P_{k+5} is the price of trade five-minutes after the kth trade. The trades are signed according to Lee and Ready's (1991) algorithm.

Corwin and Schultz (2012) introduce a new method to estimate bid–ask spreads using daily high and low prices. The authors argue that the ratio of high-to-low prices reflects both the stock's variance and its bid–ask spread. By comparing high–low price ratios over one-day and two-day intervals, they are able to estimate bid–ask spreads accurately. The authors compare their high–low estimator to alternative spread estimators and find that it is more accurate and easier to use. The high–low estimator is defined as

$$\text{High} - \text{Low Spread} = S_t = \frac{2(e^{\alpha_t} - 1)}{1 + e^{\alpha_t}}, \qquad (6.5)$$

where $\alpha_t = \frac{\sqrt{2\beta_t} - \sqrt{\beta_t}}{3 - 2\sqrt{2}} - \sqrt{\frac{\gamma_t}{3 - 2\sqrt{2}}}$, $\beta_t = (h_{t+1} - l_{t+1})^2 + (h_t - l_t)^2$, $\gamma_t = (\max\{h_{t+1}, h_t\} - \min\{l_{t+1}, l_t\})^2$ and h_t and l_t are the observed high and low prices in day t. Over a sample period of D days, the high–low spread is calculated by taking the average of the two-day estimators. Any negative values from the two-day estimates are adjusted to zero.

2. Roll's measure: Roll (1984) suggests that given market efficiency, the effective bid–ask spread can be measured by taking the square root of the *absolute value* of auto covariance of price changes. Since auto covariance of price changes is normally negative, a higher absolute value indicates a higher reversal of price changes (lower liquidity), thus resulting in a higher bid–ask spread. Roll's measure is based on the idea that the observed price series of a stock reflects both the true value of the asset and the transaction costs, primarily the bid–ask spread. As traders execute transactions at both the bid and ask prices, the observed prices will tend to "bounce" between these two levels. Roll's measure infers the bid–ask spread without the need for quote data by analyzing the covariance of successive price changes (returns). The Roll's measure is calculated using the following formula,

$$Roll's\ Spread = -2 \times \sqrt{-\text{cov}(\Delta P_t, \Delta P_{t-1})} \qquad (6.6)$$

where ΔP_t is the change in stock price from one transaction to the next and $\text{cov}(\Delta P_t, \Delta P_{t-1})$ is the covariance of consecutive price changes.

Roll's measure assumes that markets are efficient and that there are no serial correlations in true price changes, except for the bid–ask bounce. This means it assumes prices follow a random walk, and any observed serial correlation in the price changes is solely due to the bid–ask spread. The model presupposes that trading costs are uniform and unchanging over time, a condition that may not align with the dynamic nature of real trading environments. In instances where large trades shift the price beyond the bid–ask spread, the estimates of Roll's measure can become distorted. Additionally, the measure fails to take into account the market's depth or how substantial trades can influence the market price.

Furthermore, Roll's measure focuses exclusively on the cost aspect of liquidity—the bid–ask spread—and overlooks other liquidity facets such as the depth of the market and its ability to recover from trades, which are also vital components of a market's liquidity profile.

Despite these shortcomings, Roll's measure is a straightforward and accessible method for estimating market liquidity, particularly when detailed quote data is scarce. It has been extensively employed in the field of empirical finance to evaluate transaction costs and liquidity across various markets and over different periods.

3. Amihud illiquidity measure: Amihud and Mendelson (1986) argue that investors demand a premium for less liquid stocks. Amihud (2002) proposes a liquidity-based asset pricing model which suggests that expected returns are

positively related to liquidity risk. It differs from measures like the Roll's measure by focusing on the price impact of trading volumes rather than on the bid–ask spread. Amihud illiquidity measure is defined as the annual average of the ratio of absolute daily return to daily dollar transaction volume. Therefore, for stock i in year t, the mathematical expression of Amihud illiquidity $ILLIQ_{it}$ is,

$$ILLIQ_{it} = \frac{1}{D_{it}} \sum_{d=1}^{D_{it}} \frac{|R_{id}|}{VOLD_{id}} \qquad (6.7)$$

where D_{it} is the number of days for which data are available for stock i in year t, R_{id} and $VOLD_{id}$ are the return and daily volume in dollars for stock i on trading day d in year t. According to his study, illiquid stocks should have higher expected returns than liquid stocks, and empirical studies have found evidence to support this hypothesis.

While the Amihud illiquidity measure is a valuable tool for assessing the price impact of trades, it does have limitations:

It may not fully capture the dynamic nature of liquidity, as it is based on historical data and does not necessarily reflect real-time market conditions.

It can be sensitive to extreme values, which might be due to market anomalies rather than usual market conditions.

Like Roll's spread, it does not consider the depth of the market or the resilience, which are other important aspects of liquidity.

The measure assumes that the daily returns are solely due to liquidity effects and does not account for other factors that might affect returns.

4. Amivest liquidity: The Amivest liquidity ratio is another measure of price impact

$$Amivest\ Liquidity = Average\left(\frac{Volume_t}{|r_t|}\right), \qquad (6.8)$$

where r_t is the return of the tth day and the average is calculated over all non-zero return days.

In addition to these measures, Goyenko et al. (2009) proposed nine other price-impact measures: (1) Roll Impact, (2) Effective Tick Impact, (3) Effective Tick2 Impact, (4) Holden Impact, (5) Gibbs Impact, (6) LOT Mixed Impact, (7) LOT Y-split Impact, (8) Zeros Impact, and (9) Zeros2 Impact.

Liquidity holds significant practical implications for investment operations, manifesting in several key applications:

1. **Liquidity as an explanatory factor in pricing models:** Liquidity can serve as a critical explanatory variable within an asset pricing model to explain asset returns. This aspect underscores the multifaceted role of liquidity in understanding asset valuation and market dynamics.

2. **Liquidity premium:** The liquidity factor itself has a positive expected return in the long run. Assets with lower liquidity tend to have higher expected returns, acknowledging the higher risk associated with trading such assets. However, this liquidity premium is susceptible to significant drawdowns during periods of market stress when liquidity dries up, highlighting the dual nature of liquidity as both a source of excess returns and potential vulnerability.

3. **Liquidity in trade execution:** Liquidity measurements play a pivotal role in the execution of trades. Trading algorithms must adapt their parameters based on the liquidity profile of the asset in question, with less liquid stocks necessitating smaller order sizes and longer waiting periods to minimize market impact. Additionally, the efficiency of trade execution algorithms is crucial for estimating market impact and, by extension, the feasible scale of a strategy. High-frequency trading strategies, in particular, must carefully consider the detrimental effects of liquidity shortages on strategy performance.

4. **Liquidity in portfolio management:** The impact of liquidity is an essential consideration for portfolio management. Assets with lower liquidity can incur greater losses during portfolio rebalancing, necessitating risk control measures for such assets within portfolio optimization frameworks.

The aforementioned points highlight the importance of liquidity measurement, which can significantly aid not only in quantitative factor investing but in all investment strategies. Therefore, the assessment of liquidity emerges as a worthy subject of study, promising to enhance our understanding and management of investment risks and opportunities.

6.3. Probability of Information-based Trading Factors

One aspect of microstructure is to study how equilibrium prices will be affected if certain participants have superior information (informed traders) over the others (uninformed traders). In order to avoid losses due to asymmetric information, the market dealers will set the bid–ask spread accordingly. One of the earliest models is the probability of information-based (PIN) trading model proposed by Easley et al. (1996), which can be modeled as a factor.

Maureen O'Hara

Maureen O'Hara is the Robert W. Purcell Professor of Finance at the Johnson Graduate School of Management at Cornell University, and she also holds a professorship at the University of Technology Sydney in Australia. She received her PhD from Northwestern University and has since become a leading figure in the field of finance, particularly in market microstructure.

O'Hara's contributions to market microstructure are extensive and ground-breaking. She has published widely in the areas of market microstructure and high-frequency trading, liquidity, financial crises, and the relationship between market structure and public policy. Her work is known for bridging the gap between theoretical models and practical applications in finance.

One of her most influential books, *Market Microstructure Theory*, is a comprehensive examination of the subject and has become a standard reference in the field. It provides insights into the roles of various market participants, the design of trading systems, and the implications of market regulation.

O'Hara's research has not only advanced academic understanding but has also influenced policy and practice in financial markets. She has served on the board of directors for several financial institutions and exchanges, and her expertise is regularly sought in discussions about market regulation and the evolution of financial markets in the digital age.

David Easley

David Easley is the Henry Scarborough Professor of Social Science and a Professor of Economics at Cornell University. His academic career is marked by extensive research and teaching in the areas of economics, finance, and information theory.

Easley's contributions to market microstructure and finance are substantial. Alongside Maureen O'Hara, he has co-authored numerous papers that have been influential in the field. One of their most well-known theoretical frameworks is the "PIN" (probability of informed trading) model, which attempts to quantify the probability of informed trading taking place in a given stock. This model has been widely used to understand the impact of private information in financial markets.

Easley has also worked on the implications of network theory for financial markets, the risks and contagion in financial networks, and market design. His research often intersects the fields of economics, computing, and finance, particularly focusing on how information and the structure of information networks affect markets.

6.3.1. Probability of Information-based (PIN) Model

Easley et al. (1996) investigate the differences in information-based trading on the observed differences in spreads for active and inactive traded stocks. Let $i = 1, \ldots, I$ be the trading days, information events independently distributed and occur with probability α, with probability $1 - \delta$ as good news, and probability δ as bad news. Further let the value of the asset on day i conditional on good news be $\bar{V}_i$, conditional on bad news be $\underline{V}_i$, and with no news be V_i^*, with $\underline{V}_i < V_i^* < \bar{V}_i$.

Trade arises from both informed traders (who have seen any signal) and uninformed traders. On any day, arrivals of uninformed buyers and uninformed sellers are determined by independent Poisson processes, each arrives at rate ε (defined per minute of the trading day). On days for which information events have occurred, informed buyers (good signals) and informed sellers (bad signals) are also independent Poisson processes at arrival rate μ. With the above setup, on good event days (case 1), the arrival rates are $\varepsilon + \mu$ for buy orders and ε for sell orders. On bad event days (case 2), the arrival rates are ε for buys and $\varepsilon + \mu$ for sells. For no-event days (case 3), the arrival rate of both buys and sells is ε.

The market maker knows the probability of the three cases but does not know which of the three cases he is in. Let $P(t) = \big(P_n(t), P_b(t), P_g(t)\big)$ be his prior belief about the three cases of "no news" (n), "bad news" (b) and "good news" (g) respectively at time t. His prior belief at time 0 is $P(0) = (1 - \alpha, \alpha\delta, \alpha(1 - \delta))$. To determine quotes at time t, he updates his prior condition on the arrival of an order of the relevant type. Let S_t denote the event that a sell order arrives at time t and B_t represents a buy order at time t. By Bayes rule, the market maker's posterior probability on no news at time t, conditional on a sell order arriving at t, is

$$P_n(t|S_t) = \frac{P_n(t)\varepsilon}{\varepsilon + P_b(t)\mu} \tag{6.9}$$

Similarly, the posterior probability on bad news and good news, conditional on a sell order arriving at time t, are

$$P_b(t|S_t) = \frac{P_b(t)(\varepsilon + \mu)}{\varepsilon + P_b(t)\mu}, \tag{6.10}$$

and

$$P_g(t|S_t) = \frac{P_g(t)\varepsilon}{\varepsilon + P_b(t)\mu}, \tag{6.11}$$

respectively. At any time t, the zero expected profit bid price, $b(t)$, is the market maker's expected value of the asset conditional on the history prior to t and on S_t. Thus, the bid at time t on day i is

$$b(t) = \frac{P_n(t)\varepsilon V_i^* + P_b(t)(\varepsilon + \mu)\bar{V}_i + P_g(t)\varepsilon\bar{V}_i}{\varepsilon + P_b(t)\mu}, \tag{6.12}$$

Similar calculations show that the ask at time t is

$$a(t) = \frac{P_n(t)\varepsilon V_i^* + P_b(t)\varepsilon\bar{V}_i + P_g(t)(\varepsilon + \mu)\bar{V}_i}{\varepsilon + P_g(t)\mu} \tag{6.13}$$

Define the expected value of the asset conditional on the history of trade prior to time t as

$$E[V_i|t] = P_n(t)V_i^* + P_b(t)\bar{V}_i + P_g(t)\underline{V}_i. \qquad (6.14)$$

Substituting Equation (6.7) into Equations (6.5) and (6.6) gives, respectively,

$$b(t) = E[V_i|t] - \frac{\mu P_b(t)}{\varepsilon + \mu P_b(t)}\left(E[V_i|t] - \underline{V}_i\right) \qquad (6.15)$$

and

$$a(t) = E[V_i|t] + \frac{\mu P_g(t)}{\varepsilon + \mu P_g(t)}\left(\bar{V}_i - E[V_i|t]\right). \qquad (6.16)$$

As a result, the bid-ask spread, defined as $\sum(t) = a(t) - b(t)$ at time t is

$$\sum(t) = \frac{\mu P_g(t)}{\varepsilon + \mu P_g(t)}\left(\bar{V}_i - E[V_i|t]\right) + \frac{\mu P_b(t)}{\varepsilon + \mu P_b(t)}\left(E[V_i|t] - \underline{V}_i\right) \qquad (6.17)$$

It can be seen from Equation (6.17) that the spread at time t is the probability that a buy is information-based times the expected loss to an informed buyer, plus a symmetric term for sells.

The calculation of the bid–ask spread requires the estimates of parameters $\alpha, \delta, \varepsilon, \mu$. Let $\theta = (\alpha, \delta, \varepsilon, \mu)$ represent the parameter vector. A handy way to estimate θ is maximum likelihood estimation, which has been discussed in Section 4.4.1. On a bad-event day with time period T, the likelihood of observing any sequence of orders that contains B buys and S sells is

$$\frac{e^{-\varepsilon T}(\varepsilon T)^B}{B!}\frac{e^{-(\mu+\varepsilon)T}((\mu + \varepsilon)T)^S}{S!}. \qquad (6.18)$$

Similarly, on a no-event day, the likelihood of observing any sequence of orders that contains B buys and S sells is

$$\frac{e^{-\varepsilon T}(\varepsilon T)^B}{B!}\frac{e^{-\varepsilon T}(\varepsilon T)^S}{S!}. \qquad (6.19)$$

And on a good event day, the likelihood of observing any sequence of orders that contains B buys and S sells is

$$\frac{e^{-(\mu+\varepsilon)T}((\mu+\varepsilon)T)^B}{B!}\frac{e^{-\varepsilon T}(\varepsilon T)^S}{S!}. \tag{6.20}$$

With $(1-\alpha)$, $\alpha\delta$, $\alpha(1-\delta)$ being the probabilities for no-event, a bad event, and a good-event day, the likelihood function is

$$L((B,S)|\theta) = (1-\alpha)\frac{e^{-\varepsilon T}(\varepsilon T)^B}{B!}\frac{e^{-\varepsilon T}(\varepsilon T)^S}{S!} +$$

$$\alpha\delta\frac{e^{-\varepsilon T}(\varepsilon T)^B}{B!}\frac{e^{-(\mu+\varepsilon)T}((\mu+\varepsilon)T)^S}{S!} + \alpha(1-\delta)\frac{e^{-(\mu+\varepsilon)T}((\mu+\varepsilon)T)^B}{B!}\frac{e^{-\varepsilon T}(\varepsilon T)^S}{S!}. \tag{6.21}$$

Since trading days are independent, the likelihood of observing the data $M = (B_i, S_i)_{i=1}^{I}$ over I days is the product of the daily likelihood,

$$L(M|\theta) = \prod_{i=1}^{I} L(\theta|B_i, S_i). \tag{6.22}$$

The parameter vector $\theta = (\alpha, \delta, \varepsilon, \mu)$ can then be estimated by maximizing the likelihood function Equation (6.22) with respect to each parameter in the vector. With the estimated parameters, we can derive the probability of informed trade,

$$PIN = \frac{\alpha\mu}{\alpha\mu + 2\varepsilon}. \tag{6.23}$$

Empirically, Easley et al. (1996) use stock data from the year of 1990 to test their model and its implications. Specifically, they sort stocks into deciles according to trading volumes, with the first decile contains the most actively traded stocks. Their study, however, focuses on stocks in the first, fifth, and eighth volume deciles, with each decile containing a random selection of 30 stocks. For each decile, the authors first estimate the parameter vector $\theta = (\alpha, \delta, \varepsilon, \mu)$ and then apply the Kruskal-Wallies test and Mann-Whitney test to compare the parameters of different deciles. The results show that low-volume stocks have a significantly lower probability of information events than do high or medium-volume stocks. Besides, higher volume stocks have higher arrival rates of both informed and uninformed traders.

Next, the authors move on to examine the PIN measure for each decile, and their most important empirical result is that the probability of information-based trading is lower for high-volume stocks. For example, PIN trades is approximately 0.164 for the stocks in the most active sample (first decile), but it rises to 0.208 for the fifth decile stocks, and to 0.220 for the eighth decile. These numbers imply that the risk of informed trading is lower for active stocks, and as a result, the bid–ask spreads for active stocks are lower than the spreads for the less active stocks.

Empirical results show that the average spread for the first decile is 0.1763, which is significantly lower than that of the eighth decile, which is 0.2708. These results provide strong evidence that the differential behavior of spreads across trading volumes can be partially explained by asymmetric information.

6.3.2. Volume Synchronized PIN (VPIN)

Within the high-frequency trading paradigm, Easley, de Prado, and O'Hara (2012) introduce an innovative approach to time measurement termed the "volume clock". This methodology eschews traditional chronological metrics—such as years, months, days, hours, minutes, or seconds—in favor of "volume time", which entails segmenting a trading session into intervals of equal transaction volumes. This volume-based temporal framework offers several notable advantages.

First, by adopting volume time, this approach effectively neutralizes most intra-session seasonal variations, which are prevalent in financial markets due to patterns in trading activity. Second, the transformation to volume time facilitates a closer approximation to normality and the assumption of independently and identically distributed (IID.) high-frequency returns, enhancing the statistical analysis of financial data. Third, employing a volume clock metric for sampling directly addresses the challenges posed by random and asynchronous transactions—a significant hurdle in accurately computing correlations within high-frequency datasets. This volume clock concept represents a paradigm shift in temporal analysis within financial markets, offering a refined lens through which to view and analyze the rapid and complex dynamics of high-frequency trading environments.

Easley, de Prado, and O'Hara (2012) modify the PIN indicator mentioned in the previous section by using the approach of volume time, which is named as volume-synchronized probability of informed trading (VPIN).

To implement volume-dependent sampling, sequential trades are grouped into equal volume buckets of an exogenously defined size V. A volume bucket is a collection of trades with total volume V. If the last trade needed to complete a bucket is for a size greater than required, the excess size is given to the next bucket. Let $\tau = 1, \ldots, n$ be the index of equal volume buckets, the buy volume and the sell volume be

$$V_\tau^B = \sum_{i=t(\tau-1)+1}^{t(\tau)} V_i Z\left(\frac{P_i - P_{i-1}}{\sigma_{\Delta P}}\right),$$ (6.24)

and

$$V_\tau^S = \sum_{i=t(\tau-1)+1}^{t(\tau)} V_i \left[1 - Z\left(\frac{P_i - P_{i-1}}{\sigma_{\Delta P}}\right)\right] = V - V_\tau^B,$$ (6.25)

where $t(\tau)$ is the index of the last time bar included in the τ volume bucket, Z is the cumulative distribution function (CDF) of the standard normal distribution, and $\sigma_{\Delta P}$ is the estimate of the standard deviation of price changes between time bars. The procedure splits the volume in a time bar equally between buy and sell orders if there is no price change from the beginning to the end of the time bar. If the price increases, the volume is weighted more toward buys than sells, and the weighting depends on how large the price change is relative to the distribution of price changes.

With V_τ^B and V_τ^S defined, the order imbalance is then

$$OI_\tau = \left|V_\tau^B - V_\tau^S\right|, \tag{6.26}$$

and finally, the $VPIN$ measure is calculated as

$$VPIN = \frac{\alpha\mu}{\alpha\mu + 2\varepsilon} \simeq \frac{\sum_{\tau=1}^{n}\left|V_\tau^B - V_\tau^S\right|}{nV}. \tag{6.27}$$

One important empirical finding of the paper is about the trading patterns and volume distribution in E-mini S&P500 futures trades over a specific period. The results reveal a striking pattern where the largest concentrations of trading volume occur within the first few seconds of each minute throughout the trading day. This pattern is particularly pronounced at critical times such as the open and close of equities markets. It underscores the adaptability and strategic prowess of HFT in identifying and exploiting predictable trading patterns, often at the expense of Low-Frequency Trading (LFT) systems that operate on a more traditional chronological time-based paradigm. This suggests the vulnerability of LFT strategies in a market dominated by HFT that leverages volume-clock strategies.

Another empirical finding highlighted in the paper is the analysis of trade sizes, where trades of size 100 were found to be up to 17 times more frequent than those of sizes 99 or 101. This pattern is attributed to the tendency of traders, particularly those using graphical user interfaces, to prefer round numbers for trade sizes. HFT algorithms, leveraging machine learning, are adept at identifying and exploiting such predictable behaviors in the market (Kearns and Nevmyvaka 2013). This ability is further enhanced by HFT's access to big data, allowing for sophisticated pattern recognition.

6.4. Recent Advances in Liquidity Measures and Liquidity Factors

We now turn our focus to the liquidity aspect of market microstructure. We have introduced some popular liquidity measures, however, the "elevation" of liquidity as a market-wide factor in the asset pricing literature is due to a prominent work by Pástor and Stambaugh (2003), as discussed in Section 1.7.

Pástor and Stambaugh (2003) develop a liquidity factor to explain the cross-sectional variation in stock returns. The liquidity measure of stock i in month t is the ordinary least squares estimate of $\gamma_{i,t}$ in the regression,

$$r^e_{i,d+1,t} = \theta_{i,t} + \phi_{i,t} r_{i,d,t} + \gamma_{i,t} sign\left(r^e_{i,d,t}\right) \times v_{i,d,t} + \varepsilon_{i,d+1,t}, d = 1, \ldots, D,$$

$$(6.28)$$

where $\gamma_{i,d,t}$ and $\gamma_{m,d,t}$ are the returns of stock i and the market on day d in month t, respectively; $r^e_{i,d,t} = r_{i,d,t} - r_{m,d,t}$; and $v_{i,d,t}$ is the corresponding dollar volume.

The basic idea is order flow, constructed here simply as volume signed by the contemporaneous return on the stock in excess of the market, should be accompanied by a return that one expects to be partially reversed in the future if the stock is not perfectly liquid. It is assumed that the greater the expected reversal for a given dollar volume, the lower the stock's liquidity. That is, one would expect $\gamma_{i,t}$ to be negative in general and larger in absolute magnitude when liquidity is lower.

With $\gamma_{i,t}$ estimated for individual stocks, the authors future develop a market-wide liquidity measure by averaging $\gamma_{i,t}$s of all stocks in the cross-section, and move on to analyze the importance of liquidity risk, measured as the comovement between asset returns and the unanticipated innovations in liquidity. With empirical data ranging from 1966 to 1999, the study uncovers that liquidity risk is priced. Specifically, after controlling for the exposures to the market, size, value and momentum factors, the average return on stocks with high sensitivities (beta) to liquidity exceeds that of stocks with low sensitivities by 7.5% per annum.

In another investigation, Altay and Calgici (2019) propose the liquidity-adjusted capital asset pricing model (LCAPM), which incorporates a liquidity factor in addition to the market, size, and value factors. They find that the liquidity factor has a significant impact on expected returns and that it can explain a significant portion of the cross-section.

6.4.1. Trade-time Measures of Liquidity

Recent developments in the measurement of liquidity have arisen due to significant microstructure changes in equity markets, rendering traditional liquidity measures inadequate proxies for trading costs. Barardehi, Bernhardt, and Davies (2019) introduce trade-time liquidity measures that reflect the per-dollar price impacts of fixed-dollar volumes. The authors argue that traditional liquidity measures are less accurate proxies of trading costs due to changes in equity markets, such as algorithmic trading and increased trading volume. They propose measures that aggregate trade information over variable trade-time intervals corresponding to fixed dollar volumes, rather than fixed calendar-time intervals. The authors demonstrate that their trade-time based liquidity measures outperform traditional measures in explaining cross-sections of expected returns and risk-adjusted returns. They also find that liquidity premia have remained high since the financial crisis. This work highlights the importance of developing more accurate liquidity measures in the evolving trading environment. These measures effectively capture institutional trading costs and explain the cross-section of returns.

The simplest measure, BBD (named as the authors' initials), captures the average per-dollar absolute returns of fixed-dollar volumes. To construct BBD, a stock's transactions are divided into successive trade sequences, where the cumulative dollar volumes correspond to a fixed proportion of the stock's market capitalization at the end of the previous month.

The BBD metric can be likened to a trade-time equivalent of Amihud's (2002) measure, which gauges price impacts based on the intraday frequencies of trading activities. One could construct an Amihud measure with price changes and dollar volumes measured over fixed intraday time intervals. However, this approach inherently treats each time interval uniformly, disregarding the actual volume of trading activity within those intervals.

6.4.2. Liquidity Infers Tail Risks

Liquidity can also provide information on intermediate tail risks, which is a broad topic. Chapter 7 is dedicated to a full description of tail risk as a factor. This section describes a study by Weller (2019) that utilizes a cross-section of bid–ask spreads to develop a real-time measure of tail risk. Weller's work assumes that the picking-off risk is the only source of the bid–ask spread and shows that inventory risk or non-jump adverse selection risk that violates this assumption is not important in this setup.

In the setup, liquidity consumers or *fundamental traders* (FT) arrive at rate λ_{FT}, and they pay liquidity providers the half-spread h multiplied by their arrival rate per unit time. Information events arrive at rate λ_{jump}, and they shift the fundamental value of a security by a stochastic value, J. When prices experience a sudden increase, rapid traders engage in transactions using outdated or "stale" price quotes whenever the magnitude of the jump surpasses half of the bid–ask spread, resulting in a cost $J - h$ for the liquidity providers. Consequently, the anticipated expenses per time unit that liquidity providers incur due to "rapid" adverse selection are equal to the frequency of informational events, denoted as λ_{jump}, multiplied by the anticipated magnitude of the price jump on the condition that the jump size is greater than half of the spread h.

Competitive intermediation drives expected profits per unit time to zero, delivering the equilibrium condition of Budish, Cramton and Shim (2015):

$$\lambda_{FT} \times h = \lambda_{jump} \times \Pr(J > h) \times \mathrm{E}[J - h | J > h]. \qquad (6.29)$$

Weller (2019) modifies the condition in two ways: First, he allows liquidity demand and liquidity supply to exceed one share or futures contract. Denote the (stochastic) quantity demanded as q and the quoted depth as d, and assume that queue positions are random from the perspective of liquidity providers, so that all units of liquidity offered have the same expected revenues and costs per unit time. Under these assumptions, the equilibrium condition generalizes to

$$\lambda_{FT} \times h \times \{E[q|q \le d] \times \Pr(q \le d) + d \times \Pr(q > d)\} =$$

$$\lambda_{jump} \times \Pr(J > h) \times E[J - h|J > h] \times d. \tag{6.30}$$

Liquidity providers at the best bid or offer only provide for liquidity demands up to $q = d$. For demands exceeding this threshold, larger requests for liquidity transform into resting limit orders, aiming to acquire liquidity at elevated prices.

Furthermore, Weller draws a connection between the provision of liquidity by market makers and the factor structure observed in jump returns. The notion of factor structures being present in jumps is well-supported by empirical evidence and forms the foundation of a vibrant body of research focused on jump regressions, as exemplified by works such as those by Todorov and Bollerslev (2010) and Bollerslev, Li, and Todorov (2016). The decomposition of factors and idiosyncratic jumps in the fundamental value of an asset can be represented as,

$$r^d = \sum_k \beta_k r_k^d + \tilde{r}^d, \tag{6.31}$$

where k is a set of factors and $\tilde{r}^d$ is the idiosyncratic jump return. Weller adopts three simplifying assumptions for his analysis: (1) the occurrence of jumps is mutually independent across the factors and between the factors and idiosyncratic discontinuous returns; (2) idiosyncratic jumps are identically and independently distributed across different assets; and (3) the distribution of jumps associated with each factor exhibits symmetry. Combining Equations (6.30) and (6.31) leads to the following equation,

$$\left(\lambda_{FT} q^* + \lambda_{jump} d\right) \frac{h}{d} = \sum_k \lambda_k E\left[r_k^d | r_k^d > \bar{h}_k\right] |\beta_k| + \tilde{\lambda} E\left[\tilde{r}^d | \tilde{r}^d > h\right]. \tag{6.32}$$

He then uses a method similar to the two-pass Fama-MacBeth (1973) to estimate tail risk cross-sectionally. In the first-pass, rolling annual betas need to be estimated, by running time-series regression of daily returns r_{it} on candidate factor realizations f_{kt} for each stock in the filtered sample i,

$$r_{it} = \alpha_i + \sum_k \beta_{it}^t f_{kt} + {}_{it}, \forall i. \tag{6.33}$$

In the second-pass, the tail risk is estimated by running a cross-sectional regression of the form,

$$\left(\frac{Vh}{d}\right)_{it} = \tilde{\xi}_t + \sum_k \xi_{tk} |\beta_{ik}| + \delta_{it}, \tag{6.34}$$

where d represents the bid and offer depth summed across exchanges in shares, V is realized volume divided by two, h is the effective half-spread, δ_{it} is a stock-specific error term for date t, ξ_{tk} represents the average anticipated jump risk over the interval for factor k, and finally the time fixed effect $\tilde{\xi}_t$ controls for common movements in asset level tail risk unrelated to other common factors.

It can be seen that Equations (6.33) and (6.34) follow the general Fama-Mac-Beth regression framework, which is a common approach to estimating factor risk premium. However, a notable distinction arises in the treatment of the $\tilde{\xi}_t$ estimates. Unlike the Fama-MacBeth approach where $\tilde{\xi}_t$ estimates of different time t are averaged to estimate the mean of risk premium, they are of independent interest in Weller (2019). This allows the author to recover market maker expectations directly. This distinction underscores a pivotal aspect of his method: the accuracy of tail risk assessments is more closely aligned with the size of the cross-section rather than the length of the time-series under consideration.

6.4.3. Resiliency as Liquidity Factor

Hua et al. (2020) introduce resiliency as a measure of liquidity and examine its relationship with expected returns. They propose a covariance-based measure, RES, that captures opening period resiliency and use it to identify a significant non-resiliency premium ranging from 33 to 57 basis points per month.

RES encompasses both the price impact of a liquidity shock and its persistence, with a more resilient asset being one that is less likely to deviate from its equilibrium value following a liquidity shock and that quickly recovers from any deviation. Unlike other commonly used liquidity measures, such as Amihud's price impact measure and the bid-ask spread, RES differentiates between permanent and transitory price changes, accounting for both persistence and price impact.

Since the opening half-hour of trading is a period when liquidity is of major concern, Hua et al. (2020) implement RES as the covariance between a stock's opening return 9:30 to 10:00 and its rest of the day return between 10:00 and 16:00, standardized by the daily return variance, using a 22-day sample to obtain a monthly liquidity measure. Through this approach, they demonstrate the usefulness of RES as a measure of liquidity and its relationship with expected returns.

6.5. Conclusion

In this chapter, we delved into the microstructure and liquidity factors that influence the cross-sectional difference in equity returns. Our review encompassed a broad spectrum of liquidity metrics, starting from preliminary efforts like the analysis of volume impacts on absolute returns highlighted by Amihud (2002), extending to contemporary advancements that included trade-time metrics and liquidity resilience as measures. The exploration has further expanded into the realm of high-frequency data, aiming to leverage liquidity factors for tail risk deduction.

The advent of more detailed order flow data paves the way for the development of sophisticated high-frequency liquidity measures. Future studies are poised to examine the intricate interplay between market microstructure, liquidity, and additional factors, drawing upon insights from scholars such as Weller (2019). The implications of market microstructure and liquidity for portfolio construction and risk management are expected to grow in complexity, warranting more comprehensive scrutiny.

It is crucial to acknowledge that while market microstructure characteristics and liquidity can inform profitable factor-based strategies, attention must be paid to a strategy's exposure to liquidity risks. In extreme one-sided markets, assets with low liquidity are prone to significant volatility. Portfolio rebalancing under such conditions can exacerbate market squeezes, leading to amplified losses. Furthermore, in the face of shifting market environments, many enduring microstructural features may exhibit deviations from long-standing patterns. This is primarily due to unusual phenomena arising from severe imbalances in supply and demand, challenging the conventional logic derived from investor equilibrium reasoning.

Appendix

TABLE 6.1. Top HFT Hedge Funds

Firm Name	Description	Headquarters	Founder(s)	Founding Year
Allston Trading	A private HFT firm specializing in electronic market making.	Chicago, IL, USA	Bob Jordan Elrick Williams John Harada	2002
Citadel Securities	A leading HFT firm and market maker with a broad presence in multiple markets.	Chicago, IL, USA	Kenneth C. Griffin	2002
DRW Trading	A diversified trading firm that uses HFT among other strategies across many asset classes.	Chicago, IL, USA	Donald R. Wilson	1992
Flow Traders	Focuses on HFT for Exchange Traded Products (ETPs) and related instruments.	Amsterdam, Netherlands	Roger Hodenius Jan van Kuijk	2004
GSA Capital Partners	A London-based quantitative hedge fund that also engages in HFT.	London, UK	Paul Brewer	2005
Hudson River Trading	Engages in algorithmic and HFT in global financial markets.	New York, NY, USA	Jason Carroll Alex Morcos Suhas Daftuar	2002
IMC Financial Markets	A global market maker that employs HFT strategies across various exchanges.	Amsterdam, Netherlands	Rob Defares Wiet Pot	1989
Jane Street	Known for its HFT capabilities, particularly in ETF liquidity provision.	New York, NY, USA	Tim Reynolds Rob Granieri Marc Gerstein Michael Jenkins	2000
Jump Trading	A leading trading firm that uses quantitative research and HFT technologies.	Chicago, IL, USA	Bill DiSomma Paul Gurinas	1999

Firm Name	Description	Headquarters	Founder(s)	Founding Year
KCG	A former American global financial company engaging in market making and HFT.	Jersey City, NJ, USA	Merged entity (Knight Capital Group and GETCO)	2013 (merger year)
Maven Securities	A proprietary trading firm that uses HFT strategies in its operations.	London, UK	Ben Huda Ivan Koedjikov Ian Toon	2011
Optiver	An international proprietary trading house involved in market making and HFT.	Amsterdam, Netherlands	Johann Kaemingk	1986
Quantlab Financial	An HFT pioneer that focuses on technology-driven quantitative trading strategies.	Houston, TX, USA	Wilbur "Ed" Bosarge Jr. Bruce Eames	1998
RSJ Algorithmic Trading	Specializes in HFT primarily in derivatives markets.	Prague, Czech Republic	Karel Janecek	1994
Sun Trading	An HFT firm that was acquired by Hudson River Trading.	Chicago, IL, USA	Jeff Wigley	2003
Teza Technologies	A quantitative trading firm that utilizes HFT strategies.	Chicago, IL, USA	Misha Malyshev	2009
Tower Research Capital	A leading HFT firm that also operates Spire-X for cryptocurrency trading.	New York, NY, USA	Mark Gorton	1998
Tradebot Systems	One of the largest HFT firms in the US, focusing on equity markets.	Kansas City, MO, USA	Dave Cummings	1999
Two Sigma Investments	A hedge fund that employs HFT techniques as part of its various trading strategies.	New York, NY, USA	John Overdeck David Siegel	2001
Virtu Financial	A global leader in electronic trading and market making, publicly traded on NASDAQ.	New York, NY, USA	Vincent Viola	2008
XR Trading	Specializes in electronic trading and HFT across several asset classes.	Chicago, IL, USA	Matt Haraburda	2002

References

Acharya, V. V. and S. Viswanathan (2011). Leverage, moral hazard, and liquidity. *Journal of Finance* 66(1), 99–138.

Altay, E. and S. Calgici (2019). Liquidity adjusted capital asset pricing model in an emerging market: Liquidity risk in Borsa Istanbul. *Borsa Istanbul Review* 19(4), 297–309.

Amihud, Y. (2002). Illiquidity and stock returns: Cross-section and time-series effects. *Journal of Financial Markets* 5(1), 31–56.

Amihud, Y. and H. Mendelson (1986). Asset pricing and the bid-ask spread. *Journal of Financial Economics* 17(2), 223–249.

Barardehi, Y. H., D. Bernhardt, and R. J. Davies (2019). Trade-time measures of liquidity. *Review of Financial Studies* 32(1), 126–179.

Bollerslev, T., S. Z. Li, and V. Todorov (2016). Roughing up beta: Continuous versus discontinuous betas and the cross section of expected stock returns. *Journal of Financial Economics* 120(3), 464–490.

Brogaard, J. (2010). *High Frequency Trading and its Impact on Market Quality*. Northwestern University Kellogg School of Management Working Paper.

Brunnermeier, M. K. and L. H. Pedersen (2009). Market liquidity and funding liquidity. *Review of Financial Studies* 22(6), 2201–2238.

Budish, E., P. Cramton, and J. Shim (2015). The high-frequency trading arms race: Frequent batch auctions as a market design. *Quarterly Journal of Economics* 130(4), 1547–1621.

Copeland, T. E. and D. Galai (1983). Information effects on the bid-ask spread. *Journal of Finance* 38(5), 1457–1469.

Corwin, S. A. and Schultz, P. (2012) A simple way to estimate bid-ask spreads from daily high and low prices. *Journal of Finance* 67, 719–760.

Demsetz, H. (1968). The cost of transacting. *Quarterly Journal of Economics*, 82(1), 33–53.

Easley, D., N. M. Kiefer, M. O'Hara, and J. B. Paperman (1996). Liquidity, information, and infrequently traded stocks. *Journal of Finance* 51(4), 1405–1436.

Easley, D., M. M. L. de Prado, and M. O'Hara (2012). The volume clock: Insights into the high-frequency paradigm. *Journal of Portfolio Management* 39(1), 19–29.

Fama, E. F. and J. D. MacBeth (1973). Risk, return, and equilibrium: Empirical tests. *Journal of Political Economy* 81(3), 607–636.

Garman, M. B. (1976). Market microstructure. *Journal of Financial Economics* 3(3), 257–275.

Glosten, L. R. and P. R. Milgrom (1985). Bid, ask and transaction prices in a specialist market with heterogeneously informed traders. *Journal of Financial Economics* 14(1), 71–100.

Goyenko, R. Y., C. W. Holden, and C. A. Trzcinka (2009). Do liquidity measures measure liquidity? *Journal of Financial Economics* 92(2), 153–181.

Hendershott, T., C. M. Jones, and A. J. Menkveld (2011). Does algorithmic trading improve liquidity? *Journal of Finance* 66(1), 1–33.

Hua, J., L. Peng, R. A. Schwartz, and N. S. Alan (2020). Resiliency and stock returns. *Review of Financial Studies* 33(2), 747–782.

Kearns, M. and Y. Nevmyvaka (2013). Machine learning for market microstructure and high frequency trading. In D. Easley, M. Lopez de Pardo, and M. O'Hara (Eds), *High-Frequency Trading*. Risk Books.

Kirilenko, A. A., Kyle, A. S., Samadi, M., & Tuzun, T. (2017). The flash crash: High-frequency trading in an electronic market. *Journal of Finance* 72(3), 967–998.

Kyle, A. S. (1985). Continuous auctions and insider trading. *Econometrica* 53(6), 1315–1335.

Lee, C. M. C. and M. J. Ready. (1991). Inferring Trade Direction from Intraday Data. *Journal of Finance* 46(2), 733–746.

O'Hara, M. (1995). *Market Microstructure Theory*. Blackwell Publishers.

Pástor, L. and R. F. Stambaugh (2003). Liquidity risk and expected stock returns. *Journal of Political Economy* 111(3), 642–685.

Roll, R. (1984). A simple implicit measure of the effective bid-ask spread in an efficient market. *Journal of Finance* 39(4), 1127–1139.

Todorov, V. and T. Bollerslev (2010). Jumps and betas: A new framework for disentangling and estimating systematic risks. *Journal of Econometrics* 157(2), 220–235.

Weller (2019). Measuring tail risks at high frequency. *Review of Financial Studies* 32(9), 3571–3616.

Zhang, X. and L. Zhang (2015). How does the internet affect the financial market? An equilibrium model of internet facilitated feedback trading. *MIS Quarterly* 39(1), 17–38.

Zhang, L. and X. Zhang (forthcoming). Mispricing and algorithm trading. *Information Systems Research.*

7

TAIL RISK

Tail risk is an integral concept in the lexicon of risk management, referring to the potential for extreme events that lie at the outer edges, or "tails", of a probability distribution. The term paints a vivid picture of the statistical likelihood of these events: they are situated in the tails of the bell curve where fewer observations occur, and as such, they are both rare and potentially devastating. This notion of tail risk captures the attention of investors, risk managers, and policymakers because of the outsized impact these tail events, often called "black swans", can have on financial markets, economies, and investment portfolios.

The historical roots of tail risk can be traced back to the earliest days of probability theory and statistics, but it was not until the tumultuous markets of the late twentieth and early twenty-first centuries that the term gained prominence. The concept became widely recognized following the market crashes and financial crises that seemed to defy traditional risk models and expectations, such as the Black Monday of 1987 and the 2008 financial crisis. These events underscored the limitations of conventional risk assessment tools and the catastrophic potential of disregarding the tails of the distribution. During the Black Monday crash on October 19, 1987, the negative return observed was a staggering 22 standard deviations away from the mean. If we assume a normal distribution, this extreme deviation would imply an incredibly small probability of occurrence, specifically $1.440 \times 10\text{-}107$. This probability is so minuscule that it can be considered almost impossible. However, it is important to note that relying solely on the normality assumption underestimates the true probability of such extreme events happening. This highlights the limitations of assuming a normal distribution in financial markets and emphasizes the need for alternative models that better capture the dynamics of market behavior and the occurrence of rare events.

Academics have approached tail risk with a fervor for understanding and modeling these events. They delve into the mathematical underpinnings, seeking to refine models that can better capture the likelihood and impact of tail events. From

DOI: 10.4324/9781003480204-7

the development of fat-tailed distributions to the intricate construction of stress tests and scenario analyses, scholarly work aims to provide a framework for anticipating and quantifying what was once considered unquantifiable.

Meanwhile, the industry has taken a more pragmatic approach, focusing on strategies for hedging against tail risk. Financial institutions and investors have worked to develop products and strategies specifically designed to mitigate the potential losses from these extreme events. Tail risk hedging has become a cornerstone of portfolio management for those looking to protect against the unpredictable and severe market movements that can erode years of gains in a matter of days.

Despite the efforts to understand, predict, and protect against tail risks, the financial world continues to be shaken by unforeseen events, reminding us of the capricious nature of markets and the ever-present need for vigilance.

7.1. The Nature of Tail Risk

In traditional investment theory, mean-variance analysis is commonly employed to assess investment portfolios. This framework relies on average returns and variance, assuming investors have symmetrical risk preferences towards both upside and downside risks. However, real-world investor preferences are often more nuanced, with a stronger aversion to downside risk, prioritizing loss avoidance over profit pursuit.

To better reflect investors' preferences, enhanced investment models have proposed alternative methodologies. These models utilize nuanced risk metrics like downside deviation or semi-variance instead of variance, providing a more comprehensive assessment of portfolio risk. Notable contributions by studies such as Rockafellar and Uryasev (2000) and Krokhmal, Palmquist, and Uryasev (2001) address investors' asymmetric responses to downside risk versus upside gain, focusing on scenarios where portfolio returns fall below a certain threshold, better capturing investors' loss concerns.

The discourse on tail risk emerges as a natural progression from this discussion. Tail risk denotes the occurrence of rare yet profoundly adverse events that can exert a disproportionate influence on investment portfolios. These events, nestled within the extremities of the return distribution curve, have the potential to precipitate losses that far exceed the prognostications of conventional risk metrics. In the aftermath of market upheavals triggered by unforeseen calamities, the imperative to account for tail risk becomes paramount for investors striving to forge resilient portfolios.

Despite efforts to incorporate downside risk, such as the use of downside beta, directly addressing tail risk remains an incomplete task. A pivotal question in tail analysis revolves around determining investors' risk acceptance level. Bali, Cakici, and Chabi-Yo (2011) formalize a comprehensive risk measure, contingent upon investors' risk aversions.

From an industrial perspective, understanding and applying tail risk entail two main dimensions: measurement and investor perception. First, in the measurement dimension, precise analysis of objective tail risk involves employing statistical methods and mathematical models to identify and quantify factors leading to extreme events. This allows for a better understanding of market risks and the implementation of corresponding risk management measures.

Second, in the dimension of investor perception, we focus on investors' subjective perception and aversion to tail risk. This involves interdisciplinary research, including psychology and behavioral economics, to understand how investors perceive and evaluate tail risk and adjust their investment decisions accordingly. By comprehensively understanding investor behavior and emotional responses, we can predict market behavior more accurately and develop more effective investment strategies.

From a quantitative investment perspective, our goal is to leverage information from both dimensions to attain alpha. By accurately understanding and quantifying objective tail risk and investors' subjective perception and aversion to tail risk, we can construct investment strategies based on a more risk-neutral perspective. This entails investing in stocks that investors subjectively dislike but are not necessarily worse, aiming for excess returns.

This chapter will delve into existing understanding of tail risk, related concepts, and calculation methods in detail. Specifically, Section 7.2 introduces the concepts of value-at-risk and expected tail loss. In Section 7.3, we address the relationship between tail risk and asset returns, and discuss how factors can be derived from tail risk information to explain the cross-section. Section 7.4 focuses on recent developments in tail risk research. A summary of this chapter is provided in Section 7.5.

7.2. Value-at-Risk and Expected Tail Loss

The simplest yet most popular tail risk metric is Value-at-Risk (VaR). A $(1 - \alpha)$ VaR is defined as the maximum loss that is not expected to be exceeded with a $(1 - \alpha)$ level of confidence over a specified period. In other words, the probability of a loss greater than $(1 - \alpha)$ VaR is (at most) α while the probability of a loss less than $(1 - \alpha)$ VaR is (at least) $(1 - \alpha)$. Popular choices of α are 1% and 5%, which respectively represent 99% VaR and 95% VaR.

There are different ways of constructing VaR, the parametric methods and the non-parametric methods. The simplest non-parametric method is the so-called historical VaR, which is the α-percentile of a given historical sample. Figure 7.1 provides an illustration of a 95% VaR in this approach. The bars represent the frequency distribution of simulated daily returns for some asset in a given year, assuming there are 252 trading days. The dashed line indicates the VaR at the 95% confidence level. In this case, the VaR is approximately -1.44%, meaning that there is a 95% confidence that the asset will not lose more than 1.44% of its value in a single day. However, it's important to keep in mind that VaR does not predict losses beyond this threshold and does not account for extreme events in the tails of the distribution.

Another non-parametric VaR method is the resampling method. We can draw a large number of, say 10,000, samples with replacement from the same 252 daily return samples. The 95% VaR will then be the poorest 500th value out of these

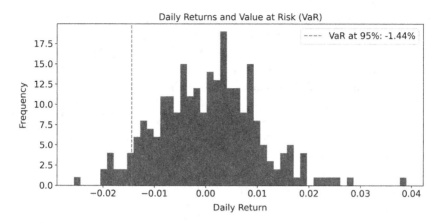

FIGURE 7.1 Historical VaR Illustration

10,000 values. The resampling method, also known as the bootstrap method, is preferred here since it accounts for the *randomness* within the sample.

Parametric VaR is based on a model's assumption of the distribution of asset returns. Suppose we assume returns are normally distributed as $N(\mu, \sigma^2)$, then the 95% VaR would be $\mu - 1.645\sigma$ where -1.645 corresponds to the z-score on the left which represents approximately the 5th percentile under the standard normal distribution. The parametric method is mainly used for portfolio VaR construction since with proper variance-covariance estimation, the portfolio VaR can be easier to handle than that of the non-parametric method.

The use of VaR as a risk measure has a main drawback. Academically, it violates one of the key properties of a coherent risk measure. A coherent risk measure $\varrho(r)$ of a risky asset with random returns r needs to satisfy the following properties:

1. Normalized: $\varrho(0) = 0$, i.e. the risk of holding zero assets should be zero.
2. Monotonicity: If $r_1 \leq r_2$ under all scenarios (r_1 being stochastically dominated by r_2), then $\varrho(r_1) \geq \varrho(r_2)$.
3. Positive homogeneity: For a constant $a \geq 0$, it requires $\varrho(ar) = a\varrho(r)$, i.e. increasing an investment a-fold will lead to the risk being a-fold as well.
4. Translation invariance: Assume a cash amount of A, it requires $\varrho(r + A) = \varrho(r) - A$, that is, the risk of an investment will be reduced by a constant cash amount if the cash is added to the investment.
5. Subadditivity: $\varrho(r_1 + r_2) \leq \varrho(r_1) + \varrho(r_2)$, i.e. the risk of two assets together as a portfolio cannot be worse than the sum of risks of two individual risks. The idea is based on the diversification principle.

VaR fulfills the first four principles but fails the subadditivity principle. To see why, let us consider an extreme example. Suppose investment A pays 100 with 99.1% probability but loses 100 with 0.09% probability. Investment B has the identical payoff as investment A but is independent of it. With the VaR definition, each investment incurs no loss under the 99% VaR. However, since (99.1%$_2$ < 99%, the 99% VaR of (A+B) will not be zero. This example highlights the problem of using VaR as a risk measure. VaR is a single point indicating the level of potential loss that can be manipulated to avoid breaching. As a result, a refined measure of VaR arises, known as Conditional Value-at-Risk (CVaR), Expected Shortfall (ES) or Expected Tail Loss (ETL). Unlike VaR, ETL is a coherent risk measure (Artzner et al. 1999, Acerbi and Tasche 2002, Tasche 2002).

We use the last term, ETL, throughout this chapter. It is defined as

$$ETL_\alpha(r) = \mathrm{E}[r|r < VaR_\alpha]. \qquad 7.1$$

Given a level of α, the ETL of an investment is the expected tail loss conditional on the $(1 - \alpha)$ VaR being breached. Using the simple historical VaR example of Figure 7.1, the 95% ETL is the average of the bars to the left of the 95% VaR vertical dashed line.

7.3. Tail Risk and Asset Returns

In Chapter 4, it has been established that low-risk anomalies represent a pivotal empirical phenomenon within stock markets, from which numerous factors can be extrapolated. This gives rise to a pertinent inquiry: could there exist factors related to low tail risk, suggesting that stocks with lower tail risks yield higher future returns? Atilgan et al. (2020) conduct a compelling empirical analysis addressing this question.

In their study, the 99% VaR metric is employed to quantify tail risk. Conventionally, these losses are multiplied by −1 to convert them into positive loss magnitudes. Descriptive statistics reveal a significant correlation between VaR and diverse factors such as idiosyncratic volatility (IVOL), MAX, beta, and size. Utilizing data from 1962 to 2014, the authors delve deeper into the relationship between tail risk and stock returns. Initial findings, based on univariate portfolio sorts, indicate that a strategy of going long on high VaR stocks while shorting low VaR stocks yields significantly negative excess returns. For instance, with market-cap weighting, the aforementioned long/short portfolio yields a mean excess monthly return of −0.78%, with a t-statistic of −2.34, thereby underscoring a negative correlation between tail risk and stock returns.

Furthermore, given that stocks with lower tail risks are characterized by lower beta and IVOL, larger sizes, higher book-to-market (BM) ratios, momentum, and coskewness, the authors consider these as control variables. They discover that, even after accounting for the influence of these factors, stocks with lower tail risks continue to exhibit higher future returns. For robustness, the authors also use ETL to measure tail risk, and the empirical findings remain the same.

Intriguingly, further examination of the relationship between VaR and future stock returns over 2 to 12 months reveals that stocks with higher tail risks not only exhibit lower returns in the subsequent month but also significantly lower excess returns over the next five months. Besides, if we consider their alphas against some benchmark factor pricing models, they remain significantly lower over the next nine months. This persistence aligns with the hypothesis of slow diffusion of private information.

Specifically, theories posited by Barberis, Shleifer, and Vishny (1998), Daniel, Hirshleifer, and Subrahmanyam (1998), and Hong and Stein (1999) suggest that investors, due to overconfidence in private information, update their beliefs gradually, leading to a sluggish dissemination of private information across markets. This, in turn, results in an underreaction to new information. Through bivariate portfolio sort analysis based on tail risk and its changes, Atilgan et al. (2020) discover that investors tend to underestimate the probability of stocks, which have suffered significant losses recently, continuing to decline. This underestimation leads to a negative correlation between VaR and stock returns over a subsequent period, highlighting the market's mispricing of tail risk.

7.4. New Advances in Tail Risk

The concept of tail risk has been increasingly recognized as a critical factor in both the theoretical framework of asset pricing and practical applications within the financial industry. There are generally four different directions in advancing the modeling of tail risk.

One approach is along the line of asset pricing models like CAPM, which construct a market-wide measure, so that assets have different cross-sectional returns due to different exposures to tail risk. The second dimension of tail risk modeling emphasizes return asymmetry, focusing on the differential sensitivity of assets to downward versus upward market movements. The third strategy explores the concept of tail dependency on the market, specifically examining the conditional distribution of asset returns in conjunction with market downturns. Lastly, the measurement of conditional tail beta represents a nuanced approach to understanding tail risk. This method quantifies the sensitivity of asset returns to extreme negative movements in the market, offering a precise metric for evaluating how assets are likely to perform during severe market downturns.

7.4.1. Market-wide Tail Risk Measure

Constructing a market-wide tail risk measure is ambitious since it needs to enter the consensus factor race like market risk premium (under CAPM), SMB and HML (under FF3), MOM (under FF3+MOM), LIQ (under FF3+MOM+LIQ, see Chapter 1 for details), to be qualified as a *universal* factor. Almeida et al. (2017) define tail risk (TR) as risk-neutralized excess ETL,

$$TR_{i,t} = \mathrm{E}^{Q(R)}\big[\big(R_{i,j} - VaR_\alpha(R_{i,j})\big)|\big(R_{i,j} \leq VaR_\alpha(R_{i,j})\big)\big], \qquad (7.2)$$

where t is the time period for which the tail risk is calculated, $j = 1, \ldots, J$ denotes the possible states of natures, α is the VaR threshold, and $Q(R)$ indicates the risk-neutral density. The aggregate market tail-risk measure is the simple average of $TR_{i,t}$ of several portfolios i. The choice of J adopted by Almeida et al. (2017) is the previous 30 days before t which corresponds to the state of nature and α is set at 10%. In forming several portfolios i, Almeida et al. (2017) uses Fama-French 25 size and book-to-market portfolios. They further extract five portfolios ($i = 1, \ldots, 5$) out of those 25 by PCA which explain around 90% of variations. The key step of risk neutralization involves assumptions of a stochastic discount kernel which is a complicated functional form with pre-assumption of risk aversion parameters. In a very recent study, Almeida et al. (2022) focuses on tail risk and its impact on asset prices in the short-term. The authors propose a new tail risk measure that combines high-frequency stock returns with risk-neutralization. They investigate the predictive power of this measure on the equity premium, variance risk premium, and realized moments of market returns. They also examine the implications of tail risk for asset pricing and its role in explaining the momentum anomaly. The authors find that their tail risk measure significantly predicts the equity premium, variance risk premium, and realized moments of market returns at short horizons. They construct a long–short portfolio based on stocks' exposure to tail risk and show that it generates abnormal returns beyond what can be explained by standard factor models. Incorporating investors' preferences through risk neutralization is crucial to their findings. The paper's incremental contribution lies in several aspects. First, it introduces a new tail measure available at a daily frequency, allowing for investigation of short-term effects. Second, it incorporates risk neutralization to capture investors' economic valuation of tail risks, which is typically done using option prices. Third, it demonstrates that short-term exposure to tail risk, as perceived by investors, helps explain differences in expected returns across stocks. Lastly, it shows that the tail risk factor improves the explanatory power for the momentum anomaly, suggesting that momentum captures short-term exposure to tail risk.

Law, Li, and Yu (2021) modify the risk–neutralization framework by constructing a minimum expected excess shortfall (MEES) measure, so that the beta exposure of each asset to this MEES is the downside systematic or the unavoidable tail risk. It can be shown that with this approach, the need for further risk neutralization can be skipped. The solution is a direct optimization solution for w_p^*,

$$w_p^* = \arg\min_{w_p} \mathrm{E}\left(abs\left(w_p' r_t - VaR_\alpha\left(w_p' r_t \right) \right) \middle| w_p' r_t \leq VaR_\alpha\left(w_p' r_t \right) \right),$$

$$subject\ to\ w_p'1 = 1, and\ 0 \leq w_p \leq 1 \qquad (7.3)$$

where $r_t = (r_1, \ldots, r_n)'$ is the vector of returns for stocks 1 to n, α is the percentile for VaR, and $1 = (1, \ldots, 1)'$ is simply a vector of ones with dimension $n \times 1$. Nonetheless, using this direct optimization, the result will be prone to choosing stocks with very low in-sample excess shortfall, resulting in a non-representative portfolio of utility-like stocks.

To mitigate this problem, the authors continue the process to extract further portfolios to ensure that the measure properly represents the market-wide cross-sectional variation of stock returns. Ideally, the succeeding portfolio p should have zero covariance to the previous ones (at least in-sample). A drawback of this approach is to search for the right number of orthogonal portfolios such that the MEES starts to flatten, i.e. no more contribution to the tail risk with further portfolio extraction.

Denoting the desired number of orthogonal portfolios by P, the idea is to solve further for $p = 2, \ldots, P$,

$$w_p^* = \arg\min_{w_p} \mathrm{E}\Big(\mathrm{abs}\ (w_p' r_t - VaR_\alpha(w_p' r_t))\,|\mathrm{w_p' r_t} \le VaR_\alpha(\mathrm{w_p' r_t})\Big),$$

subject to $w_p'1 = 1, 0 \le w_p \le 1,$ and $\mathrm{cov}\left(w_p' r_t, w_{p-1}' r_t\right) = \ldots$

$$= \mathrm{cov}\ \mathrm{left}(w_p' r_t, w_1' r_t) = 0 \tag{7.4}$$

The above problem can be transformed into a handy and direct optimization with constraints using samples for estimation. Specifically, it solves for the weight vector $w_p = \left(w_{p,1}, \ldots w_{p,n}\right)'$ for the p-th portfolio at each month-end t:

For $p = 1$,

$$\hat{w}_p = \arg\ \min_{w_p} \frac{1}{\alpha J} \sum_{j=1w_p' r_{t-j} \le VaR_\alpha(w_p' r_t)}^{J} \mathrm{abs}\ (w_p' r_{t-j} - VaR_\alpha(w_p' r_t)),$$

subject to $\mathrm{w_p'}1 = 1\ 0 \le \mathrm{w_p} \le 1 \tag{7.5}$

and $VaR_\alpha(w_p' r_t)$ is the VaR (at α-percentile) using historical method of the sample portfolio's returns $w_p' r_{t-j}$ for $j = 1, \ldots, J$.

For $p = 1, \ldots, P$,

$$\hat{w}_p = \arg\min_{w_p} \frac{1}{\alpha J} \sum_{j=1w_p' r_{t-j} \le VaR_\alpha(w_p' r_t)}^{J} \mathrm{abs}\ (w_p' r_{t-j} - VaR_\alpha(w_p' r_t)),$$

subject to $w_p'1 = 1\ 0 \le w_p \le 1\ and\ \Sigma_{j=1}^j \left(w_p' r_{t-j} - \overline{w_p' r}\right)\left(w_{p-1}' r_{t-j} - \overline{w_{p-1}' r}\right)$

$$= \ldots = \sum_{j=1}^j \left(w_p' r_{t-j} - \overline{w_p' r}\right)\left(w_1' r_{t-j} - \overline{w_1' r}\right) = 0\ and\ \overline{w_p' r} = \Sigma_{j=1}^j w_p' r_{t-j}/J.$$

$$\tag{7.6}$$

The MEES is then defined by

$$MEES_t = \frac{1}{P}\sum_{p=1}^{P}\frac{1}{\alpha J} \sum_{\hat{w}_p' r_{t-j} \leq VaR_\alpha(\hat{w}_p' r_t)} abs\left(\hat{w}_p' r_{t-j} - VaR_\alpha\left(\hat{w}_p' r_t\right)\right). \quad (7.7)$$

7.4.2. Return Asymmetry Approach

The approach focusing on return asymmetry delves into the nuanced dynamics of how an asset's returns co-move with broader market returns, particularly under varying market conditions. This perspective is pivotal in understanding the complex interplay between individual assets and the market, especially during periods of significant market fluctuations.

A key methodology within this approach is the examination of asymmetric correlation, a concept that captures the differential relationship between an asset's returns and market returns during periods of market gains versus market downturns. One contribution to this area is the exceedance correlation by Ang and Chen (2002), which aims to check the correlation between two random variables if both exceed some specified level c:

$$\rho^+(c) = \text{corr}(r_i, r_m | r_i > c, r_m > c),$$

$$\rho^-(c) = \text{corr}(r_i, r_m | r_i < -c, r_m < -c).$$

The null hypothesis (H_0) posits that the upside correlation is identical to the downside correlation, implying a symmetrical relationship between asset and market returns irrespective of market conditions,

$$H_0 : \rho^+(c) = \rho^-(c), \forall c \geq 0.$$

Conversely, the alternative hypothesis (H_1) suggests a disparity between upside and downside correlations, indicating an asymmetric co-movement between the asset's returns and the market.

Hong, Tu, and Zhou (2007) propose a model-free test for the H_0, the test statistic is

$$J_p = T(\hat{\rho}^+ - \hat{\rho}^-)' \hat{\Omega}^{-1} (\hat{\rho}^+ - \hat{\rho}^-), \quad (7.8)$$

where T is the sample size, $\hat{\rho}^+$ and $\hat{\rho}^-$ are $n \times 1$ vectors of sample exceedance correlations, and $\hat{\Omega}$ is a consistent estimator of the covariance matrix of $T(\hat{\rho}^+ - \hat{\rho}^-)$. Under the H_0 of symmetry, the test statistic has an asymptotic χ^2 distribution.

Since the correlation coefficient only measures linear dependence, to measure asymmetric co-movement at higher-order moments, Jiang, Wu, and Zhou (2018) suggest an entropy approach on the exceedance densities. They also find that higher downside asymmetric co-movement with the market indicates higher expected returns. The joint densities of two random variables conditional on the exceedance of threshold c are

$$f^+(c, r_i, r_m) = f(r_i, r_m | r_i > c, r_m > c),$$

$$f^-(c, r_i, r_m) = f(-r_i, -r_m | r_i > c, r_m > c), \forall C \geq 0,$$

and the null hypothesis is

$$H_0 : f^+(c, r_i, r_m) = f^-(c, r_i, r_m). \tag{7.9}$$

To test for H_0, the entropy test is proposed as

$$S_\rho(c) = \frac{1}{2} \int_{-\infty}^{\infty} \int_{-\infty}^{\infty} \left(f^+(c, r_i, r_m)^{\frac{1}{2}} - f^-(c, r_i, r_m)^{\frac{1}{2}} \right)^2 dr_i dr_m. \tag{7.10}$$

The test also allows for multiple exceedance levels $c_1, \ldots c_m$. The test statistic takes the simple average of S_ρ at different exceedance levels,

$$S_\rho = \frac{S_\rho(c_1) + \ldots + S_\rho(c_m)}{m}. \tag{7.11}$$

For the joint density estimation, i.e. $f(r_i, r_m)$, the authors use kernel density of the data given by

$$\hat{f}(x, y) = \frac{1}{n h_1 h_2} \sum_{i-1}^{n} k\left(\frac{x_i - x}{h_1}\right) \times k\left(\frac{y_i - y}{h_2}\right), \tag{7.12}$$

where n is the sample size of the data, h is a smoothing parameter (also known as the bandwidth), and $k(.)$ is a nonnegative kernel function. A standard kernel function is the standard Gaussian kernel, $k(z) = \frac{1}{\sqrt{2\pi}} e^{-z^2/2}$.

Bandwidth selection is another important topic. One standard approach is the likelihood cross-validation method proposed by Duin (1976),

$$\max_{h_1, h_2} L = \sum_{i=1}^{n} \ln\left[\hat{f}_{-i}(x_i, y_i)\right],$$

where

$$\hat{f}_{-i}(x_i, y_i) = \hat{f}(x, y) = \frac{1}{n h_1 h_2} \sum_{j \neq i}^{n} k\left(\frac{x_j - x}{h_1}\right) \times k\left(\frac{y_j - y}{h_2}\right), \tag{7.13}$$

which is equal to $\hat{f}(x, y)$ without the ith term. According to Hong and White (2005), the sample estimator $\hat{S}_\rho(c)$ follows an asymptotic normal distribution which does not depend on the choice of bandwidth. This completes the test of asymmetry between densities.

In another asymmetry measure, Jiang et al. (2020) propose a new asymmetry measure called Excess Tail Probability (ETP). For any stock returns, if we standardize them by subtracting the mean and then dividing by standard deviation, the standardized returns, denoted as x, will have a mean zero and unit variance. The ETP is then defined as

$$ETP = \int\limits_{1}^{+\infty} f(x)dx - \int\limits_{-\infty}^{-1} f(x)dx. \tag{7.14}$$

In other words, ETP is the probabilities evaluated at one standard deviation away from the mean. The estimation of $f(x)$ can be done by the same kernel density procedure with the bandwidth estimation suggested before. The authors present empirical evidence that the greater upside asymmetries calculated using this new measure imply lower average returns in the cross-section. In contrast, when using traditional asymmetry measures such as the skewness, the relationship between asymmetry and returns is inconclusive.

7.4.3. Tail Dependency

In the previous section, we discussed the asymmetric co-movement between individual asset return versus the market return. A natural extension would be tail dependency. Tail dependency assesses the relationship between different assets during periods of extreme losses.

Chabi-Yo, Ruenzi, and Weigert (2018) model the crash sensitivity of stocks by Lower-Tail Dependence (LTD). LTD is defined as,

$$LTD \equiv \lim_{q \to 0^+} P\left[r_i < F_{r_i}^{-1}(q) | r_m < F_{r_m}^{-1}(q)\right], \tag{7.15}$$

where r_i and r_m are returns of asset i and the market, respectively, with corresponding marginal cumulative functions F_{r_i} and F_{r_m}. The main idea of the estimation framework is to model the whole dependence structure between individual stock returns and market returns using copulas, and then estimate parameters of different copulas to compute coefficients of tail dependence based on closed-form solutions. As copulas are very mathematically involved, we will not go through the details here. Interested readers may refer to Chabi-Yo, Ruenzi, and Weigert (2018) for details.

Empirically, the authors find that stocks with stronger LTD have higher average future returns than stocks with weaker LTD. Specifically, with data ranges from 1963 to 2012, a value-weighted portfolio consisting of stocks with the strongest LTD delivers higher monthly average future return of 0.36% than a portfolio of stocks with the weakest LTD, or equivalently an annualized spread of 4.32%. Moreover, the risk premium for LTD is also higher following large stock market downturns.

Besides, industry practice often infers tail risk dependency through VaR or ETL, resulting in what is known as VaR-implied tail correlation or ETL-implied tail correlation. For instance, Liu (2021) applies the model developed by Campbell, Koedijk, and Kofman (2002), which assumes that the return distribution of an asset i takes the form,

$$r_i = \mu_i + \sigma_i Z_i, \tag{7.16}$$

Where μ_i denote σ_i the mean and standard deviation respectively, while Z_i follows a standard normal distribution. From this distribution model, along with the definition of VaR, we can deduce that the VaR at confidence level $(1 - \alpha)$ for asset i is (for simplicity of notation, we remove the subscript $1 - \alpha$ in the derivation below),

$$VaR_i = \mu_i + \sigma_i VaR(Z_i). \tag{7.17}$$

Now, considering a portfolio P composed of two assets with weights w_1 and w_2, the variance of the portfolio's returns by definition is,

$$\sigma_P^2 = w_1^2 \sigma_1^2 + w_2^2 \sigma_2^2 + 2w_1 w_2 \rho \sigma_1 \sigma_2. \tag{7.18}$$

By substituting σ_i from the VaR definition (7.17) into (7.18) and utilizing the equality $VaR(Z_1) = VaR(Z_2) = VaR(Z_P)$, we can derive the VaR-implied correlation between the two assets,

$$\rho_{VaR} = \frac{(VaR_P - \mu_P)^2 - w_1^2(VaR_1 - \mu_1)^2 - w_2^2(VaR_2 - \mu_2)^2}{2w_1 w_2(VaR_1 - \mu_1)(VaR_2 - \mu_2)}. \tag{7.19}$$

Additionally, Cotter and Longin (2006) propose a simplified formula, which does not assume asset returns to be normal, and therefore we have

$$\rho_{VaR} = \frac{(VaR_P)^2 - w_1^2(VaR_1)^2 - w_2^2(VaR_2)^2}{2w_1 w_2 VaR_1 VaR_2}. \tag{7.20}$$

The distinction between this and the previous method lies in whether the mean μ_i appears in the calculation. Given that the magnitude of μ_i is typically an order of magnitude smaller than that of VaR, the results of the two methods are very close.

However, given the fact that VaR is a single point and it is not coherent, Liu (2021) proposes a new measure called ETL-implied correlation. By extending the VaR-implied correlation based on the definition of ETL, the ETL-implied correlation follows,

$$\rho_{ETL} = \frac{(ETL_P - \mu_P)^2 - w_1^2(ETL_1 - \mu_1)^2 - w_2^2(ETL_2 - \mu_2)^2}{2w_1 w_2(ETL_1 - \mu_1)(ETL_2 - \mu_2)}. \quad (7.21)$$

In his empirical analysis, Liu (2021) finds that the VaR-implied correlation violates the [−1,1] interval frequently, while the ETL-implied correlation measure is much more stable. Besides, this new measure demonstrates that the correlations among assets under consideration increase when returns are low and decrease when returns are high. This suggests that failure to consider tail dependency appropriately could underestimate risk and cause huge losses during market declines.

7.4.4. Tail Beta

Diverging from the comprehensive ambition of tail dependency models to delineate the entire dependency structure of asset returns, a more streamlined methodology employs the principles of CAPM to focus on systematic sensitivity, commonly referred to as tail beta. This approach, in essence, involves a regression analysis of individual asset returns against market returns, conditioned on the market returns breaching VaR.

Van Oordt, and Zhou (2016) show that historical tail betas help predict the future performance of stocks in extreme market downturns. Their findings articulate that, during a market crash, stocks characterized by historically high tail betas are likely to incur losses that substantially exceed those experienced by stocks with lower tail betas—often by a factor of 2 to 3. While their research does not conclusively identify a risk premium directly attributable to tail betas, it compellingly argues that historical tail betas serve as effective indicators of future systematic tail risk. In other words, they help predict which stocks will take relatively large hits during future market crashes.

Despite the intuitive appeal and relative ease of implementation associated with the tail beta approach, it is not without its limitations. Chief among these is the inherent constraint posed by the limited number of observations that meet the VaR criteria. For example, for rolling 260 daily return observations, there are only 13 valid observations for regression under the 95% VaR assumption. This scarcity of valid data points necessitates the use of extended rolling windows for the construction of tail betas. However, this approach introduces the potential drawback of incorporating outdated or less relevant information into the analysis, thus diluting the predictive accuracy.

7.5. Conclusion

In this chapter, we delved into the concept of tail risk, a topic that has increasingly captured the attention of both the academic community and financial industry practitioners. We began by addressing a notable limitation of VaR—its failure to satisfy the subadditivity property, which is essential for a measure to be deemed coherent. To address this shortfall, we introduced an alternative measure known as ETL, which remedies some of the deficiencies associated with VaR and offers a more robust framework for assessing tail risk. We also showed that tail risk helps explain the cross-section of stock returns.

In the asset pricing literature, various sophisticated methodologies have been developed to construct and interpret tail risk, including market-wide measures, return asymmetry, tail dependency, and tail beta. Each of these approaches provides a unique lens through which to understand the influence of extreme market events on asset returns.

The market-wide measure tries to construct a universal tail risk factor such that individual assets with different cross-sectional variations in returns are explained by their different exposures to the market-wide factor. The return asymmetry factor indicates a higher risk premium when there is an asymmetry on the downside versus the upside. The tail dependency model considers how individual assets are structurally dependent on downturns. The last approach, tail beta, can be found by simple regression of asset returns with market returns conditional on the market returns falling below a VaR threshold.

The financial markets have witnessed an increasing frequency of so-called black-swan events, unpredictable and severe incidents that have profound effects on market dynamics. This trend underscores the growing importance of tail risk modeling in driving cross-sectional variations in returns. Looking ahead, the field of tail risk research could expand in several directions. One potential avenue could involve developing new measures of market-wide tail risk that complement the existing methodologies. At the individual stock level, innovative approaches to assessing a stock's resilience to tail risk could provide valuable insights, addressing the crucial question of which stocks investors should hold in anticipation of catastrophic market events. Moreover, we can extend the concept of tail risk to the realm of asset allocation, such as the increasingly recognized tail risk parity allocation method that has garnered attention in recent years. This approach has the potential to allow for more effective risk management (see, for example, Baitinger, Dragosch, and Topalova 2017).

In navigating investments, mastering the art of avoiding tail risk while accurately identifying stocks perceived as risky but potentially resilient is paramount. It requires a nuanced understanding of market dynamics, risk factors, and investor behavior. Achieving this balance represents the essence of applying the concept of tail risk in practice.

References

Acerbi, C. and D. Tasche (2002). On the coherence of expected shortfall. *Journal of Banking & Finance* 26(7), 1487–1503.

Almeida, C., K. Ardison, R. Garcia, and J. Vicente (2017). Nonparametric tail risk, stock returns, and the macroeconomy. *Journal of Financial Econometrics* 15(3), 333–376.

Almeida, C., G. Freire, R. Garcia, and R. Hizmeri (2022). Tail risk and asset prices in the short-term. Princeton University Working Paper.

Ang, A. and J. Chen (2002). Asymmetric correlations of equity portfolios. *Journal of Financial Economics* 63(3), 443–494.

Artzner, P., F. Delbaen, J. M. Eber, and D. Heath (1999). Coherent measures of risk. *Mathematical Finance* 9(3), 203–228.

Atilgan, Y., T. G. Bali, K. O. Demirtas, and A. D. Gunaydin (2020). Left-tail momentum: Underreaction to bad news, costly arbitrage and equity returns. *Journal of Financial Economics* 135(3), 725–753.

Baitinger E., A. Dragosch, and A. Topalova (2017). Extending the risk parity approach to higher moments: Is there any value added? *Journal of Portfolio Management* 43(2), 24–36.

Bali, T. G., N. Cakici, and F. Chabi-Yo (2011). A generalized measure of riskiness. *Management Science* 57(8), 1406–1423.

Barberis, N., A. Shleifer, and R. Vishny (1998). A model of investor sentiment. *Journal of Financial Economics* 49(3), 307–343.

Campbell, R., K. Koedijk, and P. Kofman (2002). Increased correlation in bear markets. *Financial Analysts Journal* 58(1), 87–94.

Chabi-Yo, F., S. Ruenzi, and F. Weigert (2018). Crash sensitivity and the cross section of expected stock returns. *Journal of Financial and Quantitative Analysis* 53(3), 1059–1100.

Cotter, J. and F. Longin (2006). Implied correlation from VaR. MPRA paper No. 3506, University College Dublin.

Daniel, K., D. Hirshleifer, and A. Subrahmanyam (1998). Investor psychology and security Market under- and overreactions. *Journal of Finance* 53(6), 1839–1885.

Duin, R. P. (1976). On the choice of smoothing parameters for Parzen estimators of probability density functions. *IEEE Transactions on Computers* C-25(11), 1175–1179.

Hong, H. and J. C. Stein (1999). A unified theory of underreaction, momentum trading, and overreaction in asset markets. *Journal of Finance* 54(6), 2143–2184.

Hong, Y., J. Tu, and G. Zhou (2007). Asymmetries in stock returns: Statistical tests and economic evaluation. *Review of Financial Studies* 20(5), 1547–1581.

Hong, Y. and H. White (2005). Asymptotic distribution theory for nonparametric entropy measures of serial dependence. *Econometrica* 73(3), 837–901.

Jiang, L., K. Wu, and G. Zhou (2018). Asymmetry in stock comovements: An entropy approach. *Journal of Financial and Quantitative Analysis* 53(4), 1479–1507.

Jiang, L., K. Wu, G. Zhou, and Y. Zhu (2020). Stock return asymmetry: Beyond skewness. *Journal of Financial and Quantitative Analysis* 55(2), 357–386.

Krokhmal, P., J. Palmquist, and S. Uryasev (2001). Portfolio optimization with conditional value-at-risk objective and constraints. *Journal of Risk* 4(2), 43–68.

Law, K. K. F., W. K. Li, and P. L. H. Yu (2021). An alternative nonparametric tail risk measure. *Quantitative Finance* 21(4), 685–696.

Liu, J. (2021). A new tail-based correlation measure and its application in global equity markets. *Journal of Financial Econometrics* 21(3), 959–987.

Rockafellar, R. T. and S. Uryasev (2000). Optimization of conditional value-at-risk. *Journal of Risk* 2(3), 21–41.

Tasche, D. (2002). Expected shortfall and beyond. *Journal of Banking & Finance* 26(7), 1519–1533.

Van Oordt, M. R. C. and C. Zhou (2016). Systematic tail risk. *Journal of Financial and Quantitative Analysis* 51(2), 685–705.

8

BEHAVIORAL FINANCE

Behavioral finance plays a critical role in factor investing by providing a framework to understand and exploit systematic behavioral biases and inefficiencies that occur in the financial markets. Traditional financial models, such as the CAPM, assume that investors are rational and that markets are efficient, meaning that all available information is fully reflected in asset prices. However, empirical evidence has shown that this is not always the case, and market anomalies persist that cannot be explained by these traditional models.

In the context of factor investing, behavioral finance contributes in the following ways:

Identification of Factors: Behavioral finance helps in identifying factors that can explain and predict returns better than traditional models. These factors often stem from systematic patterns in the way investors behave, which can lead to mispriced securities. For instance, the momentum factor, which captures the tendency of stocks to continue performing in the same direction, can be partly explained by herding behavior and the slow reaction of investors to new information.

Explaining Market Anomalies: Behavioral finance provides explanations for market anomalies that are otherwise unexplained by traditional financial theories. Anomalies such as the low volatility effect, where less risky stocks have been shown to generate higher risk-adjusted returns, can be understood through the lens of behavioral finance as a result of investor preference for lottery-like payoffs in high-volatility stocks.

Improving Factor Models: By acknowledging and incorporating how real people behave, behavioral finance allows for the development of more comprehensive factor models that better capture risks and expected returns in the market. This can lead to the creation of more sophisticated investment strategies that are attuned to behavioral biases and inefficiencies.

DOI: 10.4324/9781003480204-8

Enhancing Portfolio Construction: Understanding behavioral biases can help in constructing portfolios that are designed to capitalize on these biases. For example, a factor investing strategy might overweight stocks that are currently undervalued due to investors' overreaction to negative news and underweight stocks that are overvalued due to excessive optimism.

Risk Management: Behavioral finance recognizes that investor sentiment and psychological factors can lead to rapid changes in market conditions. By accounting for these factors, investors can better manage risk in their portfolios, potentially improving their resilience during times of market stress.

Performance and Persistence: Behavioral finance can offer insights into the persistence of factor premiums over time. Some factors may be more prone to disappearing as arbitrage opportunities are exploited, while others may persist due to deep-rooted psychological biases that are slow to change.

In summary, behavioral finance enriches factor investing by uncovering the psychological underpinnings of market behaviors that lead to the creation and persistence of factors. It allows investors to understand and harness these behavioral biases to improve investment decision-making, enhance returns, and manage portfolio risks more effectively.

8.1. The Broad Nature of Behavioral Finance

8.1.1. In Retrospect of Traditional Finance

Traditional finance theory is deeply rooted in the assumption that investors are rational. It posits that investors make investment decisions by comparing the expected utility values of available choices (Bernoulli 1738/1954, vol Neumann and Morgenstern 1944). Rational investors maximize their expected utility which is the weighted sum of utility values multiplied by their respective probabilities. Along with the rationality assumption, Markowitz (1952) introduces optimal portfolio construction by maximizing the expected return of a portfolio for a given level of risk or minimizing the risk for a given level of expected return. The so-called Markowitz's efficient frontier sets the stage for the most influential asset pricing model in finance, the Capital Asset Pricing Model (CAPM).

Further development of asset pricing theories assumes market efficiency, which was introduced by Fama (1970). The efficient market hypothesis (EMH) categorizes information into three types which gives rise to three forms of market efficiency, respectively the weak form, the semi-strong form, and the strong form. In the weak form, historical prices and returns are considered old information, so technical or trend analysis cannot beat the market. In the semi-strong form, any publicly available information is priced in such a way that fundamental analysis also fails to give superior returns. In the strong form, even non-public information like insider trading could not provide superior returns since this information could leak out and be incorporated into pricing immediately.

The key questions are, are investors really rational? Is the market truly efficient? Can we assume retail investors can perform complicated mathematics to construct an efficient frontier like PhDs on Wall Street? We might argue that, although most retail investors are not quants, they could invest their money through institutional investors or fund managers who are sophisticated and are less prone to committing emotional errors, yet fund managers are still subject to the pressure of redemption if client sentiment is influenced by market turmoil. As a result, fund managers still need to care about the *behavioral* side of finance since their clients can be affected by human factors like emotion. This is the source of behavioral factors affecting quantitative investment.

8.1.2. The Origin of Behavioral Finance

Behavioral finance, evolving over half a century, represents a significant shift from traditional finance by focusing on the psychological influences and biases that impact investor and financial practitioner behavior. This discipline emerged in response to the limitations of traditional finance theories, particularly their failure to explain market anomalies such as speculative bubbles and erratic investor reactions to new information (Shiller 1981). Unlike traditional finance, which assumes rational investor behavior and efficient markets, behavioral finance posits that investors exhibit *bounded rationality*, leading to asset mispricing and deviations from market efficiency.

Robert J. Shiller

Robert J. Shiller is an American economist, academic, and Nobel laureate recognized for his contributions to the field of behavioral economics, particularly within the subset of behavioral finance. Shiller's work has been instrumental in understanding the psychological and cultural factors that influence financial decision-making and market dynamics. Here are some key aspects of his contributions to behavioral finance.

Challenging the Efficient Market Hypothesis (EMH): Shiller is perhaps best known for his work questioning the EMH, which posits that asset prices reflect all available information and thus are always appropriately priced. His research demonstrated that stock prices often exhibit greater volatility than could be explained by changes in dividends alone, suggesting that factors other than fundamental information play a role in market movements.

Volatility of Stock Prices: In his 1981 paper, "Do Stock Prices Move Too Much to be Justified by Subsequent Changes in Dividends?", Shiller employed a variance bounds test to show that stock prices fluctuate more than can be justified by subsequent changes in dividends, highlighting the role of investor sentiment and behavior in stock price movements.

Behavioral Concepts in Economics: Shiller has been a strong advocate for incorporating psychological research into economic theory. He argued that conventional economic theories often overlook important aspects of human psychology that can dramatically affect economic decisions and market outcomes.

Exuberance and Market Bubbles: Shiller's book *Irrational Exuberance* brought widespread attention to the concept of speculative bubbles in asset markets. Published at the height of the dot-com bubble, the book warned of the dangers of market speculation driven by irrational investor optimism. The term "irrational exuberance" itself has become synonymous with market bubbles and was famously used by then-Federal Reserve Chairman Alan Greenspan.

Real Estate Economics: Shiller's work extended to the housing market, where he analyzed real estate trends and the factors driving housing prices. He co-developed the S&P/Case-Shiller Home Price Indices, which are widely used as benchmarks for measuring real estate market performance in the United States.

In 2013, Shiller was co-recipient of the Nobel Prize in Economic Sciences along with Eugene Fama and Lars Peter Hansen. The award recognized their empirical analysis of asset prices, highlighting Shiller's work on the predictability of stock and bond prices.

Shiller has been an influential voice in public discussions about the economy, contributing to debates on policy, housing, and financial market regulation. His regular columns and media appearances have made him a well-known figure beyond academia.

Robert Shiller's contributions to behavioral finance have helped shape the field and have had a lasting impact on how economists and investors understand the markets. His work underscores the importance of considering human behavior in economic models and has led to a greater appreciation for the complexity of financial systems.

One of the fundamental assertions of behavioral finance is that investors, influenced by psychological aspects, may not always make decisions based on mean-variance optimization, suggesting that considerations beyond mere risk influence expected returns (Statman 2008). This challenges the long-held belief in finance that factors represent systematic risks, offering instead the perspective that such factors might capture common sources of mispricing, often driven by widespread investors' incapability to process information efficiently.

Significant contributions to the field, such as those by Sewell (2007), Barberis and Thaler (2003), Hirshleifer (2015), and Barberis (2018), have helped map the evolution of behavioral finance, providing a systematic overview of its principles and findings. These works underscore the transition from viewing the market participants as perfectly rational to recognizing the complex interplay of psychology and market dynamics. By acknowledging the *normal* behaviors of investors—marked by cognitive biases and emotional responses—behavioral finance offers a more nuanced understanding of market movements and investor strategies, bridging the gap between theoretical finance and actual market behavior.

David Hirshleifer

David Hirshleifer is one of the prominent figures in the field of behavioral finance. His contributions have helped bridge the gap between traditional finance, which often assumes rational and efficient markets, and behavioral finance, which recognizes that psychological factors significantly influence investor behavior and market outcomes.

Some of David Hirshleifer's key contributions to behavioral finance include:

Overconfidence and Self-Attribution: Hirshleifer has examined how psychological biases such as overconfidence and self-attribution can affect trading behavior and market outcomes. His research suggests that overconfident investors trade more aggressively and can contribute to excessive volatility in financial markets.

Attention and Information Cascade: He has contributed to the understanding of how limited attention affects decision-making in finance. Additionally, he has explored information cascades, where investors make decisions based not on their private information but on the actions and inferences from other investors' actions, which can lead to herding behavior and market trends that may not reflect underlying fundamentals.

Social Transmission and Behavioral Biases: Hirshleifer has studied how social interactions and the transmission of information through social networks can impact financial decisions. He has looked at how biases and heuristics can spread through populations, influencing investment choices and asset pricing.

Mood and Weather: His research has also delved into more unconventional determinants of financial decision-making, such as the effect of weather and seasonal affective disorders on traders' moods and, consequently, on market prices.

Corporate Finance: Beyond individual investor behavior, Hirshleifer has also explored behavioral aspects of corporate finance, such as how managerial overconfidence can affect corporate investment decisions, financing, and merger activity.

Theory Development: He has developed theoretical models that incorporate psychological factors into the analysis of financial markets, helping to explain various market anomalies and phenomena that cannot be accounted for by traditional finance theories.

David Hirshleifer's work has significantly advanced the field of behavioral finance by demonstrating how systematic biases and social factors can impact financial markets. His research has been influential in showing that psychological elements are integral to understanding and predicting market movements, investor behavior, and corporate financial decisions.

In contrast to the two fundamental assumptions of traditional finance—rational expectations and decision-making based on maximizing expected utility—behavioral finance challenges these notions. It argues against the idea of rational expectations by highlighting biases related to expectations such as overconfidence and anchoring. It also challenges the assumption of timely information processing by acknowledging cognitive limitations that prevent the brain from processing all information efficiently. Furthermore, behavioral finance disputes the concept of rational risk preferences by illustrating how decision-making under uncertainty often deviates from rationality, with theories such as prospect theory providing better explanations for decision-making under uncertainty than the expected utility theory.

The concepts of expectation biases, cognitive limitations, and the nuances of risk preferences constitute the psychological foundation of behavioral finance. Together with the concept of limits to arbitrage, these form the twin pillars upon which behavioral finance is built. Each pillar is underpinned by a rich tapestry of theories and concepts, collectively encapsulating the full spectrum of behavioral finance. This comprehensive approach not only enriches our understanding of market dynamics but also offers a more realistic portrayal of investor behavior, bridging the gap between theoretical models and empirical data.

Delving into the entirety of behavioral finance within this chapter would be an ambitious endeavor. Instead, our focus will be narrowed to essential insights that pave the way for understanding and developing factors influenced by behavioral finance principles. With this objective in mind, the structure of this chapter is meticulously planned.

We begin by exploring heuristic-driven biases in Section 8.2, followed by an examination of frame-dependent biases in Section 8.3, both of which are pivotal in understanding the psychological underpinnings of behavioral finance. Section 8.4 transitions to the intricacies of risk preferences, spotlighting Prospect Theory—a seminal contribution to the field of behavioral finance that has reshaped people's comprehension of investor behavior under uncertainty.

The subsequent sections extend the discussion to the practical application of behavioral finance within the financial markets. Section 8.5 delves into sentiment analysis, a crucial tool for gauging market mood and investor attitudes. Section 8.6 broadens the perspective with a market-wide examination of behavioral factors, providing insights into how collective investor behaviors influence market dynamics. In Section 8.7, we introduce a recent development in behavioral finance—the salience theory, which offers fresh perspectives on how salient features of information impact investor decisions.

The chapter concludes with Section 8.8, synthesizing the discussions and underscoring the significance of behavioral finance in both theoretical exploration and practical application within the realms of finance. This structured approach aims to provide a comprehensive yet focused exploration of key behavioral finance concepts, enriching the reader's understanding of this dynamic and influential field.

8.2. Heuristic-driven Biases

A foundational pillar of behavioral finance is grounded in psychology, specifically focusing on the pervasive influence of heuristic-driven biases within financial decision-making. Heuristics, essentially cognitive shortcuts or rules of thumb, play a crucial role in the way information is processed and decisions are made under uncertainty.

This section discusses some of the most prominent heuristics that have been identified as significant in the realm of behavioral finance, including "representativeness", which involves judging the probability of an event by its similarity to a stereotype; "availability", where decisions are influenced by the ease with which examples come to mind; "anchoring", a tendency to rely heavily on the first piece of information encountered (the "anchor") and insufficiently adjust from it; and "overconfidence", a common bias where individuals overestimate their knowledge, ability, and the accuracy of their predictions. These heuristics and their impact on financial behavior provide revealing insights into the cognitive processes that underlie many of the decisions and actions in the financial markets.

8.2.1. Representativeness Bias

Representativeness bias is a cognitive bias that occurs when people judge the likelihood of an event based on how similar it is to a typical example or stereotype (Tversky and Kahneman 1974). This bias can lead people to overestimate the probability of an event if it appears to be representative of a certain category or stereotype, and to underestimate the probability of an event if it appears to be unrepresentative or atypical.

Amos Tversky and Daniel Kahneman

Amos Tversky and Daniel Kahneman were pioneering psychologists whose work has had a profound impact on the field of behavioral finance, among many other areas. Their collaboration, which began in the late 1960s, led to groundbreaking insights into the cognitive biases and heuristics that influence human judgment and decision-making. While Tversky's untimely death in 1996 meant he did not share in the Nobel Prize awarded to Kahneman in 2002, their joint contributions are widely recognized and celebrated.

Tversky and Kahneman's work challenged the prevailing rational-agent models in economics, demonstrating through a series of experiments and papers that people do not always act in their best financial interest and often make decisions that deviate from the predictions of traditional economic theories. Their research showed that people rely on mental shortcuts—now known as heuristics—to make complex decisions more manageable. While these heuristics are useful, they can also lead to systematic errors or biases.

One of their most famous contributions is the identification of the availability heuristic, which is the tendency for people to judge the frequency or probability of an event by the ease with which examples come to mind. This can lead to misperception of risk or overconfidence in certain areas, impacting financial decision-making and market behavior.

Another crucial concept they introduced is the representativeness heuristic, where people assess the likelihood of an event by comparing it to an existing prototype in their minds. This can result in misconceptions of randomness and can affect how investors evaluate securities.

Perhaps their most influential work for behavioral finance is the development of Prospect Theory, introduced in a seminal paper in 1979. Prospect Theory describes how people make choices in situations where they have to consider risk and uncertainty. Contrary to the expected utility theory, which assumes that individuals make decisions to maximize utility based on final outcomes, Prospect Theory suggests that individuals are more sensitive to changes relative to a reference point, typically the status quo. It also introduced concepts like loss aversion, where losses are felt more strongly than gains, and framing, which shows that the way choices are presented can significantly influence decision-making.

Their work has illuminated how human psychology can lead to systematic patterns of deviation from standard economic predictions, such as overtrading, the equity premium puzzle, and anomalies in market reaction to news.

Tversky and Kahneman's insights have not only laid the groundwork for the field of behavioral economics but have also had implications for policy-making, business, and finance. They have influenced the way economists, financiers, and policymakers think about how humans make decisions, particularly in the face of uncertainty, and have helped develop tools and strategies to address or mitigate the impact of cognitive biases in various domains, including investment and financial market regulation.

Another manifestation of the representativeness bias is people's insensitivity to sample size, a concept Tversky and Kahneman (1971) refer to as the "law of small numbers". They highlight the common yet erroneous belief that a small number of samples can adequately reflect the full characteristics of an unknown model. Statistical knowledge, however, advises that with very few data points, it is unreliable to calculate the range of variation in variables, leading to what is also known as the small sample bias.

This bias, alongside the representativeness bias, can give rise to extrapolative beliefs, where predictions about the future are often positively correlated with current data. In the context of investing, this includes extrapolation of returns and fundamentals. Investors tend to assign greater weight to recent, above-zero returns when predicting future stock performance, leading to the expectation that a stock that has recently risen will continue to rise, and vice versa for falling stocks. For example, Dhar and Kumar (2001) demonstrate this tendency, showing that investors often buy stocks with recent abnormal returns, adhering to the belief that past performance is indicative of future results. Fundamental extrapolation refers to the assumption that a company's future cash flow changes will correlate with recent trends. If cash flows have been increasing, the expectation is that this growth will continue, prompting investment and driving prices up. However, if future cash flow growth fails to meet these extrapolated expectations, disappointment can lead to asset sell-offs and price declines.

8.2.2. Availability Bias

Availability bias is a cognitive distortion where individuals assess the likelihood or significance of events based on their ease of recall or memory presence (Tversky and Kahneman 1973). This bias can lead to an overestimation of the likelihood of notable or memorable events and an underestimation of less prominent ones.

Research by Barber and Odean (2008) shows that investors tend to focus on stocks that have recently captured their attention, such as those heavily featured in recent news, exhibiting unusual trading volumes, or having experienced significant single-day returns. These stocks create a strong impression, leading to an availability bias. This phenomenon is not limited to individual investors; analysts, too, are influenced by recent experiences in their forecasts. Lee, O'Brien, and Sivaramakrishnan (2008) find that analysts' long-term earnings growth predictions for companies tend to be overly optimistic during economic expansions and unduly pessimistic during contractions, suggesting an overemphasis on the current economic condition in their long-term forecasts. Kliger and Kudryavtsev (2010) further illustrate availability bias in their finding that stock price reactions to recommendation revisions are more pronounced when aligned with concurrent market returns. This interplay between availability bias and market movements underscores the bias's impact on investment decisions, highlighting the influence of recent and easily recalled information on investor behavior. This bias is closely related to salience theory, a topic that will be explored in Section 8.7.

Terrance Odean

Terrance Odean is a noted academic researcher in the field of behavioral finance whose work has focused on the behavior of individual investors. As a professor of finance at the Haas School of Business at the University of California, Berkeley, Odean has extensively studied the ways in which psychological biases affect trading behavior and investment decisions.

One of Odean's key contributions is his research on the impact of overconfidence on trading behavior. In a series of studies, he has demonstrated that individual investors tend to trade excessively due to overconfidence in their own information and judgment. This overtrading tends to reduce their net returns, as costs such as commissions and bid–ask spreads eat into their gains.

In collaboration with Brad Barber, another leading researcher in behavioral finance, Odean has explored the disposition effect, which is the tendency of investors to sell winning investments too quickly to lock in gains, and to hold onto losing investments too long in the hope of breaking even. This behavior is contrary to what one would predict from rational decision-making models, where investors should be more willing to realize losses to offset taxes on gains and should be less inclined to sell assets that have appreciated and are likely to incur tax on capital gains.

Their research also investigated the gender differences in investment behavior, finding that men tend to trade more frequently than women, which can be attributed in part to higher levels of overconfidence. This excessive trading tends to result in lower net returns for men compared to women.

Odean's research has also looked into the impact of attention-driven buying on stock prices. He suggests that individual investors are more likely to buy stocks that have caught their attention through recent news, rather than as a result of careful analysis, which can lead to temporary price pressures and contribute to market anomalies.

Overall, Terrance Odean's work has provided valuable insights into the actual trading practices of individual investors and has highlighted the importance of cognitive biases in financial decision-making. His findings have significant implications for the understanding of market behavior, the design of investment strategies, and the regulation of financial markets. By bringing to light the systematic errors that individual investors make, Odean's research helps to explain observed anomalies in financial markets and underscores the practical relevance of behavioral finance.

Before embarking on his academic career, Terrance Odean worked as a cab driver in New York City. This experience, while seemingly unrelated to the world of finance, provided him with a rich tapestry of human behavior and decision-making. As a taxi driver, he encountered a wide variety of people, each with their own stories and biases, which could be seen as an early, informal study in human psychology.

8.2.3. Anchoring

Anchoring bias occurs when people rely too heavily on an initial piece of information (the anchor) when making subsequent judgments or decisions. This bias can lead people to adjust their judgments or decisions insufficiently away from the anchor, even when the anchor is irrelevant or arbitrary. For example, an investor may base their valuation of a stock on its current price, even though the price may be influenced by factors such as market sentiment or short-term fluctuations. Campbell and Sharpe (2009) investigate the presence of anchoring in analysts' forecasts of monthly economic releases for the period of 1991 to 2006. They find that forecasts of any given release were anchored towards the recent months' values of that release.

Another example of the anchoring bias could be seen in investors' insensitivity to a firm's good news when its price approaches the 52-week highs. The maximum price for the last 52 weeks is a psychological barrier for many analysts and investors. When the stock price approaches 52-week highs, investors will be less responsive to any good news. In this context, the ratio of current price to 52-week high has been used as a popular factor, which has a significant information coefficient with a negative sign.

8.2.4. Overconfidence

Overconfidence occurs when people overestimate their abilities, knowledge, or judgments, and underestimate the likelihood of negative outcomes. This bias can lead people to take on excessive risk, make suboptimal decisions, and fail to recognize their own limitations. For example, an investor may be overly confident in their ability to pick winning stocks and may take on excessive risk by investing in a single stock or sector. Overconfidence seems to be enhanced in those investors who have experienced high returns and thus engage in excessive trading, leading to higher trading volume.

Byun, Lim and Yun (2016) study the return predictability of continuing over-reaction based on weighted average of signed volumes. The continuing over-reaction measure is computed according to the following two steps. First, signed volume for stock i in month t is found by multiplying trading volume by the sign of contemporaneous return,

$$
V_{i,t} = \begin{cases} VOL_{i,t} & \text{if} \quad r_{i,t} > 0, \\ 0 & \text{if} \quad r_{i,t} = 0, \\ -VOL_{i,t} & \text{if} \quad r_{i,t} < 0. \end{cases} \tag{8.1}
$$

Second, continuing overreaction (CO) is defined according to the summation of weighted monthly signed volumes during the past 12 months,

$$
CO_{i,t} = \frac{\text{sum}\left(w_J \times SV_{i,t-J}, \ldots, w_1 \times SV_{i,t-1}\right)}{\text{mean}\left(VOL_{i,t-J}, \ldots, VOL_{i,t-1}\right)}, \tag{8.2}
$$

where $SV_{i,t}$ is the signed volume for stock i in month t, J is the length of the formation period, and w_J is the weight that takes a value of $J - j + 1$ at month $t - j$ (i.e. $w_J = 1, w_{J-1} = 2, \ldots w_1 = J$). The strategies of buying stocks with upward continuing overreaction and selling stocks with downward continuing overreaction generate significant positive returns. The logic behind this is high trading volume accompanied by an increasing stock price indicates that investors are overconfident about their positive private signals while high trading volume accompanied by a decreasing stock price indicates investor overconfidence about their negative private signals. It is found that continuing overreaction to negative information predicts a lower future stock price.

Building on the theme of judgment errors, we encounter optimism and pessimism biases, which similarly distort investment decision-making. Optimism bias occurs when people overestimate the likelihood of positive outcomes and underestimate the likelihood of negative outcomes. This bias can lead people to take on excessive risk, make overly optimistic investment decisions, and ignore potential risks or downsides. Pessimism bias, on the other hand, occurs when people overestimate the likelihood of negative outcomes and underestimate the likelihood of positive outcomes. This bias can lead people to be overly cautious or risk-averse, and to miss out on potential opportunities. Shefrin and Statman (2011) find that excessive optimism creates speculative bubbles by inflating the prices of securities above their intrinsic values.

Hersh Shefrin and Meir Statman

Hersh Shefrin and Meir Statman are two influential scholars in the field of behavioral finance. They are well-known for their contributions that have significantly advanced the understanding of how psychological factors affect financial markets and the behavior of investors.

One of their key contributions is the development of the Behavioral Portfolio Theory (BPT), which was introduced in the early 2000s. This theory is an extension of the traditional Modern Portfolio Theory (MPT), which assumes that investors are rational, always make decisions that maximize expected utility, and are solely concerned with the mean and variance of their portfolio returns.

In contrast, Shefrin and Statman's Behavioral Portfolio Theory offers an alternative perspective to the assumption that investors are solely motivated by maximizing the value of their portfolios. Instead, it proposes that investors have diverse objectives and construct investment portfolios that cater to a wide array of goals.. BPT posits that investors use a mental accounting framework that leads them to construct portfolios as layered pyramids of assets. Each layer corresponds to a distinct goal or mental account, such as current income or retirement security, with different layers associated with different levels of risk tolerance.

Shefrin and Statman argue that investors are influenced by biases and errors such as overconfidence, regret aversion, and the disposition effect (the tendency to sell winning investments too quickly and hold onto losing investments too long). They suggest that these biases often lead investors to make suboptimal decisions, such as failing to diversify adequately, chasing past performance, or trading too frequently.

Their work has emphasized the role of emotions and cognitive errors in financial decision-making, challenging the classical financial theory that markets are efficient and investors are always rational. Shefrin and Statman's research has broadened the understanding of how psychology intersects with economics, leading to more realistic models of market behavior and providing insights into anomalies that traditional financial theories have struggled to explain.

Overall, Shefrin and Statman's contributions have been instrumental in legitimizing behavioral finance as a crucial area of study, and their theories have had a profound impact on both academic research and practical investment strategies.

8.3. Frame Dependent Biases

While biases can be driven by heuristics, they can also be driven by "framing". Framing refers to the context or manner in which information is presented, which can significantly influence an individual's interpretation and reaction to that information, often irrespective of the underlying facts. Common frame dependent biases include loss aversion, narrow framing, mental accounting, disposition effect, herding, and status quo bias.

8.3.1. Loss Aversion

Loss aversion highlights the psychological phenomenon where the pain of losing is felt more acutely than the pleasure of an equivalent gain. This inclination towards avoiding losses can lead to decisions that are not necessarily optimal from an investment perspective. For instance, an investor might cling to an underperforming asset with the hope of recovering their initial investment, despite lacking evidence to support a potential turnaround. Such behavior is often driven by the desire to avoid the regret associated with realizing a loss, a concept intertwined with "regret theory" or the "fear of regret".

The foundational principles underlying loss aversion were initially articulated in a broader theoretical framework, which will be explored in detail in Section 8.4. Without delving into the specifics of Prospect Theory at this juncture, it's pertinent to note that this theory introduces a value function that is characterized by its concavity for gains and convexity for losses. This suggests that the experience of loss not only heightens the sensitivity to further losses but may also alter an individual's risk tolerance, potentially shifting from risk aversion to risk-seeking behavior, especially when faced with the likelihood of significant losses. Further insights into this transformative effect on risk preferences and the intricate workings of the value function will be provided in the forthcoming discussion on Prospect Theory.

Based on regret theory, one could construct factors based on the order book of the day by calculating the following:

1. Volume of buys above close (VBAC): This is the proportion of volume of buy orders with the price greater than the close price for the day,

$$VBAC = \frac{\sum_i^N volume_{buy_i} \times I_{p_{buy_i} > close}}{totalVolume}, \tag{8.3}$$

2. Average buy price above close (ABAC): This is the average price of the buy orders with the buy price above the close price,

$$ABAC = \frac{\sum_i^N \overline{price}_{buy_i} \times I_{p_{buy_i} > close}}{close} - 1, \tag{8.4}$$

3. Volume of sells below close (VSBC): This is the proportion of volume of sell orders with the price lower than the close price for the day,

$$VSBC = \frac{\sum_i^N volume_{sell_i} \times I_{p_{sell_i} < close}}{totalVolume},$$

(8.5)

4. Average sell price below close (ASBC): This is the average price of the sell orders with the selling price below the close price,

$$ASBC = \frac{\sum_i^N \overline{price}_{sell_i} \times I_{p_{sell_i} < close}}{close} - 1,$$

(8.6)

where $i = 1, \ldots N$ are the orders of the day, I_x is the indicator function if x is satisfied. For example, $I_{p_{buy_i} > close}$ equals 1 if the price of buy order i is greater than the close price of the day.

The hypothesis is that if both VBAC and ABAC are high, investors are generally bullish for the day. Because of loss aversion, the selling pressure for the stock is low, and thus a higher future return is expected. The ICs are expected to be positive for these two factors. Conversely, if VSBC is high, one can posit that the investors suffer a loss and because of regret theory, they tend not to buy back the stock even if the price rises. Thus, the momentum of the stock is expected to be weak with a lower expected return, i.e., IC should be negative in sign. ASBC should be positive in sign since the lower the ASBC, the stronger regret avoidance will be as the sold price is much lower than the close price for the day.

8.3.2. Narrow Framing

Narrow framing means that people make decisions based on a limited or incomplete view of the available options or outcomes, without considering the broader context or range of possibilities. For example, an investor may focus too narrowly on a single investment opportunity, without considering other potential investments or the broader market trends. Barberis and Huang (2006) elaborate it as when people evaluate each new gamble in isolation, they separate it from other risks. In other words, they ignore all the previous choices and derive the utility from the current risk.

8.3.3. Mental Accounting

Introduced by Richard Thaler, mental accounting occurs when people treat different amounts of money or financial assets differently, based on arbitrary criteria such as the source or purpose of the funds (Thaler 1999). For example, an investor may treat a bonus or windfall as *fun money* and spend it on discretionary purchases, rather than investing it for the long term. According to Thaler (1999), mental accounting is a set of cognitive operations used by individuals to organize, evaluate, and keep track of financial activities. It comprises three components. The first one captures how outcomes are perceived and experienced, as well as how decisions are made and evaluated. The second component assigns activities to specific accounts. The last one focuses on the frequency with which accounts are evaluated.

Like narrow framing, mental accounting could explain why investors tend to analyze securities individually instead of thinking in terms of their risk contribution to a portfolio and the performance of other securities. Each security is considered a separate account. In addition, it could somehow explain why investors hold onto losing stocks and sell the winning stocks. It is because the losing stocks belong to *unrealized loss* as an account, while selling the winning stocks belongs to another account as *realized gain*. This idea is related to loss aversion as discussed and the so-called disposition effect that we will elaborate in detail in the next section.

Richard H. Thaler

Richard H. Thaler is an American economist born on September 12, 1945, and is a central figure in the field of behavioral economics, which is a blend of psychology and economic theory. He is particularly known for his work in behavioral finance, which challenges the traditional economic assumption that markets are efficient and that market participants always act rationally.

Thaler's work has brought psychological concepts to bear on economic analysis, highlighting the fact that people often behave in ways that deviate from the rational decision-making models predicted by classical economics. He has examined the implications of such behaviors as limited self-control, lack of willpower, and the impact of social preferences on economic decisions.

One of Thaler's major contributions to behavioral finance is the concept of "mental accounting", which describes how people categorize and treat money differently depending on its source, intended use, or the mental accounts they set up. This concept helps to explain why people might, for instance, treat a dollar earned differently from a dollar won.

Another significant contribution is his work on "nudges", as popularized in the book *Nudge: Improving Decisions About Health, Wealth, and Happiness*, co-authored with Cass R. Sunstein. Thaler proposes that by understanding the biases and heuristics that influence human behavior, policymakers and organizations can design systems that "nudge" individuals toward better decisions without restricting their freedom of choice. This has implications for a wide range of areas, from retirement savings to healthcare.

Thaler has also explored the concept of "loss aversion", the idea that people experience losses more intensely than gains, which can impact their investment decisions and market outcomes. This helps to explain phenomena such as investors' reluctance to sell losing investments to avoid confronting the psychological pain of realizing a loss.

In recognition of his contributions to behavioral economics, Richard Thaler was awarded the Nobel Memorial Prize in Economic Sciences in 2017. His work has had a profound impact on various fields, including economics, finance, and public policy, and has led to a greater understanding of how human behavior affects economic decision-making and market dynamics. Thaler's research has effectively bridged the gap between economic theory and real-world human behavior, providing valuable insights into how and why markets might sometimes behave inefficiently.

8.3.4. Disposition Effect

The disposition effect is closely related to loss aversion (Shefrin and Statman 1985). It is the tendency of investors to hold on to losing investments (losers) and to sell winning ones (winners). Wang, Yan, and Yu (2017) find a negative risk–return relationship among firms if most investors face prior losses, but a positive risk–return relationship among firms if most investors face prior gains. Therefore, the authors suggest that reference-dependent preference (RDP) plays an important role in behavioral finance. RDP aims to determine whether most investors are facing prior gains or losses. A newly developed measure known as the Capital Gain Overhang (CGO), computed as the relative distance between the previous price (P_{t-1}) and the reference price (RP_t) which is the *average* price purchased by most investors who are holding the stock, is developed. It is taken from the work of Grinblatt and Han (2005), i.e.,

$$CGO = \frac{(P_{t-1} - RP_t)}{P_{t-1}}, \tag{8.7}$$

and

$$RP_t = \frac{1}{k} \sum_{n=1}^{T} \left(V_{t-n} \prod_{\tau=1}^{n-1} (1 - V_{t-n+\tau}) \right) P_{t-n}, \tag{8.8}$$

where P_t is the stock price at time t, V_t is the turnover at time t, defined as the trading volume over number of shares outstanding, T is rolling period, and k is a normalizing constant that makes the weights on past prices sum to one. Intuitively, the weight on P_{t-n} reflects the probability that the share purchased at $t - n$ has not been traded since.

Reference-dependent preference also affects investors' trading behavior in response to earnings news. Weisbrod (2019) studies stockholders' unrealized returns and the market reaction to earnings reports. It is found that investors' trading decisions vary with their unrealized returns since purchase, and they tend to sell winners and hold losers. The selling probability increases as the magnitude of either gains or losses increases, with the gain side having a steeper slope than the loss side. Stockholders in a gain position are more likely to sell as earnings news increases, while stockholders in a loss position are less likely to sell as earnings news increases. Given that post-announcement stock prices continue to move in the direction of earnings news, speculative traders should be less prone to sell as earnings news increases. Thus, the observed behavior is consistent with speculative trading motives only for stockholders in a loss position. The observed interaction suggests that, at the stock level, the disposition effect is more likely to generate a return underreaction to good news announcements than bad news announcements.

As an extension to the reference dependence, An (2016) refines the disposition effect by separating CGO into gain overhang and loss overhang. It is found that investors are more likely to sell a security when the magnitude of their gains or losses on it increases. Stocks with both large unrealized gains and large unrealized losses outperform others in the following month.

8.3.5. Herding

Herding is a behavioral finance phenomenon where investors tend to follow the actions and decisions of others, rather than making independent decisions based on their own analysis and judgment. This bias can lead to market inefficiencies and asset bubbles, as investors may buy or sell assets based on others' actions, rather than on the underlying fundamentals of the asset. Herding bias is driven by a combination of social influence and information cascades. Investors may follow others' actions to avoid being left behind or to gain a sense of security. However, this can lead to a self-reinforcing cycle where investors continue to follow the herd, even if the underlying fundamentals of the asset do not justify its price or valuation.

Lakonishok, Shleifer, and Vishny (1991) study the role of herding and how it destabilizes stock prices. Christie and Huang (1995) identify herding behavior in the market using cross-sectional standard deviation (CSSD) of individual asset returns. The CSSD is a statistical measure to assess the dispersion of individual data points around the mean in a cross-sectional data set at a single point in time. Cross-sectional data involves data on multiple subjects (such as individuals, firms, countries, etc.) at the same time point.

Andrei Shleifer

Andrei Shleifer is a distinguished economist whose research has significantly influenced the fields of behavioral finance, corporate governance, and institutional economics. Born in Moscow on February 20, 1961, he emigrated to the United States and pursued his academic career, obtaining a PhD from Harvard University in 1986.

Shleifer's research has significantly impacted the understanding of behavioral finance, particularly through his exploration of the limits of arbitrage. His work exposes the challenges arbitrageurs face, such as risks and costs, which can prevent them from correcting market inefficiencies and enforcing the law of one price. Alongside co-authors, including Robert Vishny, Shleifer has also delved into how psychological factors, such as investor sentiment and biases, contribute to market anomalies and affect asset prices.

Shleifer's academic achievements were overshadowed by controversy related to his involvement with the Russian privatization program in the 1990s. While serving as an advisor to the Russian government, he was accused of using his inside knowledge to personally invest in the Russian market, which led to a conflict-of-interest case. Harvard University, which had received government funds to support the advisory work in Russia, was ultimately sued by the US government. The case was settled out of court, with Harvard paying $26.5 million to the US government, and Shleifer paying $2 million in penalties without admitting wrongdoing.

Despite the setback due to the controversy, Shleifer's scholarly achievements have been acknowledged through various recognitions, including the John Bates Clark Medal in 1999. This medal is one of the most prestigious awards in economics, bestowed upon an outstanding American economist under the age of 40 who has made a significant contribution to the field.

In the context of finance, CSSD is often used to quantify the degree of dispersion in investment returns for a set of assets or securities at a given time. For instance, if you were analyzing the returns of stocks in the S&P 500 on a particular day, the CSSD would tell you how much the returns of the individual stocks deviate from the average return of all stocks in the index on that day.

The formula looks like this

$$CSSD = \sqrt{\frac{1}{N} \sum_{i=1}^{N} (R_i - \bar{R})^2} \qquad (8.9),$$

where N is the number of securities in the cross-section, R_i is the return of security i, and $\bar{R}$ is the mean return of the securities.

In their study, CSSD is used to measure the proximity of asset returns to the realized market average. They find that herding exists in periods of market extremes. During these times, investors follow aggregate market movement and disregard their own judgment, individual asset returns do not diverge much from overall market return as shown by the reduced CSSD value.

In the context of factor construction, the degree of herding can be reflected from the lead-lag coefficient of rank correlations. Rank correlation serves as a statistical tool to assess the similarity between two distinct sequences of rankings. To elucidate, consider the task of evaluating the rank correlation between two original data series, A_i and B_i, each comprising n observations. This process unfolds in three methodical steps:

1. Ranking Assignment: Initially, each value within the series is allocated a rank based on its magnitude, with the highest value being designated as rank 1, the next highest as rank 2, and so forth, ensuring a clear hierarchical ordering within the data set.
2. Rank Difference Calculation: Subsequently, for each observation i, the difference in ranks, denoted as d_i, is calculated by subtracting the rank of B_i from that of A_i. This step highlights the relative positioning of each paired observation within their respective series.
3. Spearman's Rank Correlation Coefficient: The final step involves the computation of Spearman's rank correlation coefficient, a statistical measure that captures the degree of association between the two ranked series,

$$\rho_{rank} = 1 - \frac{6\sum_i^n d_i^2}{n(n^2 - 1)}. \tag{8.10}$$

This coefficient provides a robust indicator of the directional alignment between the series, thereby shedding light on the presence and intensity of herding behavior within the market.

As herding measures how investors follow the actions of others, an obvious way is to measure the lead-lag rank correlations between large orders and small orders. For instance, select T trading days and two prespecified thresholds $Thres1$ and $Thres2$ with $Thres1 > Thres2$, classify each order of each day (from the order book) by net inflows into large order L_t (if net inflow exceeds $Thres1$), middle order M_t (if net inflow is between $Thres1$ and $Thres2$), and small orders S_t (if net inflow is lower than $Thres2$). Since large orders are typically institutional trades while small orders are retail trades, the herding factor could be computed as the rank correlation between L_t and S_{t+1}, which measures how likely small orders in the next period are to be affected by large orders. Similarly, another way to construct the herding factor is to use the rank correlation between L_t and S_{t+1}, i.e., the N-day herding effect of how retail investors follow institutional investors. Furthermore, we can also compute the rank autocorrelation S_t versus S_{t+1} as the herding factor between small orders.

8.3.6. Status Quo Bias

Status quo bias occurs when people have a preference for the current state of affairs and are resistant to change. This bias can lead people to maintain the status quo, even if it is not optimal or if there are better alternatives available. For example, an investor may hold onto a stock that has underperformed for a long time, even if there is little evidence to suggest that it will recover. Brown and Kagel (2009) conduct lab experiment on a simplified stock market and find that status quo bias is significant across individuals, over time, and independent of the stock performance. Further, it prevails in an environment in which there are very low costs of identifying better performing stocks. They explain that the underlying driving force behind this bias is individuals' reluctance to receive information that might question their own abilities. As a result, individuals choose to restrict their comparisons to their existing choices rather than considering other options.

8.4. Prospect Theory

8.4.1. Background and Model

Introduced by Kahneman and Tversky (1979) and further refined by Tversky and Kahneman (1992), Prospect Theory is considered to be the backbone of behavioral finance, challenging and expanding upon the traditional expected utility theory by introducing nuanced insights into human decision-making under risk. The theory delineates three critical modifications to conventional models. First, people sometimes exhibit risk aversion and sometimes risk seeking depending on the nature of the prospect. This behavior is encapsulated in the value function of prospect theory, which is concave for gains (implying risk aversion) and convex for losses (implying risk seeking). Second, investors could be risk-seeking for losses because they experience losses more acutely than they do gains. This asymmetric emotional reaction to gains and losses can lead investors to make decisions that are inconsistent with the expectation of maximizing utility. For example, an investor faced with a choice between a certain loss of $100 and a 50% chance to lose $200 might opt for the risky gamble, even though the expected loss is the same. This is because the possibility of avoiding the loss altogether (even with a risk of a larger loss) is more appealing than accepting a guaranteed smaller loss. Third, the negative emotional impact of a loss is typically greater than the positive emotional impact of a gain of the same magnitude. It implies that individuals are more sensitive to decreases in wealth than they are to increases, which can have numerous implications for financial decision-making. For instance, loss aversion can explain why investors might irrationally hold onto losing stocks or why they might purchase insurance to avoid potential losses even when the premium exceeds the expected loss. These insights from prospect theory illuminate why investors might engage in behaviors that deviate from optimal decision-making models, contributing to the emergence of various market anomalies.

In traditional utility theory, the utility of an uncertain prospect is the sum of the utilities of the outcomes, each weighted by its probability. As Tversky and Kahneman (1992) point out, empirical evidence shows two main modifications. First, the carriers of value are gains and losses relative to some reference point, not the final wealth levels. Second, the value of each outcome is multiplied by a decision weight, not by an additive probability. To see how prospect theory works, consider a game with the following outcomes

$$(x_{-m}, p_{-m}; \ldots; x_{-1}, p_{-1}; x_0, p_0; x_1, p_1; \ldots; x_n, p_n),$$

which is read as outcome x_i with probability p_i. With the assumptions that $x_i < x_j$ for $i < j$, and $x_0 = 0$, it means $x_{-m}, \ldots x_{-1}$ are losses and $x_1, \ldots, x_n$ are gains, and $\sum_{i=-m}^{n} p_i = 1$.

In the expected utility framework with utility function $U(.)$, the game is evaluated as

$$\sum_{i=-m}^{n} p_i U(W + x_i), \qquad (8.11)$$

where W is the investor's current wealth. In prospect theory, however, an investor evaluates the game with value

$$\sum_{i=-m}^{n} \pi_i v(x_i), \qquad (8.12)$$

and

$$\pi_i = \begin{cases} \omega^+(p_i + \ldots p_n) - \omega^+(p_{i+1} + \ldots + p_n) & for\, 0 \le i \le n \\ \omega^-(p_{-m} + \ldots + p_i) - \omega^-(p_{-m} + \ldots + p_{i-1}) & for - m \le i < 0 \end{cases} \qquad (8.13)$$

where $v(.)$ is known as the value function,

$$v(x) = \begin{cases} x^\alpha \, for\, x \ge 0, \\ -\lambda(-x)^\alpha \, for\, x < 0. \end{cases} \qquad (8.14)$$

are $\omega^+(.)$ and $\omega^-(.)$ *cumulative* probability weighting functions,

$$\omega^+(P) = \frac{P^\gamma}{(P^\gamma + (1 - P)^\gamma)^{\frac{1}{\gamma}}}, \omega^-(P) = \frac{P^\delta}{\left(P^\delta + (1 - P)^\delta\right)^{\frac{1}{\delta}}}, \qquad (8.15)$$

where $\alpha, \gamma, \delta \in (0, 1)$ and $\lambda > 1$. Note that in the definition above, $\omega^+(P)$ and $\omega^-(P)$ are cumulative probability functions, and therefore the Tversky and Kahneman (1992) refinement to the original prospect theory is also known as cumulative prospect theory.

Specifically, for outcomes where $x_i \ge 0$, the calculation of π_i is as follows: compute the sum of the probabilities of all outcomes not worse than x_i (i.e.,

$p_i + \ldots + p_n$) and the sum of the probabilities of all outcomes strictly better than x_i (i.e., $p_{i+1} + \ldots + p_n$). Then, substitute these sums into $w^+(.)$ and take the difference, that is, $w^+(p_i + \ldots + p_n) - w^+(p_{i+1} + \ldots + p_n)$, and this gives π_i. Similarly, for outcomes where $x_i < 0$ π_i is calculated as follows: compute the sum of the probabilities of all outcomes not better than x_i (i.e., $w^-(p_{-m} + \ldots + p_i) - w^-(p_{-m} + \ldots + p_{i-1})$ and the sum of the probabilities of all outcomes strictly worse than x_i (i.e.,). Then, substituting these sums into $w^-(.)$ and taking the difference, i.e., $w^-(p_{-m} + \ldots + p_i) - w^-(p_{-m} + \ldots + p_{i-1})$, gives π_i. In the special case where $i = n$ or $-m$, π_i simplifies to $\pi_n = w^+(p_n)$ or $\pi_{-m} = w^-(p_{-m})$, respectively. Figure 8.1 demonstrates the value and weighting functions of cumulative prospect theory with the parameters $\lambda = 2.5$, $\alpha = 0.5$, $\gamma = 0.61$, and $\delta = 0.69$.

In (cumulative) prospect theory, the value function $v(.)$ has three important properties. First, the outcome x, whether a gain or a loss, is relative to a given reference point, rather than to final wealth levels, which contrasts with the utility theory. Second, the function is kinked at the origin, which means that investors are more sensitive to losses than to gains of the same magnitude. Loss aversion represents the key difference between Prospect Theory and utility theory. Third, the value function exhibits diminishing sensitivity, whether in the domain of gains or losses. This means that the function is concave for gains, indicating diminishing marginal utility, but convex for losses, reflecting an increasing marginal disutility.

Furthermore, investors do not use objective probabilities when evaluating a gamble, but use transformed probabilities obtained from objective probabilities via the weighting functions w^+ and w^-. The weighting functions in cumulative prospect theory exhibit an important feature that for small-probability outcomes, the weight derived from w^+ or w^- is higher than the actual probability of the occurrence. This means that people tend to overestimate the probability of tail events at both ends of the outcome distribution. To see this, let us define the weights for the

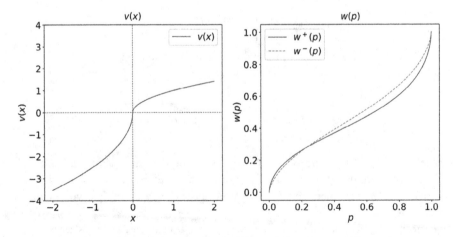

FIGURE 8.1 Value and Weighting Functions of Cumulative Prospect Theory

extreme gain outcome x_n and extreme loss outcome x_{-m} as $\omega^+(p_n)$ and $\omega^-(p_n)$, respectively. Assuming that $\gamma = \delta = 0.65$ and that the probabilities of x_n and x_{-m} occurring, i.e., p_{-n} and p_{-m}, are both 0.01, the formula of the weighting functions shows that $\omega^+(p_n) = \omega^-(p_{-m}) = 0.047$, thus $\omega^+(p_n) > p_n$ and $\omega^-(p_{-m}) > p_{-m}$. This feature of the weighting functions is meant to capture humans' tendency to overestimate the probabilities of tail events.

8.4.2. Application in Finance

To extend the work of prospect theory to finance, Barberis, Mukherjee, and Wang (2016) show that investors mentally represent a stock by the distribution of past returns and then evaluate this distribution in the way described by prospect theory. Using previous 60 monthly return data, the Prospect Theory value is defined as TK (named from Tversky and Kahneman) which depends on a multiplicative decay factor $\rho \in (0, 1)$ that downweighs distant past returns,

$$TK(\rho) = \frac{1}{\varrho} \sum_{i=-m}^{-1} \rho^{t(i)} v(r_i) \left[\omega^- \left(\frac{i+m+1}{60} \right) - \omega^- \left(\frac{i+m}{60} \right) \right]$$

$$+ \frac{1}{\varrho} \sum_{i=1}^{n} \rho^{t(i)} v(r_i) \left[\omega^+ \left(\frac{n-i+1}{60} \right) - \omega^+ \left(\frac{n-i}{60} \right) \right], \tag{8.16}$$

where $\varrho = \rho + \ldots + \rho^{60}$, $t(i)$ is the number of months ago that return r_i was realized; $\alpha = 0.88, \lambda = 2.25, \gamma = 0.61, \delta = 0.69$, being calibrated empirically; m is the number of returns which are negative, $n = 60 - m$ is the number of returns which are positive.

The article posits that there is a negative correlation between TK values and stock returns. It argues that stocks with higher TK values are more attractive, leading investors to crowd into buying stocks with high TK values and to sell off those with low TK values. This results in the former being overbought and the latter being oversold, hence the expected future returns of the stocks are negatively correlated with their current TK values. With empirical data ranging from 1931 to 2010, the authors test their hypothesis and find that a long/short portfolio, that takes a long position of stocks within the lowest TK decile and a short position of stocks within the highest TK decile, generates a monthly excess return as high as 1.35%, with a t-statistic of 5.05. The excess return remains significant, both statistically and economically, after controlling for common risk factors, such as Fama-French factors.

As mentioned before, Prospect Theory exhibits several key properties of human decision-making under uncertainty, including reference dependence, loss aversion, diminishing sensitivity, non-linear probability weighting, framing effect, endowment effect, regret aversion, status quo bias, mental accounting, overconfidence, and overestimation of tail events. These properties are manifested through the shapes of the value and weighting functions. By altering the parameters of these functions, one or more of the aforementioned properties can be turned off, allowing for an examination of the remaining properties in relation to expected returns. This approach can help identify which properties of prospect theory are most crucial for predicting future returns. In this regard, Barberis, Mukherjee, and Wang's (2016) further investigation indicates that the core property at play is the overestimation of the tail event. When this property is removed, the remaining properties, used alone or in combination, fail to generate significant excess returns.

Nicholas Barberis

Nicholas Barberis is a notable scholar in the field of behavioral finance. He has contributed significantly to the understanding of the effects of psychological factors on the financial decisions of individuals and the implications of these decisions for financial markets.

Some of Barberis's key contributions include:

Prospect Theory and Asset Prices: Barberis has conducted research that applies Prospect Theory to understand how investors make decisions under uncertainty and how these decisions can influence asset prices. He has explored how the theory can help explain various phenomena in financial markets, such as excess volatility and the equity premium puzzle.

Investor Sentiment: Barberis has investigated the role of investor sentiment in the pricing of stocks, suggesting that waves of optimism and pessimism among investors can drive stock prices away from their fundamental values.

Modeling Biases in Investment Strategies: Barberis has developed models that incorporate various cognitive biases, such as mental accounting and conservatism (the slowness in updating beliefs when presented with new evidence). These models help to explain certain investment behaviors, such as the disposition effect, where investors are prone to sell winning investments too quickly and hold onto losing investments for too long.

Style Investing: He has studied style investing, which refers to the tendency of investors to allocate funds according to certain attributes or "styles" (e.g., Growth vs. Value). His work examines how style investing can impact stock returns and market dynamics.

Learning and Belief Formation: Barberis's work also looks at how investors form and update their beliefs about future stock returns, taking into account how past experiences and representativeness bias can influence their expectations.

Barberis has co-authored a number of influential papers that have advanced the field of behavioral finance and provided a deeper understanding of how cognitive biases affect investor behavior and market outcomes. His research continues to shape the way economists and finance professionals think about the psychological aspects of financial decision-making.

In another study, Barberis, Jin, and Wang (2021) advance the field by merging insights from Prospect Theory with the concept of narrow framing from mental accounting to develop a novel investor decision model. This model integrates the full suite of characteristics from Prospect Theory's value and weighting functions, taking parameters such as stock return volatility and skewness as inputs, and its optimal solutions adhere to market clearing conditions. A key innovation of their model is its dynamic nature, which accounts for investors' historical gains and losses on stocks, thus better capturing the differential risk preferences exhibited by investors in response to gains and losses.

With this model, they try to explain 22 important anomalies observed in the stock market. The empirical evidence suggests that the model adeptly explains anomalies such as momentum, idiosyncratic volatility, idiosyncratic skewness, earnings momentum, and the post-earnings announcement drift (PEAD). However, it falls short of accounting for anomalies related to market capitalization, value, reversals, accruals, and investment. Nevertheless, this research not only provides a more dynamic representation of investor behavior but also offers a nuanced understanding of the diverse risk attitudes that come into play during financial decision-making.

8.5. Sentiment-Driven Mispricing

Another popular topic in behavioral finance is sentiment-driven mispricing. Aboody et al. (2018) study the suitability of using overnight returns to measure firm-specific investor sentiment by analyzing whether they possess characteristics expected of a sentiment measure. The work finds that the short-term persistence of overnight returns is consistent with the share demand of sentiment-influenced investors and is stronger for fundamentally anchored firms. Stocks with high (low) overnight returns underperform (outperform) over the long term, consistent with prior evidence of temporary sentiment-driven mispricing.

A similar attempt by Lou, Polk, and Skouras (2019) found that stocks with relatively high overnight returns over the last month had, on average, relatively high overnight returns as well as relatively low intraday returns in the subsequent month. A portfolio that buys the value-weight overnight winner decile and sells the value-weight overnight loser decile has an FF3 alpha of 3.47% per month with an associated t-statistic of 16.83 and an FF3 intraday alpha of -3.02% per month. The work shows that overnight and intraday component returns are likely to reflect specific client demands.

Lochstoer and Tetlock (2022) try to capture sentiment-driven mispricing with model-free mispricing factors. They analyze the factor structure of relative mispricing in closed-end funds (CEFs), which often sell at significant discounts or premiums to the net asset value of their portfolio holdings. The factor structure of relative mispricing reveals systematic discount rate shocks that affect funds and their underlying assets, which include all major securities in global financial markets.

The authors extend the analysis of closed-end fund (CEF) premiums to include locational and demographic dimensions. The locational aspect is informed by the pronounced home bias observed in global equity markets. The authors assess regional disparities in premiums between CEFs that invest in non-US developed markets and those that invest in emerging markets, termed the developed-emerging difference (DED). The DED factor aims to capture the disparity in beliefs between US investors and those in developed markets compared to the disparity between US investors and those in emerging markets. Regarding the demographic dimension, the authors calculate the differences in premiums between CEFs predominantly held by institutions and those held by individual investors, referred to as the US institutional ownership difference (UID), to reflect the divergent investment behaviors.

They found that both DED and UID are positively related to US valuations and predict negative expected returns. The authors propose an explanation that it is based on a bias in US investors' overreaction to news about future global growth. US investors could overestimate the impact of growth on developed economies, which are familiar to them, but react less to the impact of growth on emerging economies. The UID finding is consistent in the sense that overreaction is greatest for institutions' clients instead of money managers, i.e., clients' investment flows to institutions drive institutions' trading behavior.

8.6. Market-Wide Behavioral Factors

From a behavioral finance perspective, the common movements in stock returns are typically attributed to two reasons: (1) commonalities in stock mispricing; (2) commonalities in investors' incorrect reactions to new information about stock fundamentals. The former suggests that different stocks are exposed to some common style risks, and emotional shocks can cause common movements in the returns of stocks within the same style category, leading to highly correlated mispricing among stocks of the same style. The latter indicates that due to cognitive biases, investors struggle to respond timely and accurately to new information regarding stock fundamentals, which can also lead to mispricing. Since mispricing can predict future returns, this implies that behavioral factors can be used to construct a multi-factor model in hopes of better explaining the cross-section of stock returns.

In this regard, Daniel, Hirshleifer, and Sun (2020) propose two such behavioral factors. Specifically, they observe that the vast majority of anomalies in the market can be divided into two main categories based on the time scale: short and long. Anomalies on a short-term scale mostly arise from investors' limited attention, while those on a long-term scale mostly stem from investors' overconfidence. To this end, the authors propose both a short-term and a long-term behavioral factor. These two behavioral factors are designed to capture mispricing caused by overconfidence and limited attention, thereby explaining a wide range of stock-picking anomalies previously identified in academia. The authors then augment the CAPM with these two behavioral factors to create a three-factor model that outperforms traditional multi-factor models in explaining the cross-section.

The short-term factor is based on the post-earnings announcement drift (PEAD) phenomenon, which observes that firms with positive earnings surprises subsequently earn higher returns than those with negative earnings surprises. The PEAD factor is constructed by going long on firms with positive earnings surprises and short on firms with negative surprises. PEAD is based on a two-by-three sort on size and earnings surprise with value-weighted portfolios. The factor is constructed in the style of Fama and French (1993). Earnings surprise is measured as the 4-day cumulative abnormal return around the most recent quarterly earnings announcement date, following Chan, Jegadeesh, and Lakonishok (1996).

Josef Lakonishok

Josef Lakonishok is a notable figure in the field of finance, particularly known for his contributions to behavioral finance and empirical asset pricing. His work has been influential in challenging the traditional efficient market hypothesis by exploring behavioral biases and market inefficiencies.

Lakonishok earned his PhD in finance from Cornell University and has held academic positions at several universities. He served as a professor at the University of Illinois at Urbana-Champaign, where he made significant contributions to the academic literature on behavioral finance and investments.

One of Lakonishok's key contributions to behavioral finance is his work on investor behavior and its impact on security prices. Along with co-authors Andrei Shleifer and Robert Vishny, Lakonishok has written influential papers that explore the anomalies in the stock market that cannot be explained by classical theories.

Contrarian Investment Strategy: In a seminal paper titled "Contrarian Investment, Extrapolation, and Risk" (1994), Lakonishok, Shleifer, and Vishny (LSV) argued against the prevailing wisdom that buying "glamour" stocks with high growth expectations and selling "value" stocks with lower expectations would lead to superior returns. They showed that a strategy of buying out-of-favor value stocks and selling favored glamour stocks could lead to excess returns, suggesting that investors overreact to past information and that prices do not always reflect intrinsic values. This work has had a profound impact on both academic finance and investment practice.

The Behavior of Institutional Investors: Lakonishok has also investigated the trading behavior of institutional investors, challenging the perception that these investors are always rational and profit-maximizing. He found that institutional trading behavior often exhibits herd-like tendencies and can contribute to market over- and under-reactions.

In addition to his academic work, Josef Lakonishok has applied his research in the investment industry. He is a co-founder of LSV Asset Management, a firm that employs a quantitative value strategy informed by his research findings.

The firm focuses on implementing strategies that exploit behavioral biases found in the market, seeking to benefit from the mispricing of securities.

Lakonishok's research has been widely published in top finance journals, and he is recognized for his empirical analysis of equity returns. His work has had a significant influence on both the academic understanding of behavioral finance and the practical methods used by investment professionals.

Overall, Josef Lakonishok's contributions to behavioral finance have been instrumental in understanding how psychological factors and systematic biases can lead to market inefficiencies, providing a foundation for strategies that seek to take advantage of mispriced securities.

The long-term factor, known as the Financing factor (FIN), is composed of the 1-year net-share-issuance (NSI) and 5-year composite-share-issuance (CSI) measures of Pontiff and Woodgate (2008) and Daniel and Titman (2006), respectively. The FIN factor portfolio is constructed by sorting firms by size and financing characteristic, which is a 50/50 combination of the NSI and CSI measures. The portfolio goes long on the two value-weighted low-issuance portfolios and short on the two high-issuance portfolios. Daniel and Titman's 5-year CSI measure is computed as the firm's 5-year growth in market equity minus the 5-year equity return in logarithms. The NSI measure is similar to CSI, but it excludes cash dividends and uses a 1-year horizon. The FIN factor predominantly captures longer-term mispricing and correction (1 year or longer) and is less likely to capture shorter horizon mispricing due to the disclosure, legal, underwriting, and other costs associated with equity issuance and repurchase that constrain firms from issuing to exploit very short horizon mispricing.

8.7. Salience Theory

Salience theory is related to availability bias and was first introduced by Bordalo, Gennaioli, and Shleifer (2012). It was later tested empirically by Cosemans and Frehen (2021). The theory posits that the demand for risky assets is influenced by the prominence of their payoffs in different states of the world, with investors evaluating each asset by comparing its payoffs to those of available alternatives. This is in line with limited attention that investors tend to focus on what is different and unusual, the meaning of *salience*. Salience function is defined as

$$\sigma\left(r_{i,s}, \bar{r}_s\right) = \frac{\left|r_{i,s} - \bar{r}_s\right|}{\left|r_{i,s}\right| + \left|\bar{r}_s\right| + \theta}, \tag{8.17}$$

where $r_{i,s}$ is the return of stock i in state s, $\theta > 0$ and $\bar{r}_s \frac{1}{N} \sum^{N} r_{i,s}$, with N denoting the number of comparable stocks. Salience function satisfies three conditions: (1) ordering: the salience of state s increases in the distance between its payoff and the average payoff; (2) diminishing sensitivity: the salience decreases as absolute payoff levels rise uniformly for all stocks; (3) reflection: salience only depends on the magnitude of payoffs, not on their sign.

Given the salience function, a salient thinker ranks each stock's payoff and replaces the objective state probabilities with lottery-specific decision weights, which are given by

$$\tilde{\pi}_{i,s} = \pi_s \times \omega_{i,s}, \qquad (8.18)$$

with

$$\omega_{i,s} = \frac{\delta^{k_{is}}}{\sum_{s=1}^{S} \delta^{k_{is}} \times \pi_s}, \delta \in (0,1], \qquad (8.19)$$

where k_{is} is the salience ranking of payoff $r_{i,s}$, which ranges from 1 (most salient) to S (least salient). S denotes the set of states, where each state s occurs with probability πs such that $\sum_{s=1}^{S} \pi_s = 1$. In Equation (8.18), the parameter δ captures the degree to which salience distorts weights and proxies for the decision-maker's cognitive ability. When $\delta = 1$, there is no salience distortions and decision weights are equal to objective probabilities. When $\delta < 1$, the decision-maker is a salient thinker who overweighs salient states ($\omega_{i,s} < 1$) and underweights non-salient states ($\omega_{i,s} < 1$). When $\delta \to 0$, the salient thinker considers the most salient payoff and neglects all other payoffs.

Cosemans and Frehen (2021) further introduce the salient theory (ST) factor. ST for each stock i is computed as

$$ST_i = cov\left(\omega_{i,s}, r_{i,s}\right) = \sum_{s}^{S} \pi_s \omega_{i,s} r_{i,s} - \sum_{s}^{S} \pi_s r_{i,s} = E^{ST}\left[r_{i,s}\right] - \bar{r}_{i,s}, \qquad (8.20)$$

where $\pi_s = 1/S$, where S is equal to the number of states (trading days) in a period. ST suggests that if a stock's highest (lowest) past returns are salient, investors raise (lower) their expectation about its future return and push its price above (below) the fair value, thereby lowering (raising) future realized returns. Their empirical results provide strong support for the predictions of the salience model in the cross-section of US stock market. Particularly, a univariate portfolio analysis indicates that the return difference between stocks in the highest and lowest ST deciles is statistically significant and economically large over the sample period from 1931 to 2015. The monthly average excess return for the long/short strategy that buys high-ST stocks and shorts low-ST stocks ranges from 1.28% for the equal-weighted portfolio to 0.60% for the value-weighted portfolio. These excess returns cannot be explained by common risk factors, such as size, value and momentum.

Shifting our focus beyond the US stock market reveals additional insights. For example, in the context of the daily price-change limit mechanism in China's A-share market, Sun, Wang, and Zhu (2023) discover that substituting stock i's return with its turnover in the salience function (Equation (8.17)) better explains the cross-sectional variability of stock returns. The salient weight function is the same as Equation (8.19) with kis being the salience ranking of turnover for stock i in state s. The salient factor (Equation (8.20)) could be modified accordingly as the covariance between the salience weights and the turnovers for stock i for a specified period.

8.8. Conclusion

For decades, the EMH has been the academic cornerstone for understanding market dynamics. However, countless empirical findings continuously challenge the EMH. Behavioral finance emerges as a response to traditional finance theories' shortcomings in explaining market anomalies, such as speculative bubbles and momentum effects, by recognizing that investors are not always rational. This field integrates psychological factors, leading to market inefficiencies, and explores heuristic-driven or frame-dependent biases that influence investor behavior.

From a behavioral finance perspective, markets seem inefficient due to cognitive biases and limits to arbitrage, yet paradoxically, they appear difficult to outperform, suggesting a form of efficiency. This paradox is addressed by Statman (2018) through the concept of the "behavioral efficient market", which disentangles the dual implications of the EMH: "prices reflect all available information" and "markets are hard to beat". In his seminal 1986 speech titled "Noise", Fischer Black eloquently summarized this duality by stating, "The presence of noise makes markets inefficient, yet it also prevents people from exploiting this inefficiency". (Black 1986) This statement encapsulates the essence of the behavioral efficient market, acknowledging that while markets may deviate from the "price equals value" notion due to behavioral biases and limits to arbitrage, these very imperfections contribute to the market's resilience against exploitation.

Nonetheless, this field of behavioral finance is not without limitations. While it tells us the probable source of mispricing in the stock market, it does not give any technique on how to beat the stock market. We have provided some examples of how to construct factors derived from the biases based on our experience and the literature. Challenges remain that keep behavioral finance dependent on traditional theories. Nevertheless, with rapid advances in this field, it is expected that behavioral theories will become more robust and dominant in the future. Undisputedly, it has shaken the deeply rooted rationality and expected utility concepts that had dominated the literature for decades.

Appendix

In this appendix, we attempt to provide an exhaustive list of key areas where investor psychology can lead to persistent market inefficiencies that factor strategies may exploit.

The list of cognitive biases and their implications for market inefficiencies is a broad overview and should be considered with several caveats in mind. Cognitive biases are complex and often interlinked, with some positively or negatively influencing others, which adds to the intricacy of behavioral finance. For example, an

TABLE A8.1 Biases and Factor Strategies

Bias	Explanation
Affect Heuristic	Decisions are influenced by emotions, leading to investment choices that do not necessarily align with rational assessments. Factor strategies can exploit this by focusing on securities that are undervalued due to negative sentiment rather than poor fundamentals.
Affinity Bias	The tendency to favor investments in companies or sectors that the investor has an affinity for. Factor strategies can exploit this by identifying overvalued sectors due to collective affinity bias.
Ambiguity Aversion	The tendency to avoid options for which the probability of a favorable outcome is unknown. Factor strategies can exploit this by investing in misunderstood or complex securities that are undervalued.
Anchoring	Investors anchor on particular reference points, such as the initial purchase price of a stock, which can prevent them from reacting appropriately to new information. Factor strategies might exploit this by identifying and trading on stocks that are mispriced relative to recent fundamental changes.
Attentional Bias	Investors pay more attention to emotionally striking events and overlook important, non-salient information. Factor strategies can exploit this by focusing on overlooked, fundamentally strong investments.
Availability Cascade	A self-reinforcing process in which a collective belief gains more plausibility through its increasing repetition in public discourse. Factor strategies can exploit this by focusing on data-driven analysis rather than popular opinion.
Availability Heuristic	Investors might overestimate the likelihood of events associated with memorable or recent occurrences, affecting their investment decisions. Factor strategies can take advantage of securities that are undervalued due to a lack of recent attention or overvalued due to recent hype.
Bandwagon Effect	The tendency to do (or believe) things because many other people do (or believe) the same. Factor strategies can exploit this by identifying stocks that may be overvalued due to the bandwagon effect and undervalued due to a lack thereof.
Base Rate Fallacy	Investors may ignore the base rate information (general information) and focus on specific information, leading to misjudgment of probabilities. Factor strategies can take advantage of this by adhering to probabilistic approaches that incorporate base rates into their analysis.
Belief Bias	The tendency to evaluate the strength of an argument based on the believability of its conclusion. Factor strategies can exploit this by focusing on the quality of the data and the robustness of investment models.
Choice-Supportive Bias	Remembering one's choices as better than they actually were. This can lead to sticking with underperforming investments. Factor strategies can exploit this by remaining objective and regularly reassessing investment choices.

Bias	Explanation
Clustering Illusion	The tendency to see patterns in random events. This can lead to erroneous beliefs in trends and subsequently to incorrect trading. Factor strategies can exploit this by applying statistical rigor to distinguish between real trends and randomness.
Confirmation Bias	This bias leads investors to pay attention to information that confirms their pre-existing beliefs and ignore disconfirming evidence. This can result in slow price adjustments to true value, which factor strategies can exploit by using objective measures to guide investment decisions.
Conservatism Bias	Investors are too slow to update their beliefs in response to recent evidence. Factor strategies can exploit this by rapidly incorporating new information to adjust valuations.
Control Bias	Overestimating one's ability to control events can lead to an overestimation of investment skills. Factor strategies can exploit this by maintaining a disciplined, process-driven investment approach.
Denomination Effect	The tendency to spend more money when it is denominated in small amounts (e.g., coins) rather than large amounts (e.g., bills). Factor strategies can exploit this by focusing on the absolute value of investments rather than share price or denominations.
Disposition Effect	Investors exhibit a tendency to sell winning investments and hold onto losing ones due to the pain of realizing losses. This can lead to underreaction to new information. Factor strategies can exploit this by buying stocks that are being sold due to the disposition effect and may rebound upon correction.
Dunning-Kruger Effect	Unskilled individuals tend to overestimate their own abilities, leading to poor investment decisions. Factor strategies can exploit this by relying on objective measures of skill and performance.
Endowment Effect	Investors value assets they own more than those they do not, leading to a reluctance to sell owned assets even when it is rational to do so. Factor strategies can exploit this by identifying assets that are undervalued because they are not "endowed" by the majority of investors.
Experimenter's Bias	A form of confirmation bias wherein one might unintentionally influence the outcome of a study. In investing, analysts might seek data that supports their thesis. Factor strategies can exploit this by using blind or double-blind methods in analysis.
Familiarity Bias	The tendency to invest in familiar securities, such as domestic stocks or well-known companies, regardless of their fundamentals. Factor strategies can target undervalued foreign or less-known stocks that are neglected due to familiarity bias.
Functional Fixedness	The tendency to see objects as only working in a particular way. Investors might see securities in a traditional context, missing out on innovative uses or markets. Factor strategies can exploit this by seeking out securities with unrecognized potential.
Gambler's Fallacy	The belief that future probabilities are altered by past events, such as expecting a run of one outcome to be balanced by the other outcomes in the short run. Factor strategies might exploit this by investing in securities that have been irrationally devalued due to a recent run of "bad luck".

Bias	Explanation
Halo Effect	The tendency to let an overall impression shape specific judgments, including stock evaluations. Factor strategies can exploit this by objective, granular analysis of a company's fundamentals.
Herding	Investors often copy the actions of others rather than relying on their own analysis, which can lead to bubbles or crashes. Contrarian factor strategies can take advantage of the subsequent price corrections when the herd inevitably changes direction.
Hindsight Bias	After an event has occurred, investors tend to see it as having been predictable, despite there being no objective basis for predicting it. This can lead to overconfidence in predictive abilities. Factor strategies can exploit this by focusing on objective historical data rather than subjective narratives.
Home Bias	The preference for domestic investments over foreign ones, often leading to a concentration of undiversified portfolios. Global factor strategies can benefit by diversifying across countries and exploiting valuation discrepancies due to home bias.
Hyperbolic Discounting	A tendency to prefer smaller, immediate rewards over larger, later rewards. This can result in an underinvestment in long-term growth opportunities. Factor strategies can exploit this by focusing on undervalued long-term investments neglected by short-term focused investors.
Illusion of Control	The belief that one can influence outcomes over which they objectively have no control. This can lead to increased trading and risk-taking. Factor strategies can exploit this by taking a disciplined approach to investment, unaffected by this illusion.
Illusion of Truth Effect	The tendency to believe information to be correct after repeated exposure. Factor strategies can exploit this by avoiding popular, over-discussed investments that may not have solid fundamentals.
Illusion of Validity	Believing that one's judgments are accurate, especially when available information is consistent. Factor strategies can exploit this by challenging assumptions and seeking disconfirming evidence.
In-group Bias	Favoring members of one's own group or familiar entities. This can lead to a bias in stock selection favoring familiar or domestic companies. Factor strategies can exploit this by ensuring a globally diversified portfolio.
Information Bias	The tendency to seek information even when it does not affect action. Investors may trade on information that has no real relevance to stock value. Factor strategies can exploit this by focusing on relevant information that truly affects a company's intrinsic value.
Law of Small Numbers	The improper belief that small-sized samples closely resemble the population from which they are drawn. Factor strategies can exploit this by using larger and more representative data sets to inform investment decisions.
Loss Aversion	Investors' tendency to prefer avoiding losses rather than acquiring equivalent gains. This can lead to overpricing of low-volatility assets and underpricing of high-volatility assets. Factor strategies can exploit this by overweighting undervalued risky assets and underweighting overvalued less risky assets.

Bias	Explanation
Mental Accounting	Investors often segregate funds into different mental accounts for irrational reasons, which can influence their trading behavior. Factor strategies can exploit the stocks that are mispriced due to the mental accounting of a large number of investors.
Moral Credential Effect	After doing something that helps to establish a positive self-image, individuals are more likely to make decisions that could be seen as immoral, unethical, or otherwise problematic. Factor strategies can exploit this by maintaining consistent ethical standards in investment practices.
Myopic Loss Aversion	The tendency to focus on avoiding short-term losses rather than achieving long-term gains. This can lead to an overemphasis on volatility reduction at the expense of returns. Factor strategies can exploit this by taking a longer-term view in their investment approach.
Narrative Fallacy	The tendency to create a story or pattern from incomplete or random data. This can lead to overvalued "story stocks" that have appealing narratives but poor fundamentals. Factor strategies can exploit this by focusing on solid, undervalued companies that lack a compelling narrative.
Neglect of Probability	Investors often disregard the magnitude of probabilities, such as the likelihood of rare events. Factor strategies can exploit this by focusing on risk-adjusted returns rather than potential extreme outcomes.
Optimism Bias	The belief that positive outcomes are more likely than negative ones. This can lead to overvalued stocks due to irrational exuberance. Factor strategies can exploit this by taking short positions in overhyped stocks.
Outcome Bias	Judging a decision based on the outcome rather than the quality of the decision at the time it was made. Factor strategies can exploit this by focusing on process over outcomes.
Overconfidence	Investors with overconfidence bias tend to overestimate their knowledge and ability to predict market movements, leading to excessive trading and potential market mispricings. Factor strategies can exploit this by taking positions against prevailing market trends or in securities neglected by overconfident traders.
Overreaction	The tendency to react too strongly to news, leading to excessive movement in stock prices. Factor strategies can take advantage of the subsequent corrections when prices revert to mean.
Paradox of Choice	Too many choices can lead to anxiety and inability to make a decision. Factor strategies can exploit this by offering a simplified, focused investment approach.
Planning Fallacy	Underestimating the time, costs, and risks of future actions and overestimating the benefits. Factor strategies can exploit this by applying more realistic assumptions and projections.
Post-Purchase Rationalization	Justifying a purchase by overlooking any faults seen. This can lead to holding on to poor investments. Factor strategies can exploit this by being more objective about investment performance.
Projection Bias	Expecting future preferences to align with current preferences, leading to poor long-term investment decisions. Factor strategies can exploit this by taking a more dynamic approach to changing market conditions.

Bias	Explanation
Recency Bias	Overweighting recent observations compared to historical data. Factor strategies can exploit this by maintaining a long-term perspective and capitalizing on the mispricing of assets whose value is underestimated due to recent poor performance.
Regret Aversion	Fear of making an investment decision that turns out to be wrong may lead investors to not take necessary actions. Factor strategies can exploit this by taking positions in stocks that are undervalued because investors are too cautious to invest in them.
Representativeness Heuristic	Judging the probability of an event by finding a "comparable known" event and assuming the probabilities will be similar. This can lead to pattern recognition errors. Factor strategies can exploit this by relying on comprehensive data rather than heuristic shortcuts.
Restraint Bias	Overestimating one's ability to control impulsive behavior. Factor strategies can exploit this by implementing strict trading rules and discipline.
Self-Aattribution Bias	Taking credit for successes but blaming external factors for failures. This can lead to persistent overestimation of one's investment acumen. Factor strategies can exploit this by implementing strategies that are self-critical and data-driven.
Self-Serving Bias	The tendency to claim more responsibility for successes than failures. Factor strategies can exploit this by maintaining an impartial view of investment performance.
Sentiment Bias	The tendency for investors to make decisions based on human emotions and feelings rather than factual data. Factor strategies can exploit this by using sentiment indicators to identify potential mispriced securities.
Spotlight Effect	Overestimating the amount that others notice your appearance or behavior. In investing, this could translate to overvaluing the impact of one's trades on the market. Factor strategies can exploit this by recognizing the true market impact of investment decisions.
Status Quo Bias	The preference for the current state of affairs. The current baseline is taken as a reference point, and any change from that baseline is perceived as a loss. Factor strategies can capitalize on this by identifying and investing in stocks that are undervalued because they represent a change from the status quo.
Sunk Cost Fallacy	The tendency to continue an endeavor once an investment in money, effort, or time has been made. Factor strategies can exploit this by making decisions based on current and future potential rather than past costs.
Survivorship Bias	The tendency to focus on survivors rather than non-survivors, leading to an overly optimistic belief that success is more common than it actually is. This can affect stock selection and risk assessment. Factor strategies can exploit this by considering the full universe of securities, including those that have failed or underperformed.
Time Series Momentum	Investors may assume that trends will continue indefinitely. Factor strategies can exploit this by identifying when momentum is likely to reverse based on historical patterns and mean reversion.

Bias	Explanation
Unit Bias	The tendency to want to complete a unit of a given item or task. Investors may be influenced to round up their holdings. Factor strategies can exploit this by focusing on the optimal investment size based on valuation, not units.
Zero-Risk Bias	Preference for reducing a small risk to zero over a greater reduction in a larger risk. Factor strategies can exploit this by identifying and investing in assets that are undervalued due to an irrational aversion to small risks.

overconfidence bias may exacerbate confirmation bias, leading to a compounded effect on investment decisions.

It is also important to note that the impact of biases can vary widely depending on the context, including market conditions and individual characteristics. While factor strategies aim to exploit these biases, the reality of doing so is fraught with challenges. Markets are influenced by a multitude of factors beyond these biases, including economic indicators, regulatory changes, and technological advancements.

Additionally, some biases can create feedback loops, reinforcing certain market behaviors and potentially leading to bubbles or crashes. This illustrates the dynamic nature of financial markets, where the influence of cognitive biases can change over time and requires ongoing research to fully understand.

The study of behavioral finance is still evolving, and while we recognize the potential for biases to cause market inefficiencies, exploiting these inefficiencies is not straightforward. Successful exploitation of cognitive biases requires a nuanced understanding of these psychological drivers, as well as the ability to adapt to a constantly changing market environment. As such, there is a substantial need for continued research to deepen our understanding of how these biases interact with each other and with the broader economic landscape, with the aim of improving investment decision-making and market efficiency.

References

Aboody, D., O. Even-Tov, R. Lehavy, and B. Trueman (2018). Overnight returns and firm-specific investor sentiment. *Journal of Financial and Quantitative Analysis* 53(2), 485–505.

An, L. (2016). Asset pricing when traders sell extreme winners and losers. *Review of Financial Studies* 29(3), 823–861.

Barber, B. M. and T. Odean (2008). All that glitters: The effect of attention and news on the buying behavior of individual and institutional investors. *Review of Financial Studies* 21(2), 785–818.

Barberis, N. (2018). Chapter 2 Psychology-based models of asset prices and trading volume. In B. D. Bernheim, S. DellaVigna, and D. Laibson (Eds.), *Handbook of Behavioral Economics – Foundations and Applications 1*, Volume 1 of Handbook of Behavioral Economics: Applications and Foundations 1, pp. 79–175. North-Holland.

Barberis, N. and M. Huang (2006). The loss aversion/narrow framing approach to the equity premium puzzle Working paper No. 12378. NBER.

Barberis, N., L. J. Jin, and B. Wang (2021). Prospect theory and stock market anomalies. *Journal of Finance* 76(5), 2639–2687.

Barberis, N., A. Mukherjee, and B. Wang (2016). Prospect theory and stock returns: An empirical test. *Review of Financial Studies* 29(11), 3068–3107.

Barberis, N. and R. Thaler (2003). Chapter 18 A survey of behavioral finance. In *Financial Markets and Asset Pricing*, Volume 1 of Handbook of the Economics of Finance, pp. 1053–1128. Elsevier.

Bernoulli, D. (1738/1954). Exposition of a new theory on the measurement of risk. *Econometrica* 22(1), 23–36.

Black, F. (1986). Noise. *Journal of Finance* 41(3), 529–543.

Bordalo, P., N. Gennaioli, and A. Shleifer (2012). Salience theory of choice under risk. *The Quarterly Journal of Economics* 127 (3), 1243–1285.

Brown, A. L. and J. H. Kagel (2009). Behavior in a simplified stock market: The status quo bias, the disposition effect and the ostrich effect. *Annals of Finance* 5(1), 1–14.

Byun, S. J., S. S. Lim, and S. H. Yun (2016). Continuing overreaction and stock return predictability. *Journal of Financial and Quantitative Analysis* 51(6), 215–2046.

Campbell, S. D. and S. Sharpe (2009). Anchoring bias in consensus forecasts and its effect on market prices. *Journal of Financial and Quantitative Analysis* 44(2), 369–390.

Chan, L. K. C., N. Jegadeesh, and J. Lakonishok (1996). Momentum strategies. *Journal of Finance* 51(5), 1681–1713.

Christie, W. G. and R. D. Huang (1995). Following the Pied Piper: Do individual returns herd around the market? *Financial Analysts Journal* 51(4), 31–37.

Cosemans, M., and R. Frehen (2021). Salience theory and stock prices: Empirical evidence. *Journal of Financial Economics* 140(2), 460–483.

Daniel, K. D., D. A. Hirshleifer, and L. Sun (2020). Short- and long-horizon behavioral factors. *Review of Financial Studies* 33(4), 1673–1736.

Daniel, K. D. and S. Titman (2006). Market reactions to tangible and intangible information. *Journal of Finance* 61(4), 1605–1643.

Dhar, R. and A. Kumar (2001). A non-random walk down the main street: Impact of price trends on trading decisions of individual investors (Working Paper). Yale School of Management.

Fama, E. F. (1970). Efficient capital markets: A review of theory and empirical work. *Journal of Finance* 25(2), 383–417.

Fama, E. F. and K. R. French (1993). Common risk factors in the returns on stocks and bonds. *Journal of Financial Economics* 33(1), 3–56.

Grinblatt, M. and B. Han (2005). Prospect theory, mental accounting, and momentum. *Journal of Financial Economics* 78(2), 311–339.

Hirshleifer, D. (2015). Behavioral finance. *Annual Review of Financial Economics* 7, 133–159.

Kahneman, D. and A. Tversky (1979). Prospect Theory: An analysis of decision under risk. *Econometrica* 47(2), 263–292.

Kliger, D. and A. Kudryavtsev (2010). The availability heuristic and investors' reaction to company specific events. *Journal of Behavioral Finance* 11(1), 50–65.

Lakonishok, J., A. Shleifer, and R. W. Vishny. (1991). Do institutional investors destabilize stock prices- evidence on herding and feedback trading? Working paper No. 3846. NBER.

Lee, B., J. O'Brien, and K. Sivaramakrishnan (2008). An analysis of financial analysts' optimism in long-term growth forecasts. *Journal of Behavioral Finance* 9(3), 171–184.

Lochstoer, L. A. and P. C. Tetlock (2022). Model-free mispricing factors. Columbia Business School Working paper. Available at SSRN: http://dx.doi.org/10.2139/ssrn.4113272.

Lou, D., C. Polk, and S. Skouras (2019). A tug of war: Overnight versus intraday expected returns. *Journal of Financial Economics* 134(1), 192–213.

Markowitz, H. M. (1952). Portfolio selection. *Journal of Finance* 7(1), 77–91.

Pontiff, J. and A. Woodgate (2008). Share issuance and cross-sectional returns. *Journal of Finance* 63(2), 921–945.

Sewell, M. (2007). *Behavioural finance*. Working paper.

Shefrin, H. and M. Statman (1985). The disposition to sell winners too early and ride losers too long: Theory and evidence. *Journal of Finance* 40(3), 777–790.

Shefrin, H. and M. Statman (2011). Behavioral finance in the financial crisis: Market efficiency, Minsky, and Keynes (Working paper). Santa Clara University.

Shiller, R. J. (1981). Do stock prices move too much to be justified by subsequent changes in dividends? *American Economic Review* 71(3), 421–436.

Statman, M. (2008). What is behavioral finance? In *Handbook of Finance* (Vol. II). New Jersey: John Wiley & Sons, Inc.

Statman, M. (2018). Behavioral efficient markets. *Journal of Portfolio Management* 44(3), 76–87.

Sun, K., H. Wang, and Y. Zhu (2023). Salience theory in price and trading volume: Evidence from China. *Journal of Empirical Finance* 70, 38–61.

Thaler, R. (1999). Mental accounting matters. *Journal of Behavioral Decision Making* 12(3), 183–206.

Tversky, A. and D. Kahneman (1971). Belief in the law of small numbers. *Psychological Bulletin* 76(2), 105–110.

Tversky, A. and D. Kahneman (1973). Availability: A heuristic for judging frequency and probability. *Cognitive Psychology* 5(2), 207–232.

Tversky, A. and D. Kahneman (1974). Judgment under uncertainty: Heuristics and biases. *Science* 185(4157), 1124–1131.

Tversky, A. and D. Kahneman (1992). Advances in prospect theory: Cumulative representation of uncertainty. *Journal of Risk and Uncertainty* 5(4), 297–323.

von Neumann, J. and O. Morgenstern (1944). *Theory of Games and Economic Behavior*. Princeton: Princeton University Press.

Wang, H., J. Yan, and J. Yu (2017). Reference-dependent preferences and the risk–return trade-off. *Journal of Financial Economics* 123(2), 395–414.

Weisbrod, E. (2019). Stockholders' unrealized returns and the market reaction to financial disclosures. *Journal of Finance* 74(2), 899–942.

9

OPTION INFORMATION

9.1. Nature of Option Information

The integration of option trading data into quantitative investment strategies represents a dynamic frontier in the realm of financial markets. Options, as financial derivatives, are intimately connected with the underlying stock, forming a symbiotic relationship that offers unique opportunities for quantitative factor research and investment analysis.

At its core, the relationship between options and stocks is fundamental yet multifaceted. Options derive their value from the price movements of the underlying stock, effectively serving as a financial instrument that grants the holder the right, but not the obligation, to buy or sell the underlying asset at a predetermined price (strike price) within a specified period (expiration date). This linkage between options and stocks forms the basis for a myriad of trading strategies and investment approaches employed by both institutional and retail investors.

Quantitative factor research seeks to dissect and understand the underlying drivers of asset returns, aiming to identify systematic patterns and anomalies that can be exploited for profit. In this context, options trading data provides a rich source of information that can enhance the depth and breadth of quantitative factor research. By incorporating options data into quantitative models, researchers can gain insights into market sentiment, volatility expectations, and potential future price movements, thus augmenting the predictive power of their investment strategies.

One of the primary ways in which options data intersects with quantitative factor research is through the exploration of implied volatility surfaces. Implied volatility, a key parameter derived from options pricing models such as the Black-Scholes-Merton model, reflects the market's expectations of future volatility. By analyzing implied volatility surfaces across different strikes and maturities, quantitative researchers can uncover valuable insights into market sentiment, risk perceptions, and potential

DOI: 10.4324/9781003480204-9

mispricing, thereby informing their investment decisions. Additionally, we will discuss stochastic processes, including models incorporating jump processes to quantify jumps, providing yet another avenue for the development of factors.

The Black-Scholes-Merton model

The Black-Scholes-Merton model, developed by Fischer Black, Myron Scholes, and Robert C. Merton in the early 1970s, had a profound impact on the financial market. Their collaborative efforts built upon the research of Paul Samuelson and Robert C. Merton on stochastic calculus and option pricing theory. The Black-Scholes model was introduced by Fischer Black and Myron Scholes in their paper "The Pricing of Options and Corporate Liabilities" in 1973 (Black and Scholes 1973). Concurrently, Robert Merton developed a similar model and presented his results in "Theory of Rational Option Pricing" in the same year (Merton 1973). Merton's contributions included the extension of the Black-Scholes model to incorporate dividends and the application of a continuous-time finance framework.

It is ironic that when Black and Scholes first submitted such a powerful and original work, it was considered so unconventional and got rejected by the *Journal of Finance*, the *Review of Economics and Statistics,* and the *Journal of Political Economy* (JPE). As of right now, the *Journal of Finance* considers the rejection one of its biggest mistakes. It was not until two very famous American economists, Merton Miller and Eugene Fama, suggested *JPE* take another look at the work that this influential paper was eventually published in *JPE* in 1973.

The model's influence extended beyond academia. The model became widely adopted by financial institutions, options traders, and market participants around the world. It provided a standardized framework for pricing options contracts, enabling more efficient trading strategies and risk management practices. The growth of options trading on exchanges and the development of complex financial instruments can be attributed, in part, to the model's influence. Furthermore, the model's introduction sparked advancements in quantitative finance and the use of mathematical models in various areas of financial analysis and decision-making.

Myron Scholes and Robert C. Merton were awarded the Nobel Prize in Economic Sciences in 1997 for their contributions to the development of the Black-Scholes-Merton model. However, it is important to note that Fischer Black, who made significant contributions to the model's development, had passed away in 1995 and was ineligible for the Nobel Prize.

The Black-Scholes-Merton model revolutionized the options market by providing a standardized framework for pricing options contracts. Its introduction allowed traders and investors to determine the fair value of options, facilitating more efficient trading and risk management strategies. The impact of the model was particularly notable in the growth of options trading on exchanges and the emergence of derivatives markets.

Financial institutions also benefited from the model's introduction. It influenced risk management practices by providing a theoretical foundation for valuing and hedging options. The ability to hedge options using the Black-Scholes-Merton model played a crucial role in the expansion of derivatives markets and the development of complex financial instruments.

However, the model has faced criticisms. Its assumptions, such as constant volatility and efficient markets, have been questioned during periods of extreme market volatility. The financial market crashes of 1987 and the Global Financial Crisis of 2007–2008 raised doubts about the model's ability to accurately capture real-world risks and highlighted the limitations of relying solely on mathematical models for risk assessment.

Despite its limitations, the Black-Scholes-Merton model remains a foundational tool in quantitative finance. Its development, publication, and subsequent impact on the financial market have left a lasting legacy in options pricing, risk management practices, and the growth of derivatives markets.

Moreover, options data can be leveraged to develop and refine quantitative factor models designed to capture specific risk premia and market inefficiencies. For instance, factors such as option skewness, volatility risk premium, and option sentiment have been extensively studied and incorporated into quantitative investment strategies to enhance risk-adjusted returns and diversify portfolio exposures.

In this chapter, we explore the myriad ways in which options trading data can be utilized in quantitative investment research. From dissecting implied volatility surfaces to developing proprietary factor models, we delve into the intricacies of incorporating options data into quantitative strategies, offering insights and methodologies to aid investors in navigating the complexities of financial markets and optimizing their investment outcomes. Specifically, Section 9.2 provides a condensed review of the basic knowledge and mathematics of options. Some recent works on option information as factors are discussed in Section 9.3. Section 9.4 introduces the Q quant techniques to construct jump factors. Section 9.5 concludes.

9.2. Option Mathematics – A Condensed Review

In and of itself, the topic of financial options (or derivatives) is enormous. It involves sophisticated valuation frameworks, heavy mathematics like stochastic calculus, numerical algorithms like Monte Carlo, trees, and finite difference, trading strategies involving Greeks, volatility surfaces involving calibration, volatility models like geometric Brownian motion, local volatility, stochastic volatility, and stochastic local volatility, among others. These are all topics on their own, and therefore a full treatment of these topics is beyond the scope of this book. Instead, at the risk of oversimplification, we try to give a simple discussion. This is with the purpose of exploring the information that could be extracted from options for factor investing purposes.

9.2.1. Nature of Options

Options, also known as derivatives, are sophisticated financial instruments whose value is contingent upon the performance of an underlying asset. This asset can be diverse, spanning equities, fixed income securities, currencies, and commodities, offering a broad spectrum for potential strategies and applications.

The two primary types of options are call and put options. A call option empowers the holder with the right (though not the obligation) to purchase the underlying asset at a predetermined price, or the strike price, on or before a specific expiration date. On the flip side, a put option confers the right (but not the obligation) to sell the underlying asset at the strike price up to the expiration date. The acquisition of these rights requires the payment of a premium, which constitutes the cost of the option contract. This premium is influenced by several factors, including the underlying asset's price, its price volatility, the time until the option's expiration, and the prevailing interest rates.

In the nuanced landscape of options, we encounter "vanilla" and "exotic" options, each with distinct characteristics. Vanilla options, encompassing European and American options, represent the most fundamental forms of options. European options are characterized by their restriction that they can only be exercised at the expiration date, not before. American options offer more flexibility, allowing the holder to exercise the option at any point up to and including the expiration date, providing a broader range of strategic possibilities.

Exotic options, in contrast, are more complex and include a variety of non-standard options that have more complicated features and payoffs. These can include options with multiple triggers, barriers, or conditions that affect their valuation and execution, offering tailored solutions for specific hedging or speculative needs but also introducing additional layers of risk and complexity.

The classification of options extends further based on their intrinsic value in relation to the underlying asset's current price. An option is deemed "in-the-money" (ITM) if its exercise leads to profit, "at-the-money" (ATM) when the strike price equals the underlying asset's market price, and "out-of-the-money" (OTM) if exercising yields no financial gain.

Options serve a multiplicity of functions for investors, from speculative ventures aiming for significant returns to hedging strategies designed to mitigate risk, and even as mechanisms for generating income streams. Their inherent flexibility and capacity for leverage make them indispensable tools in the arsenal of modern financial market participants, catering to the diverse strategies of traders, investors, and institutional entities across the globe. For further reading on the intricacies of options, one may refer to the monograph of Hull (2014), a comprehensive resource that delves into the mechanics, valuation, and employment of derivative securities in contemporary finance.

9.2.2. Black-Scholes Formula

Valuing an option is complicated due to its non-linear payoff profile. Valuation methods can broadly be classified into three classes: Monte Carlo simulation, finite differences (with trees being a special case), and analytical solution. The analytical solution provides a closed-form formula and is the most accurate. However, analytical solutions are only available for vanilla options, with the influential Black-Scholes formula being the most well-known example.

The Black-Scholes formula for European call options is

$$C = Se^{-qT}N(d_1) - Ke^{-rT}N(d_2),$$

where

$$d_1 = \frac{\ln\left(\frac{S}{K}\right) + \left(r - q + \frac{\sigma^2}{2}\right)T}{\sigma\sqrt{T}},$$

$$d_2 = d_1 - \sigma\sqrt{T}. \tag{9.1}$$

In Equation (9.1), C is the European call option price, S is the current price of the underlying asset, and it is also known as the spot price, K is the strike price, r is the continuous compounded risk-free rate, q is the continuous dividend (or income) yield of the underlying asset, T is the maturity of the option in annual term, σ is the volatility of the option which is the key element in valuation, and finally $N(.)$ represents the cumulative distribution function of the standard normal distribution.

Similarly, for European put options, the valuation formula is

$$P = Ke^{-rT}N(-d_2) - Se^{-qT}N(-d_1),$$

where

$$N(-d_2) = 1 - N(d_2), \tag{9.2}$$

because of the symmetrical property of normal distribution. Figure 9.1 provides an example using the payoffs and prices of European call and put options. In this

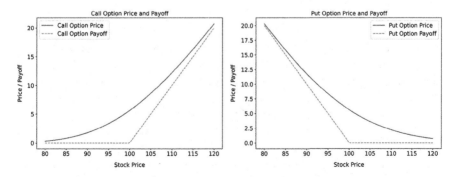

FIGURE 9.1 Payoffs and Prices of European Call and Put Options

example, the strike price for both is set to 100, $T = 0.5$, $\sigma = 20\%$, and both the risk-free rate and dividend yield are assumed to be 0. We vary the stock price from 80 to 120, and plot the price and payoff as the spot price changes.

One important property for European put and call options is the "put-call parity". It establishes a defined relationship between the price of a European call option (C) and a European put option (P) with identical strike prices (K) and expiration dates (T). This parity articulates that the difference in price between a call option and a put option equates to the difference between the present value of the strike price (discounted by the risk-free rate over the life of the options) and the current price of the underlying asset. Formally, the put-call parity is represented by,

$$C - P = S - PV(K), \tag{9.3}$$

where $PV(K)$ represents the present value of the strike price. The elegance of put-call parity lies in its ability to highlight the intrinsic connection between calls and puts, providing a framework that supports both speculative strategies and risk management techniques within the options market. It is a concept that remains central to modern financial theory and practice.

9.2.3. Implied Volatility and Implied Volatility Surface

While the Black-Scholes model represents a landmark achievement in the valuation of options, it has been observed that market prices for options often deviate from the theoretical prices suggested by the model. Notably, out-of-the-money (OTM) options tend to be priced higher in the market than the model would predict. As a consequence, the Black-Scholes formula is frequently employed in a reverse engineering manner. Specifically, when the market price of an option (be it a call or put) is known, the volatility parameter (σ) is determined in such a way that the theoretical price derived from the Black-Scholes model aligns with the observed market price. This process leads to the extraction of the so-called "implied volatility" from the market prices, based on the Black-Scholes framework.

The fundamental premise of option valuation is the replication and hedging assumption, which posits that a hedged portfolio can be constructed to be essentially risk-free. This concept is encapsulated in the risk-neutral valuation framework, wherein future financial outcomes are assessed using risk-neutral probabilities, also referred to as the Q-measure, as introduced in Section 1.1. Within the Black-Scholes formula, the probability of exercising a call option is denoted by $N(d_2)$, whereas for a put option, it is $N(-d_2)$. Given that d_2 is a function of the implied volatility σ, this parameter can be interpreted as the market's consensus on future volatility. This perspective is particularly insightful as it mirrors the market participants' expectations regarding the future risk associated with the underlying asset.

An intriguing phenomenon observed in options markets is the formation of an implied volatility surface for options tied to the same underlying asset. This surface varies across different strike prices and maturities, exhibiting dimensions of moneyness—often expressed as a ratio between the spot price and the strike price—and tenors, which denote varying expiration dates. Figure 9.2 provides an example of implied volatility surface.

A common characteristic of the implied volatility surface is that lower strike options generally exhibit higher implied volatilities than their higher strike counterparts, leading to a downward-sloping implied volatility skew. A steeper skew indicates higher implied volatilities for lower strike puts, reflecting a higher downside risk perception.

Additionally, the term structure of implied volatilities, which depicts implied volatilities across different maturities, can offer valuable information about the underlying asset. A typical term structure is mildly upward-sloping, reflecting increasing uncertainty over longer time horizons. Conversely, an inverted term structure might indicate the market's anticipation of significant short-term events or disturbances impacting the asset.

9.2.4. Stochastic Calculus and Itō's Lemma

When valuing exotic options, where analytical solutions are often not feasible due to their complexity, we are compelled to employ numerical methods. These include Monte Carlo simulations (MC) and finite difference (FD) methods, both of which are deeply rooted in the principles of stochastic calculus. Stochastic calculus provides the framework for modeling the random evolution of prices and other

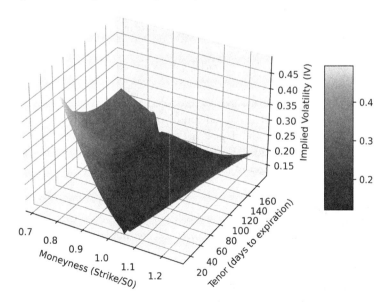

FIGURE 9.2. An Example of Implied Volatility Surface

financial variables over time, typically using stochastic differential equations (SDEs). The SDEs capture the intricate dynamics of the derivative's payoff, incorporating elements such as path dependency and early exercise features. The expected value of these payoffs, as described by the SDEs, is what MC and FD methods strive to solve, thus enabling the valuation of exotic options with a level of precision that would be unattainable through analytical means alone.

Brownian Motion

Standard Brownian motion, also known as Wiener process, is a fundamental concept in stochastic calculus and is central to the modern theory of finance, particularly in the modeling of random behavior in stock prices and other financial variables. It is defined as a continuous-time stochastic process W_t that satisfies the following properties:

1. Initiation: $W_0 - 0$, which means that the process starts at zero.
2. Independence: The increments $W_{t+s} - W_s$ are independent for all $t > 0$ and $s \geq 0$.
3. Stationarity: The increments $W_{t+s} - W_s$ are normally distributed with mean zero and variance t, i.e., $W_{t+s} - W_s \tilde{N}(0, t)$.

In addition to these properties, W_t is continuous but is nowhere differentiable. Mathematically, standard Brownian motion is a limit of random walk processes as the time steps become infinitesimally small. If we let dW_t denote the change in the process over an infinitesimally small-time interval dt, then it is normally distributed with mean zero and variance dt. Another key property of Brownian motion, for which we shall not give a proof, is nonzero quadratic variation. It states that, in infinitesimal difference form, the following holds true,

$$(dW_t)^2 = dt. \tag{9.4}$$

One of the most profound results associated with Brownian motion is Itō's lemma, which is used to find the differential of a function of a stochastic process, leading to the Itō calculus, an integral part of financial mathematics. As we will see shortly, this nonzero quadratic variation of Brownian motion has significant implications in the derivation of Itō's lemma.

Geometric Brownian Motion

Standard Brownian motion is not the most suitable model for stock prices mainly due to two reasons: it can take on negative values, which is not possible for stock prices, and it does not reflect the proportional nature of stock price movements. Stock prices are expected to change by percentages rather than absolute amounts, and the risk and return of stocks are typically proportional to the stock price itself.

Geometric Brownian motion (GBM) addresses these issues and provides a more realistic model for stock price dynamics. It models stock prices using a continuous-time stochastic process where the percentage changes in price are normally distributed. Specifically, the infinitesimal rate change of the stock price follows a continuous diffusion with a drift component. The GBM is defined by the following SDE,

$$\frac{dS_t}{S_t} = \mu dt + \sigma dW_t. \tag{9.5}$$

Here, S_t represents the stock price at time t, μ is the drift of the process, signifying deterministic growth with infinitesimal time changes, or the expected return, and σ is the volatility of the stock. This model ensures that stock prices remain positive, as they evolve in a multiplicative rather than additive manner. The GBM also incorporates the key feature of volatility scaling with the stock price. These characteristics make GBM a preferred model over standard Brownian motion for describing stock price movements in financial markets.

Itō's Lemma

Brownian motion provides a framework for people to study stock prices. However, as for financial derivatives, their prices are functions of the underlying assets. Let $f(W_t)$ be a continuous and smooth function of the Brownian motion W_t. In financial mathematics, an important topic is to study how $f(W_t)$ changes within an infinitesimal time interval, i.e., the properties of dt. As we will show shortly, classical calculus is useless in analyzing dt, but the Itō calculus proposed by Japanese mathematician Itō Kiyoshi effectively resolves the issue and lays a solid foundation for stochastic analysis.

We show first why classical calculus does not work. Suppose that we apply the chain rule to find dt,

$$df = \left(\frac{dW_t}{dt} f'(W_t) \right) dt. \tag{9.6}$$

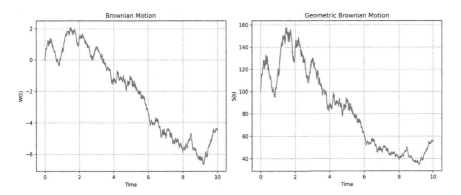

FIGURE 9.3. Brownian Motion and Geometric Brownian Motion

To see why it is incorrect, recall that W_t is not differentiable, and therefore the differentiation dW_t/dt does not exit. As a result, the above attempt fails. One possible way to work around this problem is to try to describe df in terms of dW_t, rather than dW_t/dt. In this case, we have,

$$df = f'(W_t)dW_t. \tag{9.7}$$

This new formula at least makes sense because both $f'(W_t)$ and dW_t can be computed. Unfortunately, this does not quite work. To see why, consider the Taylor expansion of $f(x)$ at x,

$$f(x + \Delta x) - f(x) = f'(x)(\Delta x) + \frac{f''(x)}{2}(\Delta x)^2 + \frac{f'''(x)}{6}(\Delta x)^3 + ... \tag{9.8}$$

When Δx approaches to 0, the dominant term in Equation (9.8) is the first term $f'(x)\Delta x$ and all other terms are of a smaller order of magnitude, which can be ignored. Therefore, we can write $df = f'(x)dx$. However, is this true for $x = W_t$? The answer is no. For $x = W_t$ we have,

$$f(W_t + \Delta W_t) - f(W_t) = f'(W_t)(\Delta W_t) + \frac{f''(W_t)}{2}(\Delta W_t)^2$$

$$+ \frac{f'''(W_t)}{6}(\Delta W_t)^3 + ... \tag{9.9}$$

Again, the first term $f'(W_t)\Delta W_t$ is still dominant. But can other terms be ignored compared to it? The answer is no due to the nonzero quadratic variation of W_t, which says $(dW_t)^2 = dt$. Since the quadratic variation is not 0, the second term in Equation (9.9) is no longer negligible. Itō calculus essentially tells us that we can make the substitution $(dW_t)^2 = dt$, and the remaining terms are negligible. Hence, we can derive,

$$df = f'(W_t)dW_t + \frac{1}{2}f''(W_t)dt. \tag{9.10}$$

Equation (9.10) is the basic form of Itō's lemma. Moving to the general case, suppose that we are given the dynamic of stochastic process,

$$dS_t = udt + vdW_t. \tag{9.11}$$

Then, by applying Itō's lemma, we can derive the dynamics of a twice-differentiable function of S_t, say $f(S_t)$, as follows,

$$df(S_t) = uf'(S_t)dt + vf'(S_t)dW_t + \frac{1}{2}v^2 f''(S_t)dt. \qquad (9.12)$$

Even more generally, the drift and diffusion coefficients, u and v, in Equation (9.11) can be functions of both S_t and t. Let $a(S_t, t)$ and $b(S_t, t)$ be the drift and diffusion coefficients. Then a stochastic process that satisfies the following SDE is called the Itō drift-diffusion process,

$$dS_t = a(S_t, t)dt + b(S_t, t)dW_t. \qquad (9.13)$$

By Itō's lemma, the expression of df in this case is,

$$df = \left(\frac{\partial f}{\partial t} + a\frac{\partial f}{\partial S_t} + \frac{b^2}{2}\frac{\partial^2 f}{\partial S_t^2}\right)dt + b\frac{\partial f}{\partial S_t}dW_t \qquad (9.14)$$

Equation (9.14) can be used to derive the Black-Scholes formula for option pricing, but we will not pursue that in this book.

Before moving on to the next topic, let us demonstrate the use of Itō's lemma with the GBM. Suppose we are given $dS_t = S_t\mu dt + S_t\sigma dW_t$ as in Equation (9.5). Now, we want to find the dynamics of the logarithm of S_t, i.e., $dlnS_t$. Compared to the general form as in Equation (9.11), we have $u = S_t\mu, v = S_t\sigma, f'(S_t) = 1/S_t, f''(S_t) = -1/S_t^2$. By Itō's lemma, we derive,

$$dlnS_t = \mu dt + \sigma dW_t - \frac{1}{2}\sigma^2 dt = \left(\mu - \frac{\sigma^2}{2}\right)dt + \sigma dW_t. \qquad (9.15)$$

Jump Diffusion Process

GBM assumes the infinitesimal rate change of stock price is a continuous diffusion with a drift component. However, stock prices usually undergo *jumps* associated with news or events. Let us discuss a more realistic stochastic process, y_t, which has the following *jump diffusion* form,

$$dy_t = a_t dt + b_t dW_t + J_t dq_t, \qquad (9.16)$$

where J_t is the jump size in case of a jump event q_t, which is a counting process, i.e., $dq_t = 1$ if there is a jump event and $dq_t = 0$ otherwise. For a twice-differentiable function $f(y_t)$, the general Itō's lemma with jump is,

$$df(y_t) = a_t f'(y_t)dt + b_t f'(y_t)dW_t + \frac{1}{2}f''(y_t)b_t^2 dt + \left\{f(y_t) - f(y_t^-)\right\}dq_t. \qquad (9.17)$$

In Equation (17), $f(y_t)$ is the value if a jump occurs, versus $f(y^{-t})$ being value immediately before a jump.

Let us work out another example which is closely related to jump factor analysis in Section 9.4. Suppose the log price process $y_t = lnS_t$ has the following form,

$$dlnS_t = \alpha_t dt + V_t^{1/2} dW_t + J_t dq_t, \tag{9.18}$$

Here α_t is the instantaneous drift, V_t is the instantaneous variance associated with the increment of Brownian motion (dWt. The process of logarithmic stock price, dlnSt, has a *smooth* component with variance growing at V_t per unit of time and a jump component, represented by J_t and q_t being a counting process. By Equation (9.17), $f(y_t) = \exp(lnS_t) = f'(y_t) = f''(y_t) = S_t, f(y_t) = \exp(lnS_t + J_t) = S_t\exp(J_t)$ in case of a jump when $dq_t = 1$, $f(y_t^-) = S_t$. Therefore, we have,

$$dG(y_t) = dS_t = S_t\alpha_t dt + S_t V_t^{1/2} dW_t + \frac{1}{2}S_t V_t dt + \{S\exp(J_t) - S\}dq_t. \tag{9.19}$$

Dividing by S_t and group the terms with dt gives,

$$\frac{dS_t}{S_t} = \left(\alpha_t + \frac{V_t}{2}\right)dt + V_t^{1/2}dW_t + (exp(J_t) - 1)dq_t. \tag{9.20}$$

We will use this result when we discuss the jump factor.

9.2.5. VIX Index

The VIX index, also known as the "fear gauge", is a widely tracked measure of market sentiment and volatility in the US equity markets. Understanding the construction of the VIX index and its implications for factor investing is essential for quantitative analysts and investors seeking to gauge market risk and incorporate volatility signals into their investment strategies.

The VIX index is calculated by the Chicago Board Options Exchange (CBOE) and is based on the prices of options on the S&P 500 index. Specifically, it represents the market's expectation of future volatility over the next 30 days. The VIX index is constructed using a formula that weights various S&P 500 options to estimate expected volatility. It is derived from the prices of both puts and calls and is calculated as a weighted average of implied volatilities.

The VIX index serves as a valuable indicator of market sentiment. High levels of VIX imply heightened fear or uncertainty among investors, while low levels indicate complacency or confidence. Factor models can incorporate VIX as a sentiment factor to adjust portfolio allocations accordingly.

Incorporating VIX information into factor investing provides valuable insights into market sentiment, risk dynamics, and volatility patterns. By understanding the construction of the VIX index and leveraging its signals effectively, quantitative analysts and investors can enhance their investment strategies, improve risk-adjusted returns, and navigate turbulent market conditions with greater confidence.

9.3. Option Information as Factors

9.3.1. Key Option Information

In Chapter 3, we explored the volatility factor, which is predominantly extracted from historical pricing data. Nonetheless, the realm of option markets unfolds a wealth of forward-looking information that has the potential to amplify quantitative factor models and enhance investment strategies. Option markets go beyond mere volatility; they unravel layers of market sentiment, highlight the dynamics of risk, and capture a picture of economic uncertainty. Such insights can endow investors with a strategic advantage as they traverse the intricacies of financial environments.

Implied Volatility

As mentioned previously in Section 9.2.3, implied volatility, derived from option prices, encapsulates market expectations of future volatility. It serves as a vital input for option pricing models and reflects traders' consensus views on future market movements.

Option Volume and Open Interest

Option volume and open interest stand as pivotal indicators of market activity and liquidity. A surge in these figures signals substantial market engagement, potentially pinpointing sectors of investor focus or indicating widespread hedging activities. The linkage between open interest, volume, and price dynamics has been subject to extensive empirical research, with studies suggesting correlations with future price movements (e.g., Pan and Poteshman 2006).

Volatility Skew

The volatility skew, observed through variations in implied volatility across different strike prices, offers insights into market perceptions of potential downside or upside risk. Skew patterns can inform trading strategies, particularly in hedging against extreme market events.

Option Greeks

The "Greeks", such as Delta, Gamma, and Theta, represent the sensitivities of option prices to various factors including movements in the underlying asset, volatility shifts, and the passage of time. Mastery of these derivatives is indispensable for crafting hedging strategies and for the dynamic management of portfolio risks. They help traders and investors understand how changes in underlying variables can impact the price and behavior of options. The five main Option Greeks are Delta, Gamma, Theta, Vega, and Rho. Let us explore each of them:

1. Delta (δ): Delta measures the sensitivity of an option's price to changes in the price of the underlying asset. It represents the change in the option price for a one-unit change in the underlying asset's price. Delta ranges from 0 to 1 for call options and -1 to 0 for put options. A delta of 0.5 implies that for every \$1 increase in the underlying asset's price, the option price increases by \$0.50 (for a call option) or decreases by \$0.50 (for a put option).

2. Gamma (Γ): Gamma measures the rate of change of an option's delta in response to changes in the price of the underlying asset. It represents the curvature of the delta. Gamma is highest for at-the-money options and decreases as the option moves further in or out of the money. A higher gamma means the option's delta is more sensitive to changes in the underlying asset's price.

3. Theta (Θ): Theta measures the rate of change in an option's price due to the passage of time. It quantifies the time decay or erosion of an option's value as it approaches its expiration date. Theta is typically negative, indicating that options lose value as time passes, assuming other factors remain unchanged. Theta accelerates as the expiration date approaches, particularly for options near or at the money.

4. Vega (ν): Vega measures the sensitivity of an option's price to changes in the implied volatility of the underlying asset. It indicates the impact of changing market expectations of future volatility on the option price. Higher vega means the option price is more sensitive to changes in implied volatility. Vega is crucial for assessing the impact of volatility changes on option prices.

5. Rho (ρ): Rho measures the sensitivity of an option's price to changes in the risk-free interest rate. It quantifies the impact of interest rate changes on the option price. Rho is generally more relevant for longer-term options. Positive rho indicates that the option price increases with an increase in interest rates, while negative rho suggests the option price decreases with higher interest rates.

Collectively, these option-derived metrics offer a multidimensional perspective on the market's future direction. When integrated with traditional financial analysis, they can bolster the robustness of investment strategies. As the financial landscape evolves, the utilization of options data in strategic planning is no longer a novel concept but a requisite for informed decision-making in the face of market uncertainties.

9.3.2. Variance Risk Premium

Beyond traditional volatility measures, option data can proxy economic uncertainty effectively. The Variance Risk Premium (VRP), introduced by Bali and Zhou (2016), captures unobserved economic uncertainty by comparing option-implied variance with realized variance. VRP has been linked to significant risk premiums in equity portfolios, highlighting its importance in risk management and asset allocation decisions.

Bali and Zhou (2016) define the expected variance under the risk–neutral measure as VIX on a monthly basis, i.e., $VIX^2/12$. Under the objective measure, the daily realized variance is calculated as $\sum_{i=1}^{78} r_i^2$ where r_i is the is the 5-minute log returns with 78 intraday 5-min returns from 9:30am to 4pm, including close-to-open interval. Monthly VRP at time t is defined as the difference between option-implied variance and the statistical expectation of the realized variance over the $[t, t+1]$ time interval.

Their empirical results from the size, book-to-market, momentum, and industry portfolios indicate that the conditional covariances of equity portfolios with market and uncertainty predict the time-series and cross-sectional variation in stock returns. Specifically, the equity portfolios that are highly correlated with economic uncertainty proxied by VRP carry a significant annualized 8% premium relative to portfolios that are minimally correlated with VRP.

9.3.3. Volatility Risk Premium

González-Urteaga and Rubio (2016) analyze the cross-sectional variation of the volatility risk premium at the portfolio level. The volatility risk premium they defined for each stock at the 30-day horizon is the difference between the corresponding realized volatility and the model-free implied volatility ($MFIV$) described by Britten-Jones and Neuberger (2000) and the extension by Jiang and Tian (2005).

Particularly, $MFIV$ for asset i over the interval $[t, t+1]$ is calculated by an integral over a continuum of strikes K,

$$MFIV_{t,t+\tau}^i = 2\int_0^\infty \left(\frac{C_{t,t+\tau}^i}{B_{t,t+\tau}} - \max\left(\frac{S_t^i}{B_{t,t+\tau}} - K, 0 \right) \right)/K^2 dK, \qquad (9.21)$$

where $C_{t,t+\tau}^i(K)$ is the price at time t of a τ-maturity call option with strike K, $B(t, t+\tau)$ is the time t price of a zero-coupon bond that pays \$1 at time $t+\tau$, S_t^i is the spot price of asset i at time t minus the present value of all expected future dividends to be paid before the option maturity.

In another study, Baltussen, Bekkum, and Grient (2018) measure uncertainty about risk as the volatility of expected volatility (vol-of-vol) and find that stocks with high uncertainty about risk (high vol-of-vol) underperform stocks with low uncertainty about risk significantly. The vol-of-vol for stock i on day t is simply the rolling 20-day standard deviation of implied volatility normalized by the mean implied volatility,

$$VOV_{i,t} = \frac{\sqrt{\frac{1}{20}\sum_{j=t-19}^{t}\left(\sigma_{i,j}^{IV} - \bar{\sigma}_{i,t}^{IV}\right)^2}}{\bar{\sigma}_{i,t}^{IV}}, \tag{9.22}$$

where $\bar{\sigma}_{i,t}^{IV} = \left(\frac{\sum_{j=t-19}^{t}\sigma_{i,j}^{IV}}{20}\right)$ and $\sigma_{i,j}^{IV}$ is the implied volatility on day j.

Furthermore, Huang et al. (2019) also show that vol-of-vol is a significant risk factor beyond the volatility itself. The volatility and vol-of-vol indices, VIX and VVIX respectively, are only weakly correlated. VIX option returns are negative on average and are more negative for strategies that are more exposed to volatility and vol-of-vol risks. In addition, volatility and vol-of-vol negatively predict future option payoffs (delta-hedged), suggesting volatility and vol-of-vol are jointly priced and have negative risk premiums.

9.4. Jump factors

As discussed, a stock price process can be described as a continuous process with jumps. Discontinuities or jumps present a risk that should be compensated. In this section, we discuss the jump factors and highlight some recent works on measuring them.

9.4.1. Variance Swap

To facilitate the discussion of jump factors, we introduce the concept of variance swap first. Variance swap is a forward contract on future realized variance of an underlying asset. It allows investors to gain exposure to future levels of volatility (square root of variance) directly. The payoff of a variance swap is

$$\left(\sigma_R^2 - K_{var}\right) \times N, \tag{9.23}$$

where σ_R^2 is the realized underlying asset's variance (quoted in annual terms) over the life of the contract, and K_{var} is the strike price for variance whose value is to be determined such that the variance swap is worth zero at inception. N is the notional amount of the swap.

Demeterfi et al. (1999) show that variance swap can be valued as the sum of a series of put options at strike K with weight $1/K^2$ for K from zero to the forward value, and a series of call options at strike K with weight $1/K^2$ for K from the forward value to infinity. Since we know equity market typically has volatility skew, that is, implied volatilities are higher for OTM puts than OTM calls, the resulted variance swap strike should be higher than the at-the-money (ATM) implied variance. At inception, the value of variance swap is zero. As time passes, the value of variance swap will be higher than or lower than zero, depending on the realized variance σ_R^2.

9.4.2. Intraday and Overnight Jumps

Jiang and Zhu (2017) find that stocks with high intraday jump returns earn higher returns than those with low intraday jump returns over the next one- and three-day investment horizons. To check whether there exists an intraday or overnight jump, they apply the variance swap jump test proposed by Jiang and Oomen (2008), a concept borrowed from the pricing of variance swaps.

Assume the instantaneous (logarithmic) change in stock price follows a jump diffusion process, i.e., $dlnS_t = \alpha_t dt + V_t^{1/2} dW_t + J_t dq_t$. According to Itō's lemma, we have $dS_t/S_t = \left(\alpha_t + \frac{V_t}{2}\right)dt + V_t^{1/2}dW_t + (exp(J_t) - 1)dq_t$ Subtracting $dlnS_t$ from dS_t/S_t and integrating from 0 to T gives,

$$2\int_0^T \left[\frac{dS_t}{S_t} - dlnS_t\right] = \int_0^T V_t dt + 2\int_0^T \left(e^{J_t} - 1 - J_t\right)dq_t. \qquad (9.24)$$

Here, $V_{0,T} = \int_0^T V_t d_t$ is the integrated variance and forms the basis of the jump test. In the absence of jumps, the difference between the simple return and the log return captures one-half of the instantaneous return variance (the strike of variance swap). Let $\{S_{t_0}, S_{t_1}, \ldots, S_{t_N}\}$ be stock prices observed over the period $[0, T]$ with $t_0 = 0, t_N = T$. Realized variance, the discretized form of $V_{0,T}$, is defined as

$$RV_N = \sum_{i=1}^N r_i^2, \qquad (9.25)$$

where $r_{t_i} = \ln\left[\frac{S_{t_i}}{S_{t_{i-1}}}\right]$ is the continuously compounded logarithmic return. The variance swap (left side of Equation (9.24)) in the discretized version is defined as

$$SWV_N = 2\sum_{i=1}^N (R_i - r_i) = 2\sum_{i=1}^N R_i - 2\ln\left(\frac{S_T}{S_0}\right), \qquad (9.26)$$

where $R_{t_i} = \frac{S_{t_i} - S_{t_{i-1}}}{S_{t_{i-1}}}$ is the simple return.

Suppose no jump occurs during the period $[0, T]$, we would expect $SWV_N - RV_N$ should be close to zero under the null hypothesis. To test the hypothesis, Jiang and Oomen (2008) show that

$$\frac{N}{\sqrt{\Omega_{SWV}}}(SWV_N - RV_N) \to N(0, 1). \qquad (9.27)$$

Defining $\mu_p = 2^{\frac{p}{2}}\Gamma\left[\frac{p+1}{2}\right]/\sqrt{\pi}$, the sample estimate for Ω_{SWV} is

$$\hat{\Omega}_{SWV} = \frac{1}{9}\mu_6 \frac{N^3 \mu_{6/p}^{-p}}{N-p+1} \sum_{i=0}^{N-p} \prod_{k=1}^{p} |r_{i+k}|^{6/p}, \text{ with } p = 6. \qquad (9.28)$$

The above test can be performed using daily return observations over a rolling window, say three-month. Let $\{r_{t_1}, r_{t_2}, ..., r_{t_N}\}$ be daily returns over the interval $[t_1, t_N]$. The sequential jump identification procedure is described as follows:

Step 1: Assume that we have performed a jump test using return observations over a three-month window $[t_1, t_N]$. If the jump test does not reject the null hypothesis of no jumps, move to the next three-month window; otherwise record the jump test statistic JS_0 (Equation 9.19) and proceed to step 2.

Step 2: Replace each daily return by the median of the sample (denoted r_{median}) and perform the jump test on the series. For example, when day i's return is replaced, we perform the jump test on the series $\{r_{t_1}, ..., r_{t_{i-1}}, r_{median}, r_{t_{i+1}}, ..., r_{t_N}\}$ and record the test statistic JS_i for $i = 1, ..., N$.

Step 3: Construct the series $JS_0 - JS_i$ for $i = 1, ..., N$. Then, the stock price change on day j is identified as a jump if $JS_0 - JS_i$ has the highest value of all days.

Step 4: Replace the identified jump observation by r_{median} and start again from Step 1 with a new sample of stock returns.

The procedure continues until all jumps are identified for all stocks.

9.4.3. Idiosyncratic Jumps

The variance swap jump test mentioned in the last section has the advantage of being model free, i.e., the test does not depend on any model assumptions. There are other works trying to follow along the factor model literature of systematic versus idiosyncratic risk and identify the so-called idiosyncratic jumps.

Kapadia and Zekhnini (2019) construct a version of idiosyncratic jump with model assumptions and find that a long–short portfolio with predicted jump probabilities earns significant mean excess return and alpha against a factor pricing model that consists of the Fama-French three factors as well as the momentum factor. The construction of idiosyncratic jump is based on the following steps:

Step 1: For day t, regress each stock return i on a 120-trading day rolling window from $t - 150$ to $t - 31$,

$$r_{it} = \alpha_i + B_i F_t + \varepsilon_{it}, \qquad (9.29)$$

where F_t is a vector of factors, e.g., Fama-French three factors plus the momentum factor.

With the estimated factor loadings $\hat{B}$, idiosyncratic returns are defined as,

$$r_{i,t}^{idio} = r_{it} - \hat{B}_{i,t} F_t. \tag{9.30}$$

To avoid the impact of outliers in the estimation, Kapadia and Zekhnini (2019) winsorize the factor loadings at the 5% and 95% levels.

Step 2: Compute the conditional volatility for day t based on the exponential weighted moving average model with $\lambda = 0.94$,

$$\sigma_{i,t} = \sqrt{(1 - \lambda) \sum_{s=1}^{t-1} \lambda^s \left(r_{i,t-s}^{idio} \right)^2}. \tag{9.31}$$

Step 3: Categorize day t as a jump day for stock i by the indicator variable J_{it}

$$J_{it} = \begin{cases} 1 & if \frac{|r_{i,t}^{idio}|}{\sigma_{i,t}} > 3, \\ 0 & \text{otherwise.} \end{cases} \tag{9.32}$$

The idiosyncratic ratio $\frac{|r_{i,t}^{idio}|}{\sigma_{i,t}}$ fits well as the definition of factor (from an industry perspective), while the indicator variable could be used as a discrete factor.

In their empirical analysis, the authors demonstrate that idiosyncratic jumps play a crucial role in explaining the cross-section of stock returns. Ex-ante, a value-weighted portfolio that buys stocks with high predicted jump probabilities and sells stocks with low predicted jump probabilities earns an annualized mean return of 9.4%, with the corresponding four-factor alphas being 8.1%. Ex-post, the annual average return of a typical stock accrues on the four days on which its price jumps. This strategy's returns are larger when there are greater limits to arbitrage. These findings align with the notion that investors generally exhibit aversion toward the risk associated with idiosyncratic jumps in stock prices.

9.5. Conclusion

In this chapter, we embarked on a journey into the realm of option data and its application in factor investing. We navigated through the intricate mathematics of options, exploring pricing models, volatility surfaces, stochastic processes, and advanced concepts like Itō's lemma and variance swap pricing. By understanding the nature of options and their inherent forward-looking nature, we uncovered valuable insights that can augment traditional factor models.

Through methodologies such as jump diffusion processes and variance swap pricing, we elucidated the decomposition of stock returns into continuous components and jumps, unveiling hidden factors that contribute to market dynamics. Moreover, we introduced model-free and model-based approaches for capturing idiosyncratic jumps, offering diverse perspectives for factor extraction and interpretation.

Looking ahead, the future of factor investing lies in embracing forward-looking information, and options present a fertile ground for exploration. The consensus expectations embedded in option prices remain underutilized in the factor-investing landscape, presenting an untapped opportunity for enhancing predictive power and refining investment strategies. As we delve deeper into the intricacies of option data, the challenge lies in devising innovative methodologies to extract actionable insights and translate them into effective investment strategies.

References

Bali, T. G. and H. Zhou (2016). Risk, uncertainty, and expected returns. *Journal of Financial and Quantitative Analysis* 51(3), 707–735.

Baltussen, G., V. Bekkum, and B. Grient (2018). Unknown unknowns: Uncertainty about risk and stock returns. *Journal of Financial and Quantitative Analysis* 53(4), 1615–1651.

Black F. and M. Scholes (1973). The pricing of options and corporate liabilities. *Journal of Political Economy* 81(3), 637–654.

Britten-Jones, M. and A. Neuberger (2000). Option prices, implied price processes, and stochastic volatility. *Journal of Finance* 55(2), 839–866.

Demeterfi, K., E. Derman, M. Kamal, and J. Zou (1999). *More Than You Ever Wanted to Know about Volatility Swaps*. Goldman Sachs: Quantitative Strategies Research Notes.

González-Urteaga, A. and G. Rubio (2016). The cross-sectional variation of volatility risk premia. *Journal of Financial Economics* 119(2), 353–370.

Huang, D., C. Schlag, I. Shaliastovich, and J. Thimme (2019). Volatility-of-volatility risk. *Journal of Financial and Quantitative Analysis* 54(6), 2432–2452.

Hull, J. C. (2014). *Options, Futures, and Other Derivatives* (9th Edition). Pearson.

Jiang, G. J. and R. C. Oomen (2008). Testing for jumps when asset prices are observed with noise—a "swap variance" approach. *Journal of Econometrics* 144(2), 352–370.

Jiang, G. J. and Y. S. Tian (2005). The model free implied volatility and its information content. *Review of Financial Studies* 18(4), 1305–1342.

Jiang, G. J. and K. X. Zhu (2017). Information shocks and short-term market underreaction. *Journal of Financial Economics* 124(1), 43–64.

Kapadia, N. and M. Zekhnini (2019). Do idiosyncratic jumps matter? *Journal of Financial Economics* 131(3), 666–692.

Merton, R. C. (1973). Theory of rational option pricing. *The Bell Journal of Economics and Management Science* 4(1), 141–183.

Pan, J. and A. M. Poteshman (2006). The information in option volume for future stock prices. *Review of Financial Studies* 19(3), 871–908.

10

UNCERTAINTY

To understand uncertainty, one must understand the essence of probability and statistical inference first.

The primary objective of probability theory is to provide a quantitative description of uncertainty by quantifying the likelihood of events. It allows us to assign numerical values to the chances of occurrence of different events, even when these events are random. Knowing the probability distribution allows us to calculate the expected frequency of each outcome over a large number of observations, to make informed decisions based on likelihoods, and to understand the long-term average results of repeated plays. The essence of probability theory is that it does not predict individual events with certainty, but rather describes the overall pattern that emerges from many individual events. Probability is the foundation of statistical inference, which involves drawing conclusions about populations based on samples. It enables statisticians to make predictions about a population's characteristics by analyzing sample data.

In the financial market, the ability to forecast individual outcomes with perfect accuracy is practically impossible due to the myriad variables that influence asset prices and market movements. However, through the application of probability and statistical inference, investors and analysts can employ quantitative methods to diminish the inherent risk and uncertainty associated with investing. By analyzing historical data and market trends, they can identify probability distributions for asset returns, which in turn inform the likelihood of future price movements. This statistical approach enables the construction of diversified portfolios that are optimized to balance expected returns against the volatility of individual assets. Moreover, by employing tools such as regression analysis, Monte Carlo simulations, and value at risk (VaR) models, financial professionals can create predictive frameworks that help anticipate the range of possible market behaviors. Although these methods cannot eliminate the inherent unpredictability of the markets, they lend a rigorous

DOI: 10.4324/9781003480204-10

approach to understanding and preparing for potential scenarios, thus providing a measure of control in an otherwise uncertain financial environment. This is the essence of quantitative finance, where the goal is not to predict the future with certainty, but to make decisions that are robust to a range of possible outcomes.

Financial markets are complex ecosystems where various participants exchange assets, services, and risks. The inherent uncertainty of the future poses a fundamental challenge to these participants, who seek to navigate through the unpredictable tides of market fluctuations, economic cycles, and geopolitical events. A core function of financial markets is to manage and mitigate this uncertainty, transforming it into actionable investment strategies. Factor investing emerges as a powerful force in this quest, providing a structured approach to capturing risk premiums and offering a semblance of certainty in the inherently uncertain world.

Although risk management models in finance are useful, they rely on an important assumption: the distribution does not change. In other words, while traditional models can deal with outcome uncertainty, they cannot deal with distribution uncertainty. This is a critical distinction because outcome uncertainty refers to the variability of results within a well-defined probability distribution. In contrast, distribution uncertainty, or ambiguity, implies that the probability distribution itself is unclear or subject to change.

This limitation of traditional models is not merely academic; it has practical implications for financial decision-making. During periods of market stress or economic upheaval, the historical distribution of asset returns can change suddenly and significantly, rendering models that assume a static distribution less effective, or even misleading. The Global Financial Crisis of 2007–2008 is a stark example where many risk models failed to predict or adequately cope with the market dynamics because they were predicated on stable historical distribution patterns that quickly became obsolete.

Moreover, the assumption of a static distribution overlooks the fact that financial markets are influenced by human behavior and by information which is often incomplete and asymmetric. Market participants do not always act rationally, and their reactions to new information can lead to changes in the underlying distribution of asset returns. This behavioral aspect of financial markets introduces additional layers of complexity and uncertainty that traditional models cannot easily capture.

For these reasons, a separate chapter on uncertainty—specifically distribution uncertainty—is warranted. In this chapter, the terms volatility, risk, and uncertainty are related but distinct concepts, each with its own implications for investment decisions and risk management.

10.1. Volatility, Risk, and Uncertainty

Volatility is a statistical measure of the dispersion of returns for a given security or market index. It is often quantified as the standard deviation of those returns. In finance, volatility is commonly used as a proxy for risk because it provides a measure of the degree to which an asset's price varies over time. High volatility implies that an asset's price can change dramatically over a short period in either direction, while low volatility indicates that the asset's price moves more steadily.

Risk refers to the possibility of an investment's actual returns differing from the expected returns, which can result in potential financial loss. It encompasses a variety of factors, including market risk, credit risk, liquidity risk, operational risk, and more. Risk is inherent in all investments, and it is typically quantified based on historical data and statistical models. However, it is a broader term than volatility and can be both quantifiable and unquantifiable.

The difference between risk and volatility lies in the scope of what they measure. Risk is a broader concept that includes the possibility of both known and unknown events affecting the returns, while volatility is a specific measure of past price fluctuations.

Uncertainty is a term that refers to the *indeterminability* of the future. It encompasses the unknown and the unforeseeable events that cannot be quantified or even predicted accurately. Uncertainty is often discussed in the context of "Knightian uncertainty" or later ambiguity in the literature, named after economist Frank Knight, who distinguished it from quantifiable risk. Knightian uncertainty describes situations where the probability of outcomes is *unknown* and cannot be measured, while risk involves scenarios where the probability of outcomes can be *known* and potentially measured.

Frank Hyneman Knight

Frank Hyneman Knight (1885–1972) was an influential American economist who made significant contributions to economic theory during the early twentieth century. He is best known for his distinction between risk and uncertainty, which has become a foundational concept in economics and finance.

Knight was born on November 7, 1885, in McLean County, Illinois. He grew up in a Christian household and initially intended to become a minister. However, his interests shifted to philosophy and then economics. He studied at the American University and later transferred to the University of Tennessee. Knight eventually obtained his PhD in economics from Cornell University in 1916.

Knight's academic career was most prominently associated with the University of Chicago, where he taught from 1927 until his retirement in 1955. At Chicago, he was a central figure in what became known as the Chicago School of Economics, influencing numerous students who would go on to become leading economists, including Milton Friedman and George Stigler.

Knight's most influential work is *Risk, Uncertainty, and Profit* (1921), where he established the distinction between risk and uncertainty. In this work, he argued that: Risk refers to situations where the probability of various outcomes is known and can be quantified. In these cases, it is possible to calculate the expected outcomes and insure against potential risks. Uncertainty, in contrast, exists when the likelihood of future events is indeterminate or incalculable. Under uncertainty, it is not possible to calculate probabilities or expected outcomes reliably.

Knight argued that this distinction was critical for understanding the functioning of markets and the role of entrepreneurs. According to Knight, entrepreneurs are compensated for bearing uncertainty, not risk. They earn profits by successfully navigating uncertain situations where outcomes cannot be predicted by statistical models.

Knight's work extended beyond this dichotomy. He also made important contributions to the areas of capital theory, social economics, and ethics. He was a profound thinker on a variety of topics, including the philosophy of economics, the function of the economic system, and the relationship between economics and education.

Knight's work has had a lasting impact on the field of economics and has been influential in the development of various economic theories and disciplines, including managerial economics, strategic management, and the study of entrepreneurship.

In finance, uncertainty can arise from events such as political instability, unexpected regulatory changes, natural disasters, or technological breakthroughs. These events can be difficult, if not impossible, to incorporate into traditional risk models, which assume that future probabilities are based on historical frequencies.

Uncertainty encompasses a deeper level of the unknown, where the probability distribution of outcomes is not readily available or cannot be precisely defined. This type of uncertainty arises in unprecedented market conditions, such as during a financial crisis or the introduction of a transformative technology, where past data may offer little insight into future trends.

Faced with such uncertainty, financial economists and investors must push the envelope of research to develop models that can navigate the uncharted waters of market behavior. Unlike risk, which can be measured and quantified through historical volatility, uncertainty demands more innovative approaches. These may include stress testing, scenario analysis, and the use of non-parametric models that make fewer assumptions about the underlying probability distributions.

In practice, as financial markets become increasingly complex and interconnected, the ability to model uncertainty becomes a critical skill. It involves discerning the difference between normal market fluctuations and those that signal a structural change. This distinction is paramount, as traditional models may fail to capture the latter's dynamic. Successfully modeling financial uncertainty could lead to the identification of unique investment opportunities and the avoidance of potential downturns. As such, the financial industry is on a continual quest for tools and frameworks that can handle uncertainty, not just to shield against potential losses but to identify and capitalize on areas of undervalued assets where the lack of clarity and consensus can lead to outsized returns.

It is crucial, both in literature and practice, to distinguish between risk and uncertainty. Numerous studies, such as those by Klibanoff, Marinacci, and Mukerji (2005), van de Kuilen and Wakker (2011) and Abdellaoui et al. (2021), have introduced theoretical models to investigate risk and ambiguity aversion.

This chapter aims to provide an introduction to ambiguity. We start with the important concept of ambiguity aversion in Section 10.2. Section 10.3 introduces five major ambiguity measures. Subsequent sections, namely 10.4 and 10.5, delve into two of the measures, i.e., the ω measure and Hellinger distance, in greater detail. Section 10.6 address the relationship between ambiguity and market crash. Section 10.7 concludes.

10.2. Ambiguity Aversion

In the intricate landscape of risk preference, the concept of ambiguity aversion emerges as a pivotal element, highlighting the decision-making tendencies of individuals when confronted with uncertainty. This phenomenon is illustrated through a seminal experiment involving two jars filled with red and blue balls, known as the Ellsberg (1961) paradox.

Consider the following experiment involving two jars, each containing a total of 100 red and blue balls. The distinction between the two jars is that in Jar 1, the numbers of red and blue balls are unknown, whereas in Jar 2, there are exactly 50 red balls and 50 blue balls. Participants are first asked to choose between the following two options:

A1: Draw a ball from Jar 1. If a red ball is drawn, receive a reward; if a blue ball is drawn, there is no reward.

A2: Draw a ball from Jar 2. If a red ball is drawn, receive a reward; if a blue ball is drawn, there is no reward.

The only difference between these two options is the jar from which the ball is drawn. In a second experiment, participants are asked to choose between two different options:

B1: Draw a ball from Jar 1. If a blue ball is drawn, receive a reward; if a red ball is drawn, there is no reward.

B2: Draw a ball from Jar 2. If a blue ball is drawn, receive a reward; if a red ball is drawn, there is no reward.

The distinction between the two experiments lies in the color of the ball that yields a reward, changing from red to blue. Faced with these experiments, a surprising outcome occurred: in the first experiment, more participants chose option A2, while in the second experiment, more participants chose option B2. The results of the first experiment suggest that people subjectively believe the number of red balls in Jar 1 to be fewer than 50, i.e., the number of red balls in Jar 2; conversely, the results of the second experiment suggest exactly the opposite, where people believe the number of blue balls in Jar 1 to be fewer than 50, i.e., the number of blue balls in Jar 2. This is the famous Ellsberg paradox in decision theory.

Daniel Ellsberg

Daniel Ellsberg was born on April 7, 1931, in Detroit, Michigan. He attended the Cranbrook School in Bloomfield Hills, Michigan, before earning a scholarship to Harvard University. Ellsberg graduated with a BA in economics, summa cum laude, in 1952. He then studied at the University of Cambridge on a Woodrow Wilson Fellowship for a year before returning to Harvard for graduate studies. Ellsberg completed a PhD in Economics at Harvard in 1962. His dissertation on decision theory was titled *Risk, Ambiguity, and the Savage Axioms*, and it is in this work that he made significant contributions to the field of uncertainty.

Ellsberg's early career was marked by a stint in the US Marine Corps, after which he joined the RAND Corporation as a strategic analyst, focusing on nuclear weapons and decision theory. He later worked at the Pentagon under Secretary of Defense Robert McNamara and was involved in the study of US military decisions in the Vietnam War.

Ellsberg's doctoral thesis on decision theory made a crucial distinction between risk and uncertainty. In a world of risk, outcomes are unknown but governed by probability distributions that are known, or can be estimated. In contrast, uncertainty refers to situations where these probabilities are themselves unknown or indeterminate.

Ellsberg famously illustrated this distinction through the "Ellsberg Paradox", which involves a scenario with two urns containing colored balls. The paradox demonstrates people's preference for known risks over unknown risks, highlighting the aversion to ambiguity and uncertainty in decision-making. This work laid the groundwork for what is now known as "ambiguity aversion" in behavioral economics and has implications for understanding decision-making under uncertainty.

Ellsberg's most famous contribution to history is not directly related to his work on uncertainty, but to his actions during the Vietnam War. In 1971, he leaked a top-secret Pentagon study of US government decision-making in relation to the Vietnam War to *The New York Times* and other newspapers. The release of the Pentagon Papers led to a significant shift in public opinion on the war and had a lasting impact on the trust between the American public and its government.

Daniel Ellsberg's contributions to the field of decision theory and his actions during the Vietnam War have left a lasting legacy. His work on the nature of uncertainty and risk has influenced not only economics but also military strategy, psychology, and political science.

Remarkably, a majority of participants exhibit a preference for drawing from the jar with a known ratio, despite identical reward structures in both scenarios. This inclination underscores a fundamental aspect of human nature: the aversion to ambiguity. When faced with a decision where the outcome distribution is known, individuals are able to gauge the risks involved. Conversely, when the outcome distribution is unknown, individuals are unable to accurately assess the risks as the uncertainty is unquantifiable.

This aversion to ambiguity is not merely an isolated behavioral quirk but inter-twines with other cognitive biases such as overconfidence and confirmation bias, often leading individuals to fare worse in domains they perceive as familiar. The interplay between ambiguity aversion and Prospect Theory (see Chapter 8 on behavioral finance) forms the bedrock of risk preference biases, offering a nuanced understanding of how individuals navigate decisions under risk.

Drawing upon Ellsberg's seminal work in 1961, research into ambiguity has evolved along two primary trajectories over recent decades. Initially, the develop-ment focused on formulating utility-maximizing preference models that extend traditional expected utility frameworks to encompass ambiguity. Notable among these are maxmin expected utility (Gilboa and Schmeidler 1989), α-maxmin expected utility (Ghirardato, Maccheroni, and Marinacci 2004, Maccheroni, Mar-inacci, and Rustichini 2006), robust control and multiplier utility (Hansen and Sargent 2001), Choquet expected utility (Gilboa 1987, Schmeidler 1989), gen-eralized prospect theory (Tversky and Kahneman 1992, Wakker 2010), smooth ambiguity model (Klibanoff, Marinacci, and Mukerji 2005), and vector expected utility (Siniscalchi 2009).

Lars Peter Hansen

Lars Peter Hansen is an American economist born on October 26, 1952. He is best known for his work in the field of econometrics and for his contributions to our understanding of ambiguity in economic decision-making. Hansen's work has been instrumental in helping economists and financial professionals understand how decisions are made when faced with uncertain outcomes.

Lars Hansen earned his bachelor's degree in mathematics and political sci-ence from Utah State University in 1974. He then went on to pursue graduate studies in economics at the University of Minnesota, where he received his PhD in 1978. His doctoral dissertation was on "Generalized Instrumental Variables Estimation of Nonlinear Rational Expectations Models".

Hansen has spent much of his academic career at the University of Chicago, where he is the David Rockefeller Distinguished Service Professor in Economics, Statistics, and the Booth School of Business. His research has focused on the economic and statistical theory and led him to develop econometric methods for modeling and measuring economic dynamics.

Hansen's contributions to the understanding of ambiguity in economics are tied to his work on the economic and financial models under uncertainty. He is well-known for his development of the "Generalized Method of Moments" (GMM), which is a statistical method that allows researchers to estimate the parameters of economic models. GMM is flexible and robust, making it parti-cularly useful when dealing with complex economic models. In recognition of his work, Lars Hansen was awarded the Sveriges Riksbank Prize in Economic

Sciences in Memory of Alfred Nobel in 2013, shared with Eugene F. Fama and Robert J. Shiller. The Nobel committee recognized Hansen for his "empirical analysis of asset prices", which includes his work on understanding the long-term average returns of assets in the face of uncertainty and his contributions to the field of econometrics.

One of Hansen's significant contributions to the subject of ambiguity, or "model uncertainty", is his work on "robust control" or "robustness". Recognizing that models used to make economic decisions are simplifications of reality and, therefore, inherently flawed, Hansen developed methods to take these imperfections into account. He introduced techniques that decision-makers could use to account for model misspecification and to make decisions that are less sensitive to uncertainty about the correct model.

Lars Hansen's work on robustness and handling uncertainty in economic models has had a profound impact on the fields of macroeconomics and finance. His methods for dealing with ambiguous situations where the probabilities of outcomes are not clear have influenced both academic research and practical financial modeling. By acknowledging the limitations of economic models and developing tools to manage these limitations, Hansen has helped pave the way for more resilient economic forecasting and policy-making.

In the second stream of works, ambiguity-based preference models are used to explain observed decision-making behavior in various contexts including participation in financial markets (Cao, Wang, and Zhang 2005), financial portfolio selection (Uppal and Wang 2003, Maenhout 2004, Garlappi, Uppal, and Wang 2007, Dimmock et al. 2016), and regulation of markets (Easley and O'Hara 2009). These applications, while significant, rely on particular assumptions subject to diverse interpretations and implementations. For an in-depth understanding, the interested reader is encouraged to consult the original publications.

With the advent and progression of artificial intelligence, coupled with the increasing application of data-driven decision-making, quantitative researchers have progressively adopted various algorithms to derive insights from empirical data. Such endeavors necessitate heightened attention to the issues arising from changes in data distribution. A common yet critically unexamined assumption in inductive algorithm application is that the data generating process remains the same, which is essential to ensure that models trained on historical data are reliable for future predictions. However, this assumption often falters in the financial markets.

Albert Einstein had a statement on mathematics and reality: "As far as the laws of mathematics refer to reality, they are not certain; and as far as they are certain, they do not refer to reality." This encapsulates the challenge of quantifying the complex dynamics of financial markets through elegant mathematical formulas. An accurate depiction of financial market characteristics must account for the potential variability in probability distributions. Overreliance on precise answers derived from such models can lead to significant drawdowns during periods of underlying market uncertainty, as exemplified by the downfall of Long-Term Capital Management. Hence, a cautious application of inductive principles is warranted, with an emphasis on analyzing and mitigating the potential adverse effects of data variability.

Long-Term Capital Management

Long-Term Capital Management (LTCM) was a prominent US hedge fund established in 1994 by John W. Meriwether, a former star trader at Salomon Brothers. Its notoriety stems from its dramatic failure in 1998, which became a significant case study in risk management and the dangers of financial uncertainty.

The fund was distinguished for its employment of complex mathematical models, designed to identify and leverage fixed-income arbitrage opportunities. Among its partners were Nobel laureates Myron Scholes and Robert C. Merton, known for their contributions to the Black-Scholes-Merton option pricing model.

Initially, LTCM saw extraordinary returns, but the fund's strategy was heavily reliant on leveraging, using borrowed money to amplify their investment capacity. The underlying assumption of LTCM's strategy was that bond yield spreads would revert to mean values, an assumption that appeared sound until the market context changed dramatically.

Events such as the Asian financial crisis in 1997 and Russia's default on its debt in 1998 led to market conditions that were highly volatile and deviated from historical norms. These conditions, representing tail events, were not fully anticipated by LTCM's models, which also failed to adequately factor in the ambiguity inherent in financial markets—such as the unpredictable nature of market participants' reactions under stress and the potential for correlation breakdowns between financial instruments.

The fund's exposure to such extreme but poorly understood risks became its undoing. With the fund's high leverage turning losses into a rapid hemorrhage of capital, LTCM's equity plummeted from over $2 billion to just a fraction of that within months. By September 1998, the fund had lost $4.6 billion and was on the brink of causing wider financial instability due to its entanglements with various major financial institutions.

To avert a potential systemic financial crisis, the Federal Reserve intervened, organizing a bailout of $3.6 billion by a consortium of banks and securities firms. The collapse of LTCM underscored the critical need for more sophisticated risk management that goes beyond conventional modeling, recognizing the limitations of predictive models in the face of market ambiguity and the potential for catastrophic tail events. It also led to increased regulatory scrutiny over hedge funds and the implementation of more robust risk management and regulatory practices in the finance industry.

In the realm of financial markets, ambiguity stems from various sources, including information asymmetry, macroeconomic uncertainties, geopolitical events, market sentiment, and behavioral biases. Ambiguity, therefore, is not only an underexplored factor but could also represent a significant, yet uncharted, source of risk, unacknowledged in existing factor literature. Integrating ambiguity into risk forecasting could enable a more comprehensive consideration of past black-swan events, potentially averting substantial investor losses. This domain warrants further investigation.

10.3. Measurements of Ambiguity

Although acknowledging the importance of ambiguity is crucial, clarity on how to measure it still eludes us. Previous studies, especially in the areas of information systems and operations management, have explored ambiguity mainly through theoretical models or questionnaires. This section offers a review of the proposed metrics that serve as potential proxies for quantifying ambiguity or for assessing the deviation between an observed distribution and a reference distribution. These measures include dispersion in analyst forecasts, CBOE VIX, ω (mho), relative entropy, and Hellinger distance.

10.3.1 Dispersion in Analyst Forecasts

Dispersion in analyst forecasts serves as a critical measure to assess the range and divergence of expectations among financial analysts concerning future earnings or the performance of stocks. This concept originates from the understanding that while agents may have considerable insights into return volatility, their knowledge regarding mean returns tends to be more limited. Anderson, Ghysels, and Juergens (2009) highlight this by introducing an ambiguity measure that capitalizes on disagreement among professional financial analysts. By analyzing the variance in forecasts, as gleaned from the Survey of Professional Forecasters, this measure provides an indication of the uncertainty levels regarding mean returns. A consensus among forecasters typically signals lower uncertainty, whereas significant disparities in their forecasts point to higher levels of ambiguity concerning future returns.

This measure of dispersion not only encapsulates the subjective viewpoints of analysts regarding market ambiguity but also encompasses the objective ambiguity present within the market itself. However, a notable challenge with this measure is its potential to conflate ambiguity with risk, particularly since the dispersion in forecasts often shows a strong correlation with stock price volatility. This overlap makes it somewhat challenging to distinctly isolate ambiguity from risk. Despite these challenges, the dispersion in analyst forecasts remains a valuable tool in understanding and quantifying the level of ambiguity that financial analysts harbor regarding future market outcomes.

10.3.2 CBOE VIX

The Chicago Board Options Exchange (CBOE) Volatility Index, better known as VIX, stands as a prominent barometer of market sentiment, often dubbed the "fear index" for its ability to reflect investor anxiety through the expected volatility of S&P 500 index options. Its fluctuations offer insights into the market's volatility forecasts, with rising values signaling heightened concerns and a potential uptick in market volatility, and decreasing values suggesting a calmer market outlook. Despite its widespread recognition and usage, particularly in volatile market conditions, the application of the VIX as a direct measure of ambiguity entails certain complexities.

Williams (2015) supports the utilization of VIX as an ambiguity metric, underscoring its reflection of market panic. However, the VIX's encompassing nature, capturing both risk and ambiguity elements, as confirmed by Miao, Wei, and Zhou (2019), poses challenges in isolating ambiguity as a standalone factor. This is further complicated by the index's theoretical framework, which does not establish a direct link to the distribution uncertainty. Such intricacies suggest that while VIX serves as a valuable tool in gauging market expectations of near-term volatility and investor sentiment, its role as a precise measure of ambiguity requires careful consideration, especially given its dual encapsulation of risk and uncertainty.

10.3.3 The ℧ (mho) Measure

The measure known as ω (mho), conceived by Brenner and Izhakian (2018), represents a novel approach to quantifying ambiguity within financial markets, particularly concerning the distribution of financial asset returns. This measure is deeply rooted in decision-making models that prioritize the role of probabilities and their mean-preserving spreads, directly linking the concept of ambiguity to these probabilistic frameworks. The essence of ω lies in its ability to encapsulate the uncertainty tied to the return distributions of financial assets, offering a quantifiable metric that captures both the expected probability and variance of returns.

Central to the application of ω is the compound probability model, which provides a robust framework for empirical analysis, as further explored in subsequent studies by Augustin and Izhakian (2020) and Izhakian, Yermack, and Zender (2022). This model's complexity and depth allow for a nuanced understanding of ambiguity in financial decision-making. However, the practical implementation of this measure is not without its challenges. The measure's reliance on the distribution of distributions necessitates access to high-frequency transaction data, which may not be readily available or accessible to all market participants. This requirement can pose significant hurdles in leveraging ω for effective decision-making, particularly when dealing with the intricate uncertainties of financial markets.

10.3.4 Relative Entropy

Relative entropy, commonly referred to as Kullback-Leibler (KL) divergence, stands as a pivotal measure in the realm of information theory, offering a robust means to quantify the divergence between two probability distributions.

KL divergence is a member of the family of distances known as "f-divergences" or "Csiszár's divergences". F-divergences are a class of functions that quantify the difference between two probability distributions. They are used to measure the "distance" between distributions in a way that satisfies certain mathematical properties.

The general form of an f-divergence is given by

$$D_f(P_1, P_2) = \int f_2(x) f\left(\frac{f_1(x)}{f_2(x)}\right) dx, \tag{10.1}$$

for continuous distributions, where P_1 and P_2 are the two probability distributions with densities $f_1(x)$ and $f_2(x)$, and f is a convex function such that $f(1) = 0$. This metric is instrumental in evaluating the extent of deviation an alternative model exhibits from a given reference model, thus providing insights into the level of uncertainty or unpredictability inherent in various systems.

The relative entropy (KL divergence) between two distributions, P_1 and P_2, is defined as follows

$$D_{KL}(P_2 \parallel P_1) = p_2(x) \log\left(\frac{p_2(x)}{p_1(x)}\right) dx, \tag{10.2}$$

for continuous distributions. The essence of relative entropy lies in its capacity to measure the informational disparity between two distributions, essentially capturing how one distribution diverges from another. This is crucial in contexts where understanding the nuances of model deviations is key, such as in assessing the reliability of predictive models in finance, where the accuracy of forecasts can significantly impact decision-making processes. However, the application of relative entropy is not without its constraints. A notable limitation arises when dealing with probability distributions that feature distinct zero probability sets, a scenario often encountered in the analysis of extreme market movements or the assessment of tail risks. Such situations demand careful consideration, as the foundational requirement of relative entropy necessitates alignment in the zero probability sets of the compared distributions, potentially limiting its efficacy in fully capturing the dynamics of rare but impactful events. Additionally, the non-metric property of the KL divergence (Gibbs and Su 2002), demonstrated by its asymmetry and failure to adhere to the triangle inequality, complicates the derivation of a consistent measure of ambiguity.

10.3.5 Hellinger Distance

Two authors of this book, Tao Lu and Michael Zhang, together with their coauthors, propose to use the Hellinger Distance (HD) as a tool for measuring the disparity between two probability distributions as a nuanced approach to quantifying ambiguity, particularly within the domain of financial markets (Lu et al. forthcoming). The idea's utility is rooted in its simplicity of computation and the provision of normalized values. The capacity of HD to adeptly capture shifts in distributions positions it as an invaluable tool for forecasting market dynamics and gaining insights into investor behavior when confronted with ambiguity.

Central to the adoption of HD as a preferred ambiguity measure are several critical criteria that it satisfactorily fulfils. These include the ease of computation without the need for exhaustive details about the true model, which is particularly beneficial in scenarios where complete information on probability distributions may not be readily available. Moreover, HD exhibits essential metric properties such as symmetry and adherence to the triangle inequality, ensuring a consistent measurement of the distance between distributions irrespective of the reference distribution chosen. The normalization feature of HD further enhances its utility by allowing for comparative analysis across varying levels of ambiguity. HD is also recommended for its integration with conventional uncertainty measures, such as volatility and entropy, with the aim of elevating the precision and efficacy of data analytics frameworks.

10.4. Ambiguity as Uncertainty in Probabilities

In this section, we delve further into the role of the $\mho$ measure introduced by Brenner and Izhakian (2018) in quantifying ambiguity. The article highlights that ambiguity is priced by positing that the equity premium comprises two distinct elements: a risk premium and an ambiguity premium. To understand the concept of the ambiguity premium, in their own words, it is useful to revisit the traditional notion of the risk premium, which can be viewed as a premium that an investor is willing to pay to exchange a risky asset for a risk-less one with an identical expected outcome. Analogously, the ambiguity premium can be viewed as the premium that an investor is willing to pay to exchange a risky and ambiguous asset for a risky, but merely risky (without ambiguity) asset, with an identical expected outcome and identical risk.

The ambiguity premium is a function of the investor's attitude toward ambiguity, and it is independent of her attitude toward risk. The work develops an empirical methodology for measuring the degree of ambiguity from market data. Specifically, the degree of ambiguity is formulated as

$$\Omega^2(r) = \int E[\varphi(r)]\mathrm{var}[\varphi(r)]dr, \tag{10.3}$$

where $\varphi(.)$ is a probability density function, $\mathrm{E}[\varphi(r)$ is the expected probability of a given rate of return r, and $var[\varphi(r)$ is the variance of the probability of r. As explained by the authors, the intuition of ω measure is that, as the degree of risk can be measured by the volatility of returns, so too can the degree of ambiguity be measured by the volatility of the probabilities of returns.

At this point, elucidating the ω measure with an example (borrowed from Brenner and Izhakian 2018) might prove beneficial. Imagine an asset with future returns that could either be -10% or 20%, each with a 50% probability. Hence, the expected return of this asset is 5%, and its risk, measured by the standard deviation, is 15%. Since the distribution of returns is known, there is no ambiguity in this scenario, i.e., $\omega = 0$ Now, let's assume the returns still have the same two potential outcomes, but their distribution could be one of two possibilities: (1) P(-10%)=0.4 and P(20%)=0.6; or (2) P(-10%)=0.6 and P(20%)=0.4, with equal likelihood for these distributions. In this scenario, investors face not just risk but also uncertainty. According to the definition of ω, the level of ambiguity is

$$\Omega = \sqrt{\sum_i E[P(i)]\mathrm{var}[P(i)])}$$

$$= \sqrt{2 \times 0.5 \times (0.5 \times (0.4 - 0.5)^2 + 0.5 \times (0.6 - 0.5)^2)} = 0.1. \qquad (10.4)$$

Back to the financial market, using historical returns, $\omega^2[r]$ can be implemented in the discrete form. To compute a rolling monthly degree of ambiguity, we can divide the range of daily returns from a left limit r_L to a right limit r_R. The range is divided into n intervals with width w. The intraday returns can be represented in the form of a histogram using a bin width of w. The degree of ambiguity can then be measured as

$$\Omega^2[r] = \frac{1}{w(1-w)}(\mathrm{E}[\phi(r_L;\mu,\sigma)]\mathrm{var}[\phi(r_L;\mu,\sigma)]$$

$$+ \sum_{i=1}^{n} \mathrm{E}[\phi(r_i;\mu,\sigma)] - \phi(r_{i-1};\mu,\sigma)] \times \mathrm{var}[\phi(r_i;\mu,\sigma) - \phi(r_{i-1};\mu,\sigma)]$$

$$+\mathrm{E}[1 - \phi(r_R;\mu,\sigma)]\mathrm{var}[1 - \phi(r_R;\mu,\sigma)]). \qquad (10.5)$$

The empirical findings of Brenner and Izhakian (2018) demonstrate that ambiguity significantly influences stock market returns, indicating that investors consider the degree of ambiguity when pricing financial assets. The study reveals that investors exhibit an aversion to ambiguity for favorable returns and a preference for ambiguity in the face of unfavorable returns. Additionally, the research shows that ambiguity aversion increases with the likelihood of favorable outcomes, while preference for ambiguity increases with the likelihood of unfavorable outcomes. The introduction of ambiguity into the model, alongside risk, illustrates that the expected market volatility has a positive and significant impact on expected returns, supporting the classical theoretical risk–return relationship.

10.5. Ambiguity as Distance from Normality

This section aims to provide a more thorough discussion about the Hellinger Distance (HD) (Hellinger 1909). HD is also a member of the f-divergence family. It is specifically derived from the f-divergence by choosing the function $f(t) = \left(\sqrt{t} - 1\right)^2$.

Lu et al. (forthcoming) propose to use the HD as a measure of ambiguity. Since ambiguity measures uncertainty in the distribution, it can somehow be described by "how far" it is from a standard reference. The obvious choice of reference is the normal distribution which is usually used in finance to model log returns, and HD is a common measure of the distance between two probability distributions. The HD can be calculated as

$$H^2(P_1, P_2) = \frac{1}{2} \int_{-\infty}^{\infty} \left(\sqrt{f_1(x)} - \sqrt{f_2(x)}\right)^2 dx. \qquad (10.6)$$

Lu et al. (forthcoming) apply an $ARMA(1,1)$ model to the daily S&P500 return in excess of the one-month Treasury rate for HD calculation based on the residuals. On the firm level, they compute HD using the residuals from the regression of individual stock returns on the market factor of Fama and French (1992), with the assumption that the residuals from these regression models adhere to a normal distribution.

Figure 10.1 displays a time-series plot of stock market ambiguity, quantified by the HD. The plot incorporates relevant variables, including SPRET, representing

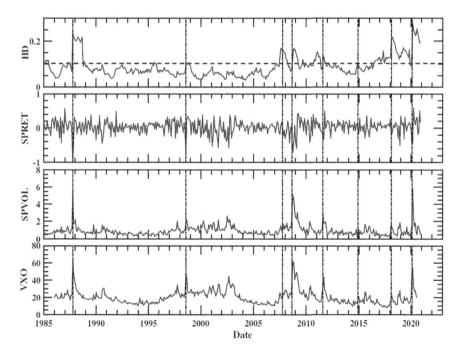

FIGURE 10.1 Hellinger Distance

the mean of daily returns of S&P 500 in month t, SPVOL, representing the standard deviation of daily returns of S&P 500 in month t, and VXO, denoting the implied volatility of an option contract on the S&P 100 index.

The top panel of the figure features a horizontal dashed line indicating the critical value (corresponding to p = 0.01) of the HD. Vertical dash-lines, from left to right, mark market crashes on Black Monday in 10/1987, during the Russian crisis in 08/1998, the Subprime crisis in 10/2007, Lehman Brothers' collapse in 09/2008, the US Sovereign Credit Degradation in 08/2011, the Russian financial crisis in 12/2014, the market crisis in 02/2018, and the COVID-19 pandemic in 02/2020.

Figure 10.1reveals that the null hypothesis that the empirical and reference distributions are identical cannot be rejected at the 1% level for more than half of the time, as HD values consistently remain below the critical value. This implies that the empirical distribution of return residuals closely aligns with a normal distribution. However, it's crucial to note periods where the null hypothesis can be rejected, indicating a deviation from normality.

The analysis underscores the relationship between the HD, VIX, SPVOL, and SPRET with market crashes. The HD experiences a noticeable decline, crossing the p = 0.01 line preceding each market crash. This decline is coupled with an upswing in VIX and SPVOL, alongside a sharp ascent in HD during the crash. This pattern suggests an opportunity to leverage two HD peaks, accompanied by a VIX surge, as leading indicators of market crashes, which is the topic of the next section.

10.6. Ambiguity and Crash Risk

Existing research suggests that leveraging an ambiguity measure can offer valuable early warnings for market crashes. This is explored in Lu et al. (forthcoming), which constructs a firm-level HD measure and studies its relationship with the occurrence of financial crashes. They begin by considering the Negative Coefficient of Skewness (NCSKEW) indicator proposed by Chen, Hong, and Stein (2001) and analyze the relationship between the HD measure in period t and crashes in period $t + 1$ using predictive regression.

Chen, Hong, and Stein (2001) argue that corporate managers possess discretion over the timing and content of information disclosures, often delaying negative news while promptly releasing positive information. This selective disclosure leads to a positive skew in return distributions. Firms with higher ambiguity or opaqueness are likely to engage more in such disclosure practices, enhancing the positive skewness effect and resulting in a lower NCSKEW value. Hence, it is expected that the ambiguity measure would inversely relate to stock crashes (NCSKEW), with HD's regression coefficients anticipated to be negative.

Empirically, using data from 1983 to 2020, Lu et al. (forthcoming) confirm these hypotheses. Without control variables, the regression coefficient of HD stands at −2.49 with a t-statistic of −25.83, and with control variables, it adjusts to −1.33 with a t-statistic of −12.77, both significantly negative, thereby validating the above hypothesis. Beyond NCSKEW, the paper also employs another metric from Chen, Hong, and Stein (2001), the Down-to-Up Volatility (DUVOL) as a proxy for financial crashes, yielding similar predictive regression outcomes. The regression coefficients for HD remain significantly negative, whether control variables are considered or not, reinforcing the predictive power of HD in signaling potential market crashes.

10.7. Conclusion

Ambiguity, distinct from the conventional understanding of risk where outcomes and their probabilities are well-defined, represents the uncertainty inherent in the probability distributions themselves, rather than in the outcomes. This concept does not constitute a separate category of factors but rather serves as a foundational theory that underpins investor behavior, suggesting that ambiguity and risk are intertwined in the decision-making process. Integrating ambiguity into the factor-investing framework allows for a more nuanced application of various factors, where the strict assumptions about underlying distributions can be relaxed. This approach not only offers a more flexible application of factors but also enhances the realism of risk models by accommodating a wider range of distributional assumptions. While this inclusion inevitably introduces complexity, it holds the potential to provide more comprehensive explanations for, or even anticipate, extreme market events, often referred to as black-swan events.

The challenge in integrating ambiguity into financial models lies in its measurement, as there is no universally accepted metric for quantifying distributional uncertainty. Our discussion introduces five popular measures of ambiguity, with a particular focus on the $\mho$ measure, which delves into the uncertainties surrounding probabilities, and the Hellinger Distance (HD) measure, which assesses the divergence between two probability distributions. These measures open new avenues for understanding and incorporating ambiguity into financial analysis and investment strategies.

As an emerging field of inquiry, the exploration of ambiguity in finance presents fertile ground for future research, particularly concerning its integration into factor investing. Future studies could extend beyond the measures discussed herein to uncover additional metrics capable of capturing ambiguity. Furthermore, an intriguing research avenue involves re-evaluating traditional factors under the lens of ambiguity, adjusting their distributional premises to account for this additional layer of uncertainty. Such endeavors could yield insights that more accurately reflect the complexities and dynamics of financial markets, thereby enhancing the efficacy of factor investing practice.

References

Abdellaoui, M., H. Bleichrodt, E. Kemel, and O. L'Haridon (2021). Measuring beliefs under ambiguity. *Operations Research* 69(2), 599–612.

Anderson, E. W., E. Ghysels, and J. L. Juergens (2009). The impact of risk and uncertainty on expected returns. *Journal of Financial Economics* 94(2), 233–263.

Augustin, P. and Y. Izhakian (2020). Ambiguity, volatility, and credit risk. *Review of Financial Studies* 33(4), 1618–1672.

Brenner, M. and Y. Izhakian (2018). Asset pricing and ambiguity: Empirical evidence. *Journal of Financial Economics* 130(3), 503–531.

Cao, H. H., T. Wang, and H. H. Zhang (2005). Model uncertainty, limited market participation, and asset prices. *Review of Financial Studies* 18(4), 1219–1253.

Chen, J., H. Hong, and J. C. Stein (2001). Forecasting crashes: Trading volume, past returns, and conditional skewness in stock prices. *Journal of Financial Economics* 61(3), 345–381.

Dimmock, S. G., R. Kouwenberg, O. S. Mitchell, and K. Peijnenburg (2016). Ambiguity aversion and household portfolio choice puzzles: Empirical evidence. *Journal of Financial Economics* 119(3), 559–577.

Easley, D. and M. O'Hara (2009). Ambiguity and nonparticipation: The role of regulation. *Review of Financial Studies* 22(5), 1817–1843.

Ellsberg, D. (1961). Risk, ambiguity, and the savage axioms. *The Quarterly Journal of Economics* 75(4), 643–669.

Fama, E. and K. R. French (1992). The cross-section of expected stock returns. *Journal of Finance* 47(2), 427–465.

Garlappi, L., R. Uppal, and T. Wang (2007). Portfolio selection with parameter and model uncertainty: A multi-prior approach. *Review of Financial Studies* 20(1), 41–81.

Gibbs, A. L. and F. E. Su (2002). On choosing and bounding probability metrics. *International Statistical Review / Revue Internationale de Statistique* 70(3), 419–435.

Gilboa, I. (1987). Expected utility with purely subjective non-additive probabilities. *Journal of Mathematical Economics* 16(1), 65–88.

Gilboa, I. and D. Schmeidler (1989). Maxmin expected utility with non-unique prior. *Journal of Mathematical Economics* 18(2), 141–153.

Ghirardato, P., F. Maccheroni, and M. Marinacci (2004). Differentiating ambiguity and ambiguity attitude. *Journal of Economic Theory* 118(2), 133–173.

Hansen, L. P. and T. J. Sargent (2001). Robust control and model uncertainty. *American Economic Review Papers and Proceedings* 91(2), 60–66.

Hellinger, E. (1909). Neue begrundung der theorie quadratischer formen von unendlichvielen ver anderlichen. *Journal fur die reine und angewandte Mathematik* 136, 210–271.

Izhakian, Y., D. Yermack, and J. F. Zender (2022). Ambiguity and the tradeoff theory of capital structure. *Management Science* 68(6), 4090–4111.

Klibanoff, P., M. Marinacci, and S. Mukerji (2005). A smooth model of decision making under ambiguity. *Econometrica* 73(6), 1849–1892.

Lu, T., L. Zhang, X. Zhang, and Z. Zhao (forthcoming). Beyond risk: A measure of distribution uncertainty. *Information Systems Research*.

Knight, F. M. (1921). *Risk, Uncertainty, and Profit*. Boston: Houghton Mifflin.

Maccheroni, F., M. Marinacci, and A. Rustichini (2006). Ambiguity aversion, robustness, and the variational representation of preferences. *Econometrica* 74(6), 1447–1498.

Maenhout, P. J. (2004). Robust portfolio rules and asset pricing. *Review of Financial Studies* 17(4), 951–983.

Miao, J., B. Wei, and H. Zhou (2019). Ambiguity aversion and the variance premium. *The Quarterly Journal of Finance* 9(2), 1950003.

Schmeidler, D. (1989). Maxmin expected utility with a non-unique prior. *Journal of Mathematical Economics* 18(2), 141–153.

Siniscalchi, M. (2009). Vector expected utility and attitudes toward variation. *Econometrica* 77(3), 801–855.

Tversky, A. and D. Kahneman (1992). Advances in prospect theory: Cumulative representation of uncertainty. *Journal of Risk and Uncertainty* 5(4), 297–323.

Uppal, R. and T. Wang (2003). Model misspecification and under diversification. *Journal of Finance* 58(6), 2465–2486.

van de Kuilen, G. and P. P. Wakker (2011). The midweight method to measure attitudes toward risk and ambiguity. *Management Science* 57(3), 582–598.

Wakker, P. P. (2010). *Prospect Theory for Risk and Ambiguity*. Cambridge: Cambridge University Press.

Williams, C. D. (2015). Asymmetric responses to earnings news: A case for ambiguity. *The Accounting Review* 90(2), 785–817.

11

ALTERNATIVE DATA

11.1. Nature of Alternative Data

Up to this point in the book, the factors discussed have been primarily constructed based on traditional trading and fundamental data. However, as more investors begin to engage with and apply these concepts, and as capital starts to trade these factors in many developed stock markets, their returns have gradually diminished, leading to a transformation of what was once alpha into beta. To acquire additional information and to capture market dynamics more accurately and timely, thereby gaining returns from other sources, industry practitioners have increasingly turned their attention to the study and use of alternative data.

Alternative data refers to non-traditional sources of information, which include but are not limited to social media data, crowdsourced data, financial transaction data, textual data, image data, satellite data, environmental indicators, and geolocation data. By leveraging these data, quantitative researchers can attempt to analyze how the concepts underlying these data influence stock returns and thus construct predictive factors. However, fully utilizing alternative data requires researchers to possess a higher level of skill. From data collection to understanding the data generation process, to data handling, and to integrating data logic to form factor logic, many challenges need to be overcome. Moreover, some data are difficult to obtain and expensive to purchase. Therefore, while alternative data holds great promise in factor construction, it also presents significant challenges.

The goal of this chapter is to explore the potential use of alternative data in factor investing. Specifically, Section 11.2 introduces common sources of alternative data. Taking technology link and stock returns as an example, Section 11.3 demonstrates in great detail how factors can be constructed using alternative data to obtain excess returns. In addition, we will present two studies on this topic to initiate a discussion on the iterative upgrading of data and its utilization methods.

DOI: 10.4324/9781003480204-11

Section 11.4 focuses on the use of machine-learning algorithms to process alternative data. Section 11.5 discusses the risks and challenges associated with the use of alternative data. Finally, Section 11.6 concludes this chapter.

11.2. Potential Sources of Alternative Data

As mentioned in Section 11.1, there exists a wide variety of alternative data types. This section provides a brief discussion for each of them, serving as a reference for readers.

11.2.1 Social Media Data

Social media data refers to information that is generated by users on social media platforms, offering a rich resource for investors and analysts to uncover insights into consumer behaviors, market trends, and potential investment opportunities. Xu and Zhang (2013) suggest that Wikipedia improves the information environment in the financial market by moderating managers' voluntary disclosure of bad news and reducing investors' negative reaction to such news, highlighting the value of information aggregation through the use of social media platforms. Through sophisticated analysis of social media activities and sentiments, valuable insights can be extracted from platforms such as Twitter, Facebook, Reddit, Wikipedia, and LinkedIn, where users freely share their opinions and sentiments on a wide array of topics.

Investors, for example, closely monitor the discussions and sentiments expressed on Twitter regarding particular stocks or companies, analyzing the volume, tone, and content of tweets to gauge market sentiment and identify potential trading opportunities (Liew and Budavari 2017). Additionally, sentiment analysis techniques can be employed to evaluate the overall sentiment polarity of social media conversations, providing quantitative measures of market sentiment that serve as a complement to traditional financial indicators.

In terms of stock market applications, Antweiler and Frank (2004) conduct a comprehensive study of over 1.5 million messages posted on Yahoo Finance and Raging Bull, related to 45 companies listed on the Dow Jones Industrial Average and the Dow Jones Internet Index. Their research indicate that stock messages could help predict market volatility and contain significant predictive information about returns. In another study, Chen et al. (2014) investigate the extent to which investor opinions disseminated through social media could predict unexpected corporate earnings and future stock returns. By conducting textual analysis of articles and their comments on the most popular investor social media platforms in the United States, the authors find that both could predict returns and unexpected earnings.

11.2.2. Crowdsourced Data

Crowdsourced data is information gathered from a large number of people, often volunteers or contributors from the general public, who provide data, ideas, or feedback. A notable source of crowdsourced data comes from platforms like Glassdoor, where employees anonymously review companies and share their experiences. These reviews offer unique insights into corporate culture, management practices, workplace satisfaction, and employee sentiment. Positive reviews that indicate high employee satisfaction and a strong corporate culture may hint at a favorable investment opportunity, while negative reviews could signal potential risks or challenges the company might be facing.

Green et al. (2019) explore the relationship between employee reviews on Glassdoor.com and stock returns. Intuitively, companies with higher scores should perform better, thus offering higher expected stock returns. To test this hypothesis, they sort stocks into three groups based on employee review changes and construct a long/short portfolio by going long on high-scoring groups and short on low-scoring ones. The empirical results support their hypothesis, showing a significant average excess return for this portfolio.

Moreover, Da, Huang, and Jin (2021) use weekly stock ratings from retail investors on the Forcerank App to study the negative correlation between investors' over-extrapolation beliefs and future stock returns. However, due to data limitations, their sample was restricted to February 2016 to December 2017, involving fewer than 300 stocks and approximately 1,000 users. Consequently, the extent to which their findings can be generalized to the entire market remains in question.

11.2.3. Financial Transaction Data

Financial transaction data offers a wealth of information that can provide valuable insights for investors and analysts. This data may include details such as online sales, payment histories, credit utilization rates, and other factors indicative of creditworthiness. Research by Yi, Zhang, and Zhao (2023) highlights the significance of online sales growth in predicting firms' future stock returns and earnings surprises.

Financial transaction data presents several advantages over traditional financial reporting. First, it often becomes available much earlier than quarterly financial reports, offering real-time insights into business performance. For instance, e-commerce transactions on business-to-consumer (B2C) platforms provide instant access to retail product prices and quantities. Second, transaction data may reveal information not disclosed in aggregated financial reports, providing a more comprehensive understanding of business operations. Finally, financial transaction data tends to be more objective compared to financial reports, which may be subject to manipulation or managerial discretion. Harnessing financial transaction data allows investors to gain timely and objective insights into market trends and potential investment opportunities, enhancing their decision-making processes in quantitative investment strategies.

11.2.4. Textual Data

Textual data encompasses any unstructured text found within documents, reports, social media posts, news articles, and more. It includes not just the words used but also the context, sentiment, and changes in language over time. Textual data analysis involves extracting meaningful information from these texts, which can provide deep insights into the behaviors, strategies, and potential future performance of companies, making it an invaluable resource for academic and financial research (Gentzkow, Kelly, and Taddy 2019, Loughran and McDonald 2020).

In recent years, numerous studies have analyzed the textual information in listed companies' financial reports to investigate stock returns, with one of the most representative works being that of Cohen, Malloy, and Nguyen (2020). This study examines whether textual changes in the quarterly and annual reports of US listed companies correlate with stock returns. As revealed by its title "Lazy Prices", the study finds that companies with fewer textual modifications in their reports tend to have higher expected future returns. An investment strategy that goes long on companies with minor textual changes and short on those with more significant changes yields an annualized excess return of over 20%.

The brilliance of this article lies in its discussion of the underlying mechanisms. Cohen, Malloy, and Nguyen (2020) identify several reasons behind the textual modifications in financial reports: more negative sentiment, higher uncertainty, increased litigiousness, and CEO/CFO changes. These factors often indicate higher operational risks and uncertainties for the companies. Furthermore, the study delves into which sections of the financial reports are most critical regarding textual changes, including Item 1A: Risk Factors.

Similarly, Lopez-Lira (2020) also analyzes the Risk Factors section of financial reports. Using Latent Dirichlet Allocation (LDA), the study extracts 25 risk topics from the Risk Factors section. Further analysis reveals that some of these represent systematic risks faced by different companies, with some of these systematic risks being priced. The pricing ability of the factor models based on these risks is comparable to that of the traditional Fama-French three- or five-factor models.

Unlike the approaches taken in the previously mentioned studies, which either construct factors from textual data or explore anomalies, Bybee, Kelly, and Su (2023) develop an empirical asset pricing model grounded in textual data analysis, drawing on the research by Bybee et al. (forthcoming). The latter develops an innovative model that leverages LDA to organize articles from *The Wall Street Journal* spanning from 1984 to 2017 into 180 distinct topics, such as small-cap stocks, commodities, and mortgages, and then computes a time-series attention score for each topic.

The underlying premise of Bybee, Kelly, and Su (2023) is the hypothesis that financial news reveals investors' beliefs about future investment opportunities, thereby influencing asset prices. To explore this hypothesis, the study employs the covariance between asset returns and topic attention data as instrumental variables, leading to the construction of a latent factor model. The empirical findings of this model offer fresh insights into asset pricing, suggesting that the attention allocated to specific topics within financial news can indeed serve as a significant determinant of asset prices.

11.2.5. Image Data

Image data refers to a wide range of visual content including photographs, charts, and graphs. This data type is particularly rich in information that is not readily captured through traditional numerical or textual analysis. Image data can convey complex information such as environmental changes, consumer behavior, corporate activities, and market sentiments in a more intuitive and immediate manner. The analysis of image data, especially with the advent of advanced machine-learning techniques like Convolutional Neural Networks (CNNs), has opened new avenues for extracting predictive information related to stock returns.

Obaid and Pukthuanthong (2022) categorize emotions in news photographs and created a daily investor sentiment index. This sentiment index is found to predict market returns and trading volumes effectively. However, it is helpful to indicate that the study explores the substitutability between pessimistic emotions in photographs and those in news text regarding stock price predictions, finding a tendency towards substitution rather than complementarity between the two.

In another study, Jiang, Kelly, and Xiu (2023) apply CNN to stock candlestick charts. It can be seen as a great advancement of the early work of Lo, Mamaysky, and Wang (2000). Unlike traditional methods that compute momentum or reversal factors based on predefined rules, their approach identifies complex price patterns that are highly correlated with future returns. These patterns differ significantly from traditional technical analysis trends (as discussed in Chapter 5) and contain more predictive information.

11.2.6. Satellite Data

Satellite data presents a unique and valuable resource for investors and analysts seeking to gain insights into various economic indicators and trends. For example, satellite imagery can be effectively utilized to track factors such as crop yields, shipping activity, and retail foot traffic, providing valuable information that can be indicative of broader economic conditions.

One notable application of satellite data in investment comes from Swiss investment bank UBS, which partnered with satellite companies like Remote Sensing Metrics LLC to analyze parking lot occupancy rates at Walmart stores. By leveraging satellite images of cars entering and leaving Walmart parking lots over specific time periods, UBS could estimate customer foot traffic and extrapolate quarterly sales figures. This approach offers a significant advantage in terms of timeliness compared to traditional methods of data collection, such as quarterly financial reports, which often suffer from delays and may be subject to manipulation or cosmetic effects.

Moreover, satellite imagery has proven instrumental during times of crisis, such as the COVID-19 pandemic, where it was utilized to track oil inventories outside the US, providing crucial insights into global macroeconomic activities. Moving forward, the integration of satellite imagery data into AI-based systems holds promise for enhancing predictive analytics in investment decision-making. As the demand for timely and accurate data continues to grow among investors and hedge funds, the competition for access to high-quality satellite imagery is expected to intensify, driving further innovation and advancements in the field.

11.2.7. Environmental Data

Environmental data encompasses information regarding various environmental factors such as climate, weather patterns, pollution levels, and natural disasters, which can significantly impact economic activities and investment decisions. Utilizing environmental data in quantitative investment strategies offers a unique opportunity to incorporate non-traditional sources of information into decision-making processes.

For instance, analysis of climate data can provide insights into the potential effects of weather conditions on agricultural yields, energy consumption patterns, and infrastructure vulnerabilities. By leveraging satellite imagery and remote sensing technologies, investors can monitor changes in land use, deforestation rates, and urbanization trends, providing valuable insights into the sustainability and resilience of companies operating in affected regions. Additionally, environmental data can be instrumental in assessing companies' environmental, social, and governance (ESG) performance, aiding investors in identifying sustainable investment opportunities and managing risks associated with climate change and environmental regulations. Overall, integrating environmental data into quantitative investment models enables investors to gain a deeper understanding of the interplay between environmental factors and financial markets, facilitating more informed investment decisions and contributing to long-term value creation.

11.2.8. Geolocation Data

Geolocation data pertains to information related to the geographical location of individuals, assets, or events, offering valuable insights into spatial trends, movement patterns, and regional dynamics. In quantitative investment strategies, leveraging geolocation data can provide unique opportunities to gain a deeper understanding of consumer behavior, economic activity, and market trends.

For instance, by analyzing mobile device data and GPS signals, investors can track foot traffic patterns, identify popular retail locations, and assess the performance of brick-and-mortar stores. This information can be particularly useful for retailers, real estate investors, and companies operating in the transportation and hospitality sectors. Additionally, geolocation data can be instrumental in analyzing supply chain logistics, optimizing delivery routes, and assessing the impact of transportation infrastructure projects on local economies. Moreover, geolocation data can offer valuable insights into urbanization trends, population movements, and demographic shifts, helping investors identify emerging markets and potential investment opportunities. By integrating geolocation data into quantitative models, investors can enhance their understanding of spatial dynamics and make more informed investment decisions based on spatial trends and patterns.

In summary, the potential sources of alternative data may extend far beyond our current understanding. Taking an abstract perspective, we can analyze the core investment viewpoint: investors allocate capital into certain assets under specific circumstances. Within this framework, three primary elements emerge: the subject, encompassing information about investors' attributes and sentiments towards different stocks; the object, consisting of data on stocks, including company performance and industry trends; and the adverbial clause, representing the conditions under which investments are made, such as micro-market environments and macroeconomic conditions. Importantly, there are no strict limitations on the use of alternative data, providing ample room for imagination and exploration of new possibilities.

11.3. An Example: T-Link and Stock Returns

In this section, we take technological linkages (T-links) among companies as an example to illustrate how alternative data can be utilized to harvest excess returns. Two pivotal academic studies on this subject are Lee et al. (2019) and Bekkerman, Fich, and Khimich (2023). These works not only underscore the increasing sophistication in utilizing information through technological advancements but also reflect on the implications of alternative data coupled with advanced algorithms on market efficiency. It's worth noting that these studies are also emblematic of the topics discussed in Chapter 2, Quantamentals, which focuses on factors derived from economically-linked firms.

11.3.1. T-Link (I)

In the age of the knowledge economy, technological prowess has emerged as a critical factor for a company's short-term profitability and long-term viability. Tech giants such as Amazon, Google, and Apple may offer vastly different products, yet they share intricate technological connections that often transcend traditional industry boundaries and are not readily discernible from financial reports. Lee et al. (2019) investigate the relationship between inter-company technological linkages and future stock returns. The underlying premise is that the spillover effects of technological advancements can impact a range of companies with high technological linkage, altering their fundamentals and eventually reflecting in their stock prices.

Building on this premise, Lee et al. (2019) reveal a lag–lead relationship between the stock return at $t + 1$ of a focal company i and the returns at t of all its technologically related companies j. By employing a proxy metric that measures technological linkage and using it as weights on returns of those related companies, we can derive the weighted return and use it as a factor for the focal company i. This weighted return possesses predictive power for the focal company's returns in the subsequent period, making it a viable factor. This lead–lag relationship is also termed as technological momentum.

From the description above, it becomes clear that calculating the technological linkages between companies is crucial to the construction of this factor, and this is where Lee et al. (2019) and Bekkerman, Fich, and Khimich (2023) differ. Specifically, Lee et al. (2019) apply the uncentered correlation between the patent distributions of two companies, a methodology also employed by Jaffe (1986) and Bloom, Schankerman, and van Reenen (2013),

$$TECH_{i,j,t} = \frac{T_{i,t}T'_{j,t}}{\left(T_{i,t}T'_{i,t}\right)^{1/2}\left(T_{j,t}T'_{j,t}\right)^{1/2}}, \tag{11.1}$$

where $TECH_{i,j,t}$ represents the technological linkage between companies i and j in period t, $T_{i,t}$ is a row vector with 427 dimensions, i.e., $T_{i,t} = \left[T_{i,t,1}, T_{i,t,2}, \ldots, T_{i,t,427}\right]$. This number originates from the 427 technology classes defined by the United States Patent and Trademark Office. Thus, in their work, a company's patent distribution is defined by the proportion of all the technological patents it has acquired in the past five years across these 427 classes. For instance, suppose a company has 10, 60, and 30 patents in the first, the 100th, and the 303rd classes, respectively, then the corresponding elements in this company's patent distribution satisfy $T_{i,t,1} = 0.1, T_{i,t,100} = 0.6$, and $T_{i,t,303} = 0.3$, while all other categories have a $T_{i,t,k}$ value of 0.

Figure 11.1 (example borrowed from Lee et al. 2019) showcases the technological patent categories of Regeneron Pharmaceuticals and Illumina between 2002 and 2006. Regeneron is a pharmaceutical company, while Illumina produces life

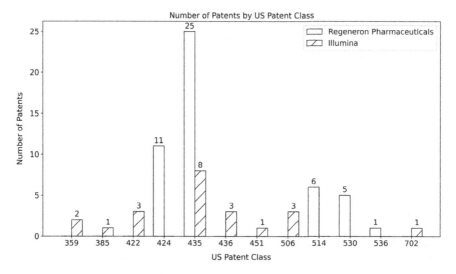

FIGURE 11.1. Patent Category Distributions
Source Data extracted from Lee et al. (2019)

science tools and offers genetic analysis services. Although these companies operate in different sectors with no apparent supply chain links, technological linkages offer a new perspective on their connection—both companies have a significant number of patents in category 435 (molecular and microbiology), resulting in a $TECH_{i,j,t}$ of 0.71. Technological linkages thus reveal relationships between companies that are overlooked by industry classifications and supply chains. Empirical evidence suggests that these linkages have considerable potential in stock selection, offering a fertile ground for investors seeking to exploit such interconnections for excess returns.

With $TECH_{i,j,t}$ derived, the calculation of the factor is straightforward, i.e.,

$$TECHRET_{i,t} = \frac{\sum_{j \neq i} TECH_{i,j,t} \times r_{j,t}}{\sum_{j \neq i} TECH_{i,j,t}}, \tag{11.2}$$

where $r_{j,t}$ is the return of the related company j at time t. Empirically, with data that ranges from 1963 to 2012, Lee et al. (2019) find that the long/short portfolio constructed by going long on stocks with the highest $TECHRET$ decile and shorting those in the lowest $TECHRET$ decile achieves significant excess returns. For example, with equal and value weights, this portfolio's average monthly excess returns are 1.17% (with a t-statistic of 5.47) and 0.69% (with a t-statistic of 3.19), respectively. Furthermore, the robustness of these excess returns persisted even after accounting for other common factors. In addition to portfolio sort analysis, the Fama-MacBeth regression reveals similar findings.

Delving into the intrinsic mechanisms of technological linkages, the study reveals that the long/short portfolio consistently generates excess returns over the ensuing months. This suggests that technological momentum represents a price discovery process, wherein the stock prices adjust as investors gradually assimilate new information about firms with technological linkages. It could be inferred that the market's absorption of news related to technological fundamentals is a slow process, potentially leading to mispricing. The authors validate this hypothesis by considering the nature of its technological innovations, the extent to which investors might be attentive to such innovations, and the costs that investors face should they attempt to arbitrage the mispricing. This line of reasoning is supported by literature that explores the characteristics of innovation news dissemination and its impact on stock prices (see, for example, Cohen and Frazzini 2008).

11.3.2. T-Link (II)

In a progressive step toward refining the measurement of T-links, Bekkerman, Fich, and Khimich (2023) utilize advanced machine learning algorithms to enhance the methodology. Unlike the study of Lee et al. (2019), which relies on patent classifications, Bekkerman, Fich, and Khimich (2023) delve directly into patent texts, extracting technical terms and computing their overlaps to gauge the similarity between companies. This approach can be considered an evolved measure of technological linkage.

In their empirical analysis, the authors first establish evidence for the existence of economic connections between technologically linked firms, which is crucial. The validity of a factor constructed based on T-links hinges on the presence of economic connections; otherwise, it would likely be a mirage. In their research, they investigate the relationships between the focal company and its technologically linked firms from the perspectives of profitability and technological innovation. For profitability, they examine the contemporaneous and the predictive relation between the Return on Assets (ROA) of focal and associated companies. For technological innovation, they conduct a similar analysis using R&D expenditure relative to total assets. The findings indicate significant positive correlations, both contemporaneous and predictive, for both profitability and innovation metrics. These empirical results underscore the economic connections between technologically similar companies, providing a foundation for asset pricing.

Furthermore, Bekkerman, Fich, and Khimich (2023) compare their new factor against the one constructed by Lee et al. (2019) and find that the new factor is superior to the old one. This is evident as the new factor continued from patent text data to achieve excess returns even after controlling for the $TECHRET$ factor of Lee et al. (2019). However, the reverse case holds not true, i.e., the $TECHRET$ factor of Lee et al. (2019) fails to deliver excess returns once the new factor is accounted for. Additionally, empirical evidence suggests that post-2000, the TECHRET factor of Lee et al. (2019) becomes less effective in yielding excess returns, whereas the new factor maintains its significance.

Bekkerman, Fich, and Khimich (2023) contributes to the literature by not only providing a refined measure of T-links but also demonstrating the enduring relevance of economic connections in an evolving market landscape. It reinforces the notion that in-depth textual analysis of patents can uncover deeper economic linkages between firms, which are vital for constructing robust investment strategies. These advancements reflect the dynamic interplay between technological innovation and financial markets, offering nuanced insights for academics and practitioners alike.

11.3.3. Implication on Market Efficiency

We conclude this section with a discussion of the implications of alternative data and advanced machine-learning algorithms on market efficiency, as exemplified by the phenomenon where the new T-link factor outperforms the older one. This is not unique to the T-link factor but a pattern that is likely to emerge across various factors as data richness and construction methods evolve, leading upgraded factors to inevitably outperform their predecessors in empirical tests.

The effectiveness of the new T-link factor post-2000, contrasted with the waning efficacy of the old factor based on patent classifications, can be interpreted from two perspectives. The first involves the issue of investors' limited attention, which leads to the slow diffusion of information—a subject previously discussed.

The second perspective concerns how investor learning affects market efficiency, drawing on the insights of Nagel (2021) and Martin and Nagel (2022). Nowadays, variable construction becomes easier, but decades ago, investors had limited access to and use of these variables, even though the data might have already been available. Patent texts exemplify this; computing similarity based on texts is more complex than using patent classifications, implying higher costs for investors to acquire and process patent data, thus making it less accessible for use. This scarcity in data accessibility can be seen as forcing investors to rely on overly sparse valuation models when pricing assets. The analysis by Martin and Nagel (2022) suggests that factors constructed with contemporary methods and advanced models can predict stock returns both in-sample and out-of-sample when they are tested on historical data. However, as alternative data and technology become more widespread, and once investors incorporate these alternative data into their valuation models, their predictive power will likely diminish.

Undoubtedly, alternative data has inaugurated a new chapter in factor investing. Nonetheless, as we employ covariates unearthed through new data and technologies, it is imperative to deeply consider the underlying reasons for their ability to generate excess returns. While alternative data and machine learning provide novel insights and opportunities for investment strategies, they also underscore the evolving nature of market efficiency.

One key way in which alternative data influences market efficiency is by providing a more comprehensive and timely view of the underlying factors that drive asset prices. Traditional financial data sources, such as company financial statements and economic indicators, have limitations in terms of their coverage and frequency. Alternative data, on the other hand, can offer real-time or near-real-time information, giving investors an edge in understanding market dynamics and making informed investment decisions. By incorporating a broader range of data points, market participants can gain deeper insights into consumer behavior, supply chain dynamics, product demand, and other factors that affect asset valuations.

Furthermore, alternative data can uncover hidden patterns and relationships that may not be evident from traditional data sources alone. By leveraging advanced analytics techniques, such as machine learning and artificial intelligence, market participants can identify predictive signals and generate alpha-generating investment strategies. These insights can lead to more accurate pricing of assets, reducing mispricing and enhancing market efficiency.

However, it is important to note that the adoption and utilization of alternative data also present challenges. Data quality, privacy concerns, and the need for robust data governance frameworks are critical considerations. Additionally, the interpretation and integration of alternative data into investment processes require sophisticated analytics capabilities and expertise. Market participants need to develop the necessary skills and infrastructure to effectively harness the power of alternative data while ensuring its responsible and ethical use.

11.4. Utilizing Machine Learning for Processing Alternative Data

In the realm of alternative-data processing, the integration with machine-learning methods plays a significant role. The complexity and diversity of unstructured data, which often presents itself in forms other than neatly formatted numbers—such as text, images, or other formats—challenge traditional data processing techniques. However, with the evolution of deep-learning technologies, we are now empowered to extract valuable insights from such data using potent machine-learning algorithms.

For instance, in text data processing, deep-learning models like Recurrent Neural Networks (RNNs) and Transformer models have proven highly effective. These models can capture semantic and emotional nuances within text, enabling tasks like sentiment analysis and topic modeling. Similarly, CNNs and Transformer models for image data have shown exceptional capabilities in extracting critical information, such as object recognition and scene comprehension. Thus, the application of machine-learning algorithms provides us with robust tools to unearth deeper insights and value from unstructured alternative data.

Upon acquiring a set of alternative data, the initial line of inquiry typically stems from its descriptive variables and collection methodology, pondering whether the data could influence stock-return predictions. While initial hypotheses may be formed, testing them rigorously is no simple task. Moreover, if initial conjectures fail, it does not necessarily render the data useless. Consequently, we can consider directly utilizing algorithms, particularly complex deep-learning algorithms, to train models and test whether the data improve the models' predictive accuracy. It is crucial to clarify that this process does not equate to deploying the trained models in trading directly. Real trading necessitates deeper research and understanding of the logic behind the data. Nonetheless, this approach is a rapid-verification method for gauging informational value. When training models with alternative data, the typical aim is to verify the data's predictive capabilities. If alternative data significantly improve predictive accuracy of a model, it may indicate the data indeed contain incremental information regarding asset returns.

Another approach to applying machine learning models involves combining trading data with machine-learning models to stabilize the information gleaned from alternative data. Since the information from various alternative data sources ultimately manifests in stock prices through investor trading actions, we can attempt to reconstruct the generation process of alternative data using trading data. This process also allows us to measure whether alternative data truly offer additional value. If a piece of alternative data can be entirely fitted and its out-of-sample performance mirrors the trend of the fitted data, its additional value may be limited.

Overall, machine learning presents immense potential in the utilization of alternative data, unveiling more information as algorithms evolve. With the continuous development and advancement of machine-learning algorithms, we can delve deeper into and leverage the information contained within alternative data. As deep-learning technology matures and its applications broaden, we can more effectively process unstructured data such as text and images to extract increasingly valuable insights. Additionally, as machine-learning algorithms improve in handling large-scale data and complex models, we can model and predict stock-market trends more accurately. Therefore, even if we have not yet fully unlocked the potential of alternative data, as long as we believe in their predictive power for stock returns, we can preserve this data through stable, long-term supply or collection methods. With the progression of machine-learning algorithms, these data may become one of the key elements in obtaining alpha in the future.

11.5. Risks and Challenges of Alternative Data

While alternative data presents a multitude of possibilities for exploring new factors in asset pricing and quantitative investment, its use comes with a spectrum of risks and challenges.

11.5.1. Risks

One potential risk is related to quality and veracity of data. The accuracy and reliability of alternative data can vary significantly. For instance, data may be incomplete, inaccurately reported, or subject to manipulation, leading to erroneous conclusions and strategies based on flawed premises.

Moreover, the supply of alternative data can be unstable, susceptible to interruptions or changes. Users must be prepared for such eventualities, particularly within quantitative investment systems by implementing measures to mitigate these risks. This includes adjusting models promptly when data updates are not forthcoming or when there is a shift in data distribution to prevent adverse impacts on other aspects of the system. Sometimes, it may even be necessary to manage each set of alternative data as a separate sub-portfolio, to safeguard against supply disruptions.

Besides, alternative data could involve sensitive commercial information or privacy concerns, posing potential regulatory risks. At the lesser end, this might lead to data supply interruptions, and at the extreme, it could result in legal scrutiny for privacy breaches or insider trading. Therefore, careful and compliant use of alternative data is paramount to ensure legality in both sourcing and application.

The use of alternative data and machine-learning technology may also shift decision-making to automated systems, thereby diminishing the role of human judgment. Investors and asset managers must maintain oversight and accountability for investment strategies and algorithms, taking responsibility for their outcomes.

11.5.2. Challenges

New data types are a double-edged sword. On the one hand, their usage is not crowded yet due to their novelty; on the other, without requisite domain knowledge, users may struggle to harness their full potential.

In the imagination of many, alternative data could be thrilling narratives, already processed into structured formats by vendors, ready to be deployed directly for factor construction. However, the reality often resembles discovering an uncharted mountain: its potential riches and points of entry are unknown until explored. In the industry, large asset management firms usually analyze data internally due to their ample talent reserves. Alternatively, data vendors often market their products with promising scenarios. Besides buyers and sellers, the market has seen the emergence of third-party research agents engaged in alternative-data analysis on investors' behalf.

Using processed data from vendors or third parties is undeniably convenient for investors. However, this practice has its downsides: processed examples may be widely known due to extensive marketing and the circulation of related reports, leading to crowded trading signals. Therefore, it is essential to delve into raw data to uncover unique insights. Thus, mastering domain knowledge—including understanding how alternative data are generated, the business processes behind them, and their financial implications—is crucial. This mastery ensures control over research and a higher likelihood of uncovering unique sources for alpha.

An accompanying challenge is the subtle evolution of data sources that can go unnoticed. Therefore, when applying alternative data, stricter monitoring of data distribution is necessary to detect anomalies and to validate research logic continually. If predictive performance changes significantly, a deep dive into the data and logic to ascertain any issues and consider discontinuation is warranted.

Furthermore, alternative data distributions may exhibit biases, necessitating careful framing to prevent unrepresentative results from analyses. Taking the previously mentioned Green et al. (2019) as an example, Glassdoor data has potential issues such as employer incentives for employees to post five-star reviews. Additionally, people are more inclined to post negative reviews when dissatisfied with their employer, raising concerns about the unbiased nature of the data. Investors and asset managers must remain vigilant of such biases and take steps to mitigate their risks.

Moreover, the short historical span of alternative data can make it difficult to draw definitive research conclusions. To address this, one might initially adopt a logic-driven research approach to reduce data-driven biases, then gradually build trust in the logic over time before applying it in practice.

11.6. Conclusion

The application of alternative data in factor investing has seen a significant uptick in recent years. Practitioners are keen to incorporate a broader spectrum of information into their investment strategies to secure a competitive edge. However, the utilization of alternative data introduces a host of challenges and risks, including issues related to data quality, coping with data discontinuities, potential regulatory scrutiny, and ethical concerns.

Despite these hurdles, the future likely holds a continued increase in the application of alternative data within factor investing. This trend is driven by investors' desire to gain a competitive edge and achieve excess returns in an increasingly crowded and competitive investment landscape. Furthermore, a reduction in the correlation of trading signals may decrease the probability of systematic risks across the market.

Factors constructed using transaction and financial data are typically easier to analyze for their efficacy. However, alternative data might be less influenced by trading activities and possess greater durability, presenting a trade-off. As markets mature and become more efficient, the effectiveness of factors derived from traditional data may diminish, prompting increased interest in alternative data. Therefore, the extent of alternative data usage in the quantitative investment industry could serve as an indicator of market maturity.

Moreover, the application of alternative data in factor investing should not be confined solely to the goal of factor discovery. Considerations should extend to understanding how alternative data can elucidate the drivers of asset returns over time as well as in the cross-section, the impact of alternative data on the behavior of various financial participants, the dynamic relationship between data richness and the informational content in asset prices, and how alternative data influences investor learning and its potential to lead to spurious predictability. These questions may be more critical than factor discovery alone.

For instance, Dessaint, Foucault, and Fresard (2022) address whether the richness of alternative data enhances the quality of financial forecasts. They find that the emergence of alternative data reduces the cost of accessing short-term forecast data while simultaneously increasing its accuracy. Consequently, alternative data leads analysts to devote more effort to acquiring and analyzing short-term forecast information, thus improving the accuracy of short-term forecasts. However, given the limited attention of analysts, this shift inadvertently reduces the accuracy of their long-term forecasts.

While the practical application and processing of alternative data can indeed be challenging, their undeniable potential cannot be overlooked. Even if failures are encountered, the exploration of alternative data remains a profoundly intriguing endeavor. Delving into alternative data not only accumulates knowledge and experience but also deepens our understanding of market dynamics. Engaging with alternative data, therefore, is not just about the pursuit of new investment factors but also about enriching our comprehension of the financial markets and their underlying mechanisms.

References

Antweiler, W. and M. Z. Frank (2004). Is all that talk just noise? The information content of internet stock message boards. *Journal of Finance* 59(3), 1259–1294.

Bekkerman, R., E. M. Fich, and N. V. Khimich (2023). The effect of innovation similarity on asset prices: Evidence from patents' big data. *Review of Asset Pricing Studies* 13(1), 99–145.

Bloom, N., M. Schankerman, and J. van Reenen (2013). Identifying technology spillovers and product market rivalry. *Econometrica* 81(4), 1347–1393.

Bybee, L., B. T. Kelly, A. Manela, and D. Xiu (forthcoming). Business news and business cycles. *Journal of Finance*.

Bybee, L., B. T. Kelly, and Y. Su (2023). Narrative asset pricing: Interpretable systematic risk factors from news text. *Review of Financial Studies* 36(12), 4759–4787.

Chen, H., P. De, Y. Hu, and B.-H. Hwang (2014). Wisdom of crowds: The value of stock opinions transmitted through social media. *Review of Financial Studies* 27(5), 1367–1403.

Cohen, L. and A. Frazzini (2008). Economic links and predictable returns. *Journal of Finance* 63(4), 1977–2011.

Cohen, L., C. Malloy, and Q. Nguyen (2020). Lazy prices. *Journal of Finance* 75(3), 1371–1415.

Da, Z., X. Huang, and L. Jin (2021). Extrapolative beliefs in the cross-section: What can we learn from the crowds? *Journal of Financial Economics* 140(1), 175–196.

Dessaint, O., T. Foucault, and L. Fresard (2022). Does alternative data improve financial forecasting? The horizon effect. Working paper.

Gentzkow, M., B. T. Kelly, and M. Taddy (2019). Text as data. *Journal of Economic Literature* 57(3), 535–574.

Green, T. C., R. Huang, Q. Wen, and D. Zhou (2019). Crowdsourced employer reviews and stock returns. *Journal of Financial Economics* 134(1), 236–251.

Jaffe, A. B. (1986). Technological opportunity and spillovers of R&D: Evidence from firms' patents, profits, and market value. *American Economic Review* 76 (5), 984–1001.

Jiang, J., B. Kelly, and D. Xiu (2023). (Re-)Imag(in)ing price trends. *Journal of Finance* 78(6), 3193–3249.

Lee, C. M. C., S. T. Sun, R. Wang, and R. Zhang (2019). Technological links and predictable returns. *Journal of Financial Economics* 132(3), 76–96.

Liew, J. and T. Budavari (2017). The "six" factor—A social media factor derived directly from tweet sentiments. *Journal of Portfolio Management* 43(3), 102–111.

Lo, A. W., H. Mamaysky, and J. Wang (2000). Foundations of technical analysis: Computational algorithms, statistical inference, and empirical implementation. *Journal of Finance* 55(4), 1705–1765.

Lopez-Lira, A. (2020). Risk factors that matter: Textual analysis of risk disclosures for the cross-section of returns. Working paper.

Loughran, T. and B. McDonald (2020). Textual analysis in finance. *Annual Review of Financial Economics* 12, 357–375.

Martin, I. W. R. and S. Nagel (2022). Market efficiency in the age of big data. *Journal of Financial Economics* 145(1), 154–177.

Nagel, S. (2021). *Machine Learning in Asset Pricing*. Princeton University Press.

Obaid, K. and K. Pukthuanthong (2022). A picture is worth a thousand words: Measuring investor sentiment by combining machine learning and photos from news. *Journal of Financial Economics* 144(1), 273–297.

Xu, S. X. and X. M. Zhang (2013). Impact of Wikipedia on Market Information Environment: Evidence on Management Disclosure and Investor Reaction. *MIS Quarterly* 37(4), 1043–1068.

Yi, Y., B. Zhang, and X. Zhao (2023). Measuring accounting quality based on real-transaction online sales data. Working paper.

12

MACHINE LEARNING IN FACTOR INVESTING

12.1. AI in Quant Finance

With machine learning and artificial intelligence achieving significant milestones across various fields, particularly the impressive potential shown by generative AI models like GPT, both the academic and industry realms of factor investing are keen to harness the formidable capabilities of machine-learning algorithms to enhance factor-investing strategies. There is a growing and enthusiastic cohort of practitioners beginning to explore the use of AI algorithms; however, it's crucial to note that while AI tools have made substantial progress in basic automation and preliminary analysis, attempts to enable AI to directly make investment decisions or to truly comprehend the underlying mechanics of financial markets have yet to achieve significant success.

Convolutional Neural Networks (CNN) and Recurrent Neural Networks (RNN) are two popular types of deep-learning architectures that have made significant contributions to modeling and analysis in the financial market.

CNNs are primarily designed for processing grid-like data, such as images or time series data, by leveraging the concept of convolution. Convolutional layers in a CNN apply filters to small local regions of the input data, capturing spatial or temporal patterns. This enables them to automatically learn hierarchical features from the data, starting from low-level features and gradually building up to more complex representations. In the financial domain, CNNs have been applied to tasks such as stock-price prediction, anomaly detection, and sentiment analysis. They can extract relevant patterns and relationships from historical price data, news articles, or social media sentiment, aiding in making more accurate predictions and identifying market trends.

RNNs, on the other hand, are designed to capture sequential dependencies in data. They are particularly effective in processing time series or sequential data,

DOI: 10.4324/9781003480204-12

where the order of observations is important. RNNs maintain an internal memory, allowing them to retain information about past inputs and utilize it to make predictions at each step. This makes them well-suited for tasks such as stock-market forecasting, portfolio optimization, and credit-risk assessment. RNN variants such as Long Short-Term Memory (LSTM) and Gated Recurrent Units (GRU) have been developed to address the vanishing gradient problem and capture long-term dependencies effectively. By utilizing the temporal dynamics of financial data, RNNs can model complex relationships and uncover hidden patterns, improving the accuracy of financial predictions and decision-making.

The combination of CNNs and RNNs has also proven to be powerful in financial modeling. Researchers have developed hybrid architectures, such as Convolutional-LSTM (ConvLSTM), where CNNs are used to extract local features from input data, and the extracted features are then fed into an LSTM layer to capture temporal dependencies. This approach has been successful in tasks such as financial time series forecasting, fraud detection, and algorithmic trading.

By leveraging CNNs and RNNs, models in the financial market can benefit from their ability to automatically learn and extract relevant features from complex data. These architectures enable the modeling of spatial, temporal, and sequential relationships, providing more accurate predictions and insights. However, it is important to note that the successful application of CNNs and RNNs in the financial domain also relies on high-quality data, proper preprocessing techniques, and robust model training and validation processes.

From the perspective of a core concept addressed in this book, and a necessary consideration in factor investing—changes in data distribution—we can see why entrusting AI with financial decisions is an immensely challenging task. Most of the algorithms that have achieved remarkable success thus far are inductive, meaning they derive patterns based on correlations from data. AI has made astounding advancements in recognizing, understanding, and generating images and text. However, it is important to understand that distribution of data may not remain the same in the future, thus defeating the reliance on historical observations of data distribution. Readers should refer to Chapter 10 of this book to see when distribution uncertainty arises and understand the limitations of machine learning.

Mathematically, this suggests that the data generating process is time-varying. Common phenomena in financial research include certain patterns or factors losing their predictive power over time or factors that work in developed stock markets but exhibit opposite effects in emerging markets (such as the momentum factor in the US versus Chinese stock markets). Therefore, one of the most crucial issues in enabling algorithms to generate intelligence might be addressing distribution changes in the data-generating process.

Moreover, data we encounter is likely biased and not representative of the entire sample space. For instance, analyzing hospital patient data might reveal a higher mortality rate among hospital visitors compared to the general population, but does that mean visiting a hospital worsens patient conditions? This paradox arises because only those who feel unwell visit hospitals. To analyze the effectiveness of hospital visits, we would need additional data on the subsequent health outcomes of individuals who feel unwell but choose not to seek hospital care. Shifting back to factor investing, the historical data we utilize represents only a tiny fragment of human history. For example, the US market in recent years has been driven by tech giants, leading to a continuous stock market rally. Such a market structure might bias the factors identified from training data to favor these stocks, mistaking large market cap as an effective predictive variable. However, a longer-term view reveals that smaller-cap stocks tend to yield higher excess returns (i.e., the famous small-minus-big factor).

The potential for distribution changes in the data generating process, compounded by the bias in observed data, makes the out-of-the-box application of machine-learning algorithms in finance unlikely to succeed. An ancient Chinese military strategy proverb states, "For a general, the anticipation of defeat precedes the consideration of victory", emphasizing the importance of recognizing and preparing for potential failures to effectively confront challenges and achieve success.

We dedicate space to these core issues because understanding the difficulties in applying machine learning to investing is the first step toward developing new technologies to overcome or mitigate these challenges or finding compromise solutions to circumvent them. These issues may remain significant academic challenges for a long time. They teach us that when employing advanced AI algorithms for factor investing, we should not abandon logical analysis in factor research; in fact, the logic behind factors requires even greater attention. Factors are merely quantifiable manifestations of stock attributes, but understanding the principles behind these manifestations is crucial. Indeed, guiding machine-learning algorithms with economic theories is key to their success, given the violation of many machine-learning model assumptions, the low signal-to-noise ratio, and non-stationarity of financial data (Nagel 2021).

This chapter will provide a comprehensive explanation of the current state and future of factor investing from the perspective of machine learning, offering forward-looking insights to the reader. Specifically, Section 12.2 discusses how machine learning can be applied throughout the entire process of factor investing practice. Section 12.3 delves into the latest advancements in applying machine learning to empirical asset pricing and factor investing. Section 12.4 focuses on the crucial issue of factor discovery and the role machine learning can play. Section 12.5 compares machine learning and econometrics in the context of factor investing. Section 12.6 concludes.

12.2. Components to be AI-fied in Quantitative Factor Investing: An Anatomy Perspective

This section begins with an analytical perspective, dissecting the primary stages involved in the entire process of quantitative factor investing. We consider how machine-learning algorithms can be introduced at each stage. Following this approach, we analyze each step sequentially, tentatively identifying areas where algorithms could significantly enhance our investment practice.

12.2.1. Data Source Expansion and Preprocessing

Beyond conventional structured financial data, there is a wealth of unstructured data rich with financial market information, encompassing broader market and individual stock insights. AI can optimize the comprehensiveness and timeliness of information gathering, with GPT-based tools offering substantial assistance.

Additionally, AI algorithms contribute to real-time monitoring of data quality and anomalies. In extracting information from unstructured data, such as news sentiment or company information knowledge graphs (Bybee, Kelly, and Su 2023, Bybee et al. forthcoming), AI can excel in deriving quantitative indicators that carry predictive information about stock returns from text and images. Furthermore, an important task in data handling is preprocessing, where AI algorithms can optimize various engineering aspects of intelligent databases, such as data updating, checking, filling missing values (Freyberger et al. 2021, Bryzgalov et al. 2022), vectorized querying, load-balanced storage, and distributed computing.

12.2.2. Factor Research

The cornerstone of factor research lies in factor discovery. The automated mining and extraction of factor logic present a promising area for AI application, albeit requiring substantial engineering and academic support for further development. Section 12.4 of this chapter will delve deeper into this discussion.

12.2.3. Factor Models

Various pricing models have been discussed to explain the expected returns of assets or portfolios in the cross-section, gradually forming a research paradigm based on machine learning in the financial academic world (to be further explored in Section 12.3).

Once numerous predictive factors are identified, integrating them effectively to form tradable signals becomes essential. However, the high dimensionality and correlation among factors pose significant challenges, offering a broad scope for applying machine-learning algorithms. Moreover, in complex factor combination models, market environment variables can be included, hoping to enhance existing linear factors through the nonlinear fitting capabilities of complex models. Of course, it is vital to consciously prevent overfitting due to increased model complexity, mitigating this risk through necessary regularization and other techniques.

12.2.4. Risk Analysis and Portfolio Optimization

After generating predictive signals for returns, the next critical step is portfolio risk analysis. Understanding that returns are derived by taking on certain risks, the core objective of risk control optimization is to maximize returns under predefined risk constraints. An emerging research direction involves establishing a reinforcement learning model and a simulation environment, which sets risk exposure levels based on asset pricing models, defines the action space (i.e., buying and selling stocks), and trains a reinforcement agent to optimize based on predictive signals and defined risk control penalties.

12.2.5. Trading Execution and Monitoring

Following the quantitative research analysis, the final step is actual trading execution. Numerous optimization opportunities exist in this process, such as the impact of liquidity on trade execution mentioned in earlier chapters.

High-frequency data reflecting short-term stock trends can be used to develop trading algorithms. Since the data used to optimize trading execution algorithms is higher frequency, the degree of data distribution change is relatively minor, allowing for optimization with complex algorithms to dissect and analyze market microstructure and short-term supply–demand dynamics.

12.3. Machine Learning and Asset Pricing

Since the work of Gu, Kelly, and Xiu (2020), which formally introduced machine learning methodologies into empirical asset pricing research, a plethora of scholars within the academic community have applied a variety of machine learning models over the past few years. These models, both linear and nonlinear, have been used for the prediction of stock returns and the identification of factors to be included in a pricing model or the stochastic discount factor (SDF). For an excellent review, see Kelly and Xiu (2023).

This shift was primarily motivated by the exponential growth in factors and the complex relationships between factors and asset returns, hallmarks of the big data and machine-learning era. These developments pose significant challenges to traditional empirical research grounded in econometric methods. While econometric techniques undoubtedly remain powerful tools for analyzing simple linear relationships and for parameter adjudication, they are not the preferred approach for dealing with high-dimensional prediction problems—an assertion we further elaborate upon in Section 12.5, where we contrast machine learning with econometrics. Machine learning algorithms, already proven in fields such as natural-language processing and image recognition, have naturally entered the fray for addressing such complex issues.

Consequently, there has been a noticeable shift in academic research from proposing parsimonious, yet ad-hoc, multifactor models, with the goal of diminishing market anomalies, towards an increasing prominence of machine-learning methods. This shift has fostered a new research paradigm around multifactor models and the stochastic discount factor (SDF). The research orientation has quietly moved from being *procedurally* developed to being *empirically* driven. The fact that numerous papers that employ machine-learning algorithms for asset pricing have been published in top-tier journals is the most compelling evidence. At the same time, various machine-learning algorithms have already made their way into industry practices of factor investing, notably in factor discovery and aggregation.

Turning our gaze back to academic research, a thorough examination of these empirical studies reveals a significant amount of commonality, both in theoretical exposition and empirical findings. A deep dive into these works can greatly enhance our understanding of applying machine-learning algorithms to empirical asset pricing and factor investing. The aim of this section is therefore to provide an objective account of the current landscape in this field for the readers. To achieve this, this section navigates the truths and misconceptions surrounding machine learning and asset pricing, via discussion of five pairs of facts and fictions.

12.3.1. Fiction 1: Data will "Speak for Itself"

The first fiction is about the fallacy of indiscriminately feeding data into sophisticated machine-learning algorithms with the mere expectation that the data will "speak for itself".

The low signal-to-noise ratio and non-stationarity inherent in financial data are sufficient to dispel the optimistic but naive hope that applying out-of-the-box machine learning to financial data alone can yield meaningful insights. In the realm of asset pricing, many aspects such as prior distributions of parameters, scaling of covariates, regularization penalties, and the choice of tuning criteria can significantly influence the outcomes.

An illustrative example, drawn from Nagel (2021), though simplistic, elucidates the aforementioned considerations effectively. Suppose we aim to predict the next day's return using the past 120 days' returns and their squared and cubed values as covariates. Table 12.1 summarizes the prediction outcomes under various settings, where the Method column indicates the regularization applied (with OLS denoting the absence of regularization), the Scaling column shows how the covariates are

TABLE 12.1 Return Prediction Examples

Method	Scaling	CV Criterion	IS R^2	CV R^2	CV Portfolio Sharpe Ratio
OLS	Equal	N/A	5.22%	−1.18%	0.35
Ridge	Equal	R^2	2.63%	0.84%	0.30
Ridge	Unequal	R^2	2.69%	1.18%	0.37
Ridge	Unequal	$E[r_p]$	1.75%	0.89%	0.35
Lasso	Unequal	R^2	3.55%	0.84%	0.36

Source Data excerpted from Table 3.2 of Nagel (2021).

standardized (with Equal meaning all covariates are standardized to a mean of 0 and a standard deviation of 1, and Unequal indicating differing standard deviations post-standardization), and the CV Criterion column indicates the metrics used for cross-validation (such as R-squared or expected return on the portfolio). In the table, OLS stands for "ordinary least squares", IS stands for "in-sample", and CV stands for "cross-validation".

The empirical results in the table reveal that model setup significantly impacts the outcomes. However, when faced with a plethora of options, it is neither feasible nor advisable to exhaustively enumerate all possible permutations. Instead, it is essential to leverage priors derived from financial theories effectively. For instance, if we assume the model to be non-sparse, we might favor Ridge regression over Lasso; if we believe the covariates have varying degrees of importance in predicting returns, we might opt for unequal scaling rather than equal; and if we approach from the core of financial theory, we might tune the model to maximize the Sharpe ratio (or minimize pricing errors) rather than relying on traditional R-squared. All these decisions are fundamentally informed by asset pricing theory.

12.3.2. Fact 1: Apply Machine Learning with the Framework of Asset Pricing

Contrary to fiction 1, the first fact states that we shall leverage big data and machine-learning algorithms within the framework of asset pricing theory.

In the domain of empirical asset pricing, the evolution from the CAPM to the APT/ICAPM, and subsequently to the extensive zoo of factors, has undeniably propelled the discipline forward through a myriad of empirical challenges. Despite the paradigm shifts, the core of research has consistently revolved around asset-pricing theories. For instance, notable recent papers such as Bryzgalova, Pelger and Zhu (forthcoming), and Chen, Pelger, and Zhu (2023) have employed advanced machine-learning methodologies—decision trees in the former and Generative Adversarial Networks (GANs) in the latter—yet both have anchored their approaches within the SDF framework to apply varying algorithms to asset pricing.

Similarly, Kelly, Pruitt, and Su (2019) with their instrumental PCA (IPCA) and Gu, Kelly, and Xiu (2021) with their autoencoder model, have utilized latent factor models, modeling factor exposures (beta) as functions of covariates (such as firm-level characteristics and macroeconomic variables). Their differences lie in the fact that Kelly, Pruitt, and Su (2019) employ linear models, while Gu, Kelly, and Xiu (2021) opt for non-linear models. Furthermore, since covariates are time-varying, both methodologies essentially represent conditional pricing models.

Empirically, a commonality among these studies is their use of a vast array of covariates—significantly more than traditional research—and they demonstrate the efficacy of their methods through the out-of-sample (OOS) performance of portfolios. Although these papers experiment with different machine learning algorithms, given the equivalence of SDF and multifactor models, their approaches can be scrutinized and understood within a unified framework, illustrating the integration of advanced machine-learning techniques with foundational asset-pricing theories.

12.3.3. Fiction 2: Machine-Learning Models Neglect Interpretability

The second fiction is related to the argument that machine-learning models are black boxes and that academic research neglects interpretability.

Interpretability is the essence of traditional multifactor models or anomaly studies. For instance, the five-factor model of Fama and French (2015) is grounded in the dividend discount model, while the q-factor model by Hou, Xue, and Zhang (2015) is based on the q-theory. Papers on anomalies also provide explanations, categorizing them as either risk-based or due to mispricing. When research objectives shift towards predicting asset returns more accurately through complex models, there appears to be a misconception that the emphasis on interpretability diminishes. However, this is not necessarily the case.

For linear models, such as the PCA by Kozak, Nagel, and Santosh (2018, 2020) and the IPCA by Kelly, Pruitt, and Su (2019), the interpretability is quite straightforward. Taking the former as an example, the authors discover that the first two principal components (PCs) derived from PCA on 25 portfolios formed on size and value perfectly correspond to the small-minus-big (size) and high-minus-low (value) factors. For the latter, although IPCA might seem mathematically intricate, its underlying intuition is essentially a linear combination of managed portfolios constructed through cross-sectional regression. Thus, for linear models, their interpretability is deeply rooted in regression and portfolio sorting, which are familiar to people.

When it comes to nonlinear models, their interpretability might not be as intuitive as that of linear models, yet academic research still places significant emphasis on this aspect (as will be discussed in Fact 2). The quest for understanding the "why" and "how" behind model predictions remains a fundamental aspect, ensuring that even the most complex models strive for a level of transparency and clarity in their explanations, aligning with the scholarly pursuit of not just predictive accuracy but also comprehensible insights.

12.3.4. Fact 2: Machine Learning Unveils Key Predictive Variables

As a response to Fiction 2, the second fact states that machine learning unveils the most important predictive variables that align with numerous empirical asset pricing findings.

In their work, Gu, Kelly, and Xiu (2020) utilize permutation importance to identify which covariates are most crucial in explaining expected returns. Their analysis reveals that: (1) The most significant covariates are consistent with previous empirical findings, broadly categorized into four main groups, including momentum/reversal, liquidity-related, risk-related (such as idiosyncratic volatility), and fundamentals (note that they are all important factors addressed in this book); (2)

The most important covariates from various machine learning models largely overlap. Furthermore, Chen, Pelger and Zhu (2023) assess model interpretability by computing the partial derivatives of SDF weights with respect to covariates. Among all covariates, the most influential ones are related to transaction frictions, value, intangible assets, profitability, investment, and historical returns.

Another noteworthy work is Kozak (2019), which ingeniously applies the kernel trick to map covariates into a higher-dimensional space without increasing computational complexity, and then performs PCA on these transformed covariates. The use of nonlinear kernels obscures the nature of the transformed covariates, yet by mapping the constructed SDF back to the managed portfolios of original covariates, it is still possible to identify the most important explanatory variables. Lastly, the significance of certain variables can also be inferred by observing common characteristics among selected stocks across different covariates, as demonstrated in Avramov, Cheng, and Metzker (2023). This approach underscores the concordance between machine-learning-derived predictors and the vast array of empirical asset-pricing results, affirming the continuity of fundamental principles within the innovative landscape of data-driven financial research.

12.3.5. Fiction 3: Complex Models Always Lead to Poor OOS Performance

At first glance, Fiction 3 may seem plausible, suggesting that complex models are susceptible to in-sample overfitting, leading to a significant increase in prediction errors ot-of-sample. This viewpoint posits that as models become more intricate, their ability to capture and replicate the nuances of the in-sample data increases, potentially at the expense of their generalizability to unseen data.

This narrative rests on the traditional understanding of model complexity and its relationship with underfitting and overfitting. With low complexity, a model tends to underfit, exhibiting low variance but high bias; conversely, as complexity increases, bias decreases at the cost of increased variance, leading to model

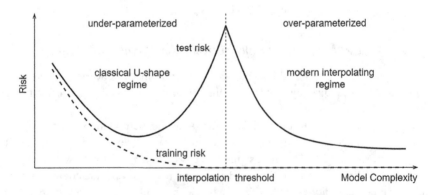

FIGURE 12.1 Risk vs. Model Complexity

overfitting. This interplay is recognized as the bias-variance trade-off, suggesting the existence of an optimal set of hyperparameters that minimizes the total out-of-sample error (i.e., test risk). Refer to the left part of Figure 12.1 which shows the classical U-shaped regime that demonstrates the trade-off.

This bias–variance trade-off can also be viewed from a different perspective. Simple models are adept at avoiding overfitting but may not serve as accurate approximations of the real world. On the other hand, more complex models may come closer to representing real-world phenomena but are indeed more susceptible to overfitting. Thus, the bias–variance trade-off can also be interpreted as an approximation–overfit trade-off. Conventional wisdom in machine learning and statistical modeling therefore suggests that over-parameterization, or having a large number of parameters relative to the size of the training data, can lead to over-fitting. This is because the model learns the noise in the training data rather than the underlying pattern. Thus, it is generally advised to keep the number of parameters in a model relatively small compared to the amount of training data.

However, in the context of deep learning, this conventional wisdom does not always hold. Despite having a high number of parameters, often exceeding the size of the training data, deep-learning models have been found to generalize well to unseen data. This phenomenon, often referred to as the "double descent" curve (Loog et al. 2020), shows that after a certain point, increasing the number of parameters beyond the size of the training data can actually improve a model's test performance.

The reasons behind this are still an active area of research. Some theories suggest that the structure of deep-learning models and the non-convex optimization algorithms used to train them may implicitly regularize the model. Others propose that over-parameterized models can represent a larger space of functions, increasing the chance of finding a model that both fits the training data well and generalizes to new data. Despite the lack of a definitive explanation, the effectiveness of over-parameterized deep-learning models is an established empirical fact.

12.3.6. Fact 3: With Proper Regularization, Model Complexity Outweighs Statistical Cost

The development of machine-learning theory offers a compelling counterpoint to Fiction 3, asserting that complex models can more accurately approximate the true data generating process (DGP). With enough regularization, the advantages brought by model complexity could surpass the statistical costs of over-parameterization.

A particularly exciting discovery in the field of machine learning in recent years is the phenomenon of double descent, where the out-of-sample error exhibits a non-monotonic relationship with model complexity. As highlighted by Belkin et al. (2019), an intriguing occurrence unfolds when model complexity surpasses the number of samples, a realm previously deemed off-limits. Contrary to expectations, the total out-of-sample error does not "explode" but instead begins to decline monotonically with increasing complexity (as illustrated in the right part of Figure 12.1). This phenomenon, characterized by a monotonic decrease in error on both sides of the interpolation threshold, has been aptly named double descent.

The intuition behind this phenomenon lies in the fact that when the number of covariates exceeds the number of samples, the in-sample solutions become non-unique. The optimal solution can be understood as the one that minimizes the variance of parameters. As model complexity increases, the variance of the optimal solution decreases. Besides, note that all models are mis-specified versions of the true DGP to some extent. When model misspecification exists, it can be shown that bias may also decrease within a certain range as complexity increases when the number of variables exceeds the number of samples. Consequently, the aggregate effect is a reduction in test risk. For those interested in the theoretical under-pinnings of the double-descent phenomenon, Hastie et al. (2022) offer a comprehensive discussion.

In the context of empirical asset pricing, Kelly, Malamud, and Zhou (2024) apply this concept to the timing of the U.S. stock market and observe a similar double descent phenomenon: the out-of-sample Sharpe ratio is improved when employing models with covariates vastly outnumbering the samples. Didisheim et al. (2023) further extend the idea to the cross-section by investigating complexity in factor pricing models.

Although the recent advancement of machine-learning theory sounds exciting, it's, however, worth noting that discussions regarding model complexity and out-of-sample performance in asset pricing are still in their nascent stages. Regularization plays a crucial role in this process, and further research in this area is highly anticipated.

12.3.7. Fiction 4: Nonlinear Models can Double Sharpe Ratio Easily

Fiction 4 refers to the misconception that nonlinear models can double the Sharpe ratio easily. However, let us first examine a set of empirical results that seem potent enough to support this fiction.

Baba-Yara, Boyer, and Davis (2021) replicate some major machine-learning asset-pricing models derived in recent years and compare their performance with traditional-factor models. A selection of representative results is summarized in Table 12.2.

TABLE 12.2 Comparison between Machine-Learning and Traditional-Factor Models

Machine-Learning Models		Traditional-Factor Models	
Model	OOS Sharpe	Model	OOS Sharpe
BPZ Random Forest	2.19	FF3	0.45
Davis Neural Network	3.21	FF5 + MOM	1.03
KNS PCA	3.21	Hou-Xue-Zhang	1.10
KPS IPCA	3.39	Stambaugh-Yuan	0.61

Source Data excerpted from Baba-Yara, Boyer, and Davis (2021).

The results vividly demonstrate that, compared to traditional factor models, the Sharpe ratios achieved by machine-learning models indeed double or even triple those of their counterparts. However, it is crucial to remember that traditional models are sparse, utilizing far fewer covariates when constructing factors, making such comparisons inherently unfair. (We will revisit these results in Fact 4.)

On the other hand, a closer inspection reveals that in the results mentioned above, the Sharpe ratios for PCA and IPCA models (both non-conditional and conditional linear models) are actually higher than those achieved by nonlinear models employing random forests and neural networks. This seems to suggest that nonlinear models, at least in the empirical results cited, do not necessarily have an edge over linear models.

12.3.8. Fact 4: Nonlinear Models Offer Marginal Incremental Contribution

It is without a doubt that there exist nonlinear relationships between covariates and asset returns. However, at this stage, nonlinear models are more likely to offer marginal incremental contributions in explaining the cross-section.

As demonstrated by Nagel (2021) and numerous recent empirical asset pricing studies, the interaction among variables plays a crucial role in these nonlinear relationships. For traditional linear regression models, considering the interaction terms between all pairs of covariates becomes impractical with an increasing number of variables. This limitation provides an opportunity for machine-learning models, which excel at handling nonlinear relationships.

However, it is essential to have realistic expectations regarding the incremental contribution of nonlinear relationships to return predictions. The empirical findings of Chen, Pelger, and Zhu (2023) indicate that their GAN can capture interactions among covariates when constructing the SDF. Yet, they also emphasize that the impact of individual covariates on the SDF is almost linear.

Now, let us revisit the study by Baba-Yara, Boyer, and Davis (2021) mentioned in Fiction 4. The table from an earlier version of their paper covers an out-of-sample empirical period from 1990 to 2020. In their latest version, however, the empirical period is curiously shortened to 1990 to 2016. It is puzzling why the

TABLE 12.3 Comparison between Machine-Learning and Traditional-Factor Models (II)

Machine-Learning Models		Traditional-Factor Models	
Model	OOS Sharpe	Model	OOS Sharpe
BPZ Random Forest	0.86 (2.19)	FF3	0.61 (0.45)
Davis Neural Network	2.39 (3.21)	FF5 + MOM	1.17 (1.03)
KNS PCA	2.77 (3.21)	Hou-Xue-Zhang	1.81 (1.10)
KPS IPCA	3.21 (3.39)	Stambaugh-Yuan	1.40 (0.61)

Source Data excerpted from Baba-Yara, Boyer, and Davis (2021).

empirical period becomes shorter in their updated version. Even more bewildering is the authors' justification that one of the traditional models used for comparison, i.e., the Stambaugh-Yuan model, only has data up to 2016. However, if the earlier version could extend empirical study to 2020, why revert to an earlier end date in the new version? The true motivation remains unknown to the public.

In this shorter empirical period, the results are summarized in Table 12.3 (data in brackets represent results up to 2020, included here for comparison). Intriguingly, when the end of the empirical period is set to 2016, all four machine learning models exhibit varying degrees of deterioration, while all four traditional models show improvement.

Focusing on machine learning models, these comparisons illustrate significant fluctuations in results across different empirical periods. Meanwhile, despite these studies employing rolling or expanding windows for training and validation before predicting out-of-sample returns for the next year, there is little (if any) discussion on the tuning process and the robustness of models under different hyperparameters. In this regard, the research ecosystem for applying machine learning in asset pricing is far from mature, calling for leaders in the field to establish a recognized research protocol.

12.3.9. Fiction 5: Machine-Learning Models can be Easily Applied in Practice

The last fiction argues that machine-learning models can be applied in practice easily. While machine-learning models have achieved encouraging results in academic research on empirical asset pricing, it does not necessarily mean they can be effortlessly applied in practice to yield substantial excess net returns, after considering all the cost.

One of the most critical empirical findings in this context is the high turnover ratios associated with portfolios constructed by machine-learning models. In this regard, Avramov, Cheng, and Metzker (2023) replicate several leading machine-learning models from the literature, including the neural network model from Gu, Kelly, and Xiu (2020), the GAN model by Chen, Pelger, and Zhu (2023), the IPCA model by Kelly, Pruitt, and Su (2019), and the conditional autoencoder by Gu, Kelly, and Xiu (2021). The average monthly turnover ratios for these models are presented in Table 12.4. To put things in context, traditional low-frequency style factors like size and value typically have average monthly turnover rates below 10% (i.e., 0.1). Through their estimation of transaction costs, Avramov, Cheng, and Metzker (2023) suggest that at such high turnover rates, it becomes challenging

TABLE 12.4 Turnover Ratios of Machine-Learning Models

Model	Monthly Turnover Ratio
Gu, Kelly, and Xiu (2020)	0.976
Chen, Pelger, and Zhu (2023)	1.664
Kelly, Pruitt, and Su (2019)	1.186
Gu, Kelly, and Xiu (2021)	1.565

for investors to earn extra excess returns through machine-learning models (though that does not preclude some sophisticated investors from successfully engineering these models to achieve excess returns despite high turnover).

To address the challenges posed by transaction costs, Jensen et al. (2022) introduce the concept of the implementable efficient frontier, which involves evaluating strategies directly through after-cost returns. This approach integrates the portfolio optimization problem, inclusive of transaction costs, into the machine-learning framework, yielding promising results. This development underscores the necessity of considering practical constraints, such as transaction costs, in the deployment of machine-learning models in investment strategies, highlighting the nuanced gap between academic success and practical applicability.

12.3.10. Fact 5: Limited Value for some Institutional Investors

The reality, contrary to Fiction 5, is that the predictabilities uncovered by advanced machine-learning models partly concentrate in stocks with high arbitrage and transaction costs. As a result, their values for some institutional investors are limited.

Empirical findings suggest that the excess returns of many anomalies predominantly originate from their short legs (Avramov et al. 2013) or stocks with tiny market capitalizations (Novy-Marx and Velikov 2016). Similarly, machine-

TABLE 12.5 Model Performance in Different Samples

Model	Full Sample	Exclude Tiny Market Cap	Exclude No Credit Rating	Exclude Financially Distressed
Panel A: Absolute Return (%)				
Gu, Kelly, and Xiu (2020)	1.56	1.05	1.02	0.72
	(4.53)	(3.24)	(3.18)	(2.49)
Chen, Pelger, and Zhu (2023)	2.13	1.08	0.82	0.92
	(6.37)	(4.06)	(2.83)	(2.91)
Kelly, Pruitt, and Su (2019)	0.95	0.91	0.89	0.73
	(5.62)	(5.57)	(5.08)	(4.08)
Gu, Kelly, and Xiu (2021)	1.16	1.11	0.87	0.67
	(4.17)	(4.22)	(2.97)	(2.22)
Panel B: Alpha (%) against FF5 + MOM				
Gu, Kelly, and Xiu (2020)	0.92	0.31	0.43	0.20
	(4.08)	(1.51)	(2.05)	(0.92)
Chen, Pelger, and Zhu (2023)	1.87	0.55	0.42	0.57
	(4.86)	(2.23)	(1.46)	(1.82)
Kelly, Pruitt, and Su (2019)	0.62	0.61	0.61	0.43
	(3.31)	(3.71)	(3.38)	(2.37)
Gu, Kelly, and Xiu (2021)	0.75	0.39	0.19	0.05
	(3.01)	(2.03)	(0.79)	(0.20)

Source Data excerpted from Avramov, Cheng, and Metzker (2023).

learning models have demonstrated proficiency in extracting predictability from stocks associated with higher arbitrage and transaction costs, thereby diminishing their practical applicability.

Taking the empirical results of Avramov, Cheng, and Metzker (2023) as an example, besides the full sample, the study also examines three subsamples: excluding tiny market cap stocks, companies without credit ratings, and financially distressed firms. The results (shown in Table 12.5, with *t*-statistics in brackets) indicate a significant performance decline in the mainstream machine-learning models (excluding IPCA) across these subsamples compared to the full sample. Moreover, the alpha of some machine-learning models against the FF5 + MOM benchmark is no longer significant in certain subsamples.

For instance, the monthly returns of the GAN model in the subsample excluding tiny market cap stocks decreased by over 50% compared to the full sample. Among the four models examined, except for IPCA, which is a linear model, the rest are nonlinear, and only IPCA shows robust results consistent across the full sample and all subsamples. It is worth noting that the subsample results are still derived using models trained on the full sample, which might raise concerns among some readers. In response, Avramov, Cheng, and Metzker (2023) further conduct training and out-of-sample prediction using subsamples but found no substantial change in results; in fact, the out-of-sample performance declines in some subsamples. In other words, the intention to constrain the models to learn from the target samples paradoxically leads to poorer out-of-sample performance due to reduced sample size.

These results imply that successfully tweaking nonlinear models to focus on stocks with lower arbitrage and transaction costs will be a crucial prerequisite for the practical implementation of machine-learning models in asset pricing.

12.4. Automated Factor Discovering

With the continuous advancements in artificial intelligence algorithms, there is a growing interest in leveraging these algorithms for factor discovering, potentially replacing manual efforts in this domain. This section explores the feasibility of this approach.

12.4.1. End-to-End Factor Fitting

One might first consider, albeit not our most recommended approach, the direct application of deep-learning models for end-to-end factor training. Deep-learning models possess formidable fitting capabilities, with gradients providing optimal directions for swiftly searching solutions. In this approach, directly predicting stock returns could be a potential goal. However, this often yields overly similar, over-fitted model outputs.

A more effective approach might involve identifying numerous intermediate objectives based on financial logic. This approach, with its diverse objectives and separate models for each, can enhance the variety of model outputs and allow for adjustments in predictive targets. For instance, models could predict basic stock attributes like turnover ratio, volatility, correlations between stocks, or distributions of returns. More complex predictions could include fundamental metrics such as earnings per share, investor sentiment towards stocks, or the likelihood of early financial report releases. Predictive targets should leverage people's understanding of financial markets, with some being predictable by models depending on the availability of data.

Besides, unsupervised learning methods can be employed to extract latent information about stock returns, such as using encoder-decoder architectures. This approach views factors as quantifiable descriptions of stocks' latent information. However, its drawback is the lack of transparency in understanding model predictions and identifying potential errors. Despite efforts to combat overfitting with necessary techniques, it remains an inherent risk.

12.4.2. Automate Symbolic Factors

Beyond direct model fitting, a more complex yet reassuring method for quantitative factor researchers involves mining data-operator combinations. Many financially logical factors discussed in this book can be decomposed into multiple sublogics, each applied by an operator to one or more variables. This step-by-step logic chain can express complex factors. Figure 12.2 illustrates this concept with an example.

To automate factor search, several components are essential:

1. Operand Space: The meta factors to be used for factor mining, such as price, volume, sector categorizations, features from limit order books, statistics from financial analysts/reports, and sentiment signals from investor emotions. This space should be enriched with variables reflecting the intrinsic attributes of stocks, as discussed in earlier chapters. A broader and higher-dimensional operand space theoretically offers more possibilities for meaningful logic discovery.
2. Operator Space: The operators to be used for processing factors like square-root, logarithm, rank, mean, and quantile, among others, along with post-processing operators like winsorization for outlier clipping and data normalization. Similar to the operand space, a diverse set of operators enhances the search's power.
3. Search Algorithms: It aims to discover effective factors, with methods ranging from Monte Carlo (MC) algorithms for random combinations to more sophisticated approaches like Markov-Chain Monte Carlo (MCMC) and genetic programming. Recent research explores using generative models and LangChain to propose operand and operator combinations based on financial logic.
4. Evaluation: Simple criteria include information coefficient (IC), annualized return, and Sharpe ratio. To avoid redundancy among highly correlated

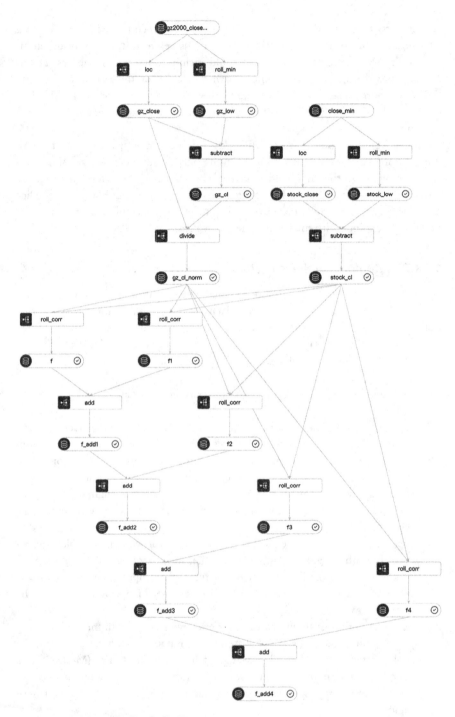

FIGURE 12.2 Automate Symbolic Factors

factors, data-driven explanatory algorithms could enhance the logical coherence of searched factors.

5. Iteration: Researchers must continuously understand the generated results, identify system flaws, and adjust the search algorithm or expand the operands and operators based on outcomes. Iterative improvement is crucial for a functional factor discovering system.

Cheng and Tang (2024) investigate GPT-4's capability of generating factors. The study demonstrates that the factors generated by ChatGPT, utilizing the capabilities of GPT-4, achieve impressive results in terms of returns and risk. These factors exhibit a commendable Sharpe ratio and an annualized return trajectory that surpasses traditional factor models. By employing a model averaging paradigm, the ensemble of 35 factors generated by ChatGPT showcases a remarkable long–short annualized return and a notable Sharpe ratio. This approach outperforms conventional data mining techniques. One notable advantage of GPT-4's factor generation process is its temporal efficiency. Unlike traditional methods that rely on extensive data mining, GPT-4's knowledge-based inference allows for faster factor generation without the need for extensive financial data. Importantly, ChatGPT provides comprehensive insights into the generated factors, grounded in economic theories. This distinguishes it from pure data mining approaches and enhances the interpretability and robustness of the factors. The study highlights the increasing relevance of large-language models (LLMs) like ChatGPT in factor generation.

The prediction of returns in financial markets has traditionally relied on the bag-of-words approach, which fails to capture the syntax and semantics of text. However, state-of-the-art LLMs in natural-language processing offer contextualized representations that provide a more comprehensive understanding of news text. Chen et al. (2024) explore the efficacy of contextualized representations in return prediction using data from 16 international equity markets and news articles in 13 different languages. These representations capture the contextual information and nuances of the text, overcoming limitations of the bag-of-words approach, particularly in cases involving negation words. The findings reveal that news information is incorporated into stock prices with an inefficient delay, but real-time trading strategies capitalizing on fresh news alerts can exploit the news-induced return predictability, resulting in higher Sharpe ratios.

Regarding factor explainability, approaches from Guo et al. (2023) include:

1. **Explanation on Stocks**: provides insights into their relationships with other stocks, stock similarity, lead-lag effects, and sector trends, allowing for a better understanding of their behavior and potential advantages in analysis and prediction compared to traditional methods. However, challenges exist in determining appropriate similarity metrics, identifying lead–lag effects, and evaluating sector contributions and feature interactions.

2. **Explanation on Time**: provides insights into market features and anomalies at specific time points, including extreme market conditions, calendar effects, style transitions, and the influence of breaking events. By decomposing

returns, identifying important calendar factors, detecting style transitions, and analyzing event influences, investors can adjust their strategies and make informed decisions in response to market dynamics.

3. **Explanation on Factor**: involves analyzing the sensitivity of stocks to different factors over time and identifying interactive effects among factors. Factors can be categorized based on various aspects, such as data sources, financial features, and time scales, and their contributions to portfolio returns can be computed. Factor interactions can be revealed through feature crossing techniques, and a hierarchical depiction of factor similarity can be created using techniques like hierarchical clustering.

This multifaceted approach to factor research using AI algorithms underscores the complexity and potential of integrating advanced technology into factor investing, highlighting the importance of continuous exploration and refinement in this evolving field.

12.5. Machine Learning vs. Econometrics

Undoubtedly, machine learning has gradually supplanted econometric methodologies, becoming a predominant tool in contemporary asset pricing and factor investing. However, before concluding this chapter, examining the differences between these two approaches from a statistical modeling perspective can be enlightening (Mullainathan and Spiess 2017, Athey and Imbens 2019). Such a comparison deepens our understanding of the methodologies, enabling the selection of appropriate techniques for the problems at hand.

12.5.1. Two Cultures

Leo Breiman, in his seminal paper "Statistical Modeling: The Two Cultures" (Breiman 2001), delves into the two prevailing cultures in statistical modeling.

The first is the *data-modeling* culture, which operates under the assumption that the data-generation process is based on a certain stochastic model and conducts statistical inference based on this assumption. The primary objective here is to comprehend the structure and relationships within the data, meaning that the essence of traditional data-modeling culture lies in understanding the mechanisms behind data generation through a series of hypotheses and theoretical frameworks. Econometric methods, well-known within this culture, rely on establishing explicit models to explain relationships between variables, often assuming linear relationships and normal distribution of errors.

The main goal of this approach is parameter estimation rather than prediction, aimed at elucidating causal relationships between variables. When data align with model assumptions, this approach can offer robust causal explanations. Empirical research methods such as time-series regression or Fama and MacBeth (1973) cross-sectional regression adhere to this culture. But what happens when prediction accuracy takes precedence over unbiased parameter estimation?

The second culture is *algorithmic modeling*, which prioritizes prediction accuracy over model interpretability. This approach does not make stringent structural assumptions about the data-generation process but employs data-driven methods to learn directly from the data. Machine-learning models epitomize this culture. Their flexibility allows them to handle complex, nonlinear, and high-dimensional data without presupposing the data's structure. However, machine-learning models are often criticized for their "black box" nature.

In this culture, no structural assumptions are made about the data; instead, a class of models (e.g., neural networks) is selected and model parameters are learned from the data based on a given loss function. The core of machine-learning modeling is to optimize the model's generalization performance out-of-sample, or equivalently to minimize generalization error, introducing the crucial concept of regularization. Compared to econometrics, machine-learning methods can approximate nonlinear, high-dimensional, and complex function relationships without explicitly defining the model's form, making machine learning a natural fit for addressing contemporary empirical asset-pricing challenges.

When viewing econometrics and machine learning through the lens of these two cultures, their differences become apparent. As Breiman (2001) emphasizes, the fundamental divergence between traditional statistical methods and machine learning lies in the former's focus on estimating model parameters and conducting statistical tests under the assumption of a known data model, whereas the latter maximizes prediction accuracy without assuming a known data model. In other words, for econometrics, parameter estimation precedes prediction accuracy; while for machine learning, prediction accuracy precedes parameter estimation. If we consider the empirical research objectives of asset pricing, econometrics mainly focuses on whether pricing models can price test assets in-sample, while machine learning concentrates on whether portfolios constructed based on model predictions can achieve optimal risk-adjusted returns out-of-sample.

12.5.2. Synergy between Machine Learning and Econometrics

In the realm of asset pricing and factor investing, the two cultures shall not be viewed as opposing forces but rather as complementary approaches (Kelly and Xiu 2023). The integration of econometric principles with the predictive prowess of machine-learning models can enrich our understanding and enhance the efficacy of investment strategies.

For instance, incorporating causality tests from econometrics into machine-learning workflows can help identify and validate the predictive factors that have a genuine economic rationale behind them, thereby reducing the risk of spurious correlation. Moreover, the econometric emphasis on understanding the underlying DGP can guide feature selection for machine-learning models, ensuring that the input variables are not merely statistical artifacts. This synthesis approach can also foster more interpretable machine-learning models. Techniques such as model-agnostic interpretability tools can be applied to machine-learning models to elucidate the relationship between input features and predictions, thereby providing insights akin to econometric models (Ribeiro, Singh, and Guestrin 2016). Furthermore, the rigorous treatment of uncertainty and inference in econometrics can augment machine-learning applications in finance. For example, studying the asymptotic distributions of machine-learning-model predictions can equip investors with a more nuanced appreciation of the risks and reliability associated with the predictive signals generated by machine-learning models.

Conversely, machine learning can unveil new empirical facts that might elude traditional econometric approaches, thereby enriching hypothesis testing and theoretical development in economics and finance. The data-driven nature of machine learning enables the discovery of complex, nonlinear patterns and interactions within financial data that might not be immediately apparent or theoretically anticipated. For instance, machine learning techniques can identify intricate relationships across a vast array of market indicators and economic signals, revealing previously unrecognized predictors of asset returns or economic cycles.

In summary, the interplay between econometric rigor and machine learning flexibility presents a fertile ground for advancing asset pricing and factor investing. By harnessing the strengths of each approach—econometrics' focus on causality, interpretability, and rigorous inference, alongside machine learning's capacity for handling complex, nonlinear relationships and large datasets—the finance community can develop more robust, insightful, and effective factors. This complementary synergy underscores the need for a multidisciplinary perspective in financial research, one that embraces both the rich traditions of econometrics and the innovative potential of machine learning (Varian 2014).

12.6. Conclusion

To conclude this chapter, we reflect upon the transformative role of machine learning within the realm of asset pricing and factor investing. The integration of machine-learning algorithms into this domain has not only augmented the analytical capabilities of researchers and practitioners but has also ushered in a new era of financial modeling and prediction.

This chapter also underscores the importance of a synergistic approach that melds the rigor of econometric theories with the adaptive prowess of machine learning. Such a multidisciplinary strategy ensures that the models we develop are not only powerful in prediction but are also grounded in economic rationale and interpretability. This balance is crucial for maintaining models' credibility and relevance in the face of ever-evolving market dynamics.

As we look ahead, the potential for machine learning in factor investing appears boundless. Yet, this journey is not without its challenges. Issues such as overfitting, interpretability, and the need for robust validation frameworks remain at the forefront of our considerations. The journey ahead will undoubtedly require a concerted effort from both academia and industry to navigate these challenges effectively. As we continue to explore this exciting frontier, the fusion of econometric wisdom and machine-learning innovation holds the promise of unlocking deeper insights and creating more effective investment strategies in the complex world of finance.

References

Athey, S. and G. W. Imbens (2019). Machine learning methods that economists should know about. *Annual Review of Economics* 11, 685–725.

Avramov, D., S. Cheng, and L. Metzker (2023). Machine learning vs. economic restrictions: Evidence from stock return predictability. *Management Science* 69(5), 2587–2619.

Avramov, D., T. Chordia, G. Jostova, and A. Philipov (2013) Anomalies and financial distress. *Journal of Financial Economics* 108(1), 139–159.

Baba-Yara, F., B. Boyer, and C. Davis (2021). The factor model failure puzzle. Working paper.

Belkin, M., D. Hsu, S. Ma, and S. Mandal (2019). Reconciling modern machine-learning practice and the classical bias–variance trade-off. *Proceedings of the National Academy of Sciences* 116(32), 15849–15854.

Breiman, L. (2001). Statistical modeling: The two cultures (with comments and a rejoinder by the author). *Statistical Science* 16(3), 199–231.

Bryzgalov, S., S. Lerner, M. Lettau, and M. Pelger (2022). Missing financial data. Working paper.

Bryzgalova, S., M. Pelger, and J. Zhu (forthcoming). Forest through the trees: Building cross-sections of stock returns. *Journal of Finance*.

Bybee, L., B. T. Kelly, A. Manela, and D. Xiu (forthcoming). Business news and business cycles. *Journal of Finance*.

Bybee, L., B. T. Kelly, and Y. Su (2023). Narrative asset pricing: Interpretable systematic risk factors from news text. *Review of Financial Studies* 36(12), 4759–4787.

Chen, Y. and B. T. Kelly, and D. Xiu (2024). Expected returns and large language models. Working Paper. University of Chicago.

Chen, L., M. Pelger, and J. Zhu (2023). Deep learning in asset pricing. *Management Science* 70(2), 714–750.

Cheng, Y. and K. Tang (2024). GPT's idea of stock factors. *Quantitative Finance* March(5), 1–26.

Didisheim, A., S. Ke, B. T. Kelly, and S. Malamud. (2023). Complexity in factor pricing models. Working paper.

Fama, E. F. and K. R. French (2015). A five-factor asset pricing model. *Journal of Financial Economics* 116(1), 1–22.

Fama, E. F. and J. D. MacBeth (1973). Risk, return, and equilibrium: Empirical tests. *Journal of Political Economy* 81(3), 607–636.

Freyberger, J., B. Hoppner, A. Neuhierl, and M. Weber (2021). Missing data in asset pricing panels. Working paper.

Gu, S., B. T. Kelly, and D. Xiu (2020). Empirical asset pricing via machine learning. *Review of Financial Studies* 33(5), 2223–2273.

Gu, S., B. T. Kelly, and D. Xiu (2021). Autoencoder asset pricing models. *Journal of Econometrics* 222(1), 429–450.

Guo, J., S. Wang, L. M. Ni, and H.-Y. Shum (2023). *Quant 4.0: Engineering Quantitative Investment with Automated, Explainable and Knowledge-driven Artificial Intelligence*. IDEA Research Report.

Hastie, T., A. Montanari, S. Rosset, and R. J. Tibshirani (2022). Surprise in high-dimensional ridgeless least squares interpolation. *Annals of Statistics* 50(2), 949–986.

Hou, K., C. Xue, and L. Zhang (2015). Digesting anomalies: An investment approach. *Review of Financial Studies* 28(3), 650–705.

Jensen, T. I., B. T. Kelly, S. Malamud, and L. H. Pedersen (2022). Machine learning and the implementable efficient frontier. Working paper.

Kelly, B. T., S. Malamud, and K. Zhou (2024). The virtue of complexity in return prediction. *Journal of Finance* 79(1), 459–503.

Kelly, B. T., S. Pruitt, and Y. Su (2019). Characteristics are covariances: A unified model of risk and return. *Journal of Financial Economics* 134(3), 501–524.

Kelly, B. T. and D. Xiu (2023). Financial machine learning. Working paper.

Kozak, S. (2019). Kernel trick for the cross-section. Working paper.

Kozak, S., S. Nagel, and S. Santosh (2018). Interpreting factor models. *Journal of Finance* 73(3), 1183–1223.

Kozak, S., S. Nagel, and S. Santosh (2020). Shrinking the cross-section. *Journal of Financial Economics* 135(2), 271–292.

Loog, M., T. Viering, A. Mey, J. H. Krijthe, and D. M. J. Tax (2020). A brief prehistory of double descent. *Proceedings of the National Academy of Sciences* 117(20), 10625–10626.

Mullainathan, S. and J. Spiess (2017). Machine learning: An applied econometric approach. *Journal of Economic Perspectives* 31(2), 87–106.

Nagel, S. (2021). *Machine Learning in Asset Pricing*. Princeton University Press.

Novy-Marx, R. and M. Velikov (2016). A taxonomy of anomalies and their trading costs. *Review of Financial Studies* 29(1), 104–147.

Ribeiro, M. T., S. Singh, and C. Guestrin (2016). *"Why Should I Trust You?"* Explaining the Predictions of Any Classifier. Proceedings of the 22nd ACM SIGKDD International Conference on Knowledge Discovery and Data Mining.

Varian, H. R. (2014). Big data: New tricks for econometrics. *Journal of Economic Perspectives* 28(2), 3–28.

EPILOGUE

As we conclude our journey through the "factor zoo", this epilogue offers a moment to reflect on the multifaceted world of factor investing. We start with a brief recap of the materials discussed in previous chapters. After that, we offer insights into the nuances between science and practice, the evolution from alpha to beta, the interplay of tradition and innovation, the dynamics of volatility and uncertainty, and the pivotal transition from theory to action. This reflection serves as a synthesis of our understanding of and introspection on factor investing, encapsulating the existing knowledge and the ongoing dialogue between theoretical rigor and practical application.

We began with "Quantamentals", exploring how fundamental analysis' detailed insights combine with quantitative techniques' precision. This synthesis challenges traditional investment strategy boundaries and advocates for a holistic approach, appreciating both data and their narratives.

Moving forward, "Statistical Moments as Factors" and "Market Beta" allowed us deeper analysis into the statistical underpinnings of risk and return, elevating our understanding beyond mere numbers to reflect broader market dynamics and investment philosophies.

In examining "Technical Analysis Factors", "Microstructure and Liquidity", and "Tail Risk", we uncovered the subtle mechanisms influencing market movements and liquidity, promoting a deeper understanding of market forces.

The integration of "Uncertainty", and "Behavioral Finance" marked a pivotal shift, encouraging us to consider the unpredictable nature of markets influenced by human behavior and external events, blending psychological insights with quantitative analysis.

We then ventured into "Option Information" and "Alternative Data", investigating how innovative methodologies and non-traditional data sources can

DOI: 10.4324/9781003480204-13

revolutionize investment strategies, underscoring finance's evolving nature where traditional models meet data-driven insights.

Lastly, "Machine Learning in Factor Investing" signaled a significant shift towards the future of investment, emphasizing the critical role of AI and machine learning in deciphering complex market signals and advocating for a synthesis of technology with economic principles.

As we conclude, view this text not as a mere collection but as an integrated framework prompting investigation, reflection, and questioning. The field of factor investing, expansive and intricate, invites continuous exploration for those who approach it with a discerning eye.

This text should serve as a catalyst, urging the reader to navigate the rich landscape of financial markets, balancing theoretical and applied knowledge with an acknowledgment of the industry's vast complexities. May this book inspire a continued journey filled with enrichment, critical questioning, and the pursuit of comprehensive understanding in the realm of factor investing.

Science and Practice: Tension and Synergy

While reading this book, readers might sense a tension between the depth of scientific research, aimed at thoroughly understanding market phenomena, and the immediacy of practical application, which targets profitable investment strategies. Scientists delve into the foundational behaviors of markets, while practitioners focus on identifying directly profitable factors, sometimes viewing extensive theoretical exploration as unprofitable and thus unnecessary.

However, we advocate for practitioners to be patient and consider the underlying theories because the conflict between science and practice can generate synergistic outcomes. Scientific insights lay a solid foundation for robust investment strategies, rooted in proven principles rather than temporary market whims. In turn, real-world applications test these theories, refining them and highlighting new research avenues. Such collaboration fosters innovative, profitable, and lasting strategies that blend academic rigor with market practicality.

For example, in the discussion about asset-pricing models, factor models like CAPM, Fama-French three-factor, and Carhart's four-factor models are grounded in academic research. However, their application and continuous improvement are driven by practitioners' experiences and challenges in real-world markets. This synergy enhances the models' relevance and applicability to diverse market conditions. Factor investing uses quantitative methods to identify and exploit investment factors, which are underpinned by substantial academic research. However, the real-world implementation of these factors requires qualitative insights, such as understanding market dynamics, investor behavior, and economic indicators. The blend of quantitative and qualitative analysis fosters a more comprehensive approach to investment, leveraging the strengths of both scientific rigor and practical wisdom. In the chapter on quantamental factors, we discussed the tension: fundamental analysis might miss short-term opportunities due to its long-term focus, while quantitative methods might overlook broader market changes due to their reliance on historical data. There is a need for a balanced approach that incorporates deep theoretical understanding and practical market insights. Also, the Global Financial Crisis of 2007–2008 exposed the limitations of relying too heavily on historical data and underscored the necessity for a more nuanced approach that integrates deep market understanding with empirical data analysis. Countless real-world events exemplify why scientific and practical insights must interact to develop robust investment strategies.

Without a deep understanding of uncertainty, the distinction between outcome uncertainty and distribution uncertainty (ambiguity) will never be an important issue in the minds of practitioners. They continue to optimize their strategies in backtesting and pursuing the highest Sharpe ratio, without recognizing and managing the types of uncertainty that cannot be easily quantified using traditional models. This recognition pushes practitioners to explore innovative modeling approaches that account for ambiguity, such as stress testing and scenario analysis, demonstrating a practical application of scientific insights into uncertainty.

The book discusses at length the tension and synergy inherent in science and practice. So, embracing both perspectives allows for a more dynamic evolution of factor investing, harnessing detailed research to inform successful market practices. Thinking from both the researcher's and the practitioner's sides will make your understanding of matters more comprehensive, enabling you to think more broadly and discover more valuable research directions or investment strategies.

From Alpha to Beta: The Lifecycle of Factors

This book underscores the continuous need for advancement in factor research, highlighting that as factors become mainstream and integrated into trading practices, their ability to generate excess returns—moving from alpha to beta—diminishes. This transition necessitates refinement or replacement of outdated factors to seize new opportunities, reflecting the fluid and dynamic nature of financial markets.

The lifecycle of investment factors, evolving from offering unique insights to aligning with market averages, underlines the critical importance of constant innovation and adaptability in investment strategies. As markets evolve, reliance on single, well-known factors must shift towards more sophisticated, multifactor approaches or entirely new paradigms.

For instance, the progression from basic statistical moments, as initially introduced by Harry Markowitz, to integrating higher-order moments and behavioral finance theories illustrates the financial industry's response to earlier model limitations. This shift towards a more holistic approach considers both quantitative models and investor behavior, emphasizing the necessity for continuous innovation to develop new logic and optimize factors.

Similarly, the evolution of technical analysis from heuristic-based methods to more quantitative, computer-assisted approaches showcases the ongoing need to develop new strategies and tools. The adoption of the Adaptive Market Hypothesis, moving from static market efficiency theories to those incorporating behavioral insights, and the balance between empirical and heuristic methods in technical analysis, reflect the industry's progression towards more sophisticated analytical frameworks.

The narrative of this book, incorporating discussions on statistical moments and technical analysis factors, highlights the perpetual cycle of discovery, saturation, and adaptation. It calls for staying ahead in the continuous evolution of factors to maintain a competitive advantage in the ever-changing market landscape. This ongoing quest for outperformance emphasizes the importance of innovation, adaptability, and a forward-looking approach in the realm of factor investing.

Tradition and Innovation: The Symbiotic Relationship

This book has introduced some innovative methodologies, yet its core remains deeply rooted in traditional approaches. The value of conventional perspectives and research methods cannot be understated; they provide a foundational bedrock of knowledge. Even in markets that have become increasingly efficient, leading to diminished returns on well-utilized factors, the application of traditional logic still yields stable, albeit lower, profits. Furthermore, we can employ modern techniques to refine and update these established concepts. Understanding quantitative factor investing through the lens of traditional logic, coupled with a growing comprehension of market dynamics, establishes a solid foundation. This groundwork is crucial when integrating machine-learning methods, enabling the creation of algorithms that are more adept at adapting to market conditions.

The book has not extensively covered new technologies such as alternative data and machine learning due to the lack of a complete consensus within the industry and academia. However, the need for these innovations is undeniable. They represent tools that can uncover new, uncorrelated sources of return beyond traditional factors. We encourage readers to further explore these emerging technologies, as they hold the potential to revolutionize our understanding and implementation of quantitative factor investing. Through this blend of time-honored techniques and cutting-edge advancements, investors can navigate the complexities of the market more effectively, paving the way for a new era of investing that honors the past while embracing the future.

In line with this perspective, the book highlights the diminishing returns from traditional factors, stressing how alternative data, including unconventional sources like social media and text data, can provide fresh insights, challenging the established norms of market analysis. This introduction of alternative data is not merely a theoretical concept; it is a response to the concrete reality of traditional trading factors yielding diminishing returns due to increased market efficiency. By offering new angles and insights, alternative data sets, as discussed in the sections on their nature and impact, underscore the necessity of evolving beyond the conventional paradigms.

Furthermore, the book delves into the technological advancements reshaping the investing landscape, particularly through T-links and the application of machine learning. These innovations represent a significant leap from traditional analytics to a more nuanced, data-driven approach, indicating an evolution towards integrating sophisticated algorithms that enhance the predictive accuracy of investment strategies. Yet, the discussion also acknowledges the challenges inherent in adopting these new methods, from data-acquisition hurdles to the complexities of machine-learning algorithms, underscoring the balanced approach required to integrate new with old.

We advocate for a holistic approach that respects and builds upon established financial theories while simultaneously embracing the advancements in technology and data analysis. This balanced approach is crucial for developing effective, robust investment strategies capable of navigating the complexities of modern financial markets, thereby charting a course that is informed by the past but geared towards the future.

Volatility and Uncertainty: The Balancing Act

In the world of quantitative factor investing, the continuous quest to improve the Sharpe ratio of a strategy plays a pivotal role. This is primarily achieved through either amplifying returns or reducing the strategy's volatility. As we explore the complexities of uncertainty, a paradox becomes evident: endeavors to reduce the volatility of a strategy, with the intention of attaining greater certainty, may inadvertently result in increased ambiguity, ultimately leading to substantial losses when confronted with challenges.

True risk mitigation within a strategy stems from a deep understanding of the logic behind each factor and the ability to discern when and under what circumstances these factors are likely to yield profits or undergo significant risk fluctuations. Moving beyond mere backtesting, factor premia, analytical charts, and statistical tests, there is a compelling need to focus more on the underlying logic and the structure of the market itself.

Furthermore, it is essential to avoid reducing the return volatility of a factor below a threshold of uncertainty. Doing so may simply replace short-term stability with significant tail risks, potentially resulting in severe losses in a single detrimental event. Hence, the real challenge lies in accurately defining the genuine risk associated with each factor, not based on its volatility, but rather on its inherent uncertainty.

In practice, this means we should endeavor to diversify by incorporating investment logics that originate from different sources of uncertainty and apply leverage based on underlying uncertainty rather than mere volatility. This approach encourages a more nuanced understanding of the factors at play, facilitating navigation through the dichotomy of certainty and uncertainty. By adopting this methodology, investors can develop strategies that are not only robust but also aligned with the inherent risks and realities of the market, ensuring a more sustainable and informed investment approach.

Our emphasis on uncertainty underscores the critical distinction between risk and ambiguity. The failure of traditional models in dealing with extreme events, especially during unanticipated crises like the Global Financial Crisis of 2007–2008, highlights the essential need for adopting strategies that align more naturally with market behavior and investor psychology, rather than forcing adherence to assumptions that seemingly improve the elegance of these models.

Furthermore, the discussion on tail risk amplifies the need for a shift towards investment strategies that genuinely reflect investor preferences against downside risks. The historical inadequacies of standard risk tools, demonstrated by the occurrences of "black-swan" events, accentuate the importance of embracing methods and models that cater to the non-symmetrical risk preferences of real-world investors.

Moreover, the narrative on the practical strategies for hedging against tail risk by the financial industry reveals a proactive approach toward managing extreme market movements. This is indicative of a growing acknowledgment within the industry that a successful risk management strategy must move beyond conventional methods to encompass sophisticated techniques that accurately capture the intricacies of market dynamics and the nuances of investor behavior.

In conclusion, navigating the realm of certainty and uncertainty in quantitative factor investing mandates a profound understanding of market nature and human psychology. It calls for a balanced approach that respects the natural tendencies of markets and investors alike, advocating for investment strategies that are not only grounded in statistical models but also in the realities of market behavior and investor sentiment. By adopting such strategies, investors position themselves to better manage the uncertainties of the financial world, aligning their pursuits with the inherent nature of the market rather than against it.

Transition to Action: From Theory to Practice

As we conclude our exploration of factor investing, the time has arrived to shift from passive absorption to active participation. Grasping the market's intricacies, understanding the subtleties of risk, and exploring innovative methods introduced here are just initial steps. True mastery is achieved by applying these theories and principles practically.

We encourage you, the reader, to extend this knowledge beyond this book. Begin by creating your own factors, conducting research, and start trading. It is through such practical applications that discussed concepts will evolve from theoretical notions to practical tools adept at navigating complex financial landscapes.

To facilitate this transition, we introduce the open-source project: "FIRE: Factor Investing Research Engine". You can find the project on GitHub at this link: https://github.com/fire-institute/fire. This platform is designed to close the gap between academic theory and real-world investment strategy. FIRE provides a space for you to experiment, exchange ideas, and craft strategies rooted in the principles detailed throughout this text.

Joining FIRE means joining a community dedicated to expanding the frontiers of financial research and strategy formulation. Regardless of your experience level, your insights and trials will enrich our collective journey.

The leap from knowledge to application is essential. Merely understanding the theories is insufficient; you must actively apply, test, and refine them to match the evolving financial landscape. Through crafting your factors, engaging in empirical research, and executing trading strategies, you'll gain a refined and profound grasp of factor investing.

This marks not an end, but a commencement. Use this book as a springboard for your ventures and discoveries in quantitative finance. Engage with the FIRE project, contributing to a forward-moving wave of informed, empirical, and cooperative investment strategy evolution.

Remember, mastering factor investing is a progressive and shared endeavor. By disseminating your discoveries, absorbing insights from others, and consistently honing your factors, you contribute not only to personal growth but to the broader advancement of this domain.

Embark on this hands-on journey with confidence in what you have learned and the wisdom to recognize the value of ongoing education. Let your contributions reflect acquired knowledge, ensuring your journey into factor investing remains as enriching and fruitful as the continuous quest for understanding. Join us to transform theory into action and collectively shape the future of investing.

INDEX

Please note that page references to Figures will be in **bold**, while references to Tables are in *italics*.

Printed in the United States
by Baker & Taylor Publisher Services